COUNSELING
· THE
DISADVANTAGED
YOUTH

PRENTICE-HALL INTERNATIONAL, INC. *London*
PRENTICE-HALL OF AUSTRALIA, PTY. LTD. *Sydney*
PRENTICE-HALL OF CANADA, LTD. *Toronto*
PRENTICE-HALL OF INDIA PRIVATE LTD. *New Delhi*
PRENTICE-HALL OF JAPAN, INC. *Tokyo*

COUNSELING

THE

DISADVANTAGED

YOUTH

Edited by

WILLIAM E. AMOS
*Chief, Division of Counseling
and Test Development
U.S. Employment Service*

JEAN DRESDEN GRAMBS
*Professor, College of Education
University of Maryland*

PRENTICE-HALL, INC., ENGLEWOOD CLIFFS, NEW JERSEY

To John Walker, friend and colleague,
whose dedication to his profession
was matched by his concern
for his fellow human beings

Barnard

HF
5382.5
U5
.A717

Library of Congress Catalog Card Number 68-21131

Printed in the United States of America

Current Printing (last digit):
10 9 8 7 6 5 4 3 2 1

PREFACE

In recent years programs and services for the disadvantaged have increased at a rapid rate. In most of these undertakings, counseling has been either the major service offered or else a supporting one for other activities. Many people have questioned whether the various counseling disciplines were ready or willing to assume this responsibility. Counselor educators have disagreed about the role of the counselor and the training needed to work with the disadvantaged. Concerned about the limited material available on the major problems in counseling the disadvantaged youngster, we invited a number of authorities to prepare papers on various topics relating to these problems. We were encouraged in this project by Robert Gibbons and Jim Clark of Prentice-Hall, and after organizing the book and selecting the authors, we submitted the completed manuscript for publication.

This book was written for both the student and the practicing counselor, as well as for all those involved or interested in working with the disadvantaged. We have not restricted the contents to any one discipline and feel that the contributions of most of the behavioral sciences are reflected in these chapters.

We are deeply indebted to the contributing authors, and we would also like to express our gratitude to many of our colleagues who have read portions of the manuscript and offered many constructive suggestions.

Special thanks are due Kit Amos for her assistance during the entire editorial process and to Shirley Smith, our typist.

WILLIAM E. AMOS
JEAN D. GRAMBS

College Park, Maryland

CONTRIBUTORS

William E. Amos	U.S. Employment Service
John J. Cody	Southern Illinois University
William C. Cottle	Boston College
S. Norman Feingold	B'nai B'rith Vocational Service
Clyde W. Gleason	U.S. Employment Service (retired)
Jesse E. Gordon	University of Michigan
Jean D. Grambs	University of Maryland
Charles Grosser	New York University
Joseph Margolin	The George Washington University
Richard Melloh	Indiana State University
Paul F. Munger	University of Indiana
Reginald C. Orem	Planning Research Corporation
Richard Pearson	Syracuse University
Edward C. Roeber	Indiana State University
Carol J. Smallenburg	California State University
Harry Smallenburg	Los Angeles County Superintendent Schools Office
Bennetta B. Washington	U.S. Office of Economic Opportunity

CONTENTS

ix

WHERE DO WE GO FROM HERE?, 353
Jean D. Grambs
William E. Amos

APPENDICES:

INTRODUCTION

WILLIAM E. AMOS AND JEAN D. GRAMBS

Today in this country we are more concerned with the health, welfare, education, and employment of all our young people than ever before in history. Particular emphasis has been placed on services to those youngsters who are classified as disadvantaged.[1] This classification is usually determined by family income and social class. The Federal antipoverty programs have fostered the development of Job Corps, Neighborhood Youth Corps, Head Start, Youth Opportunity Centers, and various other programs and agencies. Public schools and private agencies have utilized this climate of concern to shape programs aimed at the disadvantaged child. The services and resources that have poured from these programs have in most instances been based on a foundation of counseling.

Even though most program administrators are forceful in their defense of the counseling role, very few can agree on what counseling actually is. Leona Tyler has stated that "counseling is one of those words that everybody understands but no two people seem to understand in precisely the same way."[2] To some, counseling is a tool to be used in the process of

[1] The terms *disadvantaged, deprived, underprivileged,* and *culturally deprived* are used interchangeably in all chapters, primarily to refer to young people who have not had the middle-class stimulation and experiences that prepare them to compete successfully in our society. For a more detailed definition, see Chapter 2.

[2] Leona E. Tyler, *The Work of the Counselor* (New York: Appleton-Century-Crofts, Inc., 1961), p. 1.

1

personality change. To others, it is the giving of information and even guidance. However, basic to any understanding of the term is its relationship to verbal interaction between counselor and client. This relationship has historically sprung from the movements of vocational guidance and mental health. The impetus for both of these movements has come from counselor and client of middle-class society. Particular influence on counseling has been exerted by the psychoanalytic movement in the professions of psychology, psychiatry, and social work during the past two decades.

In recent years, owing to an increased emphasis on professional status and training and to an awareness that often a close relationship existed between mental health and vocational adjustment, the ranks closed; the counselor became more concerned with the total person. But, again, this total person was the verbally oriented middle-class youth or adult who, in most cases, had the ability, values, and experiences to talk through his particular problem and decide on a course of action. In recent years we have found that with many of our disadvantaged youth such an approach is not effective. Increasingly, one hears that the most successful counselor with the disadvantaged youth is the nonprofessional from the youth's own social or cultural group who can communicate on the youth's own terms and understands his problems because he has experienced them. Even though such a position has some merit, the long-term danger to the counseling profession is obvious. Unless counselors and counselor educators recognize this threat and are willing to modify curriculum roles, techniques, and procedures, additional criticism will be forthcoming.

PROBLEMS AND QUESTIONS

The more pressing operational problems facing the counseling profession include the following:

1.   The counselor's responsibility is to help all youth, including those who enjoy the cultural and other advantages of their middle-class status, to develop their potentials for leadership and creative effort, and to enter callings which can use them to the greatest advantages. No society can afford to neglect such resources. But having agreed to this, might we not then say, with equal truth, that up to now our more fortunate youth have been getting the lion's share of our guidance services, our training opportunities, and our more rewarding jobs? Have we not badly neglected the obscure and less favored young people—those whom we have recently been calling the "disadvantaged"? There is evidence of considerable talent and leadership potential among them too.

Obviously, young people who are handicapped by poverty, cultural deprivation, racial prejudice, etc., need kinds of help which are quite different from the help needed by middle-class youngsters who suffer from such liabilities as ill health or emotional disturbance or mental limitations. It is also obvious that within the culture of poverty there are major groups with very different needs—the contrast between rural and urban slum youth being a good example. And within any group of the disadvantaged, subgroups and individuals have problems that cannot possibly be solved by general rule-of-thumb prescriptions. This diversity of need is one of the reasons for our past neglect of this whole unhappy population.

On the other hand, the experience we *have* had, much of it recent, in the various experimental youth service centers, suggests that disadvantaged, culturally deprived youth have enough in common to warrant certain approaches and methods, some of which are quite unconventional, for widespread use in serving them. Let us review some of these:

A. In the past, most agencies and institutions serving youth have tended to assume that if a person old enough to need a job really wants help and is told where he might get it, he will go after it, and if he does not, it is his own fault. In contrast with this attitude, which sometimes is a rationalization prompted by shortages of staff and funds (and just possibly a little laziness), we are now beginning to realize that the very forces which make so many young people of the slums and depressed areas unemployed and unemployable also keep them from seeking help—that this is *part of the problem*, not a reason for evading it. We are learning that "outreach," going out to meet the youth on their own grounds, may be essential to future success in later counseling, remedial education, vocational training, or job finding. The use of semiprofessional workers who, so to speak, "talk the same language" and know conditions first-hand, does not seem to fit easily into the established operations of some service agencies, but we are beginning to find that this approach can work and bring results which cannot be achieved in any other way.

B. Another means of making sure that the disadvantaged youth is not lost in the shuffle and that he is understood and treated as an individual is to fix responsibility for all services on some one person, preferably in one agency; or, if that is not feasible, to use other means of keeping him off the impersonal conveyor belt of referral procedures which now shunts too many of our clients hither and yon, from one agency, or one operating unit within an agency, to another. Such youth, particularly those in the larger cities, have all too often been herded about in school, passed from teacher to teacher with few if any meaningful personal contacts with them, and all too often this has been one of the reasons for their indifference to school. They need a psychological home base, some familiar figure to personalize their relations to the organizations trying to serve them and, if possible, someone who will become a friend. The young person needs someone who comes eventually to know him, and know him well; someone who can take everything about him into account and figure out what to do next at any stage of his progress toward employability and a job. The problem, of course, is to get the full benefits of specialist services where needed while keeping this personal relationship and continuity of contact and coordination of plans. It is not easy, but the newer youth services are working toward that goal.

C.   It is also being recognized that young people who have not had the opportunity to learn informally about the vocations of their parents, relatives, and others and are hardly literate enough to read about them, and whose aptitudes and interests can hardly be appraised through such formal instruments as aptitude tests or interest inventories, must base their vocational choices on more immediate and concrete experiences. They need to get the "feel" of work activities and working conditions, and they need chances, formerly denied them, to visit establishments and see workers on the job. Numbers of special youth service projects are making increasing use of work sampling techniques, workshop tryout activities, plant visits, and other arrangements which can supplement or, where necessary, serve as practical substitutes for the more sophisticated techniques normally used with the average middle-class youth. In some projects, the young people are put on "work crews" and perform various work activities in nonprofit establishments such as hospitals and other public facilities. This gives them experience in working under supervision, helps them develop good work habits and attitudes, some familiarity with the functions of the organizations in which they are working, and the kinds of real employment possibilities that they offer. By such means, the youth reach a point at which they may be ready for full vocational training or for employment. Our national programs for work-training provide opportunities for the expansion of this approach through prevocational training.

D.   A fourth means of fitting services to the special needs of disadvantaged youth also bears on the problem of motivation. Do we not too often assume that when we can offer a young person a good, sensible, practicable course of action that will help toward his goal, he should realize what is best for him and stick to it faithfully? Suppose a given youth clearly needs a course of remedial reading before he can begin his vocational training, and we prescribe it. But soon he drops out, probably for the same reason that he previously dropped out of school. We are sorry, and that is the end of it. But should it be? Have we not overlooked his need for a constant, present motive, something concurrent with his remedial reading, such as a job (or even something that looks like a job), which lets him perform some service or produce something; a job that hopefully puts him on a payroll, even though it may be a "make-work" payroll? Many of our youth, even the best of them, need something more earthy and material than the lure of self-improvement or some distant goal. Our newer approaches must recognize this need. The old, time-tested combination of work *and* study seems to be solving many otherwise stubborn problems of motivation and growth.

2. The effort in the past has been toward directing the individual to adjust to his environment even when that environment can be destructive to the best interests of the counselee himself. We can often be more effective by seeking to modify the conditions of life in which these people live. The counselor can be an instrument for social change as well as individual change.

Counseling as a person-to-person process, providing information, guidance, insight, or support may be overemphasized in importance. It may be more important, when dealing with the disadvantaged, that we attempt to make significant changes in their conditions of life and growth. Greater stress could be placed in community and home contacts, in changing environmental conditions causing maladjustment, than in seeking to adjust the individual to these negative forces.

It has been claimed that counselors have overstated the centrality of "verbal interaction" for changing human behavior. People learn through interaction with the realities of the environment. What they learn may be more powerful in effecting change than the "verbal interaction." The way in which life is organized is more important than what the counselor is able to say. Results come from showing youth what they can do. We need to create appropriate conditions for development and support of the individual. Experience must support learning. The counselors not only have to get jobs for the young people, but also insure that they succeed in these jobs. Counseling should mean learning, and disadvantaged people do not learn a great deal by being talked to.

3. There is another aspect of this problem, calling for the community's attention—namely, that its own youth are probably restless and can thumb their way to any part of the country in a short time. No youth today, whose circumstances are at all normal, should really need either to stay at home and be resigned to poor, unsuitable employment (or none at all) or to wander to distant places, not knowing where to look for the kinds of work he can do best. But this can and will happen unless the community's educational, training, and employment agencies have specific and reliable and up-to-date knowledge of the opportunities of the home area and a good general knowledge about the principal fields of work in the American economy.

Each community which has a substantial problem of youth employment must undertake a truly community-wide effort to determine its own employment needs, giving special attention to unearthing the opportunities that may be hidden in little establishments unknown to the general public and in the equally obscure recesses of large establishments. That community can blame only itself for its failures to connect its own unemployed youth with local job opportunities. This task, it must be stated, cannot be performed adequately by only the Employment Service or any other single agency.

4.   Counseling as a service function varies widely in concept, purpose, and nature of process, depending upon (a) the type of agency or facility, (b) policy orientation—long range career planning or immediate job problem, (c) the age range and scope of problems of the clientele, and (d) the conceptual framework of the professional worker. They have in common the assertion that counseling is a helping profession. The responsibility for choice is the client's. Within these various helping professions there has long been a discussion about the degree to which the counselor may intervene in the lives of people without violating the integrity of the client. This question has particularly arisen in the relationship to disadvantaged youth.

A growing number of professional counselors are suggesting that a good counselor must be more than a good listener, a provider of information, an advisor, an appraiser of client abilities, attitudes, and interests. In addition, he must assume the role of an *enabler* who can and will take necessary action which will assist the counselee to carry out the plan which has been developed. They further suggest that counseling should be considered a process, as well as an art or a science. The counselor should create the conditions and circumstances that enable the counselee to grow and to learn.

In the secondary school the guidance counselor does not consider his responsibility limited to assistance in determining educational or vocational goals or needed changes in social behavior or attitude. He frequently takes steps to insure that goals will be achieved. Perhaps he needs only to write to a college admissions office on behalf of the student to secure his being accepted as a student, or he may help the student obtain a scholarship. Another time he may smooth the way for a better understanding and a fresh start in a student's English class, through a discussion with the teacher. He may intercede with the parent who fails to understand or appreciate the validity of his child's ambitions. Most certainly he will aid in seeking out a suitable job opportunity for his counselee in order that the student may reach his vocational goal.

In the public employment service the counselor is assuming more responsibility for the job placement of his counselees. The counselor does not need to get involved personally in the job search with *most* of his counselees. Many will be able to locate their own jobs—indeed should be encouraged to do so, or the regular placement facilities of the office may fully meet their needs. But the less able, the person with serious vocational handicaps, the school dropout, the boy with a history of delinquency, and those who are discriminated against because of race or for other reasons will very likely never reach their goals without special help of the counselor in their job search.

5. Job education or training referrals are, in some situations, a proper end product of the counseling process. When some young people are referred, the counselor may breathe a sigh of relief, wish them well, and check up on them through a phone call a month later. But not so with many of the disadvantaged. Many placements must be trial or conditional placements, made with the full knowledge of all concerned that the adjustments will be difficult and may fail. Other placements will be successful, but only if they are supported by the continuing interest of those who make them. Follow-up cannot be perfunctory. It may need to involve visits, not phone calls, and include both youth and employer. But the social and economic and psychological values of really good job adjustment are so substantial for the youth, for their employers, and for a public which otherwise may have the burden of supporting the disadvantaged youth when he no longer is a youth that an intelligent, persistent follow-through may become one of our most critical and valuable services.

Nor is job placement or referral appropriate for the young woman whose "job" is to stay home and care for her young children. Other kinds of services and programs are required for these young people, yet many if not most job-oriented programs have no room for them. The agency program may need either reevaluation or the inclusion of new services if one is to escape the referral circus.

The broad issues just presented are among those which seem to be of major significance in dealing with the problems of disadvantaged youth. Gordon [3] has stated these same issues in a series of challenging questions. These questions, presented below, are those to which the subsequent chapters of this book will provide some promising answers:

Goals of Counseling

If the target group is one for which special efforts are needed to make the group accessible to counseling, if counseling must in some sense be "sold" or the youth seduced into the agency, then there are implications for the goals of the counseling; simple statements about "felt needs" and "client self-direction" do not suffice. In most counseling, the client has to hurt somewhere to be motivated for counseling. Does this population

---

[3] The following issues were originally part of Jesse Gordon's chapter "Counseling Disadvantaged Boys" but are included here for the sake of organization.

really "hurt," or is it one that has made successful adaptations to its socio-economic-cultural world? Is behavior change *wanted*, or is it the goal of treatment to induce behavioral change anyway, in order to protect middle-class structures from being violated and inundated? Is the intent of counseling a revision of class-related behaviors (such as chronic unemployment), is it to cure trouble spots at the point of contact between lower-class integration and intruding demands for middle-class behaviors, or should counseling be reserved for disturbances in adaptations within the subculture?

Making the Youth Available to Treatment

How does "outreach" work? What psychological structures are tapped that bring the clients into contact with a counselor? What "handles" are most productive in their ability to elicit and sustain motivation for counseling? How can such "handles" be utilized in techniques? What characteristics of the population can be used most effectively for increasing accessibility to efforts designed to promote change?

Areas of Probable and Possible Change

What are the areas in which change can be produced most readily? Are there focal areas in which changes would result in modification of several areas of functioning, compared to specific changes in narrow fields? Are these areas accessible to counseling? If there are some that are more crucial than others (or in which change generalizes or spreads more than others) and if areas vary in their accessibility to treatment, can a strategy be developed in which counseling efforts are directed at relatively accessible areas which are also relatively focal? How could the counseling be scheduled to move from the accessible to the significant, or can the significant be dealt with at a level enough removed from deep defenses to enable productive change to be produced early? What are the focal areas of concern for this population? What are the limits of change that can be expected under various strategies (counseling *in situ*, removal from environment, etc.)? What is the relationship between motivation and attitude, in the context of the modifiability of each?

"Enabling" vs. Behavior Change

What areas of behavior can be worked with which require only modest redirection or supportive work to increase functioning adequacy? What areas of change would require more extensive development of new ego resources, redirection of goals, resolution of conflicts? In brief, to what extent can the "liabilities" be reduced by channeling the strengths, compared to the extent to which a more direct approach to the liabilities is required?

Counselor vs. Client Initiation

In classical counseling, it is usually assumed that environments are manageable by clients, in principle, were it not for internal blockages or inadequacies in the client. To what extent is the environment of this population manageable? To what extent does the management of such an environment require resources beyond those which the clients possess or which they can develop in treatment? To what extent, then, should the counselor become involved in environmental change management? What are the implications of such intervention for the course of the counseling? What are the implications for initiating client-activity? Are decisions on this issue related to decisions in the areas described earlier? While environmental management (or least demonstrated involvement in such management) is typically associated with supportive or "enabling" counseling more than with deeper personality change, is there reason why the reverse should not be the case? What is the relationship between counselor commitment, expectancy, hope for the client, client perception of the counselor, and success in counseling?

Group vs. Individual Methods

What are the variables influencing choice of group vs. individual methods? What areas of change are most appropriate for each approach? How do the characteristics of the population bear on decisions regarding group vs. individual methods? What are the terms of a decision regarding use of naturally occurring groups (gangs, families, spontaneous groups) vs. counselor-constructed groups? Do these have different realms of applicability, in terms of client change areas? What is known about the characteristics of groups and the characteristics of the clients which will illuminate the course of counseling in these two approaches?

Training

How can specific instruction or training be used in counseling? What areas of ego adequacy are amenable to teaching? What kind of teaching? What of the relationship between teacher and counselor? How should teaching be scheduled as a counseling resource? What kinds of teaching, in what areas, would be more productive from a therapeutic point of view? In what areas can teaching open up the client to counseling and in what areas is counseling needed to make the client available to teaching?

Talking and Showing

What are the capacities of this group for responding to verbal communications? What levels of subtlety can be used to communicate at both conscious and unconscious levels? To what extent does this population respond more completely or sensitively to nonverbal cues? What kinds of nonverbal communication techniques are available? What is the relationship between client's language, counselor's language, and the utility of modeling approaches? What, if any, is the role of direct counselor participation in the relationship compared to sublimated talk about the relationship?

Relationship—Transference

How do these clients structure their relationships with counselors? What kinds of relationships are they able to accept? What kinds of relationships are they defended against? What are the limits on the character of the relationship imposed by what the client can tolerate? What are the constraints and opportunities regarding the counselor's use of the relationship for supplementing the client's ego resources, for protecting the client against impulses, for controlling acting-out, for socializing motives, affects, and attitudes?

Rewards and Punishments

In classical counseling, internalizing of therapist approval and disapproval can be used to supplement weak ego functioning. How responsive to such reinforcers is this population? Are there other reinforcers which might also be used? What are the limitations and advantages of various kinds of reinforcers, and what are the variables which might control their best scheduling? Is there a relationship between aspects of ego functioning (e.g., impulse control, time perspective, synthesizing, abstracting, and generalizing) and the kind of reinforcement schedule which may be required for productive learning and performance?

Resistance

What are the defensive styles and preferences of this population? On what ego structures do these defenses rest? What are the concomitants of these defenses in conflict-free functioning of the ego? What are the sources of gratification which serve to inhibit change? How can change be produced, or in what areas can change occur, with least erosion of present sources of gratification? Or what new gratifications are available for replacing present ones? What is the nature of the threat to self, identity, impulses, and defenses, implied by the possibility of behavioral change, as seen by this population? What strategies of defense are available to them and used by them? What strategies and resources does the counselor have available for handling resistance? If there are disjunctures in ego functioning and an absence of an ethic of reliability and punctuality, what can the counselor use in place of pointing out inconsistencies, setting limits, etc., or how can these techniques be made effective in exposing and countering defensive maneuvers?

Counselor Characteristics

Given the demands on the counselor implied by the considerations in the above areas, what kinds of counselors are likely to be most effective? What are the personality and background features which may be essential? What features are more or less peripheral, or can be supplemented in other ways, for working productively with this population? Given the shortage of Renaissance Men who can be most things to most people, what characteristics of counselors are likely to be able to "wear" best the kinds of strategies and relationships considered to be most effective with this population? To what extent is the production of such characteristics through education and experience possible? What are the negative characteristics of therapists which must be avoided for this population in particular?

Prejudice and Value-confrontation

The target population is one which is highly prone to relatively crude and extensive prejudice; the counselor population is less likely to be strongly prejudiced (or more likely to hold prejudices subtly). These issues become particularly pertinent where prejudice plays a central role in the definition of the causes of the need for counseling and in the goals of counseling. This is especially true if counseling is thought to originate in a need to change a value structure which in itself is not neurotically determined, although it may be dysfunctional in meeting middle-class standards. What is the nature of prejudice? How does it manifest itself? Within what limits must the counselor work in conformity to the client's prejudices rather than remaining independent of them? What are the consequences of the confrontation of values between counselor and client? What strategies do these considerations dictate regarding the scheduling and programing of counseling?

End of Counseling

What kind of "way of life" (job, family structure, identity, involvement in human relationships) would be, could be, or is available which could serve as a reasonable (or minimally acceptable) level such that further counseling would not be required and which would be consistent enough with the nature and characteristics of this population so that it would make minimal demands for counseling-produced change?

WHERE ARE THE ANSWERS?

The issues presented and questions posed by the preceding pages are easily recognized as among the most pressing and difficult for any profession to solve and resolve. Fortunately, practitioners and researchers have been working to find answers in both practice and theory over the past several decades. Efforts have been sharply increased in recent years.

The aim of the following chapters is to bring, for the first time, both practical and theoretical assistance to those working in counseling and training of counselors with particular concern for the disadvantaged young person. These chapters present descriptions of promising practices in new programs, describe methods of providing needed vocational information, give the sources of this information, and discuss the special needs of the boy and girl who are handicapped by poverty and ignorance. In addition, some of the technical problems and approaches which hold promise of being more effective than previous programs are described, discussed, and analyzed.

It should be clear to all readers that there are no formulas and no general panaceas. Programs effective with one kind of young person in one region of the country may be dismal failures elsewhere. Research is so minimal that all one can say with certainty is that we need to know a great deal more than we now know about working with youth today. Finally, and most crucially, the orientation and role of the counselor himself is brought under scrutiny.

The opinions expressed by the authors of each chapter are their own; there is no implication here that these are the only, or even the best, approaches. They do, however, provide much that is worthy of serious consideration by our colleagues in the profession.

2

THE NATURE
OF DISADVANTAGED YOUTH

WILLIAM E. AMOS

THE PROBLEM

Today's counselor is facing what is perhaps the greatest challenge in his professional career in assisting youth. His typical client is vastly different from the boy or girl who needed counseling help in 1945, and there are many more of them. In 1966 an average of approximately nine million young people between 16 and 21 were in the labor force, and in any month over one million of these persons were unemployed. Not only is their total number greater today, but many of these youth have heavy liabilities that lessen their chances for success in school and later in employment.

The term "disadvantaged" encompasses a broad range of human conditions that are below par. Deficiencies in education, experiences, and the pervasive results of discrimination and socioeconomic deprivation characteristically mark the disadvantaged youth with whom we deal. The type of guidance needed by disadvantaged youth is different from and more intensive than the approach that can be used with those who have had more of the everyday advantages and opportunities. While many of the methods and techniques of vocational guidance apply equally in dealing with any youth, successful service to the culturally deprived calls for certain specific knowledge and adaptation of method to meet the special needs of this group.

There must always be recognition that each person is best served as an individual, but group characteristics must also be considered. However, it is important that no group of youth be so labeled that any feel "different." There is uniqueness in each person. Even his disadvantage is unique. And the counselor has an unparalleled opportunity: to serve disadvantaged youth in a manner and with resources never before at his disposal.

Disadvantaged youth may be found living with their families in a world where day-to-day survival—keeping a roof over their heads, getting food and clothing—takes all their thoughts and energies. Many American youth are disadvantaged from birth because they are of a minority race; they must make their way in a society still riddled with discrimination. Other youth are severely disadvantaged because of a physical environment that isolates them from opportunities for education and social experience in keeping with the requirements of modern life. These are the youth of city ghettos, of played-out rural areas; these are the children of migrant farm workers.

We may arbitrarily define culturally disadvantaged youth as those who are the products of a culture that has not provided them with the motivations, opportunities, experiences, and relationships that will enhance their chances for competing successfully with their fellow citizens in all phases of life.

From an academic standpoint, however, it must be acknowledged that there is no such person as a culturally deprived child. A person is a product of the culture to which he has been exposed. We may see a person's culture as the way of life of the group of people of which he is an integral part. One of the principal purposes of any culture is to pass its way of life on to the young. The attitudes and values of the group, as well as its artifacts and institutions, are included in this heritage. As used here, the term culturally deprived child refers to a child who has not had the stimulation of middle-class experiences and relationships that help provide a foundation for the development of his innate potentiality, yet who often aspires to acquire the same good life and its attendant material assets.

There are many criteria of disadvantage, and poverty is not the only one, although it may frequently be the factor that has contributed most. Another important factor is cultural isolation—lack of exposure to museums, trips, news media, libraries, parks, and other community offerings. The range of experiences of youth thus isolated is more limited than that of the average middle-class child. Examples of culturally isolated youth might include those growing up in rural slums (Appalachia), in an urban slum (the Bedford-Stuyvesant area of New York City), or an American Indian reservation. They miss contact with a wider and more complex cultural community that is a part of the normal mode of life of most Americans.

Geographical isolation has disadvantaged many American youth. This term signifies geographic removal from the mainstream of our life. Natural barriers such as mountains and deserts, and lack of public transportation, are as much of a disadvantage as the manmade conditions of the city ghettos. Often these geographic barriers cause entire areas to become shut off from the opportunities open to most people in our country.

Racial minority group membership in itself is a disadvantage that millions of Americans face each day. Generally included in these groups are Negroes, Indians, Puerto Ricans, and Spanish-Americans. Not all members of these groups feel, or indeed are disadvantaged. However, depending on their experiences and total environment, many have extreme feelings of inferiority and need building up as individuals, as well as members of a group. Characteristically, members of racial minorities are not only provided the poorest educational opportunities and limited employment possibilities, they are isolated from the "mainstream" of the community.

Physical disability is a disadvantage often accompanied by a lack of training and low self-esteem. Poverty is often associated with lack of medical care since uncorrected physical (and mental) disabilities are more frequent among the poor. Correctable defects may be ignored owing to lack of money or lack of access to public facilities. Subsistence living, for instance, may result in poor teeth, being severely underweight, or in other unfortunate evidences of malnutrition. Such handicaps often contribute to poor performance.

Many teachers notice the child who is suffering from physical deprivations. He may arrive at school exhausted, and fall asleep at his desk, having come from a home so overcrowded that there is not enough physical space, much less quiet, for every member of the family to sleep all night. Then there are the children who face the school day and its unwelcome demands without the sustenance of any breakfast, the ones whose debilitating colds go untreated, the ones who need glasses (and may have needed them for years), the ones who have hearing handicaps. These neglected physical problems of the schoolchild often show up in more serious and more permanent form in adolescence, a time of trial for even the most carefully nurtured child.

The high mobility and rootlessness of many families, as well as of individual youth, constitutes another disadvantage frequently noted. Moves within a city, to other cities and regions, from rural to urban surroundings, result in interruptions in education and lack of access to, and even knowledge of, desirable opportunities available through social agencies and elsewhere in the average community. There may be no participation in conventional forms of socialization, including religious institutions, schools, and youth serving organizations, for extended periods of time.

Migrant farm youth present a well-defined category of disadvantaged youth. In addition to the customary disadvantage of minority group status, most migrant farm youth suffer because of poor and intermittent educational opportunities, generally low aspirations of parents, need to supplement family income, and isolation from any normal community life and resources.

The counselor often finds himself interviewing youth who are part of a great migratory wave moving from farmed-out countrysides, mining areas, and backwoods to the urban industrial centers, there to seek a future in a city slum. Generally included in this group are Negroes, children of Spanish-American migrant families, sharecroppers, farm laborers, and rural industrial workers. Also, there are Indians, on and off reservations, and "mountain whites" from Appalachia, the Ozarks, the Cascades, and other areas isolated from contemporary American life and society.

From a broad point of view, all youth who grow up in rural areas with limited educational and other community facilities are disadvantaged to some degree when transferring to a city school, and later in looking for a job. In view of these disadvantages, many of which are compounded in one individual, it is not surprising that as a group, they usually barely manage to stay in school, and afterward can obtain and hold only jobs requiring less skill and conferring lower status than those open to urban-reared youth.

It is a rare youth who possesses only one of the generalized conditions sketched above as typical of disadvantaged youth. One problem grows out of another, and often we find a young person who faces the world with varying degrees of all the problems noted, and perhaps more.

PROBLEMS OF THE DISADVANTAGED

Low socioeconomic status brings with it the disadvantages of poor housing, marginal living, inadequate forms of social protection, few organized forms of social life, low parental motivation for youth, and damaged self-concept. Insufficient nourishment levels, inadequate clothing, neglected health conditions, and other factors such as irregular, temporary, or nonexistent residence, may preclude or interrupt satisfactory participation in local community opportunities.

Communication Skills

The great disadvantage caused by inability to handle the English language is coming to be recognized as a major handicap. Deprived living conditions tend to limit the development of middle-class language communication skills, and may result in a feeling of inferiority, coupled with a resentfulness toward others. Youth with this disadvantage may be hostile, unduly passive, or unduly uncommunicative. In this group we find the boy or girl whose grasp of English is only rudimentary because of a foreign language background in his home. And, as we are well aware, a limited vocabulary can adversely affect many test performances and can delay the establishment of a good working relationship for several interviews. This topic is discussed in more detail in Chapters 3, 6 and 7.

Financial Management

Most young people are immature in handling money; but the boy or girl from a background of deprivation is at a particular disadvantage, and is particularly vulnerable. The young person who comes to the city from a rural area finds many strange, intimidating situations with which he must learn to cope; the city youth whose family is on relief may not be much better equipped to meet such challenges. It is hard to face the reality of the amounts deducted from a paycheck (as well as their purpose), the inevitability of rent and food costs, and all of the other items that deplete income.

The disadvantaged youth is not likely to understand the pitfalls of installment buying or borrowing, the cost of credit, the possibility of legal involvements. He probably does not know how to plan his spending or his savings, nor does he understand the importance of keeping records. Usually he needs guidance in making financial decisions and clarifying goals. A good example is his attitude toward and understanding of the costs of owning and operating a car—a problem area common to youth of all strata. The financial decisions of a disadvantaged youth are guided by the desires of the moment and not by long term goals: he fails to see the continuing expenses of maintenance, insurance, and license, as well as emergencies that may arise.

Police or Institutional Record

Perhaps no youth is more disadvantaged than the one who has acquired a police record, the one who may have served time in a correctional institution. A special approach is needed; counselors should recognize the fact that these youth have assets in addition to their liabilities. On the credit side of the ledger, they often acquire a skill or skills while in detention. Various maintenance jobs are found in most institutions; but there are also numerous training programs for skills in demand in the outside labor market. Too, these young people may acquire habits of regularity and conformity, plus a new consistency of direction quite untypical of the deprived situation from which so many of them come.

It is important in dealing with such youth to help individuals understand that, while the prospective employer will know of the record, he is still willing to give the applicant a chance. This will make for a sense of security and self-confidence that could be the needed bridge to success. While each employer must be told all the positive qualifications of the youth, such as his training, experience, and attitude, the youth must be made to realize that some incontestably well-intentioned employers will not be able to give him a chance, because of regulations of bonding companies, or for other similar reasons.

Counselors recognize, too, in dealing with these youth, that they have seldom planned for the future, either as individuals or with the support and stimulus of parents or teachers. A recent study showed that 90 per cent of boys 16-18 years old in one correctional institution had given no thought to job planning for their future.[1] Therefore, a counselor working with such youth must patiently encourage them in vocational exploration, stimulate job interest, and motivate planning.

Lack of Motivation

When the disadvantaged child is old enough to try to enter the world of work, he may continue to reject the middle-class criteria for achievement, and so preserve the concept of his own worth that developed many years before. With this attitude, his progress in a job is not likely to be any more notable than was his progress in school. Further, he may think that his lack of success stems from limited opportunities in the labor force. His lack of achievement in school did not really seem relevant to him; and it comes as a shock to find that he must meet still other standards in employment if he is to compete successfully. He is apt then to continue in the unpromising pattern in order to protect his self-concept. To disown his responsibilities, he may blame the environment, the general employment picture, or the school that did not prepare him to earn an adequate livelihood. In fact, many disadvantaged youth see regular employment as "woman's work" and have little respect for males who report to work each day. The counselor's task is gigantic at this point, for the youth's negative motivations must be reversed, if possible, through skillful guidance and supportive services.

It is not surprising to note that the parents are often so involved in their own activities and personal problems that, beyond looking after the basic physical problems of their families, they find little time to encourage children in school or in social activities. It is small wonder then that so many disadvantaged youth, whose parents have so obviously failed, feel there is no incentive to try to succeed: the parents' stress on the importance of school is not borne out by their own lives. Some parents, in fact, do not encourage success in school because they themselves have failed so miserably. This seems especially paradoxical when one realizes that

[1] William E. Amos, "Job Adjustment Problems of Delinquent Minority Group Youth," *Vocational Guidance Quarterly* (Winter 1964-65), p. 88.

the parents of disadvantaged youth, in both city and country, usually place a high value on education for their children, though they themselves are largely undereducated.[2]

Yet, in spite of manifest respect for education per se, a majority of these parents cannot or do not give their children adequate support and encouragement either to attend school regularly or to study at home. This lack of family support places an extraordinary responsibility on the school system; and typically, these children go to schools with the poorest facilities, the most crowded classrooms, the most overburdened teaching staffs.

The counselor thus challenged learns to expect to observe certain characteristics. He may face an obviously distorted self-concept dating from the early pre-school years when a disadvantaged youth may have had small opportunities for creative and motivational experiences. The self-concept develops from experiences; through trial and error one learns who he is, what he can do, how others react to him, what his skills are, and what he lacks. Studies have shown that pre-school years are extremely relevant to later learning experiences.[3]

Disadvantaged children do not play like other children. They have less play equipment, less supervision, less participation and encouragement from adults. Often they have limited free space for play. The adults they know are limited, and consequently, their play models restrictive. However, such youngsters may not be confronted with an assessment of their disadvantages until they enter the structure of formal education.

A certain family may have a long history of poverty and dependency. The parents may never have completed elementary school, and may be illiterate as well as lacking in social experience; indeed, they may display consistently unacceptable social behavior which is apt to be emulated by their children. Thus, when a child of this family arrives in school, his incomplete information and experience make an inadequate foundation for the new situations he encounters, usually hampering his success in mastering subjects in competition with others who may not be so disadvantaged. The image he had developed of himself in the formative years of pre-school play is now in conflict. He may reject the importance of the school standards set for conventional achievement, and resist completely the acknowledgment that he is in any way below par.

To accept the supervision of the classroom is alien to his nature. His schoolmates' home experiences may represent a gamut of disciplinary methods, ranging from the very harsh and unreasonable, to a complete absence of restraint, or in fact, any kind of attention. The child, therefore,

[2] William E. Amos, "Disadvantaged Youth—Recognizing the Problems," *Employment Service Review,* September, 1964.

[3] Several studies conducted for the Office of Economic Opportunity have indicated that pre-school experiences are related to performance in the classroom.

must comprehend the necessity and the importance of equal supervision for all—including himself—in the school, and later in the outside world. The routine of school life may be new to him. Often requirements such as coming to school on time, coming to school every day, are beyond his imagination, and his liking. As for participating in citizenship duties of the school—sharing in the tidying tasks, the teacher-helper jobs—these are strange new events that strain his comprehension. Often the cooperation he gives is less than enthusiastic, especially after the novelty has worn off.

Understanding Procedures

Disadvantaged youth are especially deficient in understanding procedures of all types.[4] The school-age child coming from more average circumstances has already learned to value and understand procedures from his parents and general environment; he adapts more or less readily to classroom routine. But the deprived child frequently does not know how to ask and answer questions. He does not know how to study; taking tests is very difficult. His style is apt to be slow and cautious; hence he encounters still another unfamiliar attitude of society: emphasis on the importance of speed. Since he cannot quickly grasp problems, especially in the abstract, he is apt to make a poor showing when the criterion is speed. However, once he becomes truly interested in a problem, he may show evidence of his potential. Disadvantaged youth frequently display a similar orientation to a job, performing less well, or poorly, when the emphasis is on speed.

In addition to the capacity to achieve speed, such personal qualities as competitiveness, conscientiousness, and anxiety, point to success in school and career; these characteristics are not usually combined in the disadvantaged child.

The Slow Learner

Another disadvantaged child who demands special attention is the so-called slow learner. First it must be determined whether the youth is slow because he is mentally deficient, or if his slowness is related to poor educational and social experiences. As G. Orville Johnson says, "The slow learners compose the largest group of mentally retarded persons. Among the general school population 15 to 17 or 18 per cent of the children can be considered slow learners. [However,] these percentages and numbers are not true for all communities. Preferred suburban communities where executive and professional persons reside will have very few slow learners ... the subcultural areas of large metropolitan communities where the

---

[4] Frank Riessman, "The Culturally Deprived Child: A New View," *Programs for the Educationally Disadvantaged*, U.S. Department of Health, Education, and Welfare (Washington, D.C.: Government Printing Office), p. 8.

children receive little psycho-social stimulation present quite a different picture. Fifty per cent or more of the children can appropriately be designated as slow learners." [5]

Many children live under conditions that preclude their successful handling of school homework, or training preparation. As indicated above, a home may be so severely overcrowded that a youth cannot get sufficient rest to perform properly in school. Slowness is often equated with dullness, and it should be realized that many children of the slums have been shuffled into lower tracks or into special classes because most schools, like middle class society in general, reward speed. Teachers, therefore, have concluded that they should reward swiftness of learning, and have not been encouraged to develop techniques for dealing with slow pupils.

Understanding and appreciation of slow cognition could be the basis for planning a new approach to the student who is extremely careful and meticulous, and slow to respond because of failure to generalize. The slow learner *can* benefit from education; he must not be labeled a discipline problem, inattentive, or lazy. Some may move cautiously because they are physical learners, or have a one-track style.[6] Others are fearful of unbending enough to follow directions in new areas.

Most youth who have obviously limited ability to perform within a given time span can be taught to do many jobs. The notion must be avoided that the slow learner should only be given routine tasks. Good orientation and supervision are keys to this end. Counselors must try not to stereotype slow learners who, like other youth, differ in interests and temperament, and must receive appropriate assignments, again, like any other worker.

Certain assets often characterize the slow learners. Some are very careful with details, meticulous in the extreme. Thus they can be taught responsibility for specific and precise tasks, and can be depended on for handling them.

The Need to Trust

It is axiomatic that, in dealing with the disadvantaged youth, his trust and confidence must be engendered from the beginning. It is said that the youth being served in a New York slum project expressed the feeling many times that trust was the characteristic they considered of the most importance in adults; they specified the need to believe that the adult who is friendly today will not give them a brush-off the following week.[7]

[5] G. Orville Johnson, *Education for the Slow Learners* (Englewood Cliffs, N.J.: Prentice-Hall, Inc., 1963), p. 9.

[6] Frank Riessman, *The Culturally Deprived Child* (New York: Harper & Row, Publishers, 1962), p. 29.

[7] Reported to the author by counselors of the New York State Employment Service who were assigned to a youth employment project in Harlem.

The counselor's office must be a place where the youth feels he can be treated with respect. Regardless of what the counselor can or cannot do for the youth, a positive attitude is requisite. Each human being deserves to be treated with dignity by other humans, and the youth who must struggle, to preserve this dignity, who often feels abused, is alert to a negative attitude in his counselor.

Numerous pressures weigh upon the disadvantaged youth, arousing feelings of uncertainty about his own adequacy; and threats, real or implied, make him resist suggestions. Often such people go through life reacting to their repeated failures with increasing distrust of the world about them, increasingly placing the blame for these failures on others. They are always treated badly, according to their interpretation.

It is believed that youths who develop sincere confidence in their counselor may have some expectation of success from this relationship. The counselor must be a model of strength and must inspire trust in his young clients. He knows that there is no substitute for learning about people by hearing from them directly, even when a person he wants to learn about is a seemingly inarticulate youth.

Yet the counselor walks a tightrope here, for the foreseeable future does not hold jobs for all who will need them, in spite of the many constructive new programs, and we must be careful not to inspire false optimism in the youth we serve. We must impress on them the fact that the future may hold good things for them if they will take the constructive steps that are necessary to effect a change for the better. Despair and hopelessness breed demoralization and delinquency, and while education and employment are not the total answer, the knowledge that there are ways of changing one's situation is of the utmost importance.

Long-term Goals

Some of the effects of deprivation confronting the counselor are shared by most disadvantaged youth. Many, for example, are incapable of setting long-term goals because they are preoccupied with, and sometimes overpowered by immediate needs for money, food, clothing, and shelter. Desperation about the present often causes difficulty in making realistic future choices. Little interest is shown in long-term planning, either for courses in school or for a career. Talk to such a youth about his future and the importance of building for the years to come, and he stops listening. He is concerned with today and tomorrow; and his way of life only reinforces his inability to think beyond tomorrow. Counselors, therefore, should refrain from pushing plans and setting long-range goals immediately. "Ten years from now," means nothing to many they will encounter. Resentment or hostility may be reflected in the attitudes, behavior, motivation, responsibility, and levels of aspiration of a typical youth. Many times he is unfamiliar with educational and occupational opportunities; and when he is told of them, they carry no meaning for him.

Some feel that the world has treated them badly; others have developed a sense of resourcefulness and initiative. A person may assume more responsibility—a potential asset on a job—when he finds he has to look out for himself. The counselor has to determine just how far each youth is ready to go. Judgment of these factors can only be made after getting to know the individual and studying his situation and background. Then the responsibility is imposed on the counselor to help these youths into a wider world that will increase their experiences; for each job and each new experience can help in achieving upward mobility.

Unrealistic Goals

The opposite swing of the pendulum reveals the youth who has unrealistic job plans. It is apparent that he lacks realism and knowledge, and the counselor must be careful not to deflate him. He is, however, easier to deal with than the youth with limited ideas and ambition, or the kind of realism producing the conviction that there is no chance for him. The unrealistic youth's stated interest can be utilized as a point of departure for determining what steps he can take in the general area of his ambition. To tell him he cannot do something will only reinforce his weakness, as well as his hostility. The requirements for the suggested positions must be explained to him. Talking with someone in or directly concerned with an occupation may help give the youth a clear picture of what is expected of an individual working in a specific field, and can also help him realize the dignity and worth of the job.

It must be realized that an unrealistic ambition may be simply a desire to acquire a higher status. This is particularly true of many minority group youth. During the past few years, increased efforts have been directed toward increasing the aspirations of these youngsters and destroying racial stereotypes as they relate to jobs. In some instances, this has led to unfortunate confusion between dignified jobs and the dignity of work. The counselor most certainly must raise levels of aspiration where appropriate, but not to the extent that only selected status jobs are acceptable to the youth concerned.

Model Identification

Many boys seen by the employment service, social service agency, or school counselor, who may be disadvantaged in several of the ways discussed above, come from a subculture that is characteristically masculine. Physical ability carries much value with this group, and as a result individuals may tend to overestimate their own prowess in this area.[8] This masculine identification can be utilized to better advantage in rehabilitation and prevention activities in a community.

Many of the most deprived youth in our population have had no father figure in their lives, having been completely rejected by their fathers, or cared for by a female figure. Thus they turn to the gang or street corner society where the male is superior, where even leisure activities are physically oriented, and where violence and force often determine the results. Such boys need a masculine figure with whom to identify and from whom they can learn their sex roles. This factor is very important in referral to jobs, for these youth usually have no idea of what it means to be regularly and productively employed, coming as they do from homes where few male figures have set such examples.

Rural Youth

A special set of characteristics is often encountered in rural youth. Frequently they do not aspire to college as do most urban youth. Often their country environment lacks adult examples of the various professions: this limits their opportunity to gain firsthand knowledge of the varieties of professional work, and to see ways to prepare for, seek, and secure such careers. The parents of these boys and girls, like their parents before them, have always lived on a farm or in their particular rural region. Consequently, they are usually not well equipped to help sons and daughters who must leave familiar surroundings and go to the city to find a job. Successful models, not only in the professions, but in a wide range of occupations, are rare in rural environments; thus a rural youth seldom has the chance to identify with someone who is an established success in an occupation not directly related to his environment.

Another characteristic the counselor often notes in rural youths is a preference for working with their hands. Frequently, too, they aspire to be their own bosses when they go to work. Thus placement in technological and service jobs that may be in good supply in the city not infrequently brings real problems of adjustment for the rural youth.

Another disadvantage often displayed by rural youths who come to the city is the lack of social skills that are frequently requisite in urban jobs. Also, they have had limited experience in managing their financial affairs and in making arrangements for personal matters such as living space and transportation. Many a counselor has found assistance with these problems in suggesting affiliation with a recreational, educational, or religious organization where contacts and activities can facilitate the newcomers' social-personal adjustment.

[8] William E. Amos, "A Study of Self-Concept: Delinquent Boys' Accuracy in Selected Self-Evaluations," *Genetic Psychology Monographs,* **67** (1963), 45-87.

IMPLICATIONS

Sharp perception and true understanding of the nature of these disadvantages and the needs arising from them have become of the most vital necessity to our counseling programs, and undoubtedly to all counselors of youth. Traditionally, counseling has focused on problems of choice or change of occupation. Today, our imperative is to focus on the concept of role adjustments: we must look at the youth with the objective of assisting him in those areas that need strengthening so that he may be as successful as possible in our society.

We are well aware of the need to bring together elements of the various disciplines of anthropology, sociology, education, social work, and economics in order to relate our disadvantaged youth clientele to the world of work. This monumental task makes it necessary for the counselor to explore to the best of his ability and time a youth's way of life, his value system, his attitudes, his way of looking at himself and the world.

We aim to change the direction of the lives of these youth, to change the generations-old culture pattern into which they were born, so that they will be more able to cope with contemporary demands of life and employment. They will have to be taught that the treadmill of poverty can be halted. Hopefully, personalities blunted by the barriers of discrimination and rejection can be altered in today's changing social climate.

While we do not expect to correct all childhood deprivations, we can help many young people to develop the potentialities that they do have. And no matter how the disadvantaged youngster is viewed, the counselor acknowledges that he is a whole human being, bringing with him the cumulative background of a life affected by the forces he has encountered along the way. His historical, social, and economic surroundings must be taken into account, and his apparent personal conflicts weighed in relation to the conflicts of life in our communities, our entire nation, and the world itself.

Counselors do not have to be born and raised in slums to serve well the deprived clientele of these areas. As a matter of fact, it is well recognized that minority group counselors, in many cases, are among the most punitive in dealing with young people of their race. They recall only too well from personal experience what hardships the minority youth faces; they understand perfectly how discouraged he may be. Yet, at the same time, they see the child's predicament as a reflection on their race and have little tolerance for the fact that the child has not "pulled himself up" as his counselor has done. They may be prone to expect an unrealistic amount of self-insight and motivation and, not finding this, reject the youngster as unworthy. Counselors with the experiences and understanding derived from membership in minority groups should be able to make realistic appraisals, provide images of success, and thus stimulate aspirations in a very significant way. Their clue is to remain constant in their empathy with such youth, and help them to create hope, not despair.

A knowledge of human behavior and of the cultural background of each child can help free counselors from stereotyped thinking and enable them to assist even persons who come from completely alien backgrounds. The criterion of the effectiveness of "assistance" given should be whether or not the youth is receiving the power to help himself, to strengthen and maximize his individual capacities. All must be treated with respect, though they may never have been successfully employed, nor even have looked for employment.

School counselors have been generally optimistic, hoping that motivation will result from current assessment of the individual and proper placement in the curriculum. Further, there has been a tendency to trust that accurate information about available jobs and what they require will somehow automatically produce motivation in youth. But there is increasing evidence to indicate that there are, apparently, many who cannot achieve either within the school or within the labor force. It must be realized, too, that such youth may have limited participation in school activities, having been pushed aside by teachers and students because of low social status as evidenced by poor clothing and lack of verbal ability, sophistication, and acting out behavior.

Perhaps we have been too optimistic in the past. It is not the teen years that are the most important in personality development. However, it is in these years that we see the cumulative effect of environmental deprivation experienced in the years from one to five. In his pre-school life the child develops the basis for his value system, his attitudes and the feeling he has of his own place. A child who lives in circumstances of adversity will probably not be equipped to meet the competitive standards he first encounters in school. The damage started early is reinforced as he grows older, and the effect on his development becomes acutely apparent as he approaches adulthood. Educators, advisers, and counselors, who face increasing numbers of such underdeveloped and deprived personalities, are coming to the inescapable recognition that there must be intensified work with the youngest children by all who are concerned with problems of the young adult.[9]

SUMMARY

All of these disadvantages, described only superficially, but most recognizable in some degree to the counselor working with disadvantaged

---

[9] William E. Amos and Charles F. Wellford, eds., *Delinquency Prevention: Theory and Practice* (Englewood Cliffs, N.J.: Prentice-Hall, Inc., 1967), p. 142.

youth, will manifest themselves in various ways in relation to employment and school success. In all probability, these disadvantaged youths will function below their potential for any or all of the factors touched on.

In many instances, repeated failures in prior social experiences may cause these youths to see themselves as not able to perform academic tasks, or to hold jobs for which they are otherwise qualified. They may be reluctant to take training, even after they have overcome their reluctance to approach the employment service, because they "know" that nothing will be available to them. They are often withdrawn, unduly passive, uncommunicative, and in need of a good deal of "bringing out." Some may act impulsively, may have difficulty stemming from their different patterns of behavior, in getting along with coworkers and employers. These youths may recognize neither opportunities available to them, nor their own abilities. Further, they may be living under irresistible individual or social pressures that preclude conformity to behavior expected of them. For example, a youth accustomed to an environment with a pattern of late night hours may have extreme difficulty in changing his habits, should he enter a situation built for daytime hours.

It is temptingly easy to label the behavior of disadvantaged youths when they come into the counseling office. Many are suspicious, especially of those who appear to represent some sort of authority. They are not given to expressing their feelings, nor are they given to listening to those who seem not to understand them. Though they may not express their hostility, the counselor will sense a feeling that there is no use talking, and in fact, a suspicion of talk. He shows his real skill in communicating with such a youth by his "creative" listening. Long interviews are pointless with him; tangible evidence, such as referral, even to a temporary job, will often be reassuring, and provide the reality that talk will not.

Because they have seen more deprivation and hardship than youth from more sheltered environments, disadvantaged youth may in some ways appear unusually mature for their age, which can be a positive factor in getting ahead in school or in a job. As one employment counselor said, "They are often less fragile. They are often experienced in hustling for themselves." However, it is well to remember that, like most adolescents, they are immature in much more significant ways, such as desire for immediate gratification. Many require great patience because of their lack of responsiveness. These youngsters may have the same kinds of negative feelings about a counselor that many adults have toward "delinquents." They may have group or individual fears that are not easily understood by their counselor. Some of those who are bitter, disillusioned, and hostile will compensate in an overaggressive way; but more often they are inarticulate and withdrawn, particularly with adults.

The discouraged youth requires patient consideration. He is all too ready to accept the idea that he cannot succeed in school, or in life, and that his luck is all bad. Great value is derived from obvious efforts to help him—the phone calls in his behalf, and the specific, material suggestions emphasizing his potentialities. Many disadvantaged youth become easily frustrated; and the counselor must be careful not to add his own impatience to his client's other problems.

Thus, to serve these youths poses a challenge and an opportunity, whether the disadvantage present is that of poverty, geographical isolation, minority group status, physical disability, rootlessness, language deficiency, or a multiplicity of problems. They may exhibit characteristics with which it is difficult to deal, such as a poor self-concept, lack of trust in adults, short-term or unrealistic goals, poor performance on tests, slow learning, hostility, and inability to adjust to new situations. However, these youths must be shown that the world is friendly, that many people want to help them. Their basic interests must be explored, for these may provide clues to abilities that can be encouraged and channeled into new directions. And while their leisure time diversions may seem of little worth to these youth, they may contribute significantly in planning for a vocation.

It is extremely important in guidance work with deprived youth to recognize the relative validity or invalidity of all our criteria of comparison. The "average" performance standards cannot alone provide an evaluation of the performance; and while the results are measurable, the causes are not so clear. We cannot minimize the difficulties for the counselor; but neither must we minimize the fact that in serving these youth there is a real opportunity to make a major contribution to modern society.

SELECTED READINGS

1. Amos, William E., "Disadvantaged Youth—Recognizing the Problems," *Employment Service Review*, September, 1964.
2. Amos, William E., and Charles F. Wellford, eds., *Delinquency Prevention: Theory and Practice*. Englewood Cliffs, N.J.: Prentice-Hall, Inc., 1967.
3. Caudill, Harry M., *Night Comes to the Cumberlands: A Biography of a Depressed Area*. Boston: Little, Brown and Company, 1963.
4. Cohen, Albert K., and Harold M. Hodges, "Characteristics of the Lower-Blue-Collar-Class," *Social Problems*, 4 (1963), 303-333.
5. Conant, James B., *Slums and Suburbs*. New York: McGraw-Hill Book Company, 1961.
6. Faltermayer, E. K., "Who Are the American Poor?" *Fortune*, March, 1964, pp. 118-119.

7. Gowan, John Curtis, and George D. Demos, eds., *The Disadvantaged and Potential Dropout*. Springfield, Ill.: Charles C Thomas, Publisher, 1966.

8. Herzog, Elizabeth, "Some Assumptions about the Poor," *Social Service Review*, XXXVII, No. 4 (1963).

9. Johnson, G. Orville, *Education for the Slow Learners*. Englewood Cliffs, N.J.: Prentice-Hall, Inc., 1963.

10. Kerber, August, and Barbara Bommarito, *The Schools and the Urban Crisis*. New York: Holt, Rinehart & Winston, Inc., 1965.

11. Lewis, Oscar, *The Children of Sanchez*. New York: Random House, Inc., 1961.

12. May, Edgan, *The Wasted Americans*. New York: Harper & Row, Publishers, 1963.

13. National Committee for Children and Youth, *Rural Youth in Crisis*. Washington, D.C.: Government Printing Office, 1965.

14. Riessman, Frank, *The Culturally Deprived Child*. New York: Harper & Row, Publishers, 1962.

15. Silberman, Charles E., *Crisis in Black and White*. New York: Random House, Inc., 1964.

16. Strom, Robert D., and Charles E. Merrill, eds., *The Inner City Classroom*. Columbus, Ohio: Charles E. Merrill Books, Inc., 1966.

3

APPRAISAL

OF DISADVANTAGED YOUTH

JOHN J. CODY

In modern technological society terms such as statistical significance, normative data, standard deviation, and standard error of measurement have been used as verbal symbols denoting technical sophistication in recording behavior. Educators, critics of education, psychologists, business consultants, and industrial personnel agents have given much attention to the results of psychometric testing instruments.

In general, testing is purported to be one of the most scientific means of obtaining accurate information about people. Newspapers, college bulletins, psychological and educational textbooks, manuals of employment agencies (public and private) reinforce the attitude that test results are efficient and accurate descriptions of human behavior. Prediction of future behavior based on the results of standardized instruments seems to gain recognition as the need to identify individuals with specific skills and potential increases with the complexity of society. Recent efforts to deal realistically and effectively with the problems of poverty raise again some questions about these assumptions concerning psychometric devices. The purpose of this chapter is to explore some of the rationale for testing, and what seems the most effective means of utilizing test materials with the socially disadvantaged.

30

COMPARATIVE DATA

One of the obvious concerns when psychometric devices are employed with stratified populations is the appropriateness of the comparative criterion to be used in the interpretation of the results. Beginning students of measurement are acquainted with the concept of relativity in describing behavior. In the past, the results of standardized tests have been used mainly with groups; and the interpretations of the results have been based on the relative ranks of the scores within norm groups. From inspection of the directions presented in test manuals and the recommendations in measurement books, we infer that the assumption made by testers was that knowledge of comparative standing within a specific norm group was the major value to be obtained from group psychometric measures.

If the above assumption is held, testing is probably a waste of time in guidance programs. "Test and tell" seems neither effective nor reasonable as an approach to use when working with students for *individual* growth and understanding. A clarification of the merits of psychometric measures in attempts to overcome some obvious weaknesses in comparisons should be considered. An example is presented to illustrate two kinds of relativity that seem most relevant in the utilization of standardized tests. One person might identify the activity of a child as running. Another individual, seeing the same performance, labels the activity skipping. A third person might identify the method of movement as galloping and a fourth as dancing. The description of the behavior observed is relative to the observer's knowledge concerning the activity observed. This is one form of relativity.

A second form of relativity is encountered when an attempt is made to assign a value or a valence to the activity observed. It matters little whether the value is expressed in terms of quickness, slowness, beauty, achievement, adjustment, aptitude, ability, or potential. The assigning of values to a behavior requires a criterion against which the behavior is to be compared. In order to determine whether a youngster runs quickly or slowly, the observer must have a performance to which this specific trial can be compared. Even if the criterion for comparison is another trial by the same individual, the assignment of a value is relative. On occasion the comparative criterion might be drawn in the imagination only. However, this too is a comparative criterion. The second form of relativity, then, is involved whenever value or valence is given to a performance.

Since students of human behavior recognize that no absolute scales for comparison exist, the average behavior of people is a common criterion for comparison. If the average tenth grade boy runs a 100 yard dash in 15.3 seconds, then a performance can be valued as so many seconds above or below the average. Should the performances of a group of swift runners be compared to the average time for the 100 yard dash, the standard would have little meaning in the assessment of values to discriminate among the better runners. A criterion based on the average performance of swift tenth grade boys becomes more descriptive of the performance. It can be seen from this illustration that one person employing the speed criterion of all tenth grade boys would assess the time of 13 seconds in the 100 yard dash as good, while a track coach looking for a sprinter who can run the 100 yards near 10 seconds might consider the performance poor.

The same kinds of properties of measurement are encountered when value assignments are attempted in the areas of personality, ability, achievement, aptitude, and interest assessment. The criterion upon which the comparison is based is of extreme importance in the determination of values assigned to a performance. One of the basic issues in measurement with the culturally deprived involves the comparison criterion.

A standard criterion is frequently utilized in standardized testing. It is assumed that behavior observed and recorded in accord with standardized procedures results in better norms to be employed in comparing individual and group performances with the behavior of thousands of others who performed in a similar situation. Clearly evident is the fact that a concise description of criterion measures used in comparison is essential in the assignment of value to a performance. The purpose for which the performance was attempted, and the criterion to which it is related, must be clear before value can be assessed. Comparison alone does not provide an index for evaluating a performance: it does not provide a basis for evaluating the skills or varieties of knowledge incorporated in the feat. A track coach can place value on the time required to run a 100 yard dash; but the total time, as recorded by a stopwatch, reveals little in the way of running form, adequacy of the start, or personal determination on the part of the runner.

Counselors and other personnel workers seem transfixed in the stopwatch stage. Total scores and subtest scores on psychometric measures might suggest inadequate or substandard performance, but little about the causes of such behavior is found. When the socially different are the subjects of investigation, the general results of cultural biases in comparison can be predicted for groups with more test data. Considering the effect on test performance and interpretation, of the ramifications of cultural bias and its implications, psychometric measures, as currently employed, seem to offer few if any advantages.

THE CULTURAL BIAS

Whenever culturally deprived groups are compared to the general population on the results of standardized tests, the comparison usually favors the middle or upper classes. Admittedly, there is a marked degree of overlap between the groups. A few of the culturally deprived score at high levels and a few of the culturally favored achieve low level scores. Both groups are usually well represented in the middle range of performance. Generally speaking, however, the average performance of the culturally deprived falls considerably below the performance of other groups. Since there is little concrete evidence that can be construed as indicating that test scores reflect inherent potential, it is believed that many individuals are discriminated against because they lack the experiences that would enable them to do well in a testing situation. From this position it can be projected that individuals from less culturally favored backgrounds would not score high on tests, would be less likely to be selected to get further education or better jobs, and thus the majority of the poor get less opportunity to improve their status. In a real sense the tests in use today seem to discriminate against the culturally disadvantaged.

Institutions of higher learning and prospective employers view test results as a means of selecting personnel who have the kinds of background experiences that will enable the individual to demonstrate reasonable success in a short period of time. It seems expedient and profitable for employers and institutions of higher education to select those people who are most likely to succeed with the least number of hours of close supervision. Tests in this case seem to offer an advantage over the more complicated and time consuming task of evaluating each prospect in relation to recommendations of dubious validity, or performance in a trial setting. Institutional or corporate goals have the highest priority under these conditions. The feelings and plight of individuals is of little significance. On the whole, the socially disadvantaged are not likely to be selected for the better positions in industry or the finer educational opportunities.

Most students of behavior have long recognized that lower socioeconomic groups are frequently discriminated against in society. The recent emphasis on poverty and the socially different brings this sore spot into light for examination. Among the many criticized practices in education, employment, and civil rights work, standardized testing holds high rank. Much has been done to cloud the issue, and little has been accomplished in the identification of the real problem.

In a society that fosters competition, agencies, institutions, corporations, and companies vie for recognition of achievement. The institution or corporation that does not compare favorably with its competitors, theoretically fails. Recognizing such circumstances might aid the understanding of the current dilemma with the socially different.

Society, whether represented by institutions of education or corporations, rewards those who provide the most desired products. Consequently, industries and educational institutions seek to recruit individuals who appear to have the most potential in the skills and the knowledge required. Such conditions force individuals to compete for the better jobs and placement in the most prestigious positions of industry or education. The culturally deprived are forced to compete against people who are better prepared socially to engage in this competition. Since the competition is in a society that establishes the standards for performance, individuals, in order to succeed, must function under the prescribed standard for the present.

If there is evidence suggesting that workers with measured intelligence in the top 30 per cent of the general population are more likely to be productive than those who achieve a lower ranking, then those with lower standing are not likely to be selected. The cultural bias of the instrument does not seem to be the issue. The real issue seems related to whether or not the socially different are actually more likely to fail because they lack the characteristics that engender success, or because they have never been allowed the opportunity to try. In other words are the data accurate, or are the data based on assumptions and poorly substantiated evidence?

A second issue related and perhaps dependent upon the first seems apparent. Is it possible and practical, or impossible and impractical, to provide the kind of education and training for the culturally deprived that will enable them to engage in fair competition with the more socially favored? Stated differently, Can the culturally deprived, under current social standards, be helped to make themselves more competitive for better jobs and educational opportunities?

It seems unlikely that society will change drastically in the near future. Although such a possibility should never be discarded, immediate assistance for the culturally different seems most closely related to immediate attitudes and practices. Poverty restricted groups might consider some change as palatable if they are approached where they are, and assistance provided. The recent emphasis on understanding minority groups should have some impact on society. If in turn the minority groups are able to evidence consideration of change, a process of mutual evaluation might be stimulated. Special attention should be drawn to a viewpoint that the need for immediate gross change on the part of the socially different is likely to be of greater importance to specific societal groups and agencies than to the individuals concerned, or to society in general. In addition, behavior is seldom changed immediately. Some of the most intelligent humans find new modes of action difficult or even impossible to acquire.

Behavior that seems to result from long periods of learning is not easily understood. Dicta concerning rewards, perceptions, and reinforcements are at least tenuous. Providing opportunities for the culturally deprived to gain success in the less pretentious areas of behavior may constitute a potentially successful approach. The preferences for housing areas, reading materials, and recreational activities; school achievement; responsibility to the total society, and community projects are probably areas in which little change of an immediate nature will be observed.

Perhaps the historian of tomorrow will have to interpret the success of our present efforts. Today the challenge seems in the direction of providing the culturally disadvantaged with opportunities to find success in the ordinary learning settings. Knowledge that will eventually result in gross behavior change might best be acquired through several short and apparently insignificant periods of insight. An approach that might appear timid, but one which seems to have promise is *to provide the minority with opportunities to try*. At the same time, help should be extended so that success is not thwarted because of unnecessary fear of failure, or because of inadequate skills and knowledges that could have been easily acquired. Reducing the causes and consequences of cultural bias seems a better attack than reaffirming that such conditions exist and ignoring them. Cultural bias should be more than a means of describing a situation. It should be a significant signpost to direct action.

SELECTION, EVALUATION, SELF-UNDERSTANDING

A survey of the practices related to psychometric measurement suggests that instruments are usually employed in three ways. The first and perhaps the most common use of the results of standardized instruments is selection. Industries, colleges, trade schools, and civil service agencies employ test data as one criterion upon which personnel are selected. Institutions, companies, and services have discovered that many skills and knowledges apparently reflected in the results of tests seem essential elements to success. Testing becomes one method of rough screening by which groups of individuals who seem least likely to succeed are eliminated from consideration. At the same time, members of groups that seem to have acquired a sufficient amount of skill or knowledge to succeed are selected.

In the selection process many errors are admitted. Some individuals are selected who fail. Other individuals, rejected by one company, obtain placement in a similar organization and find success. Generally speaking, the practice of selecting personnel on the basis of test results might be defensible for appropriate situations. The defense is one of economy of time and money, and the fact that no better method of increasing the efficiency of the selection process has been found.

A second use of tests is evaluation or exploration. Common among the inventories and the tests employed in evaluation are: personality and interest inventories; achievement, aptitude, ability, and intelligence testing. The purpose of administering these instruments is to assess the individual's status at a specific point in time. Teachers evaluate the progress of students on the basis of test results. School administrators evaluate achievement of the student body as it relates to achievement in other schools. Psychologists employ personality instruments to evaluate a patient's behavior in relation to others on specific personality variables. Counselors employ inventories to explore different areas of counselee perceptions.

Generally speaking, the evaluative or exploratory instruments are employed to discover the present status of an individual or a group for the purpose of helping the individual modify behavior, or as a means of determining the degree of growth over time. With these purposes in mind, content and construct validity seem of supreme importance. In some cases predictive validity is of importance also; but it is not nearly as critical as it is in the selection approach. Since both content and construct validity are difficult to establish, evaluation and exploration based on the results of tests alone appear hazardous at best.

Tests used to aid the individual in self-understanding form the third category. While selection and evaluation techniques are employed to provide information for the tester, this procedure is utilized to aid the individual in better understanding himself. In the two categories mentioned above, an external figure uses data to gain insight. In this situation the information is interpreted by the external figure to the individual for purposes designed to be beneficial to the latter. Nearly all forms of inventories, tests, questionnaires, and autobiographies have been used in this process. It is not, however, the type of instrument utilized but the procedures employed in the use of the results that make the important difference between this usage of testing and those previously described. Perhaps the guidance movement has contributed greatly to the popularity of this use of psychometric data.

Although at first glance such an approach might seem able to overcome some of the weaknesses of the other uses of tests, the shortcomings are in reality magnified. In this approach, all forms of validity become equally relevant since the information gleaned from the tests is to be internalized by individual counselees with personal needs. In other approaches, the test information is used by an external figure who makes the decisions based on the best information available. In the self-understanding approach, the individual must evaluate, explore, and be selective with his personal decisions. The role of the tester is one of working out the real meaning of the test results with the individual. Obviously, a test having questionable validity is nearly impossible to interpret accurately to the individual. Few individuals claim to have a genuine knowledge of exactly how the counselee will use the information gained from tests. Thus it is imperative that the information communicated be accurate, and the counselee's perceptions "true."

When individuals attempt to understand better their personal strengths and weaknesses, they might be most concerned about prediction. On the other hand, self-evaluation or exploration might be their intent. Another consideration is information other than test data, which individuals see as meaningful points for personal insight. In addition, there must be the recognition that the most sophisticated statistic has no meaning for individual behavior. To say that 90 out of 100 men who score below the thirtieth percentile on the College Boards will fail to succeed in college has no meaning to Mr. Smith. Is he among the 90 who fail or among the 10 who will succeed? His precise chances of success or failure cannot be computed statistically. Individual test interpretation seems, at first glance, to be an ideal method of aiding an individual to understand himself better. At the same time, the practice accentuates the feature of assignment of value to performance without a meaningful criterion.

Although three uses of tests have been identified, it is recognized that there is overlap among the descriptions. Sometimes each of the three approaches is employed to nearly the same degree. Situational variables seem to be a major factor in determining to what use psychometric data will be put.

The way a test is used in a given situation depends on the nature of the setting. Of equal importance is the necessity to recognize that, used incorrectly, tests and their results are likely to lead to injustices and harm to individuals rather than improved understanding. In modern society, which emphasizes social consciousness and technological advancement, some counselors tend to believe that any procedures they employ must result in a better situation for the people they seek to help.

Little attention is given to the harm that might be perpetrated by ignorance or complacency in the use of psychometric devices with individuals. A few cases of young adults caught in a quagmire of others' complacency with the results of psychometric instruments will be presented as illustrations of this point.

Beth was an attractive 19-year-old who applied for admission to a professional school in a large university. As one of the entrance requirements she completed a personality inventory. Since the data were employed for selection, no need was recognized to provide a professional and accurate interpretation of the results to her. Beth discovered that her performance was at the extreme lower level of a heterosexual scale. Not only were the results of concern to the school, they were of personal significance to her also. In general course work she learned that, despite the questionable validity of personality measures, scores at the extremes were considered significant data. Readings and lectures in an introductory course in psychology confirmed this. Several additional hours spent in reading about abnormal psychology and homosexuality did little to reduce the student's concern. A few weeks later, Beth consulted a counselor in order to discover if, subconsciously at least, she might have homosexual tendencies.

Since problems of sex identification, moral values, and psychological self-diagnosis are not uncommon with normal young adults, the counselor made arrangements to see Beth. During counseling Beth indicated her struggle with low achievement, too much dating to allow for study time, a moral issue with which she was confronted by her steady boy friend, and finally a break away from regular dating just prior to taking the psychometric battery. At this point the counselor structured the interview around her responses to the items on the personality inventory. It was learned that her responses to items that contributed to the estimate of the degree of heterosexuality might be typical of a young adult in a similar set of circumstances. Although the counselor was reasonably assured that extreme scores in this case had little significance, Beth found it difficult to arrive at the same assurance. The degree to which this single experience will affect her attitudes toward sex, college, psychometric measures, and other facts of life remains unknown.

It is nearly impossible to establish a set of standards that will guarantee a proper interpretation of psychometric information. In the selection process, if all results were interpreted as Beth's counselor did in the case above, standardized testing as a time saving device would be difficult to justify. It seems clear, however, that personality devices are being employed in situations in which there is little justification for doing so, and only minor concern is present for possible ill effects on individuals.

A ninth grade boy who was under pressure from his parents and relatives to make a vocational choice came into the high school counselor's office. Harry was a bright boy who ranked near the top of his class in all his subjects. At Harry's insistence, the counselor administered an interest inventory. The results of the inventory suggested that the student's interests were generally undefined. His responses indicated, however, that he ranked high (the top 10 per cent) on the scale for morticians. Despite the counselor's efforts to dissuade Harry, he persisted in considering a mortician's career only. After weeks of library and occupational information research, Harry revised his course schedule and began making preparations to attend morticians school. His course selection separated him from his friends and within a two-year span he was alienated from his former pals. Harry dropped out of high school in his senior year.

No direct cause and effect relationship is implied. Perhaps Harry would have behaved similarly in a different set of circumstances. It seems clear, however, that the results of the inventory provided Harry with an excuse for his actions. The counselor had an insignificant effect on the meaning which Harry attached to his performance on the interest inventory. Whether or not Harry perceived the credence society generally holds for the results of psychometric data, and accepted the inventory results on this basis, was not ascertained. The fact that individuals' interpretations or perceptions of the results of tests and inventories cannot be accurately predicted is evident. Little justification for the assumption that standardized methods of measurement are safe procedures in dealing with individual behavior can be found in the mere existence of statistical data that seem to verify the credibility of psychometrics. Perhaps the skull and crossbones should be imprinted on each psychometric device above the words, "Potentially Poisonous, Use with Extreme Caution."

In a large suburban school the director of research, in conjunction with the curriculum director, established a basic skills testing program. The test program seemed justified since the junior high school served as the next educational step for ten elementary schools. These elementary schools served populations that varied in socioeconomic background from the upper through the lower classes. The secondary school teachers felt that grade point achievement did not represent the same level of subject matter competency for students from each of the feeder schools. The teachers were especially concerned about the grade point achievement validity of students from the "poorer" schools.

Betty was an overweight, unattractive girl from an elementary school that served the population of a socially deprived area. Betty's grades in all courses except physical education were A's and B's. Examination of her grade card suggested that her teachers regarded her as having exceptional academic promise. In spite of a relatively poor home environment, she seemed not only adjusted to the "middle class biases" of the school, but highly motivated to achieve academically. Without the dubious advantage of the results of standardized tests, it would have been assumed that Betty would continue to be an excellent student. Her scores on the screening battery and the procedures employed to disseminate the information obtained, however, resulted in a different appraisal.

Betty's scores on the test battery administered by the junior high school indicated her achievement to approximate the median level when compared to other entering seventh graders. The tests were machine scored by the test publishers and the resultant profile card was mailed to Betty's home during summer vacation. Since her parents were little concerned about school and could not read, let alone interpret, the profile cards, the results held no significance for them. To the class scheduler in the junior high school, who also had the task of grouping students, the results served as a basis for decision making. The facts spoke for themselves: Betty came from a socially disadvantaged home; her elementary school teachers had graded her in comparison with other students from similar backgrounds; she wasn't an attractive girl; she had been pitied. The halo effect must have been apparent—results from standardized tests yield objective data. Conclusion: Betty was a below average performer. She was placed in track C (vocational terminal) and became a special student in remedial reading.

After a semester in the remedial reading class, the teacher worked through the spindles of red tape and received special consideration for Betty's case. By the end of the seventh grade, Betty was in the A track (college preparatory) program and beginning to recover from a terrible experience. In actuality, if the scheduler had not mistakenly assigned her to a special reading group, Betty might have met the fate of other mislabeled students. Retesting indicated that Betty scored generally in the top 15 per cent of her class. No explanation could be found for her previous performance since the answer sheets were not available to the school any longer—just the results.

Admittedly the interpretations of this student's test results were poor. But what else might be expected? According to the test publishers, the scores were "excellent predictors . . . highly reliable and sufficiently valid." The class scheduler felt that the statistical evidence presented was sufficiently mystifying. Considering the pressures of publicity, the comments of academicians, and the results of research, a better indication of a student's potential could not be found. The scheduler was definitely in the wrong; and he had much company.

Many more examples could be presented to further accentuate a point. However, it seems clear that psychometric measurement is not an inherent good. Of equal significance is that the employment of the results of measurement might be a poor technique to use as a basis for decision making in some situations. Poor practices in test administration and interpretation are ever present. Weaknesses inherent in the instruments should never be glossed over. Individuals are likely to be treated unfairly or unjustly unless precautions are taken to analyze the test results, and the conditions under which the individual approached the test situation.

One must point out in the interests of fairness that the results of psychometric instruments have provided insight into student behavior that would possibly have gone unrecognized. The intent of this chapter is not to bury instruments of measurement in the obscurity of "for instances." Since popular practices seem involved with using the results of measurement as the "truth" criterion, it did not seem necessary to further press the advantages of testing. Rather, the cautions with which psychometric measurement should be approached seemed most relevant. It is hoped that it will not take a "thalidomide finding" in measurement to make practitioners recognize the need to exercise intelligence with data.

INDIVIDUAL ANALYSIS

Too frequently the results of measured behavior are considered only from the selection standpoint described previously. The general public seems to regard some psychometric devices as invasion of their privacy. Further, test results are often thought of as instruments for eliminating from various competitive situations individuals who seem to lack characteristics that suggest success. If these attitudes persist and become reinforced, favorable disposition toward the testing situation will be lacking in the majority of instances. Few societies have provided individuals who work with human behavior the current means to re-evaluate their present status and initiate a different set of values in an effort to help other human beings. It seems, however, that such action could result in the utilization of test scores as the first step in the process of assisting individuals to take advantage of the many opportunities afforded man in a free society.

At this point it should be recognized that total or even subtest scores become the least meaningful results of testing when working with individuals. The most relevant concern is the performance of the individual on the specific items. The case of Johnny H. should serve to clarify this point. Johnny was tested each year with a series of aptitude and achievement tests. His test scores usually fell below the fiftieth percentile. This socially different youngster was regarded as a normal achiever in comparison with students from similar environmental conditions. It was not until Johnny's test performances were analyzed item by item that he was discovered to lack specific skills that appeared essential to future learning. With additional effort on the part of the school counselor, and in cooperation with the classroom teacher, these skills were improved to the degree that Johnny now scores in the upper quartile on the same types of tests.

As further indication of the necessity to analyze test performances in depth, beyond total scores and subtest scores, the results of a pilot investigation might be of interest. Twenty students who achieved identical scores on the Numerical Ability subtest of the Differential Aptitude Test Battery (DAT) comprised the population studied. The answer sheet for each student was analyzed. As might be predicted, no two students reached the raw score value of 21 by answering the same items correctly. For all practical purposes, the students were evaluated as similar in numerical aptitude. Obviously great differences existed among the members of this pilot group. From this example it can be seen that interpreting total test scores is just the beginning. Test analysis begins where the usual raw score interpretation and item analysis leave off. The accent is on examination of individual performances, rather than group statistics.

Proponents of psychometric evaluation suggest that they consider individual performances. They present data through the results of item analysis, indicating that the items are related to the total score. Item analysis as a technique for evaluating tests is considered a respectable and necessary approach to test construction. Indeed, a test from which information about the contribution individual items make to the total score cannot be ascertained is useless for group data. Similarly, however, failure to review the individual's approach to each new item results in an aimless approach to dealing with individual performances.

Item analysis is concerned with the test items that go into the assessment of total score. Individual analysis with the test items involves the data gained from item analysis; in addition, individual analysis considers the unique approach to, and the interpretation of each item by, the person evaluated. If the culturally deprived are to be aided, the group approach seems outdated. The emphasis must be on the particular performance of each student, not on generalities that fail to describe individuals accurately. When group data are used, the socially different may miss the benefit of the spirit of "equal opportunity"; thus a different approach would appear essential if the war on discrimination and poverty is to have hope for success.

Of primary importance with the "analysis" approach seems the recognition that little can be achieved without an investment of time. If the concern for socially different individuals is sincere, the time involved seems a small price. Recognition that a test is merely a means of standardizing procedures for observing and recording behavior appears mandatory. Similarly, acceptance that visually observed behavior is only fractional, and likely to be misleading, seems critical. Verbally analyzing responses to test items with the individual enhances the preliminary aspects of test analysis. By definition, culturally deprived individuals lack experiences that enable them to compete on an equal level with the general population. The discovery of the effects of insufficient contact with the world of achievement is sought, not merely a reaffirmation that groups differ.

"ANALYSIS" WITH TESTS

In an effort to discover how much information is available through the procedures of testing, Cody, with the cooperation of the University of Indiana Test Bureau, conducted a study of 200 students. All of these students were described as slow learners. They were found to be low achievers (below the mean of standardized tests and classroom comparisons); over 60 per cent came from homes categorized as culturally deprived. Preliminary projects with arithmetic skill suggested that the "analysis" procedures described previously seemed most visible in the area of numbers. The DAT, Numerical Form B, was employed by the investigator. Freshmen students in classes of general mathematics representing northern, eastern, southern and western sections of Indiana were included in the study. The students were selected from secondary schools (grades 9 through 12) ranging in size from 150 to 700 students.

Each student completed the DAT, Numerical Form B, as part of the class requirements for the first semester's work in 1964. Prior to completing the DAT, and before the teachers were informed about the purpose of the study, the students were also evaluated on tests constructed by their respective teachers. The usual midterm evaluation was used in each case; no special instruments were constructed for this purpose. The teachers' tests were not scrutinized for validity, reliability, or relevancy. The items on the teacher-made tests were of no concern for the purposes of the study. Only the answer sheets were to be used in the study.

The teachers' tests were employed to rank the students from high to low on their performance on arithmetic skills. These ranks were then correlated with the scores achieved on the DAT. Rank order correlations were computed on the results of the two tests. No correlation fell below the .87 level and no correlation exceeded the .91 level. It was concluded that the addition of the score of a standardized test provided little new information concerning the group. For a few students, gross differences between their performances as depicted by raw scores were observed. It is clearly evident in this study that standardized tests are just another means of ranking achievement in arithmetic.

If new information about groups is the justification for standardized testing, the employment of total scores in this case would be difficult to defend. Since teachers must rank or give value to performances, information was already available concerning class rank. Comparing performances to criteria based on a national sample was accomplished by utilization of the standardized instrument. Aside from this information little that was not available through evidence already accumulated could be gained from group data. The meaning of national comparisons might be of little significance for counseling.

As a next stop, students with identical raw scores were placed in groups. As an example, all students who achieved a raw score of 19 were placed in a single group. Then each test with the score of 19 was analyzed to discover which items were answered correctly. Of the 16 answer sheets identified with raw scores of 19, no two sheets were found to have identical response patterns.

The DAT was sectioned into skill categories as the third step in the investigation. The first procedure employed was to differentiate among items that required the student to manipulate whole numbers only, fractions only, and decimals only. By this method it was discovered that three students found arithmetic functions involving whole numbers alone to be difficult. Eight students had little trouble with whole numbers; fractions were their downfall. The remaining five students seemed to encounter little difficulty with fractions and whole numbers and stumbled over decimals. It became apparent that this method of analysis was meaningful in the exploration of students' strengths and weaknesses in arithmetic skills.

A second sectioning of the test was then attempted in order to depict more specifically the competencies of the students. In this process the skills of simple addition, subtraction, multiplication, division, ratios, squares, and cubes were identified. As a result of this analysis the total scores became even less meaningful. The results suggested that each student suffered from individualized weaknesses, and that these weaknesses seemed relevant to their performance on the tests.

Inability to arrive at correct responses was related to lack of knowledge about fraction inversion, conversion of fractions to decimals, placement of decimal points, borrowing, and crossing equal signs as well as ineptitude in handling multiple numerical functions. Some of the errors were sporadic while others were consistent. Spurred to investigate these findings in depth, the investigators reviewed the tests with the students in individual interviews. As might be expected, the investigators were alerted to additional idiosyncratic behavior of students in test taking.

Five students evidenced a "test-wiseness" that enabled them to make correct responses without specific knowledge of the arithmetic functions. Typical of the performances in this category were those of students who selected responses that appeared to be far enough above or below the value of the numbers used in the items to suggest a correct response. This factor became more relevant when dollars, minutes, or similar quantities were involved. In a few cases random responses were recorded, or the same foil number checked for each question to which a correct response could not be found.

In opposition to the above, "educated guessing" was employed by three students. Most frequently this involved decimals. By counting the decimal places required for the answer and examining the last digit in the problem, sufficient information to make a correct response was found. This process seemed most important in cases when the function of borrowing was required in the hundred's digit and not in the ten's digit. Only part of the skills that seemed essential in arithmetic were in evidence; and the student employed this partial knowledge to achieve a correct response.

Examples of similar behavior as determined through a test review with the students could be cited at length. The point is not to enumerate the many techniques employed by students to respond to test items, but rather to emphasize the fact that all students do not approach test taking with similar sets. In order to really gain insight into the arithmetic skills or numerical ability of individuals, a test must be analyzed in depth.

Teachers who observed portions of the investigation and were aware of the results expressed themselves in unison. Their feelings, generally, related to the amount of time and effort spent working with individual students. It seemed to them that such efforts were not commensurate with the role defined for them by their institutions of employment. Such observations seem to point up clearly the work ahead. The usual approach to machine scored tests, group interpretations, and profile analysis will provide little new, meaningful data. Yet individual analysis of test results, as with the socially disadvantaged, is time consuming, laborious, and *rewarding*.

Since the project discussed was conducted with slow learners who in general scored below average on standardized tests, there were enough incorrect responses to provide information for analysis. Only one score grouping was presented here as an illustration. The complete study consisted of an analysis of each score obtained, individually, and again by quartile rankings. The investigators were astounded by the amount of information previously overlooked through total or subscore interpretations only.

ANALYSIS WITH INVENTORIES

Of similar interest to the experimenters were interest and personality inventories with the low-achieving student. An investigation with the California Test of Personality was instigated but was terminated at the request of parents who voiced concern over the invasion of privacy of the individual students. Such a response to the investigation provided insight into personality assessment that might be meaningful to personnel workers. It is not the results of the investigation that were important, rather the assumptions upon which parental concern was based.

Some parents, teachers, college professors, and test publishers insinuate, if not openly declare, that test results reveal what the normal student wishes to remain personal. Misinformation such as this suggests naïveté regarding standardized testing of subjects with relatively stable personalities. Previous pilot investigations conducted by this investigator with paper and pencil personality instruments indicated that personality descriptions obtained from standardized instruments are dependent upon the individual's willingness or ability to identify his self-perception. This is not to say that a test taker can portray any type of personality he desires on a personality instrument. However, the personality characteristics projected fluctuate with the set with which the student completes the inventory. It is not a question of whether or not such sets are consciously or unconsciously developed but that the picture portrayed of the student may be grossly out of focus.

The California Test of Personality, Edwards Personal Preference Schedule, and the Sixteen Personality Factor Questionnaire were given to 50 high school seniors (slow learners), 50 college freshmen, and 50 graduate students on three separate occasions, under different sets of directions. In the first administration, each group of students was informed the test results were to be kept secure and that they would have an opportunity to discuss the results with a counselor. The directions for the second administration were structured to induce the students to attempt to respond in a way that would enhance their chances of obtaining a position in public relations with a large industrial firm; they would not receive the results. In the third setting, the students were informed that their responses were to be evaluated by a group of clergy representing the Protestant, Catholic, and Jewish faiths. No names were to be included on the answer sheets and the results would not be returned to the subjects.

The concern in each case was not the relationship between the directions given and the personality pictures that resulted. The intent was to discover if the students would present three different pictures of themselves under these conditions. The results indicated that nearly all of the 150 students painted different personality portraits of themselves under the three conditions described. Eight graduate students and five undergraduate students responded in such a way that faking was detected. In the remaining 137 cases, technical analysis did not reveal conclusive evidence of faking.

Since no method thus far discovered enables examiners to determine the quality or value of responses to personality inventories, it appears that little confidence should be placed in the results. Experience with the socially different suggests that their attitudes toward testing or inventory situations are not conducive to responses that reflect genuine feelings. Attitudes of individuals toward instruments that might present an image they do not care to, or know how to reveal, are unpredictable. Furthermore, the vocabulary employed in personality instruments, and the topics presented are frequently ambiguous or outside the experiences of such students. The items apparently fail to convey meaning or interest to the individual.

Interest inventories present a situation similar to that of the personality instrument. Theoretically both personality and interest seem to be integral facets of success in given situations. Despite the quantity of research conducted with inventories, little has been found that indicates validity for these instruments. Of concern to counselors should be the possibility that interest and personality inventories given to students and cautiously interpreted might yield more false than positive data. They seem to provide cliff edges to which students cling under societal pressure to make early occupational, educational, and personal decisions. The usual assumption is that the hand hold is a saving device. On the other hand early decision making and societal pressures might just as frequently lead to false conclusions. In a time of specialization, such false conclusions might give the student a restricted view of the possibilities that exist for him.

During the spring of 1963, 100 ninth grade boys were administered the Kuder Preference Record, Vocational, Form D. A revised form of the Kuder was administered to the same population after a three week interval. The revised form included the same item topics, but each item was worded in terms of experience rather than preference. An example should help clarify the nature of the revision.

Kuder:

    R. Read about jungles of Africa.
    S. Read various peoples' ideas of how to make a better world.
    R. Read about what various well-known people do in their spare time.

These were reworded to read:

    S. Do you read about jungles of Africa?
    S. Do you read about various peoples' ideas of how to make a better world?
    T. Do you read about what various well-known people do in their spare time?

If the items were beyond the students direct experiential possibilities, they were changed as demonstrated in the examples which follow:

(1) N. Work in a candy factory
        -to-
    N. Do you know anything about work in a candy factory?

(2) P. Raise chickens
        -to-
    P. Do you know anything about raising chickens?

(3) Q. Give eye examinations
        -to-
    Q. Do you know the kind of training and skills required to give eye examinations?

Each Kuder blank was scored after the first administration according to the directions in the manual. The revised forms were designed to resemble the original answer sheet. Instead of indicating most and least acceptable responses, the students were instructed to mark each item indicating that they had had the experiences described. Patterns of responses were tabulated in the same categories as for the original administration. Response patterns for the two trials were compared.

Over 60 per cent of the students whose response patterns indicated a greater than average interest in specific areas had little or no experience related to these areas. Apparently the "most" and "least" responses were not related to activities with which the subjects were well acquainted.

After comparison of the response patterns for the 100 students, a 25 per cent sample of the parent population was randomly selected for interviews. Individual interviews seemed to be a suitable technique for checking the reasons for student responses. Of special significance to the investigator were items on the Kuder with which the student could have had experience if he had been motivated by interest. When items checked as preferences were in areas where the students had no experiential contact, the questions seemed of greater importance. Despite this decision to ignore the possibility of interesting experiences, the students indicated a preference for this response on the original administration.

Student responses in the interviews indicated two reasons for the findings. First, once experience was gained with the activity described in the item, students seemed to feel they would rather seek new experiences. Thus several items were checked simply because the students were not as familiar with the activity as they were with others to which it was compared. A second reason given by many of the subjects was that none of the activities were really appealing, but they had been instructed to respond to each entry. When there really wasn't a true preference, items were checked in a haphazard manner.

Under such conditions, it is difficult to assume much meaning for the results of the interest inventories. Perhaps the construct of interests and the inventories as they relate to the vocational selection process need further consideration. Interest profiles acquired by the forced choice method seem to offer little assistance in counseling the socially different.

As a result of the experience gained with psychometric devices in the process of analyzing performances, several conclusions have been drawn.

1. The usual methods of testing and test interpretation are not likely to be of value with the culturally deprived.
2. Tests might be used as standardized instruments to observe and to record behavior related to processes involved in responding to items.

3. Conservation of time does not appear to stand out as an advantage of testing the culturally deprived. In fact, the use of tests in analyzing individual behavior is one of the most time consuming tasks.

4. Paper and pencil tests that require interpretation of writing in order to respond seem unsuited for working with the socially disadvantaged.

5. The nature and the norms of personality inventories seem to render them of little value with youngsters who were predominantly from the lower class.

6. Perhaps fewer tests, selected for specific purposes, and used analytically in individual sessions with students, can be helpful.

7. Mass testing with currently available standardized instruments seems to provide little new information.

8. Ingenuity and creativeness on the part of counselors and others who work with the socially different seem to be the immediate requirements.

One of the most interesting propositions that seems to arise from the opportunity to help the culturally deprived is the need for creative and ingenious approaches. Too frequently gimmicks that are mere reruns of the old favorites are initiated, carrying attractive labels. Perhaps the greatest need for ingenuity can be found in attempts to stimulate people to carry out practices that have received much verbal attention and an insignificant amount of action.

The "analysis" approach, labeled by Rothney the "diagnostic approach" to utilizing test results, is not new. In fact, many people claim to be involved in similar practices as part of their daily routine. However, personal contact with school and community projects revealed that evaluation with individual tests lacks depth in the analysis of testees' behavior. If tests were used analytically, it would be impossible to administer and interpret accurately the number of tests employed in school situations specifically for counseling purposes. Many claims have been made concerning the objectives of modern guidance programs. The word counseling is used; but individuals are usually considered in conjunction with generalities drawn from group data.

Analysis of individual behavior is not dependent upon group norms. If the recognition of the necessity to work with individuals in the programs for the culturally deprived is ignored, few opportunities for success seem likely.

At this point it is critical to differentiate between the "analysis" suggested here and the clinical approach or clinical bridges described by Goldman.[1] From Goldman's viewpoint, psychometrics are used in a

[1] Leo Goldman, *Using Tests in Counseling* (New York: Appleton-Century-Crofts, Inc., 1961).

counseling setting along with other relevant data to aid the counselee in self-understanding. Goldman does not go beyond the scores achieved on the instruments; his concept is married to predictive validity. Objectively obtained data that have high predictive coefficients are essential to the process. In the analysis approach, validity must be explored in relation to the instruments, the individual performance, the resulting conclusions, the assistance given, and the evaluation of the total effort. Aid to the individual is not predicated on a "true measure" of present status or potential: the kind of assistance provided is working through the individual's approach to decision making and problem solving with a psychometric crutch. Results of this "working out" process should lead to increased knowledge of personal stature in the specific context provided by the standardized tool. Predictive validity, if critical to the practitioner, should be based on the action taken with the individual after that analysis, rather than on the individual's comparative rank as a result of test scores.

In order to avoid the charge of relegating measurement to a level below intuition, the following illustration is given to help clarify the position of supplying valid data. George is a sixth grade boy and a member of the population described as culturally disadvantaged. He reads at the second grade level, computes numbers at the third grade mean, and is dissatisfied with school. Test scores are not required to estimate group performances in the academic setting for boys with similar descriptions. What is needed is to discover why George's academic skills are retarded. As a result of investigation with tests, interviews, observations, and records, some action should be taken. Because of this intervention in the boy's life—action taken to improve skills—some predictive statements should be possible. The accuracy of the predicted performance should indicate the value of the instruments and procedures employed in analysis.

Too frequently, evaluation is lost in the furrows already plowed. Psychometrics seems to provide a structure for the study of behavior rather than a predictive or selection measure directly relating to individuals.

One of the most sobering antidotes administered to those who have been swept about by statistical jargon can be found in Anastasi's *Psychological Testing*.[2] Her comments concerning the concept of validities and reliabilities seem most conducive to inquiry. Frequently ignored is the fact that there are many concepts of validity and reliability, not one alone. Validity and reliability, if they are to have meaning, must be related to the specific use of a test at a specific time. In their book about tests in

2 Anne Anastasi, *Psychological Testing* (New York: The Macmillan Company, 1964).

guidance, Rothney, *et al.* explore a variety of weaknesses in the usual methods of employing results of standardized measurements.[3] Although their topic is not specifically related to the socially different, the fact and opinion presented seem worthy of consideration. Most books in the field of measurement touch briefly on the inadequacies of group data when they are applied to individual incidence. Typically, however, such references are hidden by flowery and technical phraseology serving to perpetuate a viewpoint that working with individuals is fruitless. The final consideration rarely exceeds the traditional contention that prediction based on scores must be the ultimate criterion.

Perhaps personnel who work with the socially different will recognize eventually the need to surpass the criterion of prediction based on total scores. Considering the probable numbers of individuals who could be assisted through considering group data is hardly an encouraging exercise. It seems dubious that anticipation of such meager rewards could stimulate development of programs with the culturally deprived. Social differences have not been diminished through mass educational or experimental techniques in the past. Recognition of the nobility of individuals despite their social description appears the most likely basis from which to proceed. Psychometric instruments used as standardized forms to analyze and record individual approaches to problem solving seem to offer one avenue of approach.

Many people who dedicate their lives to working with and for the welfare of their fellow man might sense the practices described here as too restrictive. Whenever a person becomes concerned about the apparent oversimplification of a task, it should be recalled that great strides are accomplished by what once appeared to be minor successes. Polio vaccine was not developed in one laboratory, but as a result of many research activities that ultimately led the discoverer to his successful approach to the problem. It is nearly impossible for a child to skip safely until he can walk and gain body coordination. Likewise it appears nearly impossible to try to help the "whole man" before specific developments have taken place. The elementary or secondary school child who dislikes school is not likely to change his whole personality as a result of an hour's conference. Piercing chinks in his armor of rejection with success in little things might provide personal insights for greater growth in the future.

SUMMARY

Measurement of individual behavior is still in an experimental stage. Despite claims of scientific sophistication as a result of refined statistical

[3] J. Rothney *et al.*, *Measurement for Guidance* (New York: Harper & Row, Publishers, 1959).

techniques, practitioners in the area of human behavior rely almost entirely on group data and intuition. Efforts to explore means of assisting poor children in society serve to accentuate the inadequacy of currently employed instruments and practices. Perhaps the most significant element arising from this dilemma is the need to consider individuals rather than generalities. Admission of the futility of continuing the usual interpretations of data seems a high priority measure if success is to be achieved in the future.

Results of pilot studies in which group psychometric devices were employed suggest that total score data were not sufficiently descriptive or accurate to be of much value. Investigation confirmed the conviction that there are no shortcut methods for working with individuals. Psychometric instruments seem of most value when employed to provide structure for observing and recording behavior. The reaction and response of the individual to specific items seems the most rewarding use of standardized instruments. A willingness to expend time and to understand the products of poverty apparently has no substitute.

It seems evident that different types of standardized instruments will have to be devised if psychometric measurement is to be an aid rather than a hindrance in working with the culturally deprived. The need for ingenuity, patience, and understanding on the part of individuals who work with the socially disadvantaged cannot be replaced by standardized psychometric instruments.

SELECTED READINGS

1. Ausubel, David P., "A Teaching Strategy for Culturally Deprived Pupils: Cognitive and Motivational Consideration," *School Review,* 71 (Winter, 1963), 454-463.

2. Ayer, A. L., "Labels, People and Things," *Audiovisual Instruction,* 10 (January, 1965), 84.

3. Barbe, Walter Burke, *The Exceptional Child,* Washington, D.C.: Center for Applied Research in Education, 1963.

4. Bloom, S., "Improving the Education of Culturally Deprived Children: Applying Learning Theory to Classroom Instruction," *Chicago School Journal,* 45 (December, 1963), 126-131.

5. Brown, W. M., and R. P. Russell, "Limitations of Admissions Testing for the Disadvantaged," *Personnel and Guidance Journal,* 43 (November, 1964), 301-302.

6. Clift, V. A., "Factors Relating to the Education of Culturally Deprived Negro Youth," *Education Theory,* 14 (April, 1964), 76-82.

7. Della-Dora, D., "Culturally Disadvantaged: Further Observations," *Exceptional Children,* 29 (January, 1963), 226-236.

8. Edmonds, G., "Oh, That Median Score: The Bone of Negro Pupils," *Negro Education*, 31:1 (Winter, 1962), 75-77.

9. Havighurst, R. J., "Who are the Socially Disadvantaged?" *Journal of Negro Education*, 33:210-217; also 34, 39, 46.

10. Hayes, H., "Some Ways to Teach Culturally Deprived Children," *Chicago Schools Journal*, 45 (February, 1964), 221-228.

11. Kaplan, B. A., "Issues in Educating the Culturally Disadvantaged," *Phi Delta Kappan*, 45 (November, 1963), 70-76.

12. Kvaraceus, W. C., "Emotionally Disturbed and Socially Inadequate," *Education*, 85 (October, 1964), 91-97.

13. Novak, D., "Counseling Culturally Disadvantaged Requires Special Understanding," *Chicago Schools Journal*, 45 (May, 1964), 366-372.

14. Riessman, F., "Overlooked Positives of Disadvantaged Groups," *Journal of Negro Education*, 33 (Summer, 1964), 225-231.

15. Schwebel, M., "Learning and the Socially Deprived," *Personnel and Guidance Journal*, 43 (March, 1965), 646-653.

16. Shaw, F., "Educating Culturally Deprived Youth in Urban Centers," *Phi Delta Kappan*, 45 (November, 1963), 91-97.

17. Stalnaker, G. M., "Scholarship Selection and Cultural Disadvantage," *National Association of Secondary School Principal's Bulletin*, 49 (March, 1965), 142-150.

18. Weiner, M., and W. Murray, "Another Look at the Culturally Deprived and Their Levels of Aspiration," *Journal of Educational Sociology*, 36 (March, 1963), 319-321.

19. Wolf, E. P., and L. Wolf, "Sociological Perspective on the Education of Culturally Deprived Children," *School Review*, 70 (Winter, 1962), 373-387.

20. Yourman, Julius, "The Case Against Group I. Q. Testing," *Phi Delta Kappan*, 46 (November, 1964), 108-110.

4

WORKING
WITH THE DISADVANTAGED
THROUGH GROUPS

RICHARD PEARSON

DEFINITION OF A GROUP

The term *group* has different meanings to different people. Therefore, perhaps it would be useful to start by looking at the term in order to find a common ground for discussion.

As Gibb has pointed out, one of the most common definitions of *group* centers around the idea of *number*.[1] In this sense, a group is a collection of two or more objects. For example, a grove of trees or a number of people on a bus would constitute groups from this point of view. In the terminology of the social psychologist, such collections are generally called "aggregates."

Often when people use the term "group" they refer to objects that happen to be close to each other, spatially or temporally. Thus the principle of *contiguity* constitutes another focus in defining the term. For example, the objects on top of a desk (books, papers, pencils, etc.) can be seen as constituting a group because they are together. This is another type of aggregate.

Another common way of defining a group centers around the idea of *homogeneity*. Thus, objects sharing common characteristics or attributes

[1] Cecil A. Gibb, "Leadership," in *Handbook of Social Psychology*, ed. G. Lindsey (Reading, Mass.: Addison-Wesley Publishing Co., Inc., 1954).

can be seen as a group. Something more than mere *number* is required for objects to constitute a group from this point of view, since the concept refers to qualitative as well as quantitative aspects of the entity being considered. Again, the social psychologist usually prefers to call a collection of like objects a *class* rather than a group.

Another way of looking at a group is to consider the relationship among the members of the entity. Gibb suggests that a group may be characterized by the interaction of its members, in such a way that each unit is changed by its membership in the group, and each would be likely to undergo a further change as a result of change in the group.[2]

Supporting the idea that the essence of a group lies in the relations among the members, Lewin offers as the essential criterion of a group the interdependence of the members. In a group not only do the members interact to affect each other in some manner, but they are, in some way, dependent upon each other.

A similar point of view is represented by Krech and Crutchfield who define a group as: [3]

two or more people who bear an explicit *psychological relationship* to one another. This means that for each member of the group, the other members of the group must exist in some more-or-less immediate psychological way so that their behavior and their characteristics influence him.

One of the interesting aspects of this way of looking at a group is that its emphasis on psychological relation makes it possible for group influence to operate even though spatial contiguity is absent. Thus, a person who continues to be affected by the behavior and norms of his group, though widely separated from the other members of it, can be said to remain a member of the group. The immigrant who, in the midst of a foreign culture, continues to adhere strictly to the ways of his homeland, exemplifies this type of group membership.

Finally, specifying even further the character of the relationship among group members, R. B. Cattell defines a group as a number of organisms for whom the association of the group is utilized as an instrument to satisfy some of the needs of each.[4] The group is seen as an instrument of need satisfaction for its members. This is an extremely important point; seeing the group (however inadequate and useless it may seem to the outsider) as a means of need satisfaction makes understandable some of the tremendous influence a group may have on the people in it, especially the culturally different.

[2] *Ibid.*

[3] D. Krech and R. Crutchfield, *Theory and Problems of Social Psychology* (New York: McGraw-Hill Book Company, Inc., 1948), p. 18.

[4] R. Cattell, "New Concepts for Measuring Leadership, in Terms of Group Syntality," *Human Relations*, 4 (1951), 161-184.

To summarize, the term group as used in this discussion is descriptive of two or more interacting individuals who bear an immediate psychological relation to each other and who are mutually dependent upon their interaction to satisfy some of their needs. The terms *mass* or *aggregate* will be used to refer to collections of two or more individuals of whom the above is not true.

THE SIGNIFICANCE OF GROUPS

The central significance of groups lies in the fact that they play such an important part in determining the ideas, attitudes, and behaviors of individuals. Man, as has so often been pointed out, is a social animal. He lives out his existence in the physical presence of other men; and the essential "human-ness" of man is the product of his contact and interaction with his fellows.

The human infant is born into an environment made up not only of certain geographic features and climatic conditions, but also, and more importantly, groups. What is called the socialization process can essentially be seen as the process through which the infant, child, and adult, is introduced to, and assimilates the values and behaviors of the groups in his environment.

Given this central importance of groups (i.e., that they are the source of many of the attitudes and behaviors of individuals) it would seem that a knowledge of groups, their structure, development, and influence, can be useful to any one who works with people. A knowledge of groups can help one to understand individuals. One can go a long way toward understanding the attitudes and behaviors of a particular individual by knowing the groups of which he is a member and the groups that have been significant in his development. Knowledge of this sort provides a background of meaning that adds depth and subtlety to our observations of an individual. For example, the observation that a particular teen-age girl avoids the types of recreation common to her classmates—dances, movies, etc.—means quite a different thing when we know that she is a member of a fundamentalist religious group than it would if we had considered her an "average" garden variety teen-ager.

A knowledge of groups can also suggest valuable techniques for working with and influencing an individual. If we recognize that the identity of an individual is, in large part, a result of the operation of groups, then it would follow that groups can be used as instruments to affect what an individual may become.

UNDERSTANDING THE CULTURALLY DIFFERENT USING GROUP THEORY

It has been pointed out that a knowledge of groups enhances one's understanding of the members of the groups with which he may work. What might be the value of some of these understandings with the reference to the population commonly described as the culturally deprived?

Understanding 1

Perhaps one of the most useful understandings contributed by a general knowledge of the characteristics of groups concerns the term itself: culturally deprived. This is a misleading label because it suggests that the people from many metropolitan and rural areas of poverty have no "culture," or very little of it. If culture is to be narrowly defined as "the arts," then this may be true; however, if we use Olmsted's definition—"a set of common meanings . . ." representing the group's efforts to deal with the problems it faces, and being the product of the member's on-going interaction—then it is evident that such individuals are not culturally deprived at all.[5]

In neighborhoods and areas called culturally deprived live people who, within broad limits, have similar opinions concerning what is good and bad, who attach common meanings to objects and events in their environment, and who react to these objects and events with broadly similar behavior. This can be understood by looking at the different meanings the word *policeman* has to the "culturally deprived" and to the "middle class" child. The latter child, generally thinks of a policeman as a stern, yet benevolent individual who looks after little children and protects them while, at the same time, keeps them in line. To the slum child, the same word is apt to call up an entirely different image, one of a disliked authority figure to whom is transferred much of the antagonism felt toward society in general by the child's group. This "meaning" of policemen is held in common by most of the members of the slum child's group; it is as much a part of his culture as are the very different connotations familiar to the middle-class child. Both meanings are the product of the particular group's experience with the entity represented by the word.

From the above example, one can generalize that, for the slum child, culture is not absent (as is suggested by the term "culturally deprived"); it is, however, different. One can argue that the slum culture, in many of its particulars, is maladaptive and unsuitable to the demands of life outside of the narrow slum society. But it is a mistake to assume that no culture exists. To do so would be to overlook the existence of a viable

[5] M. Olmsted, *The Small Group* (New York: Random House, Inc., 1959), p. 81.

group life that shapes and influences the development and behavior of its members just as surely as does the group life of other sectors of society.

From this perspective, perhaps the terms culturally different, or culturally disadvantaged, would more accurately describe the groups under consideration in this chapter.

This may seem to be a small and academic distinction, but let's explore some of its implications. Culture, and the common meanings attached to it, is primarily a matter of learning; it is not something we are born with. Man is not instinctively "preprogrammed" in his social behavior, like an ant or a bee. Rather, culture is acquired through contact and interaction with those around one. It takes very little sophistication to move from the recognition that culture is primarily a matter of learning to the position that, if the situation within which learning takes place is changed, the results of that learning (in this case, culture) generally will be different.

The preceding discussion does not equate an *understanding* of the culture of the slum or poor rural individual with a *condoning* of this culture. To a large extent, the success of most of what is called the War on Poverty rests upon our ability to change the culture of the disadvantaged. Effecting this change, as has been pointed out, is primarily a question of learning, and a modification of the situations in which learning takes place. Since so much of the individual's behavior and attitudes are the result of learning acquired within various group situations, there is, in the writer's opinion, great promise in the use of group procedures, not only to help individuals acquire new behavior and attitudes, but also to modify or eliminate the unfavorable results of prior learning.

Understanding 2

Another broad perspective to be derived from a knowledge of the nature of groups, for the enhancement of our understanding of the culturally different is this: the very fact that certain youths are culturally different and, in many cases, members of various minority groups, heightens the influence of those groups. At least two factors contribute to this influence. First, as demonstrated by a study carried out by Brodbeck, one generally feels more comfortable in situations in which the people around him are similar.[6] This study identified a group of individuals whose private opinions on a controversial issue (the use of wiretapping by police) were at variance with an authoritative lecture they heard on the topic. Such individuals were labeled dissonant subjects, in contrast to those who agreed with the opinions expressed in the lecture (consonant subjects). Dissonant subjects who maintained their original opinion and

[6] M. Brodbeck, "The Role of Small Groups in Mediating the Effects of Propaganda," *Journal of Abnormal and Social Psychology*, **52** (1956), 166-170.

reported no reduction in confidence in that opinion were called mildly dissonant individuals; those who, while maintaining their opinions, reported less confidence in it, were called strongly dissonant individuals.

A situation was set up in which it was possible for an individual to determine the opinions of other people on the wiretapping issue. Then, each subject was asked to list the two people with whom he would prefer to discuss the matter. An examination of the preferences showed that the "strongly dissonant" subjects more frequently preferred to discuss the matter with people who agreed with them than did the "consonant" subjects. That is, the individuals who saw themselves as different, and whose confidence in their opinion suffered as a result of this perception, tended to seek out other individuals who, they knew, would agree with them.

What does Brodbeck's study indicate in relation to the culturally different? In many cases such individuals can broadly be described as "strongly dissonant"; that is, they are often acutely aware of the difference between their own behaviors and attitudes and those of others. In accordance with the social psychologist's findings, we would expect these individuals to stick together as a means of mutual support and confirmation of worth; and so they do. A very definite result of this pattern is that the behaviors and attitudes, though perceived to be different, tend to persist. In their association, dissonant individuals tend to reinforce the variant behaviors and attitudes of each other; furthermore, such sticking together tends to isolate them from the kinds of experience that might serve to modify their behavior and attitudes.

A second factor heightening the influence of the group on the culturally different individual is the fact that often these groups are under attack (psychologically, and in some instances even physically) by various segments of the broader society. As Cartwright and Zander have pointed out, the net effect of external attack on a group is to increase the solidarity of the group.[7] This mechanism is often used by a political regime attempting to rally the support and solidarity of the people. By focusing their attention on an enemy, it is frequently possible to increase the people's devotion to the regime, and their willingness to work for and support it. Essentially the message inculcated is, It's us against the enemy; we have to stick together and protect each other against him.

Understanding 3

Another understanding of culturally different individuals to be derived from a general knowledge of groups is that, self-defeating and unrewarding as the life of the group may seem to the outsider, it is, to some extent,

[7] D. Cartwright and A. Zander, eds., *Group Dynamics, Research and Theory,* 2nd ed. (New York: Harper & Row, Publishers, 1960), p. 82.

meeting the needs of its members. It will be recalled that a true group (as opposed to an aggregate) serves as a means of need satisfaction for its members. What are some of the needs met by the groups to which culturally different individuals may belong? First, the group may provide security (physical and/or psychological) to its members. In rough neighborhoods, or in areas where the physical necessities of life are scarce, this function of the group can assume an almost life-or-death importance. The group also communicates to the individual that he is a person of importance and worth. No matter how much teachers, policemen, or other persons may reject the culturally different youth, in his group—family, gang or whatever—he feels he is "home"; he is accepted and understood. Finally, it may be pointed out that people generally feel more comfortable when they understand what is happening around them and know the appropriate kinds of responses to these events. The group culture gives an individual at least some means of "making sense" of the world.

The point of view that the group does, to some extent, serve the needs of its members has very definite implications for the person who has responsibility for working with the culturally different individual. To varying degrees, the kinds of changes that various programs are trying to promote in the culturally different can be seen as having the effect of drawing individuals away from old groups, toward membership in new groups. If these efforts are to be successful, the new groups must be perceived by the individual as capable of meeting his needs, perhaps to an even greater extent than did the old group.

The concept of the group as an instrument of need satisfaction explains why, for example, some people in Appalachia are loath to leave their barren hills and relocate in an area where opportunities are possible. "The hills, as hopeless as they are, are at least filled with others who think the way I do, and treat me with some degree of respect. Why should I go where I will be an outsider?" If one's efforts are going to have some meaning and attractiveness for the culturally different, he must give definite attention to the fact that these types of needs are met by the group.

Much of the prior experience of culturally different individuals leads them to expect to be treated as outsiders by many of the people who may be trying to assist them; unfortunately these expectations are often confirmed. The personnel and activities of various social programs can, in many ways, have the effect of driving the culturally different individual back to the security of his group. If this is true, if these programs represent values and ideas that are foreign and threatening to the culturally different individual, is there any way to minimize the threat, thus facilitating movement away from old situations?

In our relations with these young people we must offer them some of the same things that are offered by their own groups; primarily, basic acceptance as a person of worth. Schools of counseling differ in their views as to what constitutes a "good" counseling relationship; however, most agree that an individual's general reaction to threat is to become more rigid, defensive, and less open to change. A relationship (counseling or otherwise) in which an individual feels accepted, and in which he senses that he is considered a person of worth, enhances his possibilities for change and development. Culturally different individuals can be helped to change only if the avenues of change opened to them have some promise of allowing each one to retain his integrity as a person, and are perceived as need-satisfying alternatives to his current situation.

Group Work with the Culturally Different

A knowledge of groups can also be of value to the individual who works with the culturally different by providing guidelines and procedures for using groups as instruments of assistance. These procedures fall into two broad categories: mass procedures and group procedures.

Mass Procedures: General Considerations

Previously, a distinction was made between a group and other entities such as aggregates or masses. Much of what commonly passes under the name of group procedure can more accurately (at least from the perspective of this chapter) be described as mass procedure. The mass procedure is characterized by a relative independence of the persons involved, by the fact that interaction among these persons is either absent or inconsequential and, finally, by the fact that the need-fulfilling capacity of the procedure is not a function of the association of the persons involved.

A good example of a mass procedure is test interpretation as it is carried out in many schools and other agencies with programs of mass testing. Usually, on the basis of administrative or scheduling convenience, a number of individuals are called together for the purpose of test interpretation. The person in charge of the interpretation commonly begins by reviewing the tests that have been given in order to refresh the participants' memory and insure that they have an accurate idea of what the tests measure. Also, some attention is usually given to the possible uses to which the information derived from the test results might be put. For example, it is often pointed out that interest tests, while not specific indicators of which occupation a person should enter, can suggest broad areas or types of work to be explored as a means of helping him progress toward a vocational choice.

Another common component of these test interpretation procedures is an explanation of the form in which the results are expressed. Thus, if the test results are presented in percentiles, the interpreter attempts to help the participants arrive at an understanding of percentiles as a quantitative concept clear enough to permit them to know what their scores mean in comparison to the relevant norm group. Usually, test profiles are handed out to the participants; then, on the basis of the information previously given, they are expected to understand and internalize the results of their own tests. If necessary, some individual assistance is provided by the interpreter.

Without considering the efficacy, or lack of it, of such a procedure, one can point out that, essentially, the individual participant makes his way through the process as an independent unit. It is true that there are other persons seated around him, but any interaction that takes place is fortuitous and not an integral part of the procedure. While it is also true that some of the individual's needs might be met by the procedure (e.g., a more accurate understanding of his abilities and interests thus gained could help him in making various vocational/educational decisions), the main agent of need satisfaction is the test interpreter rather than interaction with the participant's peers. It would make little actual difference if the individual participant had not been able to see or hear the other persons: they have no active part in the procedure for him. They, like him, were recipients of the interpretation procedure rather than participants in it.

Goldman has pointed out that it is possible to conceptualize group guidance procedures in terms of two variables: content and process.[8] *Content* refers to the subject matter of the procedure—the topic or area with which it deals. Content varies along a continuum ranging from predominantly factual material with which the individual deals on a cognitive level, to material that is predominantly attitudinal or emotional in nature, and with which he deals on an affectual level.

Process describes the techniques and methods employed to achieve the objectives of the procedure. Goldman sees process also as varying, from the traditional lecture-type, teacher-dominated classroom at one extreme, to the group-centered and directed counseling or therapy groups. Within this frame of reference, the test interpretation procedure just described falls toward the lecture end of the process continuum; that is, the interpreter carries primary responsibility for determining the direction and pace of the process, as well as the specifics of its content and technique. Unlike the group-centered procedures at the other end of process continuum, mass test interpretation must be described as a leader-centered procedure.

The reader may feel at this point that mass procedures, and the process that characterizes them, are about to be pictured as useless things, to

---

[8] F. Goldman, "Group Guidance: Content and Process," *Personnel and Guidance Journal,* **40** (1962), 518-522.

be avoided by the intelligent group worker. Such is not the case. Obviously, for many situations involving work with numbers of individuals, mass procedures are most appropriate, both in terms of efficiency and efficacy. The criticism one may make of mass procedures is, as is suggested by Goldman, that the process characteristic of them is often applied to inappropriate content. That is, while the lecture-type, leader-oriented process may be appropriate for presenting relatively factual material with which individuals can deal on an intellectual or cognitive level, it is clearly inappropriate when linked to content that engages the individual at an affective level—content he must grapple with and internalize emotionally.

Thus, for many individuals, at least some of the content of test interpretation is not appropriately dealt with in a mass situation. Anyone who has worked closely with individuals to help them understand the meaning and ramifications of their test scores knows that these are not just bits of factual information with which the individual can deal on a completely cognitive level; rather, such scores often elicit a definite emotional response because they are perceived as reflecting upon what the individual is, and what he can or will become. Therefore, to carry out test interpretation (as well as many other procedures for working with people) through mass procedures, is to fail to comprehend the unique characteristics and strengths of various types of group processes; it also represents a failure to recognize the effect that our efforts have on people.

One can, in a mass procedure, present material aimed at influencing the participants at an emotional or attitudinal level; however, the results of such an undertaking are usually negligible or unfortunate. On the one hand, this inappropriate linking of process and content may lead the participants to reject the material as invalid, or not applicable to them; if, on the other hand, material is accepted at a cognitive level, it may not really affect the participants' underlying values or attitudes. In connection with this latter point, Lewin and Grabbe, commenting upon re-education procedures, make the following observation: "In the use of mass procedures, then, one must be sensitive to the relationship which content and process bear to each other, to the manner in which each affects the participants, and to the contributions which each can make to the goals of the procedure." [9]

There are many situations in which mass procedures are appropriate both in terms of efficiency and efficacy. What is the nature of these situations, and what are some instances?

Intelligent use of mass procedures rests initially upon a recognition that, in working with people, consideration of the *efficacy* of a procedure

[9] K. Lewin and P. Grabbe, "Conduct, Knowledge, and Acceptance of New Values," in *Perspectives on the Group Process,* ed. Kemp (Boston: Houghton Mifflin Company, 1964), p. 331.

must always set limits for efforts to achieve *efficiency*. That is, a procedure that allows the efficient "processing" of large numbers of individuals, but makes very little contribution to the goals being pursued, represents false efficiency. If one is genuinely concerned with affecting the lives of people, he must pay attention to the results of his actions and be willing to fall back on more costly, or time-consuming methods when the objectives of his work demand it. Within the limits set by considerations of efficacy, mass procedures are most appropriately used when one can, with a fair degree of certainty, assume that the following conditions are present:

1. The material dealt with in the procedure is meaningful and relevant to the participants;
2. The material can, in the mass situation, be presented in a manner that will engage and sustain the attention of the participants;
3. The individual participants have sufficient intellectual skills to comprehend and deal with the material in a mass situation;
4. The material is of such a nature that it can be adequately dealt with and internalized on a cognitive level.

One of the chief criticisms of mass procedures is that they are apt to be ponderous and inexact in meeting the needs of individuals. While the general content of a particular mass procedure may touch upon the needs of all the participants, a given aspect of the subject may be meaningful only to a small portion of them. Mass procedures are aimed at meeting the needs of a mythical "average" that, in its particulars, corresponds to the real individual. This may not be too serious a situation if the number of individuals is small and if they are fairly homogeneous with reference to the needs to be filled by the mass procedure; when such is not the case, however, large segments of the procedure are apt to be unmeaningful to the participants. The participants will then "tune out" much of what is happening, including portions that would be useful to them.

Many mass procedures are based on the assumption that material that may eventually be useful and significant to the participants is perceived by the participants as being so at the time of presentation. Thus, mass orientation procedures, often given at the beginning of a program, tend to be built around the idea of providing the participants with all the information they will, at some point during the program, need. Obviously, the participants in many orientation procedures, since they are at the beginning of the program and often have very little knowledge of, or experience with, its workings, are not in a position to judge immediately what is or is not useful. Thus some may be overwhelmed in an effort to internalize all the information presented, while others arbitrarily pick and choose which material they will concentrate on. The outcomes of both courses of action are generally unsatisfactory.

Mass procedures tend to assume that the verbal, lecture-type presentation is the most effective way to introduce individuals to the content in question. Yet even when the material being considered is currently meaningful to the participants, a lecture-type presentation (even when enlivened by audiovisual effects, or a variety of speakers) is often inefficient and/or uninteresting. Much of the time spent in actually presenting material to the participants could be more effectively put to use in telling them where the information can be obtained. Mass procedures can better be used to provide contact with the information in the form of handbooks or other printed materials, or, alternatively, to provide participants with the resources they need to seek out and obtain information on their own.

As indicated above, the most serious fault with the way mass procedures are commonly used, is the unwarranted assumption that participants in a mass situation can deal with and internalize material that is affective or attitudinal in nature in the same way that they can absorb material of a cognitive or intellectual nature. At the very least, use of mass procedures with the former sort of material may be ineffective. At the worst, inner concerns or conflicts may be created in a mass situation that is insensitive to a participant's needs as an individual, and allows him very little opportunity for the support or assistance he may need to deal with these concerns. Thus it is one thing to present, by means of mass procedure, material concerning trends in the labor market, the changing pattern of job availability in various fields, and quite another matter to use the same means to attempt to directly modify deeply entrenched attitudes toward the necessity for, and value of work.

Returning to Lewin and Grabbe's ideas concerning re-education, we too may conclude that supplying new information, or indeed effecting a change in the cognitive structure does not necessarily result in a change in the individual's values or attitudes.[10] Such changes rest on a basic acceptance by the individual of the material as valid for, and applicable to him. Such acceptance typically does not occur as a result of the conditions present in mass procedures.

A recognition of the importance of meaningfulness of content to the success of mass procedures should have at least these practical results: 1) the scope of the procedures (in terms of the coverage) usually becomes more limited; 2) it is necessary, usually, to work with smaller numbers of individuals in order to obtain the homogeneity of need demanded by the mass procedure; 3) rather than attempting to anticipate

[10] *Ibid.*

the future needs of the participants, and deal with them in one setting, provision must be made for a series of mass meetings, timed to capitalize on immediacy of need and the concomitant increase in meaningfulness. The procedures to be considered are: mass treatment procedures, information transmission procedures, and orientation procedures, with particular reference to the needs of culturally different individuals.

Mass Treatment Procedures

Mass treatment procedures are those in which the participants are submitted to a process, or expected to complete some sort of task, more to meet the administrative or procedural demands of a program, or to receive material objects, than to receive information that will prepare them for other situations. Examples of mass treatment procedures are: making out application or personal data blanks; mass testing; issuance of clothing or other material; mass physical examinations.

Such mass treatment procedures vary in the extent to which the participants' cooperation and good will are necessary to the success of the procedure. At one extreme is the issuance of clothing, in which situation the individual can be seen as a passive object to be fitted with the standard line of equipment, irrespective of his preference or opinions. At the other extreme lies mass testing in which the involvement and cooperation of the participant are crucial to the obtaining of reliable and valid results.

Whatever level of involvement and cooperation is demanded by a given mass treatment procedure, the participant should know at least the outline or main events of the procedure, so that he will have an idea "where he is." Even though the individual may not be in a position to influence the course of the procedure, a knowledge of what is coming next can serve to dispel much of the feeling of helpless depersonalization that often accompanies the mass treatment procedure. Such information can be transmitted to the individuals in a brief pretreatment orientation, or with printed schedules.

When the involvement and cooperation of the participants become important, they must know not only what is going to happen, but also why it is going to happen. The transmission of the latter type of information generally requires a somewhat more elaborate orientation procedure, one that attempts to point out the manner in which the participants' cooperation will pay dividends in terms of future benefits.

There are many situations in which an effort is made to convey a body of information to a large number of individuals. Within the context of programs for working with the culturally different, such situations are either eventually a result of administrative consideration (i.e., a need to tell the participants about the operation of the program), or are part of the educational aspects of the program.

Perhaps the most specific guidelines applicable to the wide variety of procedures falling into this category are embodied in what can be called the Principle of Largest Mass Size. This term stems from Thelen's Principle of Least Group Size.[11] According to Thelen, groups used for instructional purposes should be as small as containment of the resources in terms of socialization and achievement skills demanded by the task permits. When one is involved in the transmission of information, the Principle of Largest Mass Size holds that the number of individuals involved in the procedure can be as large as possible, always allowing the content of the procedure to remain meaningful or relevant to all the participants. Obviously, this principle operates within the broad limits set by such physical factors as availability of room, sound transmission, etc. However, within these limits, the principle underlines the importance in setting up a situation for transmitting information, not of answering questions such as, How many people can we accommodate? and To whom is it meaningful? In other situations, when one *must* work with a given number of individuals, the primary question becomes, What information is relevant to all these individuals?

The manner in which introductory courses are handled in many colleges and universities provides a convenient example of the operation of the Principle of Largest Mass Size in the transmission of information. Typically, mass lectures are arranged in which the central, factual material of the course is presented to all persons enrolled in the course. Theoretically, an enormous number of students can participate in such a procedure through the use of closed-circuit television, or other media.

In conjunction with mass lectures, provision is often made for students to meet in small discussion groups. In these small groups the students, ideally, have an opportunity to pursue specific, individual questions they might have, or to think through the various personal implications that the material might have for them. This college practice provides a good illustration of the manner in which a mass procedure may be dovetailed with a small group procedure to efficiently and effectively meet the needs of individuals.

In terms of Goldman's scheme, the *process* of the mass information procedure is that of the traditional lecture presentation. The appropriate *content* for this process is factual information with which the participants can deal on a cognitive level. When one moves away from this type of content, it is necessary to fall back on a different type of process.

Actually, orientation procedures are an instance of the mass transmission of information procedures, but because of their widespread use, and because their results often color and influence the participants' reactions

[11] H. Thelen, "Group Dynamics in Instruction: Principle of Least Group Size," *School Review,* 57 (1949), 139-148.

to succeeding aspects of the program, orientation procedures will be considered separately.

Orientation procedures can be seen as serving two general functions: 1) providing the individual with (or giving him access to) information concerning content, sequence, goals, etc. of a future event or series of events, and his role in these events; 2) preparing the individual psychologically for participation in the events.

Entrance into a new situation or program may be a threatening or unsettling experience for the participants because, for most people, it represents a venture into unknown territory. An orientation procedure can, however, have the effect of bringing some structure to the unknown; that is, the participant can acquire through orientation information about what is coming next, and where he stands in relation to the program. Effective orientation can contribute to the smooth operation of a program by letting the participants know what will be expected of them, as well as where they will be and what they will be doing at various times.

Structuring the unknown through orientation can make a valuable contribution to the emotional security of participants by bringing the light of reality to bear on their apprehensions, and by offering them some measure of support in the face of these apprehensions. Much of the uneasiness precipitated by new situations stems from the fact that the individual does not know if he will be able to respond adequately to as-yet unknown demands that the situation may present; hence, he may worry about being found lacking.

Often the fear of inadequacy can grow to unrealistic proportions both in terms of the actual demands of the procedure, and the individual participant's ability to meet these demands. Proper orientation, while obviously incapable of completely dispelling unrealistic apprehension in all cases, can give the individual enough information and perspective to put him in a better position to judge what will be demanded of him. For example, culturally different young people entering training programs very often have behind them a long history of failure in various types of educational situations. In the absence of any definite information concerning the various remedial steps included in the program in anticipation of their deficiencies, these young people may have unrealistic concerns about the level of academic attainment required for successful participation in the program.

Proper orientation can also serve to correct unrealistic complacency with regard to the demands of a program. An intelligent appreciation of these demands can decrease the likelihood that an individual will let himself in for more than he can manage; it can also help to prevent the situation in which an otherwise capable individual impairs his chances for success because he feels he can get along with less effort than is actually required.

Finally, the orientation procedure can contribute to the participants' psychological readiness by serving as a symbol of the program personnel's willingness to offer support and assistance. Such meaning is not necessarily conveyed by means of a welcoming speech by an important figure in the program. Rather, the orientation procedure itself—when approached with a desire to let the participants know where they stand, and a sensitivity to the kinds of concerns that often accompany a new undertaking— can serve to communicate the support of the personnel. Let the room be comfortable, the schedule carefully planned, meals promptly served, etc., to demonstrate this good will.

While it is important to convey to the participants *enough* information about coming events so that they can form realistic expectations, it is important to avoid the error of trying to cover the program completely in one sitting. It is often much more reasonable to provide for a series of short orientation programs, timed to meet the participants' developing needs for information, than to attempt to dispose of the orientation function in one effort. Short, concise orientation procedures that have content meaningful to the participants can allow the orientation personnel to devote more time and effort to the second aspect of orientation: psychological preparation of the participants for the program.

GROUP PROCEDURES: GENERAL CONSIDERATIONS

Group procedures are those in which interaction and interdependence among members, as well as the need-satisfaction capabilities of the group, play an integral role in the achievement of goals. Whereas the participant makes his way through mass procedures as an independent unit, in group procedures the other participants are not only close to him physically, they also impinge upon him psychologically. In mass procedures, participants can be added or taken away with very little, if any, effect on the experience of the other participants, or on the nature and progress of the procedure. In small group procedure, each participant is influenced by the presence or condition of the other participants; the progress and outcome of the procedure may be drastically altered by a change in the status of any of the participants. In mass procedure, the agent of need satisfaction is typically the leader; in the group situation, the participants' needs are met through the group's functioning.

Several bases can serve to justify the use of small group procedures. Probably the most common is that these are timesaving devices. Theoretically, small group procedures allow the worker to deal with more persons per unit of time than would be the case if individual procedures were used. When one moves from the realm of theory to that of practice, he encounters several limitations serving to moderate enthusiasm concerning the timesaving features of group procedures.

First of all, in order to allow for the interaction essential to the group procedure, it is usually necessary to place certain limits on the size of the group. Through there is no hard-and-fast rule applicable to all situations, Warters, reviewing the literature on group counseling, suggests that groups of from 6 to 15 members seem most suitable.[12] As group size increases, there is simply less time per participant; also, members' inhibition toward contributing to the functioning of the group rises. Kelley and Thibaut, commenting on the influence of various factors upon group problem-solving, note that as group size increases there is often also an increase in the proportion of group members who report feeling inhibited about participating in the group activities.[13] Thus, while group procedures may, indeed, be more efficient than *individual* procedures (ignoring, for the moment, considerations of efficacy), it is most unrealistic to expect to work with more than 15 individuals at one time, and still retain the essential characteristics of small group procedure.

When the primary rationale for the use of group procedures is the saving, or more efficient use of time, the result is often a mass procedure. In an effort to achieve greater efficiency, more and more participants are added until interaction among participants becomes nonexistent, or limited to a very small portion of them. Often, in face of people "just doing nothing," the person with responsibility for the procedure assumes the role of lecturer or director. Serving to encourage this assumption of a directive role by the leader is the tendency, noted by Hemphill, for groups to be more comfortable with authoritarian leadership as group size grows.[14]

Small group procedures are often claimed to be effective as a preparation for individual procedures, and capable of serving as a screening device for locating those who are in need of individual procedures. Behind this point of view often is the assumption, stated or unstated, that group procedures are generally less effective than individual procedures. Thus, group procedures of various sorts are used to "prepare the soil" so that the "real work" can be done in the individual setting. Though this chapter does not allow space for a comprehensive consideration of the group vs. individual techniques question (nor, for that matter, does the

---

[12] H. Warters, *Group Guidance* (New York: McGraw-Hill Book Company, Inc., 1960), p. 174.

[13] H. H. Kelley and J. W. Thibaut, "Experimental Studies of Group Problem Solving and Process," in *Handbook of Social Psychology*, ed. G. Lindsey (Reading, Mass.: Addison-Wesley Publishing Co., Inc., 1954), pp. 735-785.

[14] J. Hemphill, "Relation Between the Size of the Group and the Behavior of 'Superior' Leaders," *Journal of Social Psychology*, 32 (1950), 11-32.

writer necessarily consider the question a useful, meaningful one), it is believed that a stout maintenance of the general superiority of individual techniques is based more on faith than upon fact.

Existing research [15] is at best suggestive rather than authoritative. It is possible that during the course of group procedures one will encounter participants for whom individual procedures seem more appropriate. However, it is just as reasonable to assume that, as a result of individual procedures, one will encounter persons for whom group procedures are most appropriate; indeed, this seems to be the case with girls. At present it does not seem justifiable to relegate group procedures to the status of "feeder activities" for the supposedly more efficacious individual procedures. Perhaps a more reasonable position in this regard is that group and individual procedures should complement or supplement each other, as Froelich suggests.[16]

The use of small group procedures should be determined by the demands of the situations within which one works, and the demands of the goals being pursued. The decision to use a particular procedure should be based on a careful consideration of the characteristics of the situation, and the relevancy of various procedures to these characteristics, rather than an a priori decision based primarily on considerations external to the situation. There are many situations for which small group procedures are most suitable. As Wright [17] has pointed out, the existing research concerning the distinctive merits of group procedures (in this case group counseling) is inconclusive; thus, it is not currently possible to make general statements concerning the group procedures most suitable for specific situations.

The use of group procedures, at least from the perspective of this chapter, assumes that the group can serve as an agent of need satisfaction for its members. When various factors raise doubts about this basic assumption, the use of a group procedure also becomes open to question. Thus, if the needs to be satisfied by the group demand of the members resources they do not possess, the group clearly cannot be an effective agent. The use of therapeutic group procedures with young children, for example, has been questioned on the grounds that youngsters have neither the experiential background, the intellectual sophistication, nor the emotional maturity to be of help to each other in the group therapy situation.

The general limits set by the group's ability to meet the needs of its

[15] F. Baymur and C. Patterson, "A Comparison of Three Methods of Assisting Underachieving High School Students," *Journal of Counseling Psychology*, 7 (1960), 83-90.

[16] C. Froelich, "Must Counseling Be Individual?" *Educational and Psychological Measurement*, 18 (1958), 681-689.

[17] E. W. Wright, "Group Procedures," *Review of Educational Research*, 33 (1963), 205-213.

members stands as an important consideration in working with the culturally different. There is often a tendency to see these individuals as deficient with regard to the various attributes commonly deemed necessary to the give-and-take of a group situation. One could, perhaps, point to their limited verbal skills or their circumscribed experiential background as examples of factors serving to reduce the usefulness of group procedures with the culturally different. While it is true that certain characteristics of these individuals may limit the usefulness of group procedures in some instances, there are also grounds for maintaining that, in some respects, group procedures are *specially suitable* in working with them.

Implementation of Group Procedures

Jennings's [18] division of groups into the categories of socio and psyche will be used as a basis for discussing the general implementation of group procedures with the culturally different.

Socio Groups

Socio groups as, described by Coffey, are characterized by the following features: [19]

1. Existence of definite group goals;
2. Formal structure;
3. Heterogeneity of membership in most cases.

The socio group is a task-oriented group. The interaction and efforts of the group members all tend toward the attainment of the group's goal. Perhaps the most common example of the socio group is the work committee. Typically, such committees are set up to accomplish a given purpose, the committee's structure and organization being designed to facilitate this. Interaction among the members tends to be restricted to topics related to the committee's goals. Generally, relations among group members may be somewhat formal: members tend to relate to each other on a cognitive or intellectual level.

As is suggested by the above description, the socio group is most useful when the object of the work with individuals takes the form of a relatively circumscribed, cognitive task (e.g., a committee report, the compilations of information relating to an occupational field, the building of scenery for a play).

The behavior of the leader is central to the functioning of the socio

---

[18] H. Jennings, *Leadership and Isolation*, 2nd ed. (New York: Longmans, Green & Co., Inc., 1950).

[19] H. S. Coffey, "Socio and Psyche Group Process: Integrative Concepts," *Journal of Social Issues*, 8 (1952), 65-74.

group. He coordinates the efforts and resources of the group members to aid the group in achieving the task at hand. As described by Fleishman *et al.*, he is an "initiator of structure," establishing patterns of organization, assigning roles to the group members, pushing them to get the task done.[20] Fleishman and his colleagues found that industrial production groups with foremen who showed this type of leadership tended to have higher proficiency ratings than groups whose foremen manifested a more group-centered "consideration" type of leadership. These findings are also consistent with those of Fiedler, who found that groups whose leaders were characterized by greater psychological distance or objectivity vis à vis the members' ability to contribute to the group's task tended to be more effective, according to various criteria of group effectiveness.[21]

While considering the effectiveness of the socio group for accomplishing various tasks, perhaps one should point out that the research also suggests that the effectiveness of these groups is achieved somewhat at the expense of friendly interpersonal relations among the group members. Fleishman, for example, found that workers preferred working under "consideration" type foremen, and that absenteeism under "initiation" leaders was higher than under "consideration" foremen.[22] Fiedler reports that, among surveying crews observed, "the . . . good teams in effect seem to trade, or sacrifice, some of the personally more comfortable intrateam relations, for the later satisfaction which can be derived from outside the team for good performance." [23]

These findings suggest that it is important to examine carefully the ends toward which the use of small group procedures is directed. It is essential to determine if the primary concern is to accomplish certain very definite tasks, or if there is also concern with the type of interpersonal relationships existing among the group members, and their satisfaction with the group situation. In the former case, the socio group process and "initiation of structure" type of leadership may predominate; in the latter, it is less appropriate.

In working with the culturally different, socio groups are most frequently used in connection with either residential or continuing programs. For example, the governing bodies or councils set up in Job Corps Training Centers can be seen, essentially, as socio groups. In educational or training classes, committees can be used to enhance the students' interest

[20] E. Fleishman *et al., Leadership and Supervision in Industry: An Evaluation of a Supervisory Training Program* (Columbus, Ohio: Ohio State University Bureau of Educational Research, 1955).

[21] F. Fiedler, "The Leader's Psychological Distance and Group Effectiveness," in *Group Dynamics, Research and Theory*, 2nd ed. (New York: Harper & Row, Publishers, 1960).

[22] Fleishman *et al., op. cit.*

[23] *Ibid.*, p. 594.

in the material being covered, and to give them some responsibility for presenting or dealing with this material.

One of the most valuable contributions that socio group experience can make to the culturally different is to give them an opportunity to participate in the give-and-take of the group process, offering them a chance to develop skills and attitudes that can contribute to the success of a group undertaking. This is not to suggest that the opportunity for such experience is necessarily absent in the culturally different individual's environment; however, such experience is usually offered within the context of situations in which the culturally different individual feels "out of place."

It has often been observed that students from the lower socioeconomic levels tend to participate less than other students in extracurricular activities of the schools. To the extent that clubs and other extracurricular activities offer students a chance to enhance their group skills, the culturally different may be cut off from a major source of socializing experiences. As Warters points out, activities like student government groups tend to be open to and dominated by the "better" students; therefore, the availability to the culturally different student of these and other group experiences is typically and drastically limited.[24]

Psyche Groups

Psyche groups, as described by Coffey, are characterized by: [25]

1. No stated, specific goal;
2. Informal structure; lack of rules or regulations;
3. Typically voluntary membership;
4. The purpose of the group, though usually not stated, is to meet the emotional needs of its members.

In contrast to the socio group, the psyche group is not a task-oriented group with a definite, well-defined goal. The focus of the group is not upon a task or other goal that exists outside of the group; its primary concern lies in the nature of the interpersonal relations among group members. These interpersonal relations are typically friendly, informal, and relaxed. Members are concerned with each other as people rather than as functionaries who carry out certain tasks. Generally the member is involved as a total individual rather than having a relatively narrow aspect of his functioning engaged. Also, in contrast to the socio group, the members of the psyche group tend to interact and affect each other on the affective as well as on the cognitive level. Within the context of the psyche

[24] Warters, *op. cit.*, p. 289.
[25] Coffey, *op. cit.*

group, one is sensitive to and concerned with the attitudes, opinions, and feelings of the other members.

A very common example of the psyche group is the neighborhood gang or peer group. Certainly the family would also stand as an example of this type of group. While most socio groups exist as means to an end, both the family and the neighborhood gang exist as ends in themselves. The therapy group is an example of a psyche group established as an instrument for working with people.

From the point of view of professional staff who work in various educational or personnel programs, the most important aspect of psyche groups is the involvement of individuals on the attitudinal and affective levels. While efforts are aimed at affecting the behavior of individuals, most people think this is done by dealing with the perceptions, attitudes, values, etc. that serve as the bases of behavior. As has previously been pointed out, Lewin and Grabbe suggest that meaningful, permanent behavior change rests not necessarily on the acquisition of new information or experience by the individual, nor on a change in his cognitive structure, but rather on "... real acceptance of a changed set of facts and values, a change in the perceived social world. ..." [26] They point out that an effective way to bring about a change in underlying perceptions and values is to establish an "in group."

> The changes for re-education seem to be increased whenever a strong feeling is created. The establishment of this feeling that everybody is in the same boat, has gone through the same difficulties, and speaks the same language is stressed as one of the main conditions facilitating the re-education of the alcoholic and delinquent. ... [27]

The characteristics of the psyche group seem to most completely provide the conditions in which the process Lewin and Grabbe broadly call re-education can take place.

Group counseling is probably one of the most common applications of the psyche group to the task of working with culturally different individuals. On a theoretical level, there seems to be some basis for considering group counseling an extremely suitable procedure for working with the culturally different.

Counselors whose experience and background differ greatly from that of the culturally different individual may, because of these differences, be somewhat limited in their ability to be sensitive to and to understand certain aspects of these individuals. This is not to take the position that, "to counsel one, you have to be one." Nevertheless, the background and experience of the middle class counselor can present certain barriers to his

---

[26] Lewin and Grabbe, *op. cit.*, p. 332.
[27] *Ibid.*

efforts to understand and work with the culturally different. Even if the group counselor is, indeed, sensitive to, and understanding of the situation of the culturally different, the prior experience of these participants may dispose them to perceive the counselor as an outsider who could never really appreciate their situation; or, even granting empathy on the counselor's part, the culturally deprived client may feel that he has no meaningful assistance to offer.

To the extent that both of these factors (i.e., the counselor's inability to understand the individuals, and their tendency to perceive him as an outsider) come to the fore in the counseling situation, the conditions generally seen as contributing to the change and growth will be impaired. *Group counseling can minimize the influence of these two factors.*

First, the group bears a large amount of the responsibility for the progress and direction of the counseling group. This being the case, the counseling situation has access to information, attitudes, and experiences that the counselor may not independently possess. Secondly, the group counseling situation is apt to be seen by the culturally different individual as less threatening than individual counseling. In the words of Lewin and Grabbe, "... everybody is in the same boat, has gone through the same difficulties, and speaks the same language...." [28] Group counseling being a "safer" situation, the culturally deprived individual should be able to lower his defensiveness, thus enhancing his openness to new attitudes, values, and experiences and—ultimately—to change.

One can raise the question of whether or not the security and support of the group situation might lead to a continuation of old attitudes and behaviors, rather than change. Might not the grouping of individuals, all sharing similar backgrounds and values, merely serve to reinforce and strengthen existing attitudinal behaviors? Certainly, one would have to agree that this possibility exists in work with groups such as the culturally different. However, for people who have entered a program out of a desire to become more effective members of our society, the small group situation allows the freedom and security to change, rather than forcing them to change; and to the extent that the group counselor is skilled in assisting the group to a position of responsible self-direction, the possibility that the group will remain becalmed in inadequate attitudes and behaviors is reduced. In fact, Lewin and Grabbe suggest that the opportunity to reject change and denounce the new actually seems to facilitate change. It is almost as if, in the opportunity to reject the new, one finds the freedom to accept it.

In working with a group of this nature, the counselor's behavior is of the type that Fleishman *et al.*[29] have identified as "consideration." The

[28] *Ibid.*
[29] Fleishman *et al., op. cit.*

counselor reflects a concern for the atmosphere or climate which exists in the group. The counselor tries to establish a situation in which warmth, mutual respect and trust are present. Unlike the "initiation of structure" leader described in connection with socio groups, the "consideration" counselor holds interpersonal relations rather than task accomplishment, of primary importance.

Socio and Psyche Groups: Conclusion

The foregoing discussion may give the impression that a group must be either a socio or psyche group. Actually, as Coffey points out, these two group types do not represent distinct, independent entities; rather, they are separate ends of a continuum of group process.[30] Any group will usually display, to varying extents, the characteristics of both types. The skillful group counselor is able to draw upon the characteristics of both groups in his work. Even a strictly task-oriented group can benefit from an effort by the worker to make the group situation "interpersonally comfortable" to the participants. Rarely are we so interested in efficiency of task fulfillment that we are willing completely to sacrifice the good will of the group members.

Conversely, even in a group primarily set up to help the participants deal with attitudinal or emotional concerns, it is not uncommon for the group to encounter areas that can be handled most effectively through the socio group process. A counseling group set up to help adolescents clarify and work through their vocational objectives may, at some point, find it necessary to organize itself into a task-oriented group to gather information concerning various aspects of the "world of work." Essentially, the group worker can be seen as one who can use his knowledge of, and experience with groups to nurture and support a variety of group situations calculated to meet effectively the needs of individuals.

SELECTED READINGS

1. Baymur, F., and C. Patterson, "A Comparison of Three Methods of Assisting Underachieving High School Students," *Journal of Counseling Psychology*, 7 (1960), 83-90.

2. Bilovsky, D., *et al.*, "Individual and Group Counseling," *Personnel and Guidance Journal*, 31 (1953), 363-365.

3. Brodbeck, M., "The Role of Small Groups in Mediating the Effects of Propaganda," *Journal of Abnormal and Social Psychology*, 52 (1956), 166-170.

4. Cartwright, D., and A. Zander, eds., *Group Dynamics, Research and Theory* (2nd ed.). New York: Harper & Row, Publishers, 1960.

[30] Coffey, *op. cit.*, pp. 65-74.

5. Cattell, R., "New Concepts for Measuring Leadership, in Terms of Group Syntality," *Human Relations*, 4 (1951), 161-184.

6. Coffey, H. S., "Socio and Psyche Group Process: Integrative Concepts," *Journal of Social Issues*, 8 (1952), 65-74.

7. Davis, D., "Effects of Group Guidance and Individual Counseling on Citizenship Behavior," *Personnel and Guidance Journal*, 38 (1959), 142-145.

8. Fiedler, F., "The Leader's Psychological Distance and Group Effectiveness," in *Group Dynamics, Research and Theory* (2nd ed.), ed. Cartwright and Zander. New York: Harper & Row, Publishers, 1960.

9. Fleishman, E., *et al.*, *Leadership and Supervision in Industry: An Evaluation of a Supervisory Training Program*. Columbus, Ohio: Ohio State University Bureau of Educational Research.

10. Froelich, C., "Must Counseling Be Individual?" *Educational and Psychological Measurement*, 18 (1958), 681-689.

11. Gibb, Cecil A., "Leadership," in *Handbook of Social Psychology*, ed. G. Lindsey. Reading, Mass.: Addison-Wesley Publishing Co., Inc., 1954.

12. Goldman, F., "Group Guidance: Content and Process," *Personnel and Guidance Journal*, 40 (1962), 518-522.

13. Hemphill, J., "Relation Between the Size of the Group and the Behavior of 'Superior' Leaders," *Journal of Social Psychology*, 32 (1950), 11-31.

14. Jennings, H., *Leadership and Isolation* (2nd ed.). New York: Longmans, Green & Co., 1950.

15. Kelley, H. H., and J. W. Thibaut, "Experimental Studies of Group Problem Solving and Process," in *Handbook of Social Psychology*, ed. G. Lindsey. Reading, Mass.: Addison-Wesley Publishing Co., Inc., 1954.

16. Krech, D., and R. Crutchfield, *Theory and Problems of Social Psychology*. New York: McGraw-Hill Book Company, Inc., 1948.

17. Krumboltz, J., and C. Thoreson, "The Effect of Behavioral Counseling in Group and Individual Settings on Information Seeking Behavior," *Journal of Counseling Psychology*, 11 (1964), 324-333.

18. Lewin, D., "Field Theory and Experiment in Social Psychology: Concepts and Methods," *American Journal of Sociology*, 44 (1939), 868-896.

19. Lewin, K., and P. Grabbe, "Conduct, Knowledge, and Acceptance of New Values," in *Perspectives on the Group Process*, ed. Kemp. Boston: Houghton Mifflin Company, 1964.

20. Marx, G., "A Comparison of the Effectiveness of Two Methods of Counseling with Academic Underachievers," *Dissertation Abstracts,* **20** (1959), 2144-2145.

21. Olmsted, M., *The Small Group.* New York: Random House, Inc., 1959.

22. Stockey, M., "A Comparison of the Effectiveness of Group Counseling, Individual Counseling, and Employment Among Adolescent Boys with Adjustment Problems," *Dissertation Abstracts,* **22** (1961), 491.

23. Thelen, H., "Group Dynamics in Instruction: Principle of Least Group Size," *School Review,* **57** (1949), 139-148.

24. Warters, H., *Group Guidance.* New York: McGraw-Hill Book Company, Inc., 1960.

25. Wright, E. W., "Group Procedures," *Review of Educational Research,* **33** (1963), 205-213.

5

THE MENTAL HEALTH
OF THE DISADVANTAGED

JOSEPH MARGOLIN

The ways of science are strange indeed. Given marvelous though fallible machines in both man and society, we proceed to carve them up in the service of scientific analysis. The magic of aseptic surgery prevails. We, like the committee of blindmen researching the elephant, forget to reassemble our subject. We ignore the synthesis; yet synthesis is necessary if our efforts are to lead to the understanding of human phenomena rather than of bits and pieces.

The problem of dealing with psychological phenomena is enhanced by a wide range of perceptions based on the characteristics and circumstances of the individuals studied.

Mental illness provides a particularly good example. It is a complex entity, variously perceived at different times, and from different stations in life. The excited behavior of a middle-aged executive suffering from a manic-depressive process would probably be much less alarming to the middle class bystander than comparable excitement on the part of a young Negro laborer, entailing a policeman required to subdue the sufferer and, unfortunately, a psychiatrist who may or may not treat him.

There are many reasons for such differences in perception of mental illness. It is undoubtedly true that a capable adult relative or colleague will be available to help the hypothetical executive. He can obtain adequate hospitalization. He can communicate better with those seeking to help him; and he does not feel the continuing fear and hostility that exist between the lower class Negro and a representative of white middle class society.

We must say from the outset that the mental illness of the individual Negro or impoverished individual is not different only because of the disadvantages possessed by one group. There is an interesting parallel in the recent flareups in Watts, Harlem, etc. Herzog suggests that, "what is new for the Negro minority is not a sudden acceleration of family break-down. What is new is an injection of hope that attacks apathy and fatalism and sparks insistence on full justice." [1] The onset of such expectation before the dominant culture is prepared to offer to relate hope, effort, and reward can prove tragic to the individual and to the community. How-ever, the work of Deutsch, Bloom, Whiteman, Pettigrew, and others suggests that the primary problem is not race but social class status, or, even more, the pressure of severe impoverishment.

Yet this statement is still an oversimplification. We are reminded re-peatedly of the deprivation of the Greek and Jewish immigrant population of a generation or two ago; but these groups produced relatively effective citizens, with a low rate of severe mental illness.

Hylan Lewis, in a recent article, warns against the oversimplification implicit in the concept of a "culture of poverty." [2] Such a term, he states, diverts attention from the real causes and consequences of poverty: "It might be more fruitful to speak of people as being in poor situations. . . ." Lewis speaks of the complexity of the experience of being poor, and suggests as well the diversity of the situations in which the poor live their lives. He notes, in particular, the tendency of many low income families to be "frustrated victims of middle class aspirations." He observes that "heavy goods [television sets, furniture] are easily obtained on credit whereas expendable items [food, clothes] are characteristically bought for cash."

The tendency of low income families to show greater conformity to middle class standards in what they say they want than in their actual behavior is also cited as a source of conflict and confusion for the young. For instance, mothers had high educational and occupational aspirations for their children, yet were unable to provide the means or the motivation toward such goals.

However, low income group, lower class, and lower class culture are not synonymous concepts.

---

[1] Elizabeth Herzog, "Is There a 'Breakdown' of the Negro Family?" *Social Work,* 11, No. 1 (January, 1966), 9.
[2] Hylan G. Lewis, "Culture, Class and Poverty," *Cross-Tell,* February, 1967. Sponsored by the Health and Welfare Council of the National Capitol Area.

Neither the quality of life in most low-income neighborhoods nor the varying child-rearing behaviors of low-income families is to be interpreted as generated by, or guided by a cultural system in its own right with an integrity of its own. Rather they appear as a broad spectrum of pragmatic adjustments to external and internal stresses and deprivations.[3]

It is important that we get our conceptual "ducks" in a row. We may assume either that: (1) mental illness is a physical process determined at least in part by genetic or physical factors, or (2) mental illness is environmentally determined, and related to a variety of noxious or inadequate environmental factors that are psychological in nature.

Probably both assumptions are true. We may further suppose that: (1) functional processes do have physiological equivalents; and (2) harmful environment or deprivation of medical and nutritional care may produce birth injuries or other damage, or change contributing to mental illness. It is also abundantly evident that social and psychological conditions resulting from deprivation and poverty contribute to personal ineffectiveness; conflict with, or alienation from the environment can also stem from these circumstances.

Apparently, then, if mental illness is broadly conceived, we may assume that economic and social disadvantage will predispose to mental illness or ineffectiveness.

When we consider the mental health problems of the poor, we are faced with vastly different perceptions of who the poor are. Are they those who have little now, but are gaining in their capacity for coping and earning? Are they those who have had some means but who, like the retired person in a time of inflation or the laborer in a period of advancing technology, are losing ground? Or are they those whose circumstances preclude their making use of opportunities available to the population at large? Relevant factors might include race, education, developmental deficit, or other considerations.

The point of view of each subgroup is different, and the scientist's perception of the circumstances and the character of each group is also different.

We may also ask where the disadvantaged person works and lives—in a city, suburb, farm, rural mining community? Does he experience only the slum ghetto, or does he traverse a wide social spectrum daily, traveling to another milieu to work (and to observe the life style of other more fortunate citizens)?

We need to know many of the day-to-day experiences that determine the ecology of life under circumstances of disadvantage. Early childhood experiences; school; work; the cultures of the nuclear family, the extended

[3] *Ibid.*, p. 11.

family, and the community all provide gross or subtle factors that influence the quality of "disadvantage."

Our search, then, is for some simple approaches to a complex problem and, subsequently, for some description of those we consider to be "the poor."

It is vital for the middle class to distinguish the blue collar or working class from the poor. Indeed, the surfeit of jokes featuring comparisons of plumbers' and construction workers' wages with those of language instructors is enough to disabuse one of such confusion. Thus, the blue collar worker, as his lot currently stands, is not necessarily impoverished.

Let us also distinguish between the poor and what Leighton describes as "poverty in the context of social disintegration." [4] These are the profoundly poor: the inhabitants of the Appalachian highlands or the rural or urban ghettos, the Indian on the reservation, and the migrant laborer. Most have experienced many generations of poverty; yet there is a stability to their cultures and to their circumstances as long as they remain in the familiar physical and ecological setting. It is only movement within or to the city, or the city to them, that creates crisis. Other than that, the profoundly poor are a segment of the population that does not benefit from the largesse of our society in equal share with others. However, crisis is common, our culture is a dynamic one, and the invasion of the bastions of stable poverty by the mass media and industry produces some unsettling results. These are the poor of the "culture of poverty" described by Oscar Lewis,[5] the "unstable poor" of S. M. Miller;[6] they are described by Beiser[7] as "the disintegrated poor."

This group, which is a reservoir and an incubator of psychopathology, has been and continues to be subjected to the stresses of a society with which its members cannot cope, and wherein they fall farther and farther behind in the race. Its characteristics include unstable family conditions, unreliable social institutions, material deprivation, lack of a sense of community, and inadequate and distorted relations with the remainder of society. These are the ingredients that produce hostility or apathy, psychopathology and rebellion.

We have alluded to some of the several populations that make up the

[4] Charles C. Hughes et al., People of Cove and Woodlot (New York: Basic Books, Inc., Publishers, 1960); Alexander H. Leighton, My Name Is Legion (New York: Basic Books, Inc., Publishers, 1959); ———, "Poverty and Social Change," Scientific American, May, 1965; Dorothea C. Leighton, et al., The Character of Danger (New York: Basic Books, Inc., Publishers, 1963).

[5] Oscar Lewis, The Children of Sanchez (New York: Random House, Inc., 1961).

[6] S. M. Miller, "The American Lower Classes: A Typological Approach," in Mental Health of the Poor, ed. Frank Riessman, et al. (New York: The Free Press of Glencoe, Inc., 1964), pp. 139-154.

[7] Morton Beiser, "Poverty, Social Disintegration and Personality," Journal of Social Issues, XXI, No. 1 (1965), 56-78.

segment we call disadvantaged. Negroes, the most numerous minority in the population, certainly constitute the largest percentage of this group. However, a large part of the American Indian population lives under poor conditions, as do people of Spanish, Mexican, and Puerto Rican origin. We must also include the poor rural dweller or marginal farmer, notably from the Appalachian region; he is usually of northern European stock. Our migrant population is a mixture of all of these elements, and even this categorization does not fully depict the heterogeneous quality of the poor in America.

Their conditions of life range from the seemingly limitless space of a New Mexico reservation to the jammed squalor of a Harlem tenement. Yet who can measure human stress or suffering in order to make comparison? It is clear that the factors contributing to stress vary as widely as do the forms of pathology. The latter, in turn, are as wide as the range of mental and somatic illness in the middle class population. There is reason to believe that the spectrum of mental illness in our society is more heavily weighted at the impoverished end because of the preponderance of factors conventionally perceived as contributing to mental illness or incapacity. These range from birth injury to chronic stress.

What are the traits that go with poverty? The happy, carefree Negro, the bitter ghetto dweller, the moonshining mountaineer, the indolent Indian; genetic inferiority versus sexual virility; the inability to cope versus the carefree psychopath—our stereotypes are sufficiently contradictory to be ridiculous. Yet there are characteristics, related not to geography or race, but to antecedent and current circumstances that are probably meaningful.

Weakness of the capacity to defer gratification, a difficulty in orientation to the future, apathy, hostility, suspiciousness, an inability to cope with changed circumstances—these we find in our work with deprived children and adults. They are significant signs, causes, and results of the conditions under which these groups have existed, and continue to exist.

A wide range of traits has been studied in an effort to distinguish between Negro and white populations, and among social class groups. Almost universally, most of the variability appears to be associated with social class. Herzog,[8] in discussing family life, states, "... adequately controlled comparisons within different income levels show that the differences associated with color, family structure, for example, differ more between different income levels than between Negro and white families." The same is true of differences between Negro and white children in educational achievement. When income is controlled, the relative posi-

[8] Herzog, *op. cit.*, p. 7.

tions of men and women, economically and educationally, are the same for whites as for nonwhites.

It would be unreasonable to assume that the factor of race does not contribute to existing circumstances, particularly those producing frustration and anxiety. The high visibility of the Negro, and the attitudes of the middle-class white, for good or for ill, make the factor of being a Negro a significant one. However, despite this burden, Herzog states that "descriptions of white families at the very low income levels read very much like current descriptions of poor Negro families with a high incidence of broken homes, 'mother dominance,' births out of wedlock, educational deficit, crowded living, three generation households, and failure to observe the norms of middle-class behavior." [9]

Hollingshead and Redlich's [10] descriptions of the white population they studied offer vivid evidence of the accuracy of Herzog's position. Thus, many of the factors that contribute to mental disability and illness appear to be class-centered, and to relate inversely to the social structure.

It is unlikely that any single system will explain the condition of the poor. Deutsch [11] effectively describes the sad, and sometimes contradictory condition that has arisen, despite seeming scientific rigor. Significant correlations with poverty are achieved by any number of variables including intelligence (as measured by intelligence tests), social and economic opportunity, race, religion, and developmental experience. It is even possible that a modest genetic factor could be introduced if the researcher ignored some very obvious fallacies.

In the approach to this problem, we have all too frequently been satisfied with correlational studies that show some vague relationship but give us neither a theoretical basis nor a handle by which to grasp the problem. We will attempt to present at least two approaches that provide a theory whereon intervention and program may be built.

In assessing poverty, we will make an effort to penetrate some of the social psychological variables affecting "mental illness " on the assumption that they promise both a fruitful etiological yield and a useful methodological one. This will be attempted with full awareness that in some cases the clinical personality areas will also prove useful.

What do we know of the demography of mental illness, and incapacity in this context? We are immediately faced with the methodological problem of whether to use prevalence or incidence statistics. Included in the

[9] *Ibid.*

[10] August B. Hollingshead and Frederick C. Redlich, *Social Class and Mental Illness* (New York: John Wiley and Sons, Inc., 1958).

[11] Martin P. Deutsch, "Social Intervention and the Malleability of the Child" (lecture, Cornell University, 1965).

former group could be persons in treatment in a given community, or those in need of treatment. The numbers of first admissions, or of all admissions, may be used to define incidence. Each serves its purpose but should be carefully distinguished in terms of definition, and with respect to the institutions providing the data, and their criteria for mental illness.

When Hollingshead and Redlich [12] studied the relation of mental illness to place of origin of their subjects' parents, they found no significant relation between foreign- and native-born status. What differences there were were minimized by adjustment for social class status, suggesting again the potency of that factor.

Despite this, and despite the extensive and intensive study of multi-problem families who are considered reservoirs of psychopathology, we really do not have enough firm information on the frequency of mental illness in the several social class groups. Parker and Kleiner [13] refer to the literature on the relation between socioeconomic status and mental illness as "confusing." They note the frequent failure of reporters to distinguish between prevalence and incidence studies.

Early, Faris and Dunham [14] found an inverse relation between social class and the incidence of schizophrenia in the Chicago area. Tietz, Lemkau and Cooper [15] reported the same finding in Baltimore; they also reported a tendency toward manic-depressive psychoses in upper class populations. Clark,[16] in 1949, supported these findings but felt they were more true of whites than Negroes. Morris reported the same inverse relationship of schizophrenia and social class in England, in 1959.[17]

Hollingshead and Redlich,[18] in a somewhat more refined study, demonstrated the highest rates of psychoses in the lowest of the five classes investigated. There was little distinction among the other four classes except in schizophrenia, which increased inversely in a linear manner with social class.

Later studies by Jaco [19] in Texas brought out an interesting relationship in which rates of psychosis were highest in the highest and lowest educational and occupational groups in the "non-Anglo" population: nonwhites

[12] Hollingshead and Redlich, *op. cit.*

[13] Seymour Parker and Robert J. Kleiner, *Mental Illness in the Urban Negro Community* (New York: The Free Press of Glencoe, Inc., 1966).

[14] R. E. Faris and H. W. Dunham, *Mental Disorders in Urban Areas* (Chicago: University of Chicago Press, 1939).

[15] C. Tietze *et al.*, "Schizophrenia, Manic-Depressive Psychosis, and Socio-Economic Status," *American Journal of Sociology*, 47 (1941), 167-175.

[16] R. E. Clark, "Psychosis, Income, and Occupational Prestige," *American Journal of Sociology*, 54 (1949), 433-440.

[17] Parker and Kleiner, *op. cit.*

[18] A. G. Hollingshead and F. C. Redlich, "Schizophrenia and Social Structure," *American Journal of Psychiatry*, 110 (1945), 695-701.

[19] E. G. Jaco, *The Social Epidemiology of Mental Disorder: A Psychiatric Survey of Texas* (New York: Russell Sage Foundation, 1960).

in the upper classes showed remarkably high incidence of mental illness. There was a negative relation between education and mental illness in the "Anglo" population, and a positive relation in the "non-Anglo" groups.

Doubts about the simplicity of the above relationship have been raised: neither in 1959 [20] nor in 1960 [21] did Clausen and Kohn report evidence of this connection; nor were Kleiner, Tuckman, and Lavell [22] able to show any such evidence in the case of the Negro population. The latter authors, however, offered some support for the postulated inverse relation of schizophrenia and social class in the white population.

If there is one conclusion that is supported, it is the positive relation of psychosis, particularly schizophrenia, with the lowest class. This is consistent with the experience of a large number of public health officers and social researchers who have studied the multiproblem family. It is also apparent that these statistics represent prevalence, in large part. Thus, the continuation of the illness becomes the significant variable, not its initial incidence.[23]

Hollingshead and Redlich's study also tended to support the curvilinear relation suggested by Jaco.[24] In their study, when the lowest group was eliminated, there was evidence of a growth in difficulty with increase in level of social class. Also, the prevalence of neurotic disorders tended to be positively related to social class.

The results of attempts to study nonpatient populations are quite ambiguous (Pasamanick, Roberts, Lemkau, and Krieger; [25] Srole [26]). These studies, while carefully conceived, suggest that differences in the results are a product of different criteria and methods of data collection.

The literature appears to indicate certain trends. It would seem to be more important to develop a theory or a system for dealing with the phenomena than to allow an unspoken theory to be operative when we select social class as an independent variable. On the basis of what we

[20] J. A. Clausen and M. L. Kohn, "Relation of Schizophrenia to the Social Structure of a Small City," in *Epidemiology of Mental Disorder,* American Association for the Advancement of Science, Publication No. 60, ed. B. Pasamanick (Washington, D.C., 1959), pp. 69-95.

[21] ———— and ————, "Social Relations and Schizophrenia: A Research Report and a Perspective," in *The Etiology of Schizophrenia,* ed. D. D. Jackson (New York: Basic Books, Inc., Publishers, 1960), pp. 295-320.

[22] R. J. Kleiner *et al.,* "Mental Disorder and Status Based on Race," *Psychiatry,* **23** (1950), 271-274.

[23] Parker and Kleiner, *op. cit.*

[24] Jaco, *op. cit.*

[25] B. Pasamanick *et al.,* "A Survey of Mental Disease in an Urban Population: Prevalence by Race and Income," in *Epidemiology of Mental Disorder,* American Association for the Advancement of Science, Publication No. 60, ed. B. Pasamanick (Washington, D.C., 1959), pp. 183-201.

[26] Leo Srole *et al., Mental Health in the Metropolis: The Midtown Manhattan Study* (New York: McGraw-Hill Book Company, Inc., 1962).

have observed, it is even less advisable to accept conventional "disease entity" concepts of mental illness. This would seem to have been the tendency of most of the demographers who have investigated the problem. Competent epidemiology demands more complete conceptualization of the process under study, and fewer a priori assumptions.

In dealing with mental illness, we will use the increasingly popular social competence model derived from psychology. The disease model may occasionally creep in—it is the nature of much of the training and conditioning of this generation. Indeed, in view of the need for a chemical or electrical process to mediate the behavior of the central nervous system, the disease model may prove to have some ultimate merit. However, we must now consider which model or theory offers the best basis for prevention and intervention.

By and large we will again employ a social psychological model, or more precisely, a field theoretical model. This model is consistent with the constructs developed by Erikson.[27] The field theoretical model offers a psychological medium for the descriptive process by which Erikson presents the dynamics of development.

The question of the relation between mental illness and poverty may appear at first blush to involve an encounter between two different systems: the economic, and the psychological or psychiatric. Psychology deals with human behavior, and it would be unfortunate if we did not make an effort to reconcile the several elements of the elephant that has so effectively been divided by blind men.

We have observed that no current research variable offers a high correlation with mental illness. This is very likely so because of the highly complex etiology and/or the wide range factors contributing thereto. Perhaps a common psychological meaning is the element most desperately needed.

It will be useful to establish the relation between the various poverty-related traits and mental incapacity or illness. We have mentioned the problems of deferment of gratification, apathy, suspiciousness, etc. We must also consider the inadequacy of intellectual, cognitive, and social skills that maintains the "culture of poverty." Beiser describes these skills: [28]

During the process of socialization, an individual must acquire an armamentarium of skills, the use of which will enable him to function within the larger cultures technology. Depending upon circumstances, these necessary skills may embrace anything from canoe-building to literacy. If he fails to acquire such skills, he will probably be unable to partake in the consumption of

[27] Erik H. Erikson, *Childhood and Society* (New York: W. W. Norton & Company, Inc., 1963).
[28] Beiser, *op. cit.*, p. 58.

goods and services available to those who are better endowed. Individuals living in conditions of social disintegration characteristically fail to develop these abilities.

The definition of skills can be expanded to include even more basic aspects of personality functioning such as perception, cognition and the use of language. Accumulating evidence suggests that the poor suffer deficits in these areas as well.

Between these two levels of skills, there exists an intermediate body which might be collectively termed, "social skills." Their importance has largely been neglected. The ability to know where to go for appropriate help in a situation seems mundane enough, but its lack may be paralyzing for the individual.

A rather broad repertoire of skills is called for in complex social situations. These include the recognition of nuances in behavior, the ability to assess another's motivations accurately and the discrimination of affects both in one's self and in other people. There is some evidence that the disintegrated poor tend to see others in block terms and lack such discriminatory facilities.

Such a change in perspective would be based on a developmental approach to the problem. It would be an approach not unlike that of Erik Erikson, for whom proper development requires, as a beginning, effective achievement of a sense of basic trust and security in our neighbors—derived, to be sure, from early positive experience with them, and appreciation of their characteristics.

Autonomy, initiative, industry, and a sense of identification with one's surroundings are necessary successive elements in this development, as are the abilities to love and to appreciate the role of assisting the new generation and, lastly, the feeling of satisfaction with one's life.

Early development of a sense of the dependability of the environment, self-mastery, initiative, etc. are critical factors in the ability of the individual to rise from poverty, or to avoid falling into it.

The incapacity for future orientation so frequently associated with poverty may well be derived from an absence of support for future plans or expectations of the child. Difficulties in causal thinking have a similar etiology. The inability to tolerate ambiguity of idea or person is another significant product of deprived childhood. Each of these factors, and a host of others, contributes to the durability of what has been perceived as a culture of poverty. In large part they also contribute to the entrenchment of the conventional forms of psychopathology.

The skills whereby the intelligence of the individual, or his capacity for success, are judged weigh heavily in his predisposition toward mental "illness." The ability to feel inwardly secure throughout a crisis, the sense of one's own identity, a feeling of competence, the capacity for delay of gratification, and tolerance of ambiguity are essential to emotional well-being. Absence of these qualities may result in stresses so severe that the constructive ego may not endure, or may never develop.

Certainly atypical modes of development usually do not bode well for the socialization or the social effectiveness of the individual. In school, at work, and in marriage, an excessive gap between the expectations of the environment and the functioning person predispose to stress, failure, and breakdown. At each stage of development, the situation becomes worse and the real and perceived anxiety and alienation of the person increase.

In 1949, Leighton's description of a disintegrated community in Stirling County [29] indicated that:

There were strong sentiments of self-disparagement, mistrust of outsiders, especially those in positions of authority. Work was regarded as virtueless, a necessary evil to be avoided when possible; and the people were little permeated with ideas of foresight and planning. The future was thought to be uncontrollable and most people felt that the best thing to do with a dollar was to spend it at once, for only in that way could one be assured of getting full use of it.

The community had a very low level of educational achievement and occupational effectiveness. Broken marriages, conflicts, and child neglect were much more prevalent than in other parts of the county; but such difficulties were much like those in the multiproblem groups in San Mateo, California, and a variety of other communities where they have been studied.

In 1952, a mental health survey undertaken in the same Stirling County revealed a high prevalence of mental illness in the form of depression, anxiety, and psychosomatic conditions. Beiser describes the result as [30]

a vicious spiral in which the lack of skills, the sentiments and the psychopathology militated against satisfactory interactions with each other and against effective interdigitation with the larger society. Their poor performance at schools, jobs, etc., reinforced the impression of surrounding communities that this was a collection of inferior people. Rejection by the larger society in turn reinforced the focus community members' feelings of apathy and suspiciousness and thus the self-perpetuating spiral continued in its downward direction.

It should be added that the history of the region does not lend support to a "misery seeking each other out" hypothesis nor to an explanation of this community's existence as a result of genetic inferiority. Rather, it seems that cultural isolation and a precipitous loss in the community's economic base initiated the trend towards disintegration.

Apparently, then, inadequate skills and high stress can interact to predispose to mental breakdown, or to serve as an actual causal agent.

What can we learn of the individual psychological process that mediates such breakdown? If we examine the external psychological conditions, we may perceive better the field in which this process operates.

---

29 Leighton, *op. cit.*, p. 29.
30 Beiser, *op. cit.*, p. 72.

We have established the frustrating and goal-defeating characteristics of both the individual and his environment. As a result of his incapacity, his attitude, and that of the enveloping society, the path of upward mobility is closed or at best limited; yet, while he endures these conditions, he is deluged by the mass media with exhortations to consume and to appear respectable. With legitimate avenues to goal areas closed, the individual may be even further alienated from his environment should he try (unsuccessfully) any other approach. Even more than the "content" skills, the absence of formal skills makes the movement of the ill-prepared individual toward his goals difficult to achieve.

The invisibility of poverty makes the individual seem even more culpable and unmotivated. This may be the case; but motivation and skill are frequently the products of opportunity and training. Moreover, the latter may not achieve their purpose if they are too long deferred. Even today we are learning that the sense of mastery and the cognitive skills must be acquired very early, perhaps by the age of two or three, if they are to assist in the proper development of a personality in society. The work of Deutsch, Hess, Grey, Kirk, and a host of others attests to this. And now Schafer [31] has begun to unearth evidence that supports the Skeels and Dye [32] principle that deficit, perhaps partly irreversible, may develop if the infant is not properly stimulated.

Who are the emotionally or mentally incapacitated, or those most vulnerable to such incapacity? It would seem that in many walks of life they are those who are alienated from their surroundings; those who are, out of defeat and frustration, depressed or agitated.

It is assumed that an irrational process operates. One might even take the seemingly heretical position that it is likely that the irrationality is evident only to the observer, not to the victim. Perhaps we can accept the "there's a reason for everything" school of psychiatry and psychology and suggest that people who live in depressed or disturbed settings may be depressed or agitated. They may be, as Michael Harrington put it, "victimized by a mental suffering to a degree unknown in suburbia." [33] Harrington develops a theme of J. K. Galbraith in declaring that [34]

physical and mental disability are . . . an important part of poverty in America. The Poor are sick in body and in spirit but this is not an isolated fact . . . an

[31] Earl Schafer, "Intellectual Stimulation of Culturally Deprived Infants" (Washington, D.C.: National Institute of Mental Health, in press).

[32] H. N. Skeels and H. B. Dye, "A Study of Effects of Differential Stimulation on Mentally Retarded Children," *Proceedings*, American Association on Mental Deficiency, 44, No. 1 (1939), 114-136.

[33] Michael Harrington, "The Invisible Land," in *The Disadvantaged Learner, Part I: Knowing the Disadvantaged*, ed. Staten W. Webster (San Francisco: Chandler Publishing Co., 1966), p. 7.

[34] *Ibid.*, p. 14.

individual "case," a stroke of bad luck. Disease, alcoholism, low IQ's, these express a whole way of life. They are, in the main, the effects of environment not the biographies of unlucky individuals. Because of this, the new poverty is something that cannot be dealt with by first aid. If there is to be a lasting assault on the shame of the other America, it must seek to root out of this society, an entire environment, and not just the relief of individuals.

One need say little more about the "therapeutic approach" to poverty.

What then is the situation of the poor in this milieu? Many of the poor are alienated, as members of minority groups, from a reasonable reference group. Kardiner and Ovesey [35] make a useful comparison of Jewish and Negro ghetto life. The life of the ghetto Jew was derogated by the outsider; but in his daily life, in the ghetto, his behavior was independent and rewarded according to his system. For the Negro, first in slavery, then after 1865, it was necessary to find a place in the white man's system. He had no religious or traditional defenses against the pressure of the white man's values. The old culture of Africa and of slavery had no functional relevance, even within the Negro group. Thus the ghetto operated not to protect him but to limit his physical, economic, and spiritual mobility. In its final effect, the ghetto was ego destructive. More significantly it symbolized the Negro's economic, physical, and psychological state.

What is the psychological state of the poor? We have suggested a field theoretical model as a way of conceptualizing the relation between poverty and mental illness. We need only conceive of the goal areas representative of the needs and desires of each individual. To achieve his goal, the individual P must traverse a psychological field containing both barriers and facilitators. Movement toward the goal is motivated by the valence of the goal for P. Yet it is not a completely simple mechanical system. P is subjected to a variety of more complex phenomena including a degree of goal-striving stress that affects his performance in complex ways. The positive factors in goal-striving stress include:

1. The discrepancy between P's current position and the one sought;
2. The perceived probability of success; and
3. The value to P of the success.

The perceived probability of failure and the expected social or personal consequences of failure constitute important negative factors.

Parker and Kleiner [36] have made effective use of a field system in studying mental illness in a Negro community in Philadelphia. In developing their theory, they took note of other factors. For example, stress is also

---

[35] Abram Kardiner and Lionel Ovesey, "The Social Environment of the Negro," in *The Disadvantaged Learner, Part I: Knowing the Disadvantaged*, pp. 141-160.

[36] Parker and Kleiner, *op. cit.*

seen as being determined by the discrepancy between reference group achievement and *P*'s own achievement. Other important considerations in the development of stress include:

1. *P*'s perception of his own appearance to others and to himself (the weight is dependent on degree of self- or other orientation);
2. *P*'s sensitivity to success or failure; and
3. *P*'s awareness of his success (or upward mobility) relative to others.

Parker and Kleiner developed an elaborate system demonstrating the effectiveness of this conceptualization in the study of factors affecting mental illness in the Negro community, and among the several social and class levels. Several of their findings are interesting; a few are unexpected. Negroes native to the Philadelphia area had a higher rate of mental illness than migrants from the South (or the North).[37] This surprising finding may be explained in a number of ways. Perhaps, however, it is most meaningful to suggest that a person native to an area has the greatest stake in success, and is most sensitive to any discrepancy between reference group forces and perceived achievement.

Parker and Kleiner's [38] study probed the complex effects of goal-striving stress under different field and personal conditions that cannot be fully presented here. They demonstrated that goal-striving stress and reference group behavior determine the self-esteem of the individual which, in turn, interacts with his self-perceived success to determine his susceptibility to mental illness. There appeared to be a clear relation between low social class, downward mobility, and mental illness; but fuller study revealed some surprising qualifications of the generalization.

In studying the relation of social mobility and mental illness, it must first be reported that the subjects who were classified as patients tended to regard the opportunity structure as *much more open* than did the relatively normal individuals: apparently the former were much more vulnerable to discouragement and frustration. (There may be a chicken-egg quality to this relation.) In short, they may be disturbed because of frustration in the face of perceived opportunity.

The investigators concluded that relative downward occupational mobility is related to mental illness. In an earlier report, Kleiner and Parker [39] noted that the tendency of the downwardly mobile to higher illness rates was more observable in residents of large urban areas than in residents of smaller communities.

[37] Seymour Parker and R. J. Kleiner, "Status Position, Mobility, and Ethnic Identification of the Negro," *Journal of Social Issues,* **20** (1964), 85-102.
[38] ———— and ————, *Mental Illness in the Urban Negro Community.*
[39] R. J. Kleiner and S. Parker, "Goal-Striving, Social Status, and Mental Disorder: A Research Review," *American Sociological Review,* **28** (1963), 189-203.

Refinements of the results parallel other findings—the same researchers report, for instance, that the downwardly mobile at the lower end of the status continuum show higher illness rates, but that the upwardly mobile at the upper end of the status spectrum also show higher rates.

Though somewhat unexpected, the results with regard to goal-striving also support the conclusions. A nonlinear relation appeared between *goal-striving stress and mental disorder*. Within an optimal range of goal-striving, mental disorder was lower than among those who demonstrated either a high or low level of goal-striving. Beyond these limits it is likely that those at the higher end of the goal-striving continuum were dissatisfied and frustrated in their efforts, while those at the lower level considered themselves to be failures. It is unlikely that members of the high goal-striving group can reduce their striving, even after a degree of success. This continued goal-striving suggests the *anomie* effect of the differentially restricted opportunity structure that the Negro faces.

Kleiner and Parker [40] have brought us to several very useful conclusions. The first would establish the general significance of relative downward mobility as the most frequent basis for mental illness. This appears to be a product of unrealistically high goal-striving stress coupled with low self-esteem. However, the presence of a group of upwardly mobile individuals, "patients" in the high status groups, suggests that the most effective measure is a "high level of goal-striving stress," rather than the direction of mobility in its own right. Thus, the failure of the downwardly mobile to reduce high levels of aspiration associated with past status affiliations results in pathogenically high levels of stress. In the upwardly mobile, unrealistic levels of aspiration produce the appearance of relative downward mobility, and anxiety.

It follows from our previous observations that the above view is quite consistent with Merton's [41] presentation of *anomie* and resultant psychological disability as a disjunction between socially valued goals and the socially provided means to attain these goals. It also relates closely to Durkheim's conceptualization of *anomie* and the stress derived from an insufficient association of the individual's goals and achievements with the standards of his significant social groups.

. Thus, Durkheim [42] and Merton [43] have systems for understanding the sociological process contributing to emotional illness in the lowest socioeconomic class, and among members of minority groups. We also have a conceptually consistent psychological description derived from field

[40] Parker and Kleiner, *Mental Illness in the Urban Negro Community.*

[41] R. K. Merton, *Social Theory and Social Structure,* rev. ed. (New York: The Free Press of Glencoe, Inc., 1957).

[42] E. Durkheim, *Suicide,* trans. J. A. Spaulding and G. Simpson (New York: The Free Press of Glencoe, Inc., 1951).

[43] Merton, *op. cit.*

theory, based on early formulations by Lewin and Escalona [44] and the more recent work of Parker and Kleiner.[45] It provides us with both evidence and explanation of the unfortunate psychological consequences of disadvantage and limited opportunity.

The relevance of this theoretical system to the plight of the disadvantaged should be clear. Contemporary centers of poverty are alienated from the mainstream of our society primarily insofar as the opportunity structure is concerned. In other respects they are subject to the "American dream" and to the constant reality of the mass media's hard sell of tangible and expensive items. It is made to appear so easy to "buy one's way into the middle class" that the disadvantaged, and those who would help them to make the transition to the middle class, are blinded to the solid economic, sociological, and psychological bases necessary to make a firm transition.

What are the solutions? We have established that conventional methods of psychotherapy, even if they were available in sufficient quantity, could not solve so great a problem. In any event, such measures would be prohibitively expensive. As Rae-Grant, Gladwin and Bower [46] observe, "If mental health had been able to find solutions there would have been no need for the War on Poverty." It is very likely that conventional welfare methods are at best a maintaining diet.

It is evident that a revision in thinking about psychopathology is called for. The helping professions cannot continue to devote their attention only to the neurotic whose conflicts and symptoms interfere with the ability to learn new tasks, to function in a family setting, or to work satisfactorily. *Experience with disadvantaged groups highlights the importance of recognizing the possibility of a reverse order of cause and effect. A deficit in skills may have direct implications for the development of mental illness, and may in itself constitute the point of attack in attempting to alleviate such distress.*

Sociological, psychological, and educational alterations in the nature of the opportunity system or the channels to upward mobility are needed, in close association with methods that effect an improvement in social competence. The two add up to what has been described as the social competence model.

[44] J. N. Morris, "Health and Social Class," *Lancet*, I (1959), 303-305; S. K. Escalona, "The Effect of Success and Failure upon the Level of Aspiration and Behavior in Manic-Depressive Psychoses," *University of Iowa Studies in Child Welfare: Studies in Topological and Vector Psychology* 1, **16**, No. 3 (Iowa City: University of Iowa Press, 1940), 199-302; ———, *An Application of the Level of Aspiration Experiment to the Study of Personality* (New York: Teachers College, Columbia University, 1948).

[45] Parker and Kleiner, *Mental Illness in the Urban Negro Community*.

[46] Q. A. F. Rae-Grant *et al.*, "Mental Health, Social Competence, and the War on Poverty," *American Journal of Orthopsychiatry*, **36**, No. 4 (July, 1966), 644-652.

The tendency to perceive the opportunity system unrealistically can be corrected by opening the system somewhat more than it is. But perhaps as critical is the kind of educational and developmental experience that enables the individual to make a more accurate estimate of the opportunity offered to him by the society, and prepares him for the best utilization of that opportunity.

Most important, this new approach opens the possibility of a variety of interventions assisted by a much larger range of disciplines than those that had previously cornered the market. Psychiatry, psychology, and social work can be significant in such interventions, as can educators, economists, urban planners, group workers, etc. This broadening trend has constituted much of the thrust of current programs, including the poverty and educational efforts of the Great Society.

We must intervene in a manner that will increase the capacity of the disadvantaged to cope with their situation. If we are to achieve maximum benefit, the intervention must affect the individual in his social matrix. In short, familial and social supports must reinforce the more effective functioning of the individual. It may be profitable to examine the critical steps in such intervention begun in the early years. A psychologically disturbed child, or a child whose development has been markedly limited, is a handicapped learner—handicapped not only in learning academic subjects, but also the multitude of formal "bits" that he must acquire if he is to function as a constructive member of society.

A considerable body of literature offering both formulation and solution has been developed by Deutsch, Hess, Levine, Gray, Bloom, Whiteman, and others. We have noted that Schafer,[47] in an unpublished work, supports the work of Skeels and Dye [48] and Skodak and Skeels,[49] demonstrating the effect of very early experience on learning. If we can accept the principle that the development of a personality capable of perceiving the environment accurately and coping with it without breakdown is learned, then we can accept the significance of early learning in the prevention of mental disorder. The thesis concerning the learning process is difficult to dispute. It is even fundamental to psychoanalytic theory. To reject it would seem to send us back to disease, or genetic, or endocrine theories of mental illness. These will find few advocates among those who are familiar with the mental disability of the poor or, indeed, of any segment of society. Such approaches, moreover, have little utility for current intervention.

Moynihan and others in the antipoverty movement stress changing

[47] Schafer, *op. cit.*
[48] Skeels and Dye, *op. cit.*
[49] Marie Skodak and H. M. Skeels, "A Final Follow-up Study of 100 Adopted Children," *Journal of Genetic Psychology,* **75** (1949), 85-125.

the poor to fit the institutions. Riessman and others insist that institutions should be changed to fit people. Undoubtedly both are right. One way of effecting structural change is to use the positive elements in the traditions, style, and culture of the poor. New social technology has been developed by building on the traditions of the poor. These techniques have implications for potential change within some of our major institutions—education, mental health, and services to name a few.

New mental health approaches have been developed for low-income people. These include peer intervention, as in the various forms of self-help groups or group therapy. Sociotherapy proposes indirect models as an added tool for improving mental health. These developments may result in better treatment for all classes.

Changes in the education of the disadvantaged that would revitalize the entire educational system include use of nonprofessionals to aid teachers, and development of a teaching technology that makes available more varied styles of learning.

The time of intervention is critical. Hunt [50] has indicated that the extent to which modification of function is possible depends on the "match" or correspondence between individual developmental stages and external stimulation. As Deutsch has expressed it, "the extent of malleability [of the child] then, is related to the appropriateness and power of the entire social intervention process." [51]

If this is so, then a network must be fashioned to nurture the development of the child who today is denied such support. It would begin with prenatal consultation and care, proper obstetrical and pediatric services, and the provision of a stimulating and supportive environment practically from birth. We have begun to enlarge the preschool activity of our educational system. For some time, the forces of medicine and welfare have been active in the maternal and child health areas. Their work must be fitted into the fabric of social policy.

Psychology, psychiatry, and social work can do much to improve the character of the family matrix of the developing infant and child. It is important, however, that an effective program be planned, one that provides the economic, social, and attitudinal underpinnings for the type of family needed. Tranquilizers and psychotherapy will not suffice, nor could they reach the right places in the right doses in time.

The mastery of objects, of self, and ultimately of language, is more than the key to proper development. The nature of the relation to objects, to people, and to the self, as well as the use of language, are the models, the final determinants of behavior. They spell the difference be-

[50] J. McVicker Hunt, "Experience and the Development of Motivation: Some Reinterpretations," *Child Development,* 31 (1960), 489-504.
[51] Deutsch, lecture, p. 39.

tween sound mental functioning and functional retardation or emotional illness.

As one example, Graham,[52] in a book distributed by the Anti-Defamation League of B'Nai B'Rith for use by Head Start teachers describes methods that have proven successful for teaching culturally deprived children in preschool centers.

The children in Head Start programs frequently lack a sense of self-worth. Therefore, teaching the child to value himself and to interact with others constitutes a basic goal of the program. "Though some will have known parental love or at least acceptance, many others do not know what it means to be wanted, or to matter." They hide their feelings of insecurity behind masks of passivity and sullenness. Many have to be taught how to play. They rarely laugh; and giving these children reasons for laughter is a considerable achievement.

Since the children's range of experience is small, they have developed little curiosity; and they lack self-confidence in new environments. In order to reach them, the Head Start teacher must encourage every effort, no matter how small. Enthusiasm is essential to build communication.

The most perplexing barrier for the middle class teacher is the children's silence. They communicate with shrugs, nods, or sentence fragments, or they remain impassive when spoken to. In their homes, speech is sparingly used for social interaction. The ability to ask questions and to learn depends upon the development of speech. One technique of establishing communication is to talk with each child at intervals throughout the school day. The subject matter progresses from the teacher's interest in the child to her approval of his appearance, clothing, and activities, and finally to her sharing mutual experiences with him. Speech is encouraged by listening to sounds indoors and out, and by discrimination between sounds for loudness, pitch, rhymes, and the sounds of letters of the alphabet.

The children's curiosity increases as they learn to observe. Some subjects for observation are the environment, "likeness and differences," pictures (to be "read"), shapes (to be distinguished), and objects (to be classified). Curiosity is further aroused by simple scientific experiments, classroom pets, time concepts, premathematics work, field trips, and short walks. Even learning to form a line for walks or for classroom games requires special teaching methods, because the acutely disadvantaged children have no concrete concept of what a line is.

Building a sense of self can be accomplished in several ways. Each child needs his own possessions and storage place. Snapshots and long

---

[52] Jory Graham, "Handbook for Project Head Start," under the direction of the Urban Child Center, University of Chicago, and the New York Anti-Defamation League, 1965.

mirrors help the children learn who they are; and proper names should be used frequently. Personal cleanliness should be stressed partly for the sense of self it develops. Demonstrations in social behavior teach the children that they are members of a group, and that they can relate to each other by taking turns, sharing, making room for someone to sit down, shaking hands, offering something to another child, and so on.

Creativity and expression of personal feelings should be encouraged through physical activity, rhythm, artwork, music, and woodworking. The effect of these activities is dramatic in easing tensions and preparing the child emotionally for entrance into the public schools.

When the child has reached school age, it is important that the opportunities to achieve education be maintained. Education in the formal processes that ultimately provide the roots of mental health—the sense of mastery and security in himself and his environment, and the capacity to communicate—is as important to the child as education in curricular content.

Operating as an effective part of the social organism, the educational system can do as much as any other agency to prevent mental illness, not only in the more depressed parts of the population, but at all levels.

If the concept of *social competence in an open society* can be maintained, we will have taken a great stride toward the elimination of "mental illness." We have the means. Advances in the understanding of the cognitive process, and of man's relationship to his environment, work hand in hand in the service of a major new function for education. Educational technology can give the teacher new freedom and flexibility. The awakened awareness of the importance of education provides the green light. Such programs will be expensive in money, in effort, and in concessions from the several components of our society who may applaud the goals but question the methods. The goal area is a worthy one; our society must develop for itself the plan and the program for achieving that goal.

SELECTED READINGS

1. Beiser, Morton, "Poverty, Social Disintegration and Personality," *Journal of Social Issues,* XXI, No. 1 (1965), 56-78.

2. Erikson, Erik H., *Childhood and Society.* New York: W. W. Norton & Company, Inc., 1963.

3. Faris, R. E., and H. W. Dunham, *Mental Disorders in Urban Areas.* Chicago: University of Chicago Press, 1939.

4. Herzog, Elizabeth, "Is There a 'Breakdown' of the Negro Family?" *Social Work,* XI, No. 1 (1966), 3-10.

5. Hollingshead, August B., and Frederick C. Redlich, *Social Class and Mental Illness.* New York: John Wiley & Sons, Inc., 1958.

6. Hollingshead, August B., and Frederick C. Redlich, "Schizophrenia and Social Structure," *American Journal of Psychiatry*, **110** (1945), 695-701.

7. Jaco, E. G., *The Social Epidemiology of Mental Disorder: A Psychiatric Survey of Texas*. New York: Russell Sage Foundation, 1960.

8. Kleiner, R. J., J. Tuchman, and M. Lavell, "Mental Disorder and Status Based on Race," *Psychiatry*, **23** (1950), 271-274.

9. Kleiner, R. J., and S. Parker, "Goal-Striving, Social Status, and Mental Disorder: A Research Review," *American Sociological Review*, **28** (1963), 189-203.

10. Miller, S. M., "The American Lower Classes: A Typological Approach," in *Mental Health of the Poor*, ed. Frank Riessman, *et al.* New York: The Free Press of Glencoe, Inc., 1964.

11. Parker, Seymour, and Robert J. Kleiner, *Mental Illness in the Urban Negro Community*. New York: The Free Press of Glencoe, Inc., 1966.

12. Rae-Grant, Q. A. F., T. Gladwin, and E. Bower, "Mental Health, Social Competence, and the War on Poverty," *American Journal of Orthopsychiatry*, XXXVI, No. 4 (1966), 644-652.

13. Srole, Leo, *et al.*, *Mental Health in the Metropolis: The Midtown Manhattan Study*, Vol. 1. New York: McGraw-Hill Book Company, Inc., 1962.

14. Tietze, C., P. Lemkau, and M. Cooper, "Schizophrenia, Manic-Depressive Psychosis, and Socio-Economic Status," *American Journal of Sociology*, **47** (1941), 167-175.

6

LANGUAGE AND THE
CULTURALLY
DISADVANTAGED

R. C. OREM

Recent work of many researchers in the behavioral sciences points to the profound importance of environmental influences upon the individual's physical, emotional, intellectual, and social development. Given a normal or even superior genetic endowment, the individual can develop his capacities only within the limits of environmental nurture. For example, if English is absent from a child's environment, he will not learn that language.

The early years of childhood are now acknowledged to be an especially critical or sensitive period—a time when basic patterns of perception, communication, cognition, and other behavior patterns are formed. The importance of the pre-school years is also readily seen in the matter of language learning.

The child, as a creature in process of formation, displays a remarkable capacity for absorbing whatever language he is exposed to during his first six years of life. If he is exposed to standard English under suitable conditions of learning, he can be expected to master standard English. If the same child were exposed during his formative years to the imprecise and restricted language of the urban slum ghetto, however, one could predict that he would just as readily learn this language.

The young child learns spoken language through exposure, largely in his home, without the necessity of formal schooling. In fact, if two languages are adequately presented in the home, he will learn both. And if, on the other hand, the child has only one poor language model to imitate, his language learning will reflect all the errors in vocabulary, syntax, and pronunciation to which he is exposed. A language-rich environment, then, promotes language development; an unstimulating or defective language environment retards it. The implication is clear enough: All children need, from birth, the best surroundings that can be provided, to facilitate optimum development of their language aptitude and of their potentials in all other areas of human development as well.

Students of human behavior generally acknowledge that man's language is his greatest intellectual achievement—his most distinctive, complex, and powerful tool for mastering his environment. Language enables man to order and analyze his experience. By abstracting and organizing elements of his experience, he is able to use reason in problem-solving. Language makes possible the various forms of communication that underlie social life. Finally, language enables man to record, and to transmit through time his accumulated cultural heritage. It would be difficult to overestimate the importance of language, especially reading, to the educative process in our culture.

Because language deficits impair the individual's psychological, intellectual, and social development and functioning, the quality of the child's language environment should be of paramount concern to society. The young child, who is really at the mercy of his environment in the matter of language learning, can only utilize models and materials that are available. We may fairly ask, then, Do all children in America now enjoy the benefits of a "prepared" environment, conducive to good language learning?

We must answer with a resounding No! For there are some ten million "disadvantaged" families in the United States. One third or more of the children in many of the larger urban areas may come from such families. But the facility with which the label may be applied should not mislead us: in the final analysis, the disadvantaged are disadvantaged *individuals,* and one must be careful to avoid easy generalizations and stereotypes. Although we shall focus primarily on selected problems of the urban slum Negro family, it is recognized that other disadvantaged groups (e.g., Puerto Ricans, Mexicans) with somewhat similar problems exist in many American cities. Also, of course, there are the rural disadvantaged, comprised of certain groups of American Indians, migratory workers, Appalachian poor, etc.

EFFECTS OF DEPRIVED ENVIRONMENTS

The plight of the Negro in the urban slums has been detailed in many books of the past decade, and there is no need to elaborately review all of the sordid conditions found in the ghettos' self-perpetuating poverty. The inhabitants are generally "lower class" socioeconomically, and their existence is precarious. They suffer the adverse effects of unhygienic housing, substandard diet, weak family structure, limited medical and recreational facilities. It has been estimated that by 1970 at least 50 per cent of the school children in many of our major cities will come from deprived environments. Of particular concern to us is the unfavorable language environment to which such children are exposed.

We have already indicated that the child "builds himself" through interaction with his environment. At birth, he has virtually no IQ, language or personality; but in the space of a few years, and long before his formal education begins, he will have established the foundations for all three. However, the child must "build" with whatever he finds in the environment; and deprived environments result in deprived children.

Recent research in sensory deprivation, language development, and the deficits of certain institutionalized children illustrates dramatically how the external environment must match the inner needs of the young organism if maximum development is to occur. Performance of youngsters from "advantaged" backgrounds demonstrates that environments rich in sensory stimuli tend to promote perceptual development. Youngsters with such backgrounds likewise have been provided the means and motivation for extensive language development. The lower class child, however, is blocked at every turn.

The adults with whom the lower class child comes in contact are usually poor speech models. Their vocabulary is restricted, imprecise, and reflects a low level of conceptualization. Sentences tend to be short or incomplete, and syntactically simple; they often take the form of shouted commands, accompanied by grunts and gestures. As a rule, lower class parents do not talk over at length with the child what has happened, is happening or will probably happen.

When the adult does talk his pronunciation is likely to be blurred. Thus the child does not learn to make the fine auditory discriminations learned by his middle class peer; and the former's speech, mirroring all the defects to which he has been exposed, will need extensive remedial work. The slum youngster's failure to master a high standard of spoken English leads to serious problems with beginning reading which, in turn, multiply his failures and frustration in the classroom situation.

Many other features of the lower class Negro subculture may retard not only the child's language, but his intellectual development generally. Let us examine some of these features and their implications for the child's learning.

Instead of a stable male head of the household, there may be a series of men who move into and out of the family constellation. The male child in particular may have difficulty relating to these mobile figures and learning a positive masculine role.

Investigators have noted that books, magazines, and newspapers are often lacking in lower class homes. Middle class children, in contrast, have ready access to general reading materials, dictionaries, encyclopedias, and other reference works.

Overcrowding in the slums contributes to noise and lack of privacy. The child may learn "not to hear" the blare, not to attend to the chaos about him. He still will not have the opportunity to concentrate on a task and bring it to completion. Even if materials such as learning games were available, there would be a lack of space, and surfeit of interruptions. The young child may have to repeat a new task many times before it is learned. While the adult learner may be able to master a task quickly, repetition is essential to the child. He has not yet developed the perceptual and cognitive fluency that characterizes the mature adult. The ghetto child may have virtually nothing to call his own—not even a bed—in his constantly shifting environment.

Mastery of one's environment implies the presence of a minimum of order, consistency, and predictability in that environment. The lack of patterns, routines, and rituals in the lower class environment is so striking that some researchers have been led to speak of the "nonculture" or "protoculture" of poverty. A child caught in the randomness of such an environment fails to grasp any logical connections between means and ends, between his actions and their consequences. He lacks the confidence of competence in dealing with his surroundings, and may perceive himself as constantly threatened by powerful external forces.

What of the dynamics of the lower class family as they relate to language development?

Family Functioning: A Study in Contrasts

The lower class family is often loosely structured in terms of organization and functioning. Children are left to fend for themselves much of the time. Discipline is inconsistent: children are treated harshly one moment and indulged the next. They learn, by example, to gratify their impulses immediately whenever possible. The family may do few things together as a cohesive unit. Of course, there are varying patterns of family interaction among the different groups in the lower class, but we are speaking here primarily of the lower class urban slum Negro.

If meals in the ghetto are unscheduled, slapdash affairs, for the typical middle class family they are but one aspect of a regular rhythm of activities. Meals provide opportunity for discussion and for the learning of manners, as do excursions to the zoo, and to historic sites. In short, the average middle class child benefits from an informal "cultural agenda" planned by his parents, often with his help. He can expect considerable supervision. At a certain hour he is to be in bed, not in the street. From an early age he hears about the value of education.

Middle class parents tend to promote language learning in their off-spring. The parents provide cues, feedback, reinforcement to help the child along the path to mastery of spoken English. Questioning is encouraged. The child is constantly "testing" his speech on his parents. Books are valued in the home. He is told stories and read to, perhaps daily. Once in school, his academic performance is of real concern to his parents, who continue to provide whatever outside support is needed. He leaves in the morning with food in his stomach, adequate clothing, homework done. Although lower class parents often voice high aspirations for their children, little if any action may be taken toward achieving such aspirations.

Parents who are preoccupied with the day-to-day struggle for survival may have little motivation and few resources for aiding the development of their children.

At this point in our discussion, let us summarize briefly: That the effects of the environment are far-reaching, especially in the pre-school period, is demonstrated in language development. Environments vary widely with regard to opportunities offered for learning of language. Through no fault of their own, lower class urban Negro children are at a terrible disadvantage from the very start, developmentally. They are unable to master and utilize a high standard of English. Physical conditions in the slums, poor adult speech models, and other factors limit the quality and quantity of the slum child's language learning. In contrast, the environment of the middle class, including family structure and functioning, tends to enhance language development, and learning generally.

LANGUAGE AND EDUCATION

Because language plays a crucial role in virtually all phases of personality development, an individual's language proficiency may be the most important determinant of his adjustment to the school situation. It is through language that his experience can be organized and internalized. The individual gradually learns to bring his motor behavior under verbal control, as he uses words to mediate between feeling and action. The self-disciplined individual is not at the mercy of every fleeting impulse. Faced with a particular situation, he weighs the probable consequences of various actions. He finally makes a conscious decision to act in a certain manner. He has learned to reason. He has developed habits of self-control; and he brings these habits into the middle class school situation. He understands and responds to the verbal signals of the teacher. He knows how to be obedient.

In the typical middle class school, orderliness, quiet, obedience, sitting still are all prized. The student is expected to "do what the teacher says." He must pay attention for relatively long periods of time, and not talk out of turn. He is supposed to forego immediate pleasures for long-term goals. Traditionally, practices and programs in the schools have been geared to middle class students, with only token efforts to adapt to the needs of other groups. Middle class schools are "anxiety factories" for the disadvantaged child. Deutsch, for example, has found that lower class Negro and lower class white children alike are subject to a "cumulative deficit phenomenon" between the first and fifth grade years.[1] Children who come to school with language and experience handicaps do not catch up, or even hold their own. They fall ever farther behind their more fortunate classmates until, by grade five, their academic situation may already be hopeless. What can be done?

The implementation of Title I Public Law 89-10 (the Elementary and Secondary Education Act) represents one approach to meeting the language learning needs of the child of poverty. During 1965-66, the first year of Title I programs, approximately one billion dollars was spent on more than 20,000 projects in the 50 states and six territories.

Title I funds are aimed at helping disadvantaged children overcome the limitations of their environment, primarily through the process of education. In view of the importance of the early years, and of language development as stressed throughout this chapter, it is encouraging to note that some 70 per cent of the children affected by Title I funds are in pre-primary classes through grade six. As the National Advisory Council on the Education of Disadvantaged Children has put it, ". . . the principal target of local programs is the young child, from three to twelve years old."[2] The major thrust of these programs is directed at the improvement of language arts skills in these children: reading, writing, speaking, and listening. Language competency, especially reading, is the most important prerequisite to success in school. Disadvantaged children are weakest in this area; therefore their greatest educational need is for specialized programs that enhance language development.

Project Head Start, initiated in the summer of 1965, represents a major endeavor to strengthen education in the preschool years. During fiscal year 1967, more than $100 million in federal funds were used to help improve language skills of 500,000 disadvantaged children. Although this program, administered by the Office of Economic Opportunity, is de-

---

[1] Martin Deutsch, "The Role of Social Class in Language Development and Cognition," *American Journal of Orthopsychiatry*, **35** (1965), 78-88.

[2] *Report of the National Advisory Council on the Education of Disadvantaged Children*, March, 1966, p. 6.

signed to aid the various aspects—physical, emotional, intellectual, social—of child development, increasing emphasis is being put on language learning.

Introduced early enough, and in sufficient measure to counteract negative environmental influences, new curricula, programming, teaching strategies, language training, and enrichment could help alleviate the situation. But the school, as one of many social institutions, does not operate in isolation. All family, community, and governmental resources must be mobilized in a coordinated effort to provide a "responsive" environment, sensitive to the developmental needs of every child.

Grambs [3] has discussed many of the shortcomings of contemporary schools: the competition of the classroom, resulting in repeated failure of the slum child; the subtle rejection of the slum child by many school personnel; the unrealistic and uninteresting programs and books; the whole bias toward "proper" middle class values. She suggests that we experiment with the use of tape recorders to build language, bring successful Negroes into the classroom to raise levels of aspiration, and give Negro students greater responsibility in program planning to increase their motivation.

We must not depreciate or be scornful of lower class language which, it should be noted, is constantly influencing the development of the standard English used by the middle class. The American middle class child really uses two languages: the standard English he encounters throughout his school career and in informal language that he uses, for example, in peer group interaction.

The dilemma of the Negro child lies in his possession, basically, of only one language—the informal or "public" speech, which, while appropriate to his slum environment, will penalize him academically. This informal language is the only one he has, and therefore the only one he can bring to the schooling (and counseling) situation. He must also learn enough of the standard English necessary for academic success and access to that large portion of our culture's literary heritage which is "recorded" in standard English.

Riessman and Alberts have described as "linguistic inversion" [4] the social situation in which the "dialect" of the disadvantaged child constitutes his primary language.

The middle class student's primary language is the customary English of our schools—essentially standardized in pronunciation. The urban slum child does not have this language at his command. For him, a "dialect" functions as the primary language. Riessman and Alberts suggest that

[3] Jean Grambs, "The Culturally Deprived Child: Achieving Adequacy Through Education," *National Elementary School Principal*, 44 (1964), 9-15.

[4] Frank Riessman and Frank Alberts, "Digging 'The Man's' Language," *Saturday Review*, September 17, 1966, p. 80.

school personnel must accept this nonstandard primary language of their disadvantaged students. The basic point is that the teaching process should be additive. The teacher *"builds on* what the pupil brings to the teaching situation; he does not *take away* from the pupil." [5]

Just as the disadvantaged child must learn standard English, so must the teacher and counselor of middle class background learn enough of the lower class language to communicate effectively. And this is not accomplished by merely memorizing a list of "street" words and their meanings. He must develop some fluency with the style of lower class communication. There is currently a great deal of interest in presenting (standard) English to disadvantaged students as a second language, as one would teach a foreign language. More consideration needs to be given to the feasibility of teaching nonstandard English to school personnel, to whom the language of the disadvantaged is indeed "foreign."

Basil Bernstein, the English sociologist, has differentiated between the formal language of the middle class and what he terms the "public" language of the English "working class." [6] Children of the latter group are characteristically sensitive to the content of objects, and are predisposed to thinking of a descriptive order. The middle class child, on the other hand, is sensitive to the structure of objects, and is predisposed to thought involving the discovery and classification of symbolic relations. The logically simpler public language "limits the type of stimuli to which the speaker learns to respond." [7] He becomes progressively more dependent upon short simple statements and commands, and descriptive, concrete visual symbolism of a low order of generality—more emotive than logical. The user of a public language relies heavily upon nonverbal aspects of communication—gesture, facial expression, tone, etc.

In a public language, emphasis is upon things rather than processes. Vocabulary is restricted, and expression of curiosity is limited. The language tends to reinforce loyalty to the group, and dependence upon its power structure. Expression of tender feeling, and the experiencing of shame and guilt are discouraged. While for the American cultural context the full implications of Bernstein's interesting formulations have yet to be extensively researched, the work of Minuchin [8] and his colleagues in this country generally substantiates Bernstein's writings.

Minuchin and his coworkers have been studying low socioeconomic

[5] *Ibid.*, p. 81.
[6] Basil Bernstein, "Social Class and Linguistic Development: A Theory of Social Learning," in *Education, Economy, and Society,* ed. A. H. Halsey, J. Floud, and C. A. Anderson (New York: The Free Press of Glencoe, 1961), pp. 288-314.
[7] *Ibid.*, 292.
[8] Salvador Minuchin *et al.,* "The Study and Treatment of Families Who Produce Multiple Acting-Out Boys," *American Journal of Orthopsychiatry,* **34** (1964), 125-133.

families including those who produce "acting-out" boys. Among these boys is found a characteristic lack of development of self-observation. They think and feel in action and, because of an inability to verbalize experience, they have difficulty organizing their experience and learning from it. The changeability of the physical and personal environment prevents the child from developing the sense that he is effective and responsible. The outcomes of his behavior, or his impingement upon others are not clear to him; thus, uncertain about his own boundaries, he needs to continuously use other people for definition of himself and his social situation.

These children are exposed to the insecurity of a never-ending power struggle; and communication in their families "tends to be a chaotic network of jammed messages ..." [9] There are two levels of meaning in these messages. The first has to do with the content of the subject under "discussion." The second, and often more important, concerns a defining of the power structure. The content tends to be obscured by this expression of the "me-you" relationship.

The lower class child learns not to share information about himself and his motivations. Frequently such knowledge is not part of his own awareness anyway. Asked about an action, he genuinely may not know what he did, why he did it, or "how he feels about it."

This is by no means to say that the disadvantaged child lacks entirely positive potentials, and achievement in language specifically or intellect generally. Riessman [10] and others have noted that investigators must be willing to search for strengths as well as to acknowledge weaknesses. We tend to find what we are looking for. Our schools and our society have traditionally favored speed of performance, formal language fluency, and verbal teaching techniques. We must recognize that there are different styles, rates, and rhythms of learning. Some disadvantaged children may benefit more from modes of teaching that are visual, tactile, and kinesthetic than oral-aural methods.

Though the lower class child usually has language deficits ranging from mild to severe, in certain situations he may display considerable verbal facility. In a role-playing situation, for example, he may be able to express himself adequately. However, it is true that our society is generally placing an increasingly greater emphasis on proficiency in formal language. Vocationally, survival in our complex economy demands

[9] Salvador Minuchin, "Family Structure, Family Language, and the Puzzled Therapist" (Paper presented at the American Orthopsychiatric Association, 41st Annual Meeting, Chicago, March, 1964), p. 2.

[10] Frank Riessman, "The Culturally Deprived Child: A New View," *Educational Leadership*, **20** (1963), 337-347.

ever-higher levels of skill in listening, speaking, reading, and writing. There are few places left for the functional illiterate.

SELF-IMAGE OF THE DISADVANTAGED

We have noted that the middle and lower classes are essentially two different cultures featuring two different languages. Children of each class are exposed, from birth, to separate and distinct patterns of living and learning characteristic of their respective environments. These patterns of living and learning involve different modes of perception, communication, and cognition.

In the lower class culture, differences and disagreements are likely to be settled by direct action, by fighting it out rather than talking it out. The appeal is to brute force, rather than reason. The tone and volume of the speaker carries the authority, not the content or logic of his message. The vocabulary itself reflects the value placed on physical prowess. A "hard hitter" is not to be "messed with," but a "lame" won't "do you in." He doesn't have any "heart."

In addition to definite language handicaps, the lower class child typically has, at best, an inadequate self-concept. He spends his formative years in an environment that is insensitive to his needs. His earliest attempts to explore his environment and master a segment of it are thwarted; his curiosity is stifled. The reactions of the significant adults in his life are unpredictable: adults are too preoccupied with the problems of their precarious existence to guide the child's development. The child is not understood; he may not even be heard. He lacks the self-confidence of competence stemming from success. If all he has known is failure, he will be threatened by the challenges of new endeavor. He craves immediate gratification of his impulses. Given the impermanence of his world, it is only natural that he be concerned with the here and now. In such a child's perception of time, next week may be as remote as next year.

What could be termed the lower class child's "social self" should also be considered. The lower class child has poor work habits. He has not learned to finish what he starts, and has great trouble adjusting to the demands of a definite time schedule. He may be unable to tolerate even constructive criticism and will "blow up" at his supervisors. His relations with people are likely to take the form of attempts to manipulate them. He has a low frustration tolerance. The very nature of his language may be offensive or threatening to those outside his own group. His failure to internalize the so-called social graces creates friction in his dealings with others. In addition to his language and cognitive deficits, then, the lower class child has psychological, emotional, and social shortcomings that may preclude successful participation in the cultural mainstream.

REVIEW

Receptive and expressive language is the chief vehicle for internalizing the culture to which one is exposed. Therefore, how effectively one perceives, interprets, and organizes his experience will depend, in large measure, on his language proficiency. By age five, the average middle class child displays an essential mastery of the elements of English, far outdistancing the lower class child.

Language is central to personality development; and language deficits are related to the lower class child's inadequate "psychological self" and "social self." The cumulative worsening of these deficits after the child enters school reflects the failure of the school, and of other social institutions oriented to middle class values and expectations, to meet the unique needs of the disadvantaged child. A rethinking and restructuring of the entire educational experience for this child is in order. For this task, the research of such investigators as Bernstein and Minuchin, concerning communications processes in the lower class, may have a number of important implications.

LANGUAGE AND COUNSELING

The school counselor's general functions usually include: helping the individual to increase the accuracy of his self-percepts and environmental perceptions; helping the individual to integrate his self-percepts with environmental realities and perceptions; presenting relevant information; helping the individual to increase his ability to make and execute plans.[11]

Middle class children are typically prepared to be helped in these areas. They have been encouraged from a very early age to develop grammatically and syntactically correct English. There is frequent opportunity in their pre-school years for vocabulary enlargement through vacation travel and other experiences. They have been encouraged to express their feelings and needs in language; and they learn that adults will respond positively to appropriate verbal behavior. In fact, the counselor in the suburban school may have to cope with the problem of parents who, in their concern for a child's welfare, may be "too helpful."

The structure of the formal language that the child masters makes it possible for him to organize his experience into complex patterns. Ac-

[11] Alfred Stiller, "School Guidance Needs Research," *Personnel and Guidance Journal*, 41 (1963), 798-802.

curate and comprehensive concepts of time, space, and causality can be developed. The significance of long-term goals can be grasped.

His school experience has afforded him many opportunities for success. His home situation, with its printed materials, games, discussions, has been building readiness for years; and the positive self-concept he brings to school is further enhanced there. In the classroom he is "at home" listening to an adult speak. The schedules, routines, orderliness parallel the preparedness of his home environment.

The middle class child is ready to share information, to communicate in verbal channels. He and the counselor "speak the same language."

The lower class counselee will likely find the typical one-to-one counseling situation confusing and anxiety-provoking, especially if the counselor is of "nondirective" leanings. The counselee, needing some definition of the "power structure," may attempt to plumb the nature of what is to him a puzzling interpersonal relationship by listening more for evidence of the "me-you" message than for "guidance information." He has to know "what this man's game is." The behavior of the nondirective counselor who waits for the child to help structure the situation by volunteering information about himself may be foreign to the child—in his experience, it is the adult who structures any adult-child relationship, however vaguely and inconsistently. The child has no set for engaging in democratic verbal transactions with an adult. The child has been let down by adults so frequently that he has little motivation for cooperating with a counselor.

Perhaps the most tragic aspect of deprivation is its basic inhumanness —the massive deviation of human development and dissipation of inborn potential. At birth, a lower class Negro baby has the same drives for full development, and the same capacities in all areas of human functioning as his environmentally "advantaged" Caucasian peer. But in the face of unrelentingly harsh conditions, his drives and capacities are thwarted and aborted. Despite normal intellectual endowment at birth, for example, he is likely to be classified as a slow learner in the space of a few years.

Because of adult insensitivity to his needs during his formative period, this child is likely to have a negative attitude toward adults in general. He may see the counselor as yet another authority figure, and show hostility in some manner—perhaps by withdrawing. The counselor should understand that such generalized hostility is not directed to him personally, but to him as one symbolizing authority.

The counselor must be conscious of his own feelings regarding race and class. He must look inward while observing externally, recognizing and overcoming any antipathies that could block the establishment of rapport with students. Often the disadvantaged child can quickly pick up nonverbal cues that betray the counselor's real feelings: a grimace, a tone may convey far more than words. The counselor should become adept at understanding the nonverbal signals and signs used by the lower class child in expressing himself.

Some school systems provide in-service training for counselors and teachers who are or will be working with the culturally deprived. Field trips, handbooks, films, conferences, seminars, talks by individuals experienced in working with these children, may all be helpful.[12]

Some persons are rather quickly able to gain considerable insight into the cultural forces at work in the lower class environment by reading fiction and autobiography concerning persons from this environment. The novelist may better capture realities of lower class life than the statistician or sociologist.

Children, as we have noted, tend to learn that to which they are exposed. The lower class child who has to shift for himself "in the street" becomes sophisticated at an early age in techniques for survival. The skill he develops in sizing up people may awe the professional social worker. It is this skill, incidentally, that enables the child to spot the insincere adult—the one who is indifferent or hostile. The street-wise child knows how to play on the weaknesses of people, to manipulate and con them in order to get what he wants. Perhaps we may learn how to tap this ability and direct it into more positive channels.

If the counseling situation is to be productive, there must be a maximum of communication between the parties involved.

Words, whether spoken or written, are symbols for various aspects of man's experience. They represent objects, actions, relationships, etc., and constitute, in effect, a code. In order for verbal communication to occur between parties, there must be shared understandings, common ideas, concerning these words. When the counselor speaks, the words he uses must have meaning for the listener. Likewise, when the counselee speaks, the counselor must know what the words, as used by the speaker, stand for. Both persons, in short, need to know the code. Because the middle class counselor and the lower class child have such divergent experiential backgrounds, communication may be impeded by the lack of a pool of shared understanding. The word bread for example, may have a particular meaning for the middle class counselor and another, different one, for the lower class child.

Concepts are built up from percepts which, in turn, result from a person's experiences. For example, a lower class child may only see store front churches in his neighborhood. After a number of experiences with

[12] *Baltimore Bulletin of Education,* **41**, 1963-64. Issue devoted to education of disadvantaged.

one or more of these churches, his concept of church may be restricted to a mental association featuring such a store front building where loud and demonstrative services are held. The middle class child's concept of church may embrace a large spired building where services of a different nature are held.

Likewise, the lower class child's concepts of sex, employer, the law, etc. will be functions of his particular experiences. Whereas, for example, middle class parents may encourage their children to seek out a policeman when in need of assistance, lower class parents are more likely to instill in their children the idea that policemen are to be avoided whenever possible. And the youth's own experiences may reinforce this idea.

Richard Adams, speech therapist with the Washington, D.C. Department of Public Welfare has made an informal compilation of terms often used by disadvantaged youngsters in our nation's capital. A few examples are given below. Although some of the terms have several meanings, only one is given for each. A feature of street language is its fluidity, with new terms being incorporated as others are dropped. This speech is subject to great geographic variations.

Batman is coming.—Something is about to happen.

chee-chee—warning—look out!

chop—chewing gum

cool—enjoyable

flat sandwich—bologna sandwich

man—authority figure (old man—father)

mud—peanut butter

not with it—stupid

out of sight—spectacular

miser—one who won't share (to "mise," to hoard)

nub—fight

race right along with—to keep up, be savvy

slings—open-heeled shoes

swift—clever

tens—$10 pair of shoes (twenties—shoes costing $20)

threads—suit

torture—punishment

up tight—o.k.—fine

vine—necktie

(to) waste—confuse, upset

UTILIZING INDIGENOUS PERSONNEL

The counselor should strengthen the lines of communication between himself and the parents of disadvantaged children. Such parents have often had only a brief and unhappy stay in school themselves; they may, knowingly or not, transfer to their children attitudes of hostility toward school. Feeling unwanted or looked down upon, they will avoid contact with the school. The counselor may have to seize the initiative if he is to meet and talk with them. Some school systems are experimenting with methods of communicating with mothers and fathers in the evenings, since both parents often work during the day.[13]

Earlier, we noted the importance of the family in shaping a child's behavior, especially during his formative years. As public educational programs become more comprehensive in scope, efforts are made to encourage parent participation in many phases of the educational process. Parents from deprived areas are serving as "auxiliary school personnel" in a variety of roles: teacher aides, teacher assistants, health aides, family and community liaison workers, and guidance aides. These subprofessionals or nonprofessionals as they are sometimes called, can help break down the communication barrier that typically exists between middle class professionals and lower class pupils.

A recent report of auxiliary school personnel notes:

The auxiliary who has actually lived in disadvantaged environments often speaks to the disadvantaged child or youth in a way that is neither strange nor threatening. He may help the new pupil to adjust to the unfamiliar world of the school without undue defensiveness; to fill the gaps, if any, in his preparation for learning; and to build upon his strengths, which may have more relevance to the new situation than the child himself realizes.[14]

In addition to helping in the classroom, the guidance office, the health suite, and on the playground, auxiliary workers drawn from the ranks of the indigenous can serve as chaperones on study trips and tours. Such workers do more than aid pupils by providing more individualized services. They can also help the teacher to learn the language of the culturally disadvantaged, and to better understand the values and motivations of the child of poverty.

In the process, the parents themselves are being helped, often directly in the form of salary, and indirectly by gaining knowledge.

[13] *School Programs for the Disadvantaged,* Educational Research Service Circular No. I (Washington, D.C.: National Education Association, 1965), p. 9.
[14] Garda Bowman and Gordon Klopf, *Auxiliary School Personnel: Their Roles, Training and Institutionalization* (New York: Bank Street College of Education, October, 1966), p. 4.

According to the National Advisory Council on the Education of Disadvantaged Children, many schools are using Title I funds to provide guidance and counseling services at the *elementary* level for the first time. Leaders in elementary education and guidance must "combine their judgments to formulate a clearer definition of the term 'elementary school guidance,' and to plan new approaches to the training of counselors." [15] The Council members consider counseling in the elementary grades to be a vital aspect of the disadvantaged child's school experiences. The counselor, in addition to guiding and assisting the child, can help parents realize the importance of the role they play in their children's education.

FLEXIBILITY OF TECHNIQUE

Whenever possible, when working with the disadvantaged child, the counselor should help him center his attention, at least initially, on a concrete and rather immediate task. This is more easily said than done; the child may be unable at first to attend actively for more than a few moments to a problem that is in the least remote. Long, abstract involved explanations, which lower class children have not learned to follow, should be avoided.

The counselor may want to make use of audiovisual aids when these are available. Some counselors are able to use a sense of the dramatic to advantage: they can impart an enthusiasm that more reserved colleagues may have trouble generating.

The middle class oriented counseling format, appropriate as it may be for certain children, is not designed for lower class children. With the latter, we often find that action, rather than talk gets through.

The counselor may find it necessary to structure the counseling situation to a considerable degree with lower class children, who may have great difficulty in framing logical questions. Such children may have had neither training nor practice in defining a problem, considering possible solutions, selecting a line of attack, and pursuing it steadily. The counselor must know how to help them develop such abilities. He must be skillful at keeping the objective in the forefront, and keeping discussions on the track.

The counselor, then, must help the counselee to identify and accept a clear, realistic goal. The behavior required to reach the goal must be specified. This behavior must be broken down into small, manageable steps that the counselee can master one at a time.

The counselor must be part of a concerted team approach to improve

[15] *Report of the National Advisory Council on the Education of Disadvantaged Children,* March, 1966, p. 14.

language. He must accept the informal public language of the lower class counselee while using every opportunity for promoting formal language development.

Ultimately, the solutions to the lower class child's language problems specifically, and developmental problems generally, lie in prevention rather than the application of remedies. There is considerable evidence that some of the effects of early deprivation are irreversible, no matter how extensive and well-funded later programs to overcome these effects may be.

Basic social and economic inequities, and other factors causing disadvantage, must be corrected. Adequate housing, employment, and education for example, must be available to everyone. The school counselor, together with all citizens, must be concerned with ways to achieve equality of opportunity as soon as possible.

FINAL NOTE

In summary, let us note that the counselor who utilizes only traditional procedures will find it difficult if not impossible to achieve middle class counseling goals with lower class children. These children bring to the counseling situation perceptions, language, and motivations derived from their different culture. Training and experience will enable the sincere and insightful counselor to appreciate such differences, and to communicate with these children and their parents. He must employ a counseling structure and style appropriate to the unique background and needs of his counselee. Hopefully, as more knowledge is gained through research into the (until recently) neglected challenges of counseling the disadvantaged, we shall see the emergence of imaginative and effective strategies for assuring full "counseling parity" for all youngsters.

SELECTED READINGS

1. *A Chance for a Change: New School Programs for the Disadvantaged*. Washington, D.C.: U.S. Office of Education, 1966.

2. Bereiter, C., and S. Engelmann, *Teaching Disadvantaged Children in the Preschool*. Englewood Cliffs, N.J.: Prentice-Hall, Inc., 1966.

3. Bloom, Benjamin, *Stability and Change in Human Characteristics*. New York: John Wiley and Sons, Inc., 1965.

4. "Education for Socially Disadvantaged Children," *Review of Educational Research*, 34, 1965.

5. Fowler, W., "Cognitive Learning in Infancy and Early Childhood," *Psychological Bulletin*, 59 (March, 1962), 116-152.

6. Hope: *A School Administrator's Guide to State and Federal Programs for Educating Deprived Children.* Hartford, Conn.: Connecticut State Department of Education, 1966.

7. Hunt, J. McV., *Intelligence and Experience.* New York: The Ronald Press Company, 1961.

8. Hurst, Charles, *Higher Horizons in Speech Communications.* Washington, D.C.: Communication Sciences Research Center, 1965.

9. Kvaraceus, William, *et al., Negro Self-Concept.* New York: McGraw-Hill Book Company, Inc., 1965.

10. Kemp, Barbara, *The Youth We Haven't Served.* Washington, D.C.: U.S. Dept. of Health, Education, and Welfare, 1966.

11. *Language Programs for the Disadvantaged.* The Report of the NCTE Task Force on Teaching English to the Disadvantaged. Champaign, Ill.: National Council of Teachers of English, 1965.

12. McCarthy, Dorothea, "Language Development in Children," in *Manual of Child Psychology,* 2nd ed., L. Carmichael, ed., 1954.

13. Newton, Eunice, "Verbal Destitution: The Pivotal Barrier to Learning," *Journal of Negro Education,* **29** (1960), 497-499.

14. Orem, R. C., ed., *Montessori for the Disadvantaged.* New York: G. P. Putnam's Sons, 1967.

15. ———, ed., *A Montessori Handbook.* New York: Capricorn Books, 1966.

16. ———, "Preschool Patterning and Language Learning," *National Catholic Kindergarten Review* (Spring, 1966).

17. Record, Wilson, "Counseling and Communication," *Journal of Negro Education,* **30** (1961), 450-454.

18. *Report of the National Advisory Council on the Education of Disadvantaged Children* (November 25, 1966, and January 31, 1967). Washington, D.C.

19. *Universal Opportunity for Early Childhood Education.* Washington, D.C.: National Education Association, 1965.

20. White, Robert, "Motivation Reconsidered: The Concept of Competence," *Psychological Review,* **64** (1959), 297-333.

7

COUNSELING
THE DISADVANTAGED BOY

JESSE E. GORDON

As the poverty program has progressed, with its unique power for eliciting strong commitment and the strong feelings that energize such commitment, it has become increasingly difficult to talk in a detached manner of "the disadvantaged"; every claim, every description, every assertion, every hypothesis is scrutinized and evaluated in terms of prior sociopolitical attitudes, until only the more callous are bold enough to offer anything other than sympathetic platitudes and apologies. Even the term disadvantaged, and its assumption of a classifiable group of people who may be discriminated from those not so labeled, may be seen as a denial of the positive regard that demands that the uniqueness of individuals be perceived and appreciated. This is not the place to argue that even so crude a distinction as disadvantaged-nondisadvantaged represents a gain in recognition of individual differences over the more typical teaching that speaks of adolescents all lumped together, though dealing in fact with only the middle class. Yet love is not enough; for love that cannot survive knowledge, love that does not demand use of all our knowledge resources in determining and taking the most effective action made possible by that knowledge, is a poor love—the poor have had enough of that kind of regard.

However, to admit, if only for heuristic purposes, the concept of the disadvantaged puts us on the path of an infinite regress into finer and finer discriminations within such a heterogenous group, until we have reached groups with N's of 1—clearly an impossible situation for the codification and transmission of scientific knowledge. But to stop anywhere short of this end is likely to arouse the charge that one is treating all the disadvantaged as if they were alike, with the added implication that to do so is evidence for the very prejudicial overgeneralization ("All Negroes look the same to me") whose bitter fruit we are now tasting. My solution to this paradox is to make a virtue of the necessity. I shall describe some disadvantaged as they are known to the social and behavioral scientist and the clinician, discuss the implications for counseling that arise from this "knowledge," and leave it to practitioners to apply these materials to those among the disadvantaged who fit the description from which this chapter proceeds.

The literature to which I will address myself is largely that concerned with "the lower class," the delinquent, the school dropout, the young gang member; by and large, this is a literature that refers to the inner-city adolescent, the so-called hard-core youth studied by Miller [1] rather than to the poor rural young man, or what used to be called (before we had rid ourselves of the invidious comparison that the expression implied) "the deserving poor." Certainly not all disadvantaged boys are "hard-core" school dropout delinquents; and there is no intention to suggest that all disadvantaged boys are like those with whom this chapter will deal. It is manifestly impossible in a brief chapter to deal with all kinds of poor boys in all their variety; and the alternative, to deal only with the features common to all disadvantaged, is to restrict oneself to the most banal generalizations, unproductive of enough directives for the practice of counseling to be useful. Given the necessity for choosing from among the disadvantaged, I have selected the inner-city delinquent or delinquentlike lower class slum youth, very likely Negro or Puerto Rican. This choice is based on personal interest, and the private conviction that study of this group will ultimately do for the behavioral and social sciences what atomic research did for chemistry: it will provide us with the impetus and the concepts for one of the most thoroughgoing revisions that our field has ever known, one that may finally rid us of a great deal of our embarrassing and long outmoded baggage of social and cultural chauvinisms in scientific guise.

We are already dumping the conception of intelligence as an innate status trait, serving Darwinian natural selection in the socioeconomic world. This is at least partially a result of the demand for better opportunities by people who used to be defined by tests (developed by those

[1] W. Miller, "Implications of Lower Class Culture for Social Work," *Social Service Review*, 33 (1959), 219-236; ———, "Lower Class Culture As A Generating Milieu of Gang Delinquency," *Journal of Social Issues*, 14 (1958), 5-19.

for whom the concept served to guarantee survival as a species-class) as lacking the intellectual qualifications required for deserving the chance to make a decent living. And this dumping was well deserved as we moved past the Newtonian world of finiteness of energy, the Marxian world of finite wealth, and the Darwinian world of a finite supply of the needs of life for which individuals had to compete, into the world of the new physics and the new economics, in which there is no longer a natural limit on the creation of energy or wealth, and the means of life.

Competition for survival once required high intelligence as a resource that fitted the individual for the conditions of his environment enough to enable him to compete successfully; this, however, is no longer necessary as a precondition of having access to the needs of life, except as an artificial and outmoded barrier whose removal is constrained by no natural law beyond lack of will. Other concepts that grew out of a different world are also likely to change, as we widen our concerns to include the masses of people we used to define as "not suitable" for our techniques and concepts—people who will no longer allow us so cheaply to preserve our techniques from challenge, who now refuse to agree that when the techniques don't work, it is because something is wrong with the client. These are the visible, demanding, "social problem" young: the ghetto Negroes, the inner-city delinquent gang members, the unemployed who, lacking access to jobs, pull "jobs." Thus I wish to focus this chapter on them.

CHARACTERISTICS OF DISADVANTAGED BOYS

The presumed characteristics of many disadvantaged boys will be discussed under the following headings: conceptual vs. motoric style, verbal style, time perspective and delayed gratification pattern, ego functioning, family background, educational background, interpersonal operations, and role mastery. Very little is conclusively known in these areas; and the only scientifically proper judgment that may be made about each of the hypotheses discussed is "Not proven." Nevertheless, they represent the closest we have to knowledge; if counseling is not to await the millennium in which perfect knowledge will exist, then it must be based on the inadequate, incomplete, and partially false knowledge that is all that we have so far. Thus the following notions are presented as suggestive rather than definitive.

One final caveat: the definitions and hypotheses presented in psychoanalytic, social psychological, or learning theory terms are not intended to prejudge the issues: the theoretically sophisticated reader may treat any of the ideas so designated in alternative language systems and from other theoretical perspectives.

Conceptual vs. Motoric Style

One of the most oft-observed (or frequently hypothesized) characteristics of the disadvantaged boy is that for him the balance or relation between verbal conceptual activity and direct expression in bodily terms favors the motoric or acting-out style more than it does for members of the middle class. These two styles "describe the relative extent to which a person employs his muscles and his mind in resolving his problems. Some people can think through a problem only if they can work on it with their hands. Unless they can manipulate objects physically, they cannot perform adequately. Other people feel more comfortable if they can get a picture of the task and then solve it in their heads." [2] This orientation has been demonstrated for the lower class in a preference for action dramas over other kinds of entertainments, as well as in other ways; [3] Gans points out that this preference describes not only American poor, but the poor in other countries also.

Adolescents tend to act out more than adults, boys more than girls, and the lower class more than the middle class, so that the lower class adolescent boy appears to be the most motoric of all. Gans describes lower class adolescent milieu as "peculiarly suited to the episodic life. The routine portions of existence, such as school and work, are usually based on adult rules, and unsatisfying to the adolescent. Thus, the teenage boy can be himself only during adventurous episodes that are interspersed between periods of time-killing." [4] Empirical support comes from studies such as that by Amos [5] which found delinquent boys overestimating their physical prowess, though their self-perceptions in other areas were not noticeably askew; and that by McNeil [6] which compared lower and middle class adolescent boys on a motoric task (expressing an idea by striking a body pose) and a conceptual task (making an abstract drawing to express an idea). McNeil found that the lower class boys did better on the former task than the comparison group.

The orientation toward motor expression in the lower class male adolescent playing a part in the style described by Gans as "action-seeking" is

[2] D. Miller and G. Swanson, *Inner Conflict and Defense* (New York: Holt, Rinehart & Winston, Inc., 1960).

[3] H. Gans, *The Urban Villagers* (New York: The Free Press of Glencoe, Inc., 1962); B. Berger, *Working Class Suburb* (Berkeley: University of California Press, 1960); H. Gans, "American Films and Television Programs on British Screens: A Study of the Functions of Popular American Culture Abroad" (Philadelphia Institute for Urban Studies, 1959, mimeographed).

[4] Gans, *The Urban Villagers.*

[5] W. Amos, "A Study of Self-Concept: Delinquent Boys, Accuracy in Selected Self-Evaluations," *Genetic Psychological Monographs,* **67** (1963), 45-87.

[6] E. McNeil, "Conceptual and Motoric Expressiveness in Two Social Classes" (Doctoral dissertation, University of Michigan, 1952).

itself very probably related to a number of other factors, several of which will be discussed in more detail below: restriction on range of verbal expressiveness; tendency to seek immediate gratification; an orientation to the present such that covert planning through mental conceptualizing is less frequently engaged in; lower level of impulse control; relative absence of inhibitions over display; gratification of stimulation needs through interoceptor stimulation rather than through fantasy;[7] weaker synthetic ego functioning creating uncertainty about the status of reality, thus requiring frequent immediate reality-testing through action on the environment;[8] and emphasis on demonstrating masculinity. Whatever the source, the behavioral effect has been noted sufficiently often to give some confidence in the hypothesis that acting-out and body language are more likely to be expressive and functioning modes for the lower class boy than for his middle class contemporary. In psychoanalytic terms, impulses have greater access to the motor system than they do to the verbal-conceptual system, the result being somewhat lower levels of autonomy of the ego with respect to id impulses. As Brenman and Gill[9] point out, such reduced autonomy from the id inevitably brings with it lower autonomy from the environment; this latter characteristic will be discussed later with reference to the stimulus-bound and concrete thought of the disadvantaged boy.

Several implications of the motoric style for counseling should be briefly noted here.

1) The counselor who has not learned to "read" body language and to interpret the meanings of actions will receive a more restricted range of information from a lower class counselee.

2) Counseling that does not provide opportunities for trying out decisions and activities, and for tying the content of talk to direct action by the counselee will probably be less effective.

3) Clients are likely to express responses to the counseling through acting out that may have serious consequences (e.g., resentment of or disappointment in the counselor may be expressed through stealing, or effacing property associated with the counselor or his agency). Because of the public nature of the acting out, these may make problems for reputations of the counselor and the agency in the community, and may elicit kickback from the community.

4) Tolerance for long verbal interviews is probably low, so that counseling sessions requiring motor passivity should be briefer than customary,

---

[7] J. Gordon, *Personality and Behavior* (New York: The Macmillan Company, 1963).

[8] F. Riessman, *The Culturally Deprived Child* (New York: Harper & Row, Publishers, 1962).

[9] M. Gill and M. Brenman, *Hypnosis and Related States* (New York: International Universities Press, Inc., 1960).

or the counseling session should be interspersed with opportunities for motoric behavior (e.g., role playing, rehearsals of planned actions, counselor-client interaction during the course of some shared activity).

Verbal Style

It has been frequently asserted, and vehemently denied, that the poor are nonverbal. Gordon refers to "weaknesses in the utilization of abstract symbols and complex language forms to interpret and communicate . . . [and] weaknesses in the utilization of abstract cognitive processes with marked tendency to favor concrete, stimulus-bound cognitive processes." [10] Riessman,[11] on the other hand, has observed that deprived children do not verbalize well in response to words alone, as in a conversation or question-response interchange; but he reports that their verbal performance is markedly improved when, as in discussion periods following role-playing sessions, they talk about some action they have just seen. It is clear that poor people do relatively poorly on verbal and vocabulary tests; but, as Walter Murray suggests in the Riessman work just cited, it seems equally clear that the inner-city slum culture, like the southern Negro culture that gave rise to jazz and the jazz vocabulary, is one of the most fertile and imaginative sources for new language concepts (e.g., slang).

It seems to me that there are several related aspects of the asserted nonverbal nature of the poor. Inner-city youth exist within a subculture that overlaps general American culture in language, but is not identical to it.[12] Thus there are subcultural language patterns not shared or understood by nonmembers of the subculture; and there are language patterns, vocabulary, and usage common to and required by the larger culture, primarily through its educational institutions, that are not shared by the subculture.[13] Thus to some extent the disadvantaged boy is qualitatively different from the middle class individual in his use of verbal language; however, his usage is not necessarily quantitatively different. The nature of these qualitative differences and their implications will be discussed later in this chapter.

A second factor refers to the use of available language. There is a good deal of evidence indicating that in social interactions with representatives of the large culture (i.e., "the man"), minority group members tend to become verbally inhibited. Thus they speak less in structured situations

---

[10] E. Gordon, "Counseling and Guidance for Disadvantaged Youth," in *Guidance and the School Drop-Out*, ed. D. Schreiber (Washington, D.C.: National Education Association and American Personnel and Guidance Association, 1964), pp. 173-208.

[11] Riessman, *The Culturally Deprived Child.*

[12] J. Yinger, "Contraculture and Subculture," *American Sociological Review* 25 (1960), 625-635.

[13] K. Eells and R. Havighurst, *Intelligence and Cultural Differences* (Chicago: University of Chicago Press, 1951).

such as employment and counseling interviews, and in individual test sessions (therefore achieving lower IQ scores).[14] I observed a dramatic instance of this reaction when visiting a group of Negroes living in a small "tent city" in rural Alabama. They had been evicted from their plantation shacks for having registered to vote. I was introduced to some of the residents of the tent city by a Negro worker who, in a sense, transferred his rapport with the residents to those of us accompanying him. Our conversation was quite animated and showed no dearth of expressive verbal activity on the part of the residents, until we were intruded upon by a strange white man taking movies of the tents. He was a local resident who revealed stereotyped segregationist and paternalistic sentiments. During the period of his participation in the group conversation, the Negroes spoke very little, assumed a passive expression, and gave monosyllabic answers. They stared off blankly into space, and looked "dumb" and un-comprehending, which attitude completely disappeared with the departure of the intruder.

It should also be noted here that the lower class youth ethic of non-commitment—playing it cool—in achievement situations, itself a response to other conditions of lower class life, further contributes to the impression of lower verbal ability and facility in the very situations in which middle class children are most likely to show verbal sparkle. Thus the lower class youth avoids speech as his way of meeting threat, while the middle class youth uses speech as his defense.

A third factor affecting the verbal behavior of the poor is related to the above. Hess has demonstrated that lower class mothers, and their vocabularies, are more frequently abusive, the words often being used critically and aggressively. Hess suggests that this accounts for reduced motivation for imitating parental verbal behavior;[15] it also leads to reduced opportunities for imitation since the child avoids interaction with the mother who is, for most children, the best available teacher of verbal usage. Deutsch[16] observes that the tasks assigned to children in lower class homes tend to be motoric and thing-oriented, while the tasks assigned in middle class homes are more likely to involve verbal and conceptual processes. He also finds lowered auditory discrimination among poor children during the period when children ordinarily pay attention to parents' speech, imitate it, and receive corrective feedback. Thus there

[14] B. Pasamanick and H. Knoblock, "Early Language Behavior in Negro Children and the Testing of Intelligence," *Journal of Abnormal and Social Psychology*, **50** (1955), 401-402.

[15] O. Mowrer, *Learning Theory and the Symbolic Processes* (New York: John Wiley & Sons, Inc., 1960).

[16] M. Deutsch, *et al.*, "Some Considerations as to the Contributions of Social, Personality, and Racial Factors to School Retardation in Minority Group Children," Paper read at American Psychological Association, Chicago, September, 1956.

appears to be less opportunity for and encouragement of verbal development in poor families. These poor language backgrounds are further compounded when the children enter school, as will be discussed later.

It may be further added that the phenomena noted by Hess may also account for the restriction on verbal activity when "the man" is present; Hess's results suggest that words, for the lower class child, are connected with the expression of anger and hostility. This notion receives added support from such highly verbal lower class games as "playing the dozens," in which sexual-aggressive quips and insults are traded among the protagonists.[17] If words function so strongly as the media for aggressive acts, it is reasonable that there should be a bias in the syntax available for use in structured, formal social situations. This bias will then look like low verbal ability on middle class tests, and in informal situations emphasizing the verbal domains scanted in lower class culture and failing to tap domains in which lower class culture is particularly rich.[18] The aggressive function of language will also produce a restriction on verbal activity in threat situations.

A fourth factor that may be cited in connection with the alleged nonverbal nature of the poor is restriction of experience with cultural artifacts, leading to a restriction of concepts, i.e., of experienced events for which words are required as labels. Thus some restriction of vocabulary may be the result of a lack of a wide range of things and experience to talk about. The irrelevance to the lower class child of the activities of Dick and Jane in the basic readers is the classic illustration of why poor children do not learn to read well—i.e., to learn words in association with actions, objects, concepts and relations with which they have had no direct experience. Such deprivation will be discussed more fully later, with reference to its effects on the poor child's repertoire of thoughts and actions.

A final factor to be cited is the lower class adolescent's emphasis on masculinity. Talk is feminine, and the verbal facility so valued and stressed in school is further perceived as feminine because of the perception of school as dominated by women's values.[19]

Thus several factors participating in the lack of verbal responsiveness in formal situations, such as counseling, characterize the disadvantaged boy. But before discussing the implications of these factors for the conduct of counseling, it is important to note some important qualitative aspects of the language structures used by the poor.

[17] E. McNeil, "Psychology and Aggression," *Journal of Conflict Resolution,* **3** (1959), 195-293.

[18] On the CAUSE II Selection Test, disadvantaged applicants achieved lower scores on a standard civil service-type test of vocabulary, but scored higher than nondisadvantaged on a test of slum slang.

[19] Riessman, *The Culturally Deprived Child.*

Several studies find that the poor are relatively nonintrospective in their talk.[20] Their referents are largely external, concretistic events, with internal events represented by the externals assumed but unverbalized. A young male client with whom I worked typified this: he would describe an experience he had had and, in some response to my probe about how he felt about the event, would, with some astonishment, describe the objective events again. He seemed to be saying, "Why, I felt like you feel when that happens to you." In counseling with disadvantaged youth, this kind of interaction gives some advantage to the counselor who shares enough of the youth's subculture to understand what those unverbalized and unverbalizable feelings were. Such understanding helps the counselor to avoid getting hung up in intrusive and extensive probing.

To some extent the lack of a psychological frame of reference that makes for easy access to descriptions of internal states may be a product of the youth's socialization. There is evidence that lower class parents are much less psychologically oriented in their childrearing practices than the middle class. They respond more often to actions and their consequences, rather than to the reasons and motivations for their children's acts; they use direct physical punishment rather than deprivation of love, and manipulation of shame and guilt; they are more concerned with behavioral conformity than with their children's psychological states; they want obedience, cleanliness, and neatness compared with higher middle class parental values for such psychic states as curiosity, happiness, and consideration.[21]

Thus the lower class child grows up without attention to internal states, and therefore without a vocabulary for labeling that which he has not learned to discriminate. If one adds to this the boy's notion that talk about feeling is a femininity to be avoided, plus the observation that if discriminated, many of the feelings experienced by these boys would be anxiety-arousing feelings of hopelessness, copelessness, powerlessness, and despair, it becomes apparent that the counselor is faced with a powerful array of forces operating against the kind of dissection of feeling states that so characterizes much of traditional counseling content, especially in the client-centered mode. This difficulty has raised the possibility that the counselor of disadvantaged youth might well proceed without explicit

[20] Gans, *The Urban Villagers;* G. Gurin, J. Veroff, and S. Feld, *Americans View Their Mental Health* (New York: Basic Books, Inc., Publishers, 1960); Riessman, *The Culturally Deprived Child.*

[21] E. Duvall, "Conceptions of Parenthood," *American Journal of Sociology,* **52** (1946), 193-203; M. Kohn, "Social Class and Parent-Child Relationships: An Interpretation," *American Journal of Sociology,* **68** (1963), 471-480; ———, "Social Class and Parental Values," *American Journal of Sociology,* **64** (1959), 337-351; V. Bronfenbrenner, "Socialization and Social Class Through Time and Space," in *Readings in Social Psychology,* E. Maccoby, T. Newcomb, and E. Hartley, eds. (New York: Henry Holt and Company, 1958).

reference to feelings—not by denying their existence, but by taking a stance that implicitly assumes them. In this way he would not risk destroying the relationship by inopportune probing, asking the client to talk about what he cannot talk about, and opening access to floods of feelings that neither he nor the client in his life circumstances can do much about except struggle to repress again. Thus the counselor might well take the stance that, if he concentrates on the objects of the client's available experience—the events of his life—and deals with the client's behavior, the feelings will take care of themselves, as the youth tries out new behaviors, builds them into his repertoire of roles, and begins to experience success in his undertakings.

The most original and exciting work on the language of the poor has been done by the English therapist, Basil Bernstein, with reference to the English poor and the appropriateness of their language usage to the demands and requirements of psychotherapy. Much of what he says rings true for the lower class American, and has equal applicability to counseling. Bernstein describes the role of the therapy patient as one that requires him to manipulate words to structure and restructure his experience, from an internal frame of reference. The authority relations within therapy are unclear and ambiguous (to which one might add that the patient is expected to recognize the authority of the therapist in fact, but to act as if there were mutual sharing of authority).

The effectiveness of therapy rests on the ability to use speech in a social relationship in which the effects of experiences are changed through changes in the words used to describe and account for the experiences. Bernstein then points out that the coding operations of the poor patient almost eliminate the possibilities for playing this kind of role, in that the verbal style required for the role is not available. He describes the lower class patient's speech as being poor in qualifiers, adjectives, adverbs, and words to describe feelings.

The restricted code [of the poor] is played out against a back-cloth of assumptions common to the speakers, against a set of shared interests and identifications . . . which reduces the need for the speakers to elaborate verbally their intent and make it explicit. If you know somebody very, very well, an enormous amount may be taken for granted; you do not have to put into words all that you feel because the feelings are common. But knowing somebody very well is a particular kind of social relationship. . . . In these social relationships . . . the speech will tend to be fast, fluent, with reduced articulatory clues, the meanings are likely to be condensed, dislocated, and local to the relationships. There will be a low level of vocabulary and syntactic selection. Finally, and of critical importance, the unique meaning of the person will be implicit and not verbally elaborated.[22]

[22] B. Bernstein, "Social Class, Speech Systems, and Psycho-Therapy," in F. Reissman, J. Cohen, and A. Pearl, *Mental Health of the Poor* (New York: The Free Press of Glencoe, Inc., 1964).

Bernstein further suggests that, in poor families in which a restricted code is the only code, and in which speech is not used for communicating unique experiences, aspects of the self as the object of special perceptual activity to be encoded in speech are not likely to be differentiated. He also notes that in interpersonal relations, some degree of separateness as a person leads to the elaborate code through which individuals relate themselves to others; where the relation is status- and authority-controlled, as parent-child relations in lower class families tend to be, the linguistic system is restricted. A restricted code

is generated in social relationships where the intent of others may be taken for granted. This sharing of expectation of common intent simplifies the structure of the speech and so makes it predictable. It removes the need in the speakers to elaborate verbally their unique experience. Hence the reduction of qualifiers of various kinds. . . . The code functions to permit the signalling of social (i.e., membership in the group)* rather than personal identity. The latter tends to be signalled through non-verbal means rather than through elaborate varying of verbal selections. The code tends to make relevant the concrete here and now action situation rather than point to reflective, abstract relationships. It does not facilitate a sustained interest in processes, particularly motivational processes. The self is rarely the subject of verbal investigation. . . . Behavior is controlled in a social context in which status is unambiguous and in which the intent of the regulated and the regulator is rarely verbally explored and so feelings of guilt (arising from consciousness of intent)* and personal involvement in misdemeanors may be reduced. The code strengthens solidarity with the group by restricting the verbal signalling of personal difference. This does not mean that no differences will be signalled but that they will rarely be systematically explored.** A strong sense of social identity is induced probably at the cost of a sense of personal identity.[23]

It is obvious that this kind of code is unsuited to traditional counseling, with its explorations of feelings, its implication of a separate and uniquely different personal identity, its demand for introspective exploration of motivations. The lower class youth often responds to such demands with dependency and confusion, tempting the counselor into taking a more active and leading role than he feels comfortable with, a role to which the client responds with passivity. The counselor will then tend to see the client as negative and sullen, and will find the relationship unrewarding. Thus Miller and Swanson [24] stress the "desirability of exploring a variety of new . . . techniques, particularly those in which words and concepts are subordinated to nonverbal and even motoric activities."

[23] *Ibid.* * Words in parenthesis added. ** Lower class clients often respond to explorations of their feelings by denying them, out of the assumption that to have feelings that one must explain is to admit that one is different (else why have to describe and explain what others share); the thought of being different is intolerable to many youth with strong needs to be a part of a security-lending and supporting group or gang.

[24] Miller and Swanson, *Inner Conflict and Defense.*

These factors reinforce the suggestions for counseling that arose from consideration of the motoric preference of the disadvantaged boy: counseling content should be tied closely to current events and experiences of the client; discussion should be concretized rather than in terms of abstract relations and structural systems; exploration of feelings may contribute little, and in many cases may appear so irrelevant or so threatening to the client that he terminates the relationship; the counselor may find it appropriate to provide differentiating labels for the client's actions and experiences, rather than expect the client to provide them; the counselor may find concentration on behavior to be more productive than concentration on psychological states of the client. Furthermore, the long tutoring in experiencing the self, that functions as a value in its own right in psychoanalysis and in all the systems of therapy (including the Rogerian) ultimately derived from it, is inappropriate and nonproductive for members of a subculture in which such introspection is nonfunctional and may even be shattering of the only accommodation to the actual conditions of life available to disadvantaged youth.

The counselor may also find that translating decisions and attitudes developed verbally during the counseling into appropriate action is more likely to occur if the counseling provides opportunity for rehearsing and coaching the client in the actions and behaviors for which the words are referents. Finally, the client's poor ability to represent verbally important aspects of the experiences he has outside of the counseling may require that the counselor engage in direct contact with those experiences, in the client's home and family, in his neighborhood, in his recreations, and even on his job. A joint on-site visitation may be advisable in which the things seen, heard, and experienced in their immediacy are labeled and put into words by the counselor and the client as a part of *in situ* counseling.

Time Perspective and Delayed Gratification Pattern

Theoretically, words and thoughts and the covert ratiocination made possible by words, mediate delays in gratification, and enable the individual to derive symbolic gratifications while putting off real ones until the situation is most propitious.[25] There is, then, a close connection between verbal-cognitive style, time perspective, and tolerance for delayed gratification. It is, therefore, no surprise that the lower class child has difficulty in making time judgments [26] and, as an adolescent, has often been described as living in the present (compared with the future orienta-

[25] J. Gordon, "Family Interaction Around the Deaf and Non-Verbal Brain-Injured Child," *Journal of Speech and Hearing Disorders* (in press).

[26] M. Deutsch, "The Disadvantaged Child and the Learning Process," in *Education in Depressed Areas*, A. Passow, ed. (New York: Bureau of Publications, Teachers College, Columbia University), 1963, pp. 163-179.

tion of the middle class), and as not being able to delay gratification.[27] Thus a basic theme of the lower class adolescent is said to be "short-run hedonism."[28] The classic illustrative experiment is that of Mischel who offered delinquent boys the option of taking a five cent candy bar immediately as a reward for engaging in an experimental task, or waiting a week for a twenty-five cent bar, on the pretext that the experimenter, who did not have enough five cent bars with him for everyone, would be helped if the boy waited.[29] In contrast to the nondelinquents, the experimental subjects more frequently chose the smaller but immediate reward.

Miller, Riessman, and Seagull[30] vigorously contest this interpretation, pointing out controverting behavior patterns and explaining the apparent nondeferred gratification pattern as a product of disbelief in the future reward, and the lack of reinforcement value of the presumed delayed gratifiers. Thus it has been suggested that the conditions of childrearing in lower class families, and in American society as it impinges on the lower class, are such that promises (of equality, of affluence, of opportunity, of reward for efforts in school, of new clothes or new toys when the money comes in) have been too infrequently redeemed for the promise of a future reward to serve as a secondary reinforcer.[31] And Dollard and Miller point out that many symbols that function as reinforcers for middle class children because they know them to be associated with primary reinforcers —good grades in school, for instance, are known to the middle class child to lead to academic success, getting into a good college, having a good business or professional career—are not so known to the lower class boy.[32] To the latter, who has too often seen hard work rewarded only by financial failure and insecurity, such symbols as good grades, savings accounts, etc., have no reinforcement value, and do not function to sustain behavior for some long range goal. Hyman finds that there is less optimism about possibilities for advancement, less belief that personal effort is an important factor in who gets advanced, and less belief in the rewards of work.[33]

[27] Ibid.

[28] L. Schneider and S. Dornbusch, "The Delayed Gratification Pattern: A Preliminary Study," American Sociological Review, 18 (1953), 142-149.

[29] W. Mischel, "Preference for Delayed Reinforcement and Social Responsibility," Journal of Abnormal and Social Psychology, 62 (1961), 1-7.

[30] S. M. Miller, F. Riessman, and A. Seagull, "Poverty and Self-Indulgence: A Critique of the Non-Deferred Gratification Pattern," in Poverty in America, L. Ferman, J. Kornbluh, and A. Haber, eds. (Ann Arbor: University of Michigan Press, 1965), 285-302.

[31] J. Gordon, Personality and Behavior.

[32] J. Dollard and N. Miller, Personality and Psychotherapy (New York: McGraw-Hill Book Company, Inc., 1950).

[33] H. Hyman, "The Value Systems of Different Classes: A Social Psychological Contribution to the Analysis of Stratification," in Class, Status, and Power: A Reader in Social Stratification, R. Bendix and S. Lipset, eds. (Glencoe, Ill.: The Free Press, 1953), pp. 426-442.

Cloward and Ohlin point out that this does not mean that the poor do not value the same things the middle class does; they indicate that desire for money and status are characteristic of the poor and of the middle class alike, but that the poor do not believe (for realistic reasons) that personal sacrifice of time and energy in schooling and work are means to those ends in American society as they know it.[34] Their contention is supported by several published studies,[35] and an as yet unreported study in which it was found that disadvantaged boys being served in a vocational counseling program placed high values on income and status, and good jobs as routes to these ends, belying the agency's impression that the boys were not motivated (Gurin, personal communication). However, Clark and Winniger also found that there was a difference between middle class and lower class children, in the direction indicated here, in commitment to middle class goals, in samples drawn from areas dominated by large concentrations of lower class people.[36] In other words, when the poor live in a homogeneous slum, they do develop different goal orientations from the middle class.

It may also be argued that tolerance for delayed gratification implies a habit of thinking in terms of a future, with the implication that the future will be better than the present. This is a characteristic middle class attitude, embodied in the notion of progress and upward social mobility. For those in which the future leads only to frustration, unexpected and new problems, and further decline into poverty, thinking about the future is nonfunctional and anxiety-arousing; it is better to avoid such thoughts.

Thus several lines of argument combine to indicate that, at least with respect to standard middle class goals and motivations, lower class youths are not inclined to delay an immediate gratification; their present orientation, together with the weight of frustrations that they experience, combine to orient them to the concrete present and the gratifications available within it. The picture of low impulse control is complete when one adds to this: [37]

[34] R. Cloward and L. Ohlin, *Delinquency and Opportunity: A Theory of Delinquent Gangs* (New York: The Free Press of Glencoe, Inc., 1960).

[35] J. Clark and E. Winniger, "Goal Orientations and Illegal Behavior Among Juveniles," *Social Forces,* Vol. 42, 1963; F. Kelley and D. Veldman, "Delinquency and School Dropout Behavior as Functions of Impulsivity and Nondominant Values," *Journal of Abnormal and Social Psychology,* Vol. 69, 1964; M. Sherif and C. Sherif, *Reference Groups* (New York: Harper & Row, Publishers, 1964).

[36] Clark and Winniger, *op. cit.*

[37] Nevertheless, this is a relative matter. We are dealing here not with an absence of capacity for impulse control and deferred gratification, but rather with a life situation that characteristically does not elicit impulse control. That deferment of gratification, endurance, and commitment to long range goals is possible for the disadvantaged has been dramatically demonstrated by the impressive personal changes wrought by the Black Muslim movement, and by the success of such programs as Rev. Sullivan's Opportunities Industrialization Centers, in which lower class Negroes

1. The acting-out style discussed earlier;

2. Resentment of the agencies of social control (schools, police, social agencies, and their representatives) which disapprove of impulse display;

3. The need for immediate reality testing through direct action (predicated on an underlying weakness in understanding the environment, to be discussed in a later section);

4. The need to emphasize the "rocky" male who takes what pleasures he can; and

5. Superego and ego structures in which inhibitory controls are less emphasized than in the middle class (also to be discussed later).

The nondeferred gratification pattern and present orientation that many disadvantaged youth bring to counseling agencies suggest a number of counseling strategies.

1. Counseling should not be scheduled as a step to be accomplished *before* the client begins activities more clearly related to his goals in coming to the agency; it would be more appropriate for counseling to accompany real activity connected with the client's goals. Thus the client who comes to an Employment Service office or other employability development agency wants a job, and will not often stay with a long course of counseling to get him ready for work *before* he is actually put into a work situation. Regardless of the client's level of job and work skills, in many cases he should be placed in some kind of work tryout with the counseling scheduled to be intercurrent with the work. This has the added advantage, related to the points made earlier in this chapter, of providing a ready source of current and highly relevant experiences as content for the counseling.

2. Someone once said that agency apathy could be measured by the length of its waiting list. When a disadvantaged youth seeks counsel-

---

undertake long term literacy and job training programs, with no supporting pay or allowances such as MDTA provides. When I asked a young Negro employment service counselor who was working with an Opportunities Industrialization Center what Rev. Sullivan's group had going for it that produced such success in an area where MDTA job training programs, with their pay and allowances, were considerably less successful in getting disadvantaged Negroes to stick with the training, his answer was immediate and simple: "Pride." But for the purposes of this chapter I will assume that most agencies in which counseling of disadvantaged youth takes place will not be initially perceived by their constituents in such a way as to permit the agency to tap into such motivations, and therefore will not provide the kinds of conditions that will easily elicit impulse control and delayed gratification. Thus counseling in such agencies should proceed on the assumption that these traits are generally low; the task of the agency must then be to set up a program that will broaden the range of stimuli that will elicit impulse control and deferred gratification, through gradual lengthening of its clients' tolerance for delay from the low level initially displayed in relation to the agency's goals.

ing help, he wants it when he seeks it. It is important for intake and initial counseling to be scheduled at once. The quite successful program of the Jewish Employment and Vocational Service of Philadelphia may owe some part of its clients' stick-to-it-iveness to the fact that when a disadvantaged youth indicates interest in the program, he is given a starting appointment within 24 hours.[38]

3. Counseling might best proceed with a program of frequent and closely spaced rewards and reinforcers in which the intervals are gradually lengthened. Thus, if possible, the youth should be placed in the kind of program in which he can get a raise in pay after only one or two days, then after a week, after two or three weeks, and so on, until he has come to believe that the future reinforcers are reliable, and that his work will be ultimately rewarded.

4. It is of utmost importance that the youth recognize the close relation between his present activities and his long-term goals. Scheduled activities should be clearly related to his goals and identified as such. Those not related, but possibly having other values, should be separately identified so that the client is not misled into thinking that they are steps toward his goals of income and status, and thus not disappointed by their lack of direct payoff. If he is to be placed in an entry level job at once, it should be made clear that such placement is to function as a steppingstone to something better.

5. The reliability of the agency's and the counselor's commitments to the youth are crucial. An unkept promise, even when the promise is only implied, or may even be a misperception by the client, will reconfirm the client's disbelief in the availability of delayed gratifications. A missed appointment by the counselor can be a disaster. If the implicit program of the counseling is to help the client make choices, the counselor must be sure that the alternatives exist and are available. Counseling for work that is not available to the disadvantaged youth is utterly destructive. As Conant has said, "One finds a vicious cycle of lack of jobs and lack of ambition; one leads to the other. . . . It does no good whatever to prepare boys and girls for nonexistent jobs." [39]

6. Planning with the youth should emphasize immediate and short term plans upon which the client can act at once, with longer range plans introduced gradually. Opportunities for testing actions and plans should be provided with minimal delay.

7. Counseling sessions might well be closely scheduled, perhaps on a daily basis at first, to reduce the demands for long term carry-over from week to week.

[38] S. Leshner and G. Snyderman, "Preparing Disadvantaged Youth for Work I: Jobseeking Patterns of Disadvantaged Youth," *Employment Service Review*, November, 1965.
[39] J. Conant, *Slums and Suburbs: A Commentary on Schools in Metropolitan Areas* (New York: McGraw-Hill Book Company, Inc., 1961).

8. The counselor and the agency should be prepared to accept and tolerate losses in impulse control, and to handle them in such a manner as to keep the client in contact with the agency and the counselor. In many cases, the client has no other resources for counseling help; and if the agency gives up in response to the client's acting out of his ambivalences or limits testing, the youth's last chance will have been used up.

9. Leshner and Snyderman describe several "types" of failure cases in their program at the Jewish Employment and Vocational Service, all of which were marked by such extreme impulsiveness or inability to sustain effort that they could not be fit within the agency's program as it existed.[40] Such boys may require a more fully controlled environment—a residential program such as Job Corps, or a quasi-residential program such as Highfields, in which there is greater opportunity for influencing a wider range of situations in which delays or gratification can be scheduled may be required for such boys.

Ego Functioning

Several characteristics of the disadvantaged adolescent's thinking may be subsumed under the heading of ego functioning.

Synthetic Functions. The most subtle, frustrating, and ultimately striking aspect of the thought of many disadvantaged youth is a certain freedom from the constraints of verbal logic. Compared to the middle class, lower class youth are less responsive to the commands of words. Haggstrom indicates that the poor

frequently verbalize middle-class values without practicing them. Their verbalizations are useful in protecting their self-conceptions and in dealing with the affluent rather than in any pronounced relationship to non-verbal behavior. This does not imply deliberate falsification; a poor person may have the necessary sincerity, intention, and skill to embark on a course of action but there is so much unconscious uncertainty about achieving psychological returns through success that the action may never be seriously attempted. As has been discovered in social surveys, the poor may not only pay lip service to middle class notions, but may, for similar reasons, say to any powerful person what they believe he wants to hear.[41]

This account is also implied in Bernstein's comments, cited earlier, about the signaling function of language to denote group membership, rather than to communicate aspects of oneself as a separate identity. Thus the

---

[40] S. Leshner and G. Snyderman, "Preparing Disadvantaged Youth for Work V: The Failure Cases in a Vocational Development Program," *Employment Service Review*, March, 1966.

[41] W. Haggstrom, "The Power of the Poor," in *Mental Health of the Poor*, pp. 205-223.

link between words and actions is a tenuous one for the disadvantaged. It is the weakness of this link which may account for the finding that disadvantaged youth often verbalize and report high aspirations for vocational success (and goals that are often completely unrealistic, given their educational backgrounds) without apparent concern about the mismatch between their stated goals and their current positions and the low level dead-end jobs that they actually seek and apply for.[42]

This characteristic is often dismaying to the counselor who expects words to invoke their associated actions, and who is therefore puzzled by his observations of discontinuity between the verbal and motoric behavior in disadvantaged young men. In this connection, recall Bernstein's earlier comments on the two separate functions of the verbal and nonverbal communication systems. Because of the diminished authority of words, the lack of introspective activity discussed earlier, and the limited time perspective in which future and past are less potent than the immediate present, the disadvantaged youth is also likely to appear inconsistent in his verbal behavior from one counseling session to another, thus further demonstrating a low level of synthetic ego functioning, and further confusing the counselor.

One of the implications of this reduced synthetic functioning is that disadvantaged youth often have difficulty following directions. Again, the action-evoking power of the words in which directions are given is responsible (together with the youth's restricted perspective that operates against the ability to sustain a set over the time interval between the directions and the performance they dictate). These factors combine to limit the youth's ability to solve imposed problems requiring toleration of a delay in action. For example, he may not be able to locate an object or place if there has been much of an interval since his last contact with it, or the directions for reaching it. He is much like deaf children who show limited ability to locate the cup under which they saw a piece of candy placed, if they are required to delay identifying the cup for some time after they saw the candy put there.[43] Thus the youth appears stupid, and this difficulty, plus his lack of familiarity with many of the objects and events of the American culture, means that he does indeed have difficulty in solving many of the problems life presents to him. Unsurprisingly, these circumstances reinforce his feelings of copelessness and inferiority.

[42] Hyman, "Value Systems of Different Classes"; S. Korbin, "Sociological and Cultural Foundations of the Youth Employment Problem," Paper read at School Achievement Conference, Hull House, Chicago, February 24, 1961.

[43] J. Gordon, "Tolerance for Delay in Deaf and Hearing Children" (in preparation).

These characteristics of the disadvantaged boy's ego functioning add to his difficulty in translating the verbal interchange of counseling into action, in a setting outside the counseling, that will be appropriate to secure results in the real world of his day-to-day activities. Even sessions that seem to "go well" and to be productive of insights, understanding and plans, may in fact ultimately go nowhere, in terms of later behavioral implementation; and the counselor's initial feelings of satisfaction with what appeared to be a successful session will turn to disappointment, bitterness, and often resentment of the client when he discovers that the client behaves outside the counseling as if the session had never taken place.

These considerations underscore the suggestions made earlier that counseling include opportunities for direct rehearsal and coaching of the client in carrying out actions and plans discussed in the counseling. This may mean, in some counseling settings, that the counselor or his delegate may do much of his work with the client in the various locales in which the client carries out his real world operations—his work place, his home, his recreation sites. The client's verbal assent during an office counseling session that he understands some direction or plan is an insufficient guarantee that he will at a later time be able to translate the plan into action.

A further implication of the kind of synthetic ego functioning described here is an admonishment that the counselor concern himself with the client's actions and behaviors, and be less beguiled by his verbalizations than is usually the case in counseling middle class adolescents. To a great extent, counseling can become a learning situation in which the counselor coaches the client to match words with actions by the counselor's labeling of client actions and experiences in the course of direct participation with the client in his activites. This approach appears to be implicit in the counseling program of the Philadelphia Jewish Employment and Vocational Services, referred to earlier, in which counseling took place concurrently with the youth's work tryout. "The function of counseling in the work adjustment process was a supporting and reinforcing one. As the youth developed suitable attitudes and coping behaviors [on the job], counseling enabled him to bring to awareness the changes that were occurring within him." [44] This approach presumes that attitudes and self-concepts will change as behavior changes, which hypothesis is directly the reverse of that held by many youth-serving agencies that direct their efforts toward modifying attitudes and motivations as the primary source of behavioral change. Nevertheless, this hypothesis has received a great deal of empirical support from the research on cognitive

[44] S. Leshner and G. Snyderman, "Preparing Disadvantaged Youth for Work III: Work Adjustment Training," *Employment Service Review*, January, 1966.

dissonance reduction, and is consistent with recent finding calling into question the notion of a motivational deficit in the disadvantaged youth.[45]

Activity. There is a reverse side to the coin of freedom from the command of words; it lies in the unstereotyped thinking that leads to creative problem-solving.[46] Thus several workers have remarked on the resourcefulness, ingenuity, and creativity of many disadvantaged people. Reissman quotes Irvin Taylor: "...that deprived individuals are not as restricted by verbal forms of communication, but tend to permit language to interact more with non-verbal means of communication, such as gestures and pictures. This interaction with other kinds of communication gives them the potential for 'breaking through the language barrier'; they are not forced to think in terms of the structure of language as are so many people. *They are less word-bound.*"[47] Gordon describes disadvantaged youth as possessing "ingeniousness and resourcefulness in the pursuit of self-selected goals and in coping with the difficult conditions of life peculiar to states of economic insufficiency and poverty, low social class status, and low racial-caste status."[48]

This ingeniousness, this potential for creativity, may manifest itelf to the counselor in colorful and original figures of speech, and in unexpected and disarmingly different ways of approaching tasks familiar to the counselor. The counselor should not be put off by unusual problem solutions simply because they are not *comme il faut;* he should recognize the necessity to evaluate independently the manner in which a job gets done and the extent to which the job is accomplished. Conformity to stereotype and conventionality of manner need not be requirements for task success.

A further implication refers to the kinds of jobs for which such youth are particularly suited. The disadvantaged boy's love of adventure, physical activity, and variety; his needs for masculinity; and his capability for adaptable "make do with what is available" problem-solving recommend him particularly for certain kinds of nonroutine jobs requiring action without extensive planning. Thus one city mobilized its disadvantaged youth into a disaster corps which was called on in cases of flood, fire, and other civil disasters. Newark and New York City are training some disadvantaged youth as junior policemen, with the training to lead to regular police jobs. Claims surveying also suggests itself as a kind of work that

[45] L. Festinger, *A Theory of Cognitive Dissonance* (Evanston, Ill.: Row, Peterson, 1957); ——— and Carlsmith, "Cognitive Consequences of Forced Compliance," *Journal of Abnormal and Social Psychology,* **58** (1959), 203.

[46] J. Gordon, *Personality and Behavior.*

[47] Riessman, *The Culturally Deprived Child.*

[48] E. Gordon, "Counseling and Guidance."

would tap the style and resources of many disadvantaged boys. The list is limited only by the ingenuity of the counselor and job developer.

Person Orientation. A further characteristic of the thinking of many disadvantaged people has been described as person-oriented thought, in which bureaucracies, agencies, and other abstract entities tend to be personalized, to be seen in anecdotal terms as actions of individuals directed toward them.[49] Thus the disadvantaged client is likely to react to agency policies, and to features of the structure and system of the counseling setting, as personal choices of the counselor having relevance directly to himself. He does not think in terms of administrative styles, constraints, or the needs of the agency to account for and deal with problems beyond the client as an individual. Similarly, he is more likely to interpret failures to get a job as an instance of prejudice against himself than he is to entertain the idea that there may have been no positions open in the company. This tendency to personalize is thus a great potential threat to the counseling relationship, and the counselor should take pains to emphasize and assert his interest in and commitment to the client within the constraints imposed by the agency; the counselor may take the stance that he himself is not personally identified with the rules of the institution, though he accepts them and works within them. On occasion he may find it appropriate to become the client's advocate against structural features that inhibit or limit the client's ability to make his way successfully.[50]

Concreteness. Almost all of the characteristics of thought and action described above combine in a trait of concreteness. This characteristic may be thought of as a derivative of those just discussed, and requires no further elaboration, except to reinforce the point that counseling discussions with disadvantaged youth are likely to be most effective if they deal with the palpable and the here and now, rather than generalized instances and abstract qualities.

Copelessness. A final characteristic of the ego functioning of many disadvantaged youth may be described as copelessness—the lack of cognitive and intellectual resources appropriate for solving many of the problems they encounter in attempting to move in the middle class worlds of school and work. Such copelessness, experienced simply as not knowing

---

[49] S. M. Miller and F. Riessman, "The Working Class Subculture: A New View," *Social Problems,* 9 (1961), 86-97.

[50] Participation by the client or his representatives in agency policy-making would seem to be an effective means for dealing with the relationship problems arising from the tendency to personalize.

what to do or how to go about finding out, is a product of the ego styles described above, and a lack of available knowledge and cultural concepts. An appreciation of the meaning of copelessness must therefore await discussion of the home and educational backgrounds of disadvantaged boys.

Family Background

The baby born into a disadvantaged home, often to an unwed mother who may already have had other children and who may be living in her parental home, is born into an environment that is seldom organized around the needs of the new infant in the manner of the young middle class family. Usually, there has been no ritualistic build-up of expectations through baby showers, no celebration through the extended family, no elaborate preparations for baptism of the newborn, etc. Instead, there may be only a brief period in which the mother is able to remain home to take care of the baby; then she must return to work, and the baby must be fitted into an already chaotic family schedule, marked by tension and insecurity, in a crowded and noisy apartment. The new baby is likely to be taken care of by a shifting array of relatives, neighbors, and older siblings, as the mother's work schedule and the siblings' school schedules permit. To speak of reliable and stable mothering, of consistency in interactions with the baby, of appropriate feeding schedules, in such circumstances, is almost irrelevant.

Understanding the Environment. The kind of early infancy described above gives rise to two important products: first, weakness in reality contact resulting from a lack of gratification from reliable others that would function to direct the infant's interest and attention to the environment and to the persons and objects in it; [51] and second, failure to establish basic trust in nurturant figures and, by generalization, in other adults.[52] Thus from the very beginning the disadvantaged infant is prepared to be suspicious of the behavior of people and objects, to be always doubtful of their status, and thus to need to engage in repeated reality testing through manipulating and touching objects at hand and avoiding those that may be avoided, acting out, testing and provoking, in search of reduction of ambiguity.

This initial uncertainty is given added impetus during the growing years by the lack of contact with toys, objects, manipulanda, and cultural artifacts through which the child ordinarily learns space and size relations, size constancy, and other aspects of the psychophysical world. Deutsch describes the situation thus:

[51] J. Gordon, *Personality and Behavior.*
[52] E. Erikson, *Childhood and Society* (New York: W. W. Norton and Company, Inc., 1950).

Visually, the urban slum and its overcrowded apartments offer the child a minimum range of stimuli. There are usually few if any pictures on the wall, and the objects in the household, be they toys, furniture, or utensils, tend to be sparse, repetitious, and lacking in form and color variations. The sparsity of objects and lack of diversity of home artifacts which are available and meaningful to the child, in addition to the unavailability of individualized training, gives the child few opportunities to manipulate and organize the visual properties of his environment and thus perceptually to organize and discriminate the nuances of that environment. These would include figure-ground relationships and the spacial organization of the visual field. The sparsity of manipulable objects probably also hampers the development of these functions in the tactile area. For example, while these children have broomsticks and usually a ball, possibly a doll or a discarded kitchen pot to play with, they don't have the different shapes and colors and sizes to manipulate which the middle class child has in the form of blocks which are bought just for him, or even in the variety of sizes and shapes of cooking utensils which might be available to him as playthings.[53]

Deutsch goes on to suggest that these perceptual handicaps, plus the learning to not attend to sound that occurs in a noisy household, handicap the child in school learning, especially reading. It must also be added that these represent handicaps in the basic notions of the physical world upon which ability to learn to understand, predict, and control the objects of the environment depends. Thus these children are handicapped in the basic constructs that make much learning possible.

This point can be overstressed, however. While the deprived child lacks the kinds of educational toys and manipulanda that middle class people accept as standard, it must also be pointed out that he has access to a large variety of discarded objects and junk, with which he plays quite imaginatively. This early training in making toys out of whatever stray objects come the way of the disadvantaged child may play a part in the resourcefulness and ingenuity mentioned earlier in this chapter.

It thus seems fairly clear that a lack of contact with traditional cultural objects, whose generalized and related forms constitute much of the content of school learning, produces a child and adolescent who is uncertain about his environment, fearful of it, and who appears stupid to his teachers and to others who judge him later.[54]

[53] Deutsch, "The Disadvantaged Child and the Learning Process."
[54] This is dramatically illustrated by an anecdote related to me by a kindergarten teacher who, after several years of teaching emotionally disturbed children, went to work in a special enrichment kindergarten for disadvantaged children. Despite her experience, she was amazed when, after the children had done several paintings, she gave them paper clips with which to put the drawings together so that they could conveniently carry them home to show their parents: none of the children knew what the clips were or how they worked; it is unlikely that any of them had seen them at home. Thus a simple matter of carrying several pieces of paper home was problematical for these children. Had these children been interspersed in a classroom of middle class children with a less alert teacher, they would surely have been seen as

If the disadvantaged young man finds the environment difficult to understand, it must also be admitted that his environment is a difficult one for anyone's coping capacities. The powerlessness of his position, the readiness of agents of social control to assume that it is others who need help and protection from him, rather than realizing that he needs help and protection, the wanton waste and brutality he sees around him, the humiliating subjection to prejudice and rejection masked by pious sentiments and patriotic rhetoric—in short, an environment without logic or order in which words do not match actions and meanings approach double-think, would leave the most intelligent and capable bewildered. The Negro in his ghetto is in a position not very different from that of the Jews in the ghettos of Europe; and it must be admitted that they, with their education and ego resources, were no more successful in understanding the environments of Nazi persecution than are the urban poor in coping with life in America today. The environments of the disadvantaged are in some respects quite un-understandable and irrational. Sherman Barr reports, for example, that "the poor cope, somehow, with a welfare system so bureaucratic that it allows 90 razor blades a year for employed males but only 50 for unemployed males; 12 haircuts a year if a man is working, and 9 if he is not." [55] Thus even the welfare systems becomes a representative of all that is cruel, unjust, and illogical in American society.

Role Taking. In deprived neighborhoods, children have few opportunities to learn about the social roles characterizing the varieties of statuses and positions that people in middle class America occupy. They do not visit and know their friendly fireman, our helpful policeman, the dairyman who delivers our milk, etc. They thus have limited opportunity to learn, through play imitation, to take on a variety of social roles. The result of this limitation will be discussed later, when the disadvantaged boy's inability to "take the role of the other" to see things from a variety of perspectives, or to play a variety of important roles, is explored.

Theoretically, role-taking ability is associated with early identification with the parents from whom middle class children derive their status. In lower class, disorganized homes, identification with parents is limited in a variety of ways. Lower class parents tend not to use psychological control techniques [56] and there is evidence that the use of psychological

---

individuals of low intelligence, rather than related as a group product of a sociological crime. Such a teacher would then, appropriately, have lowered her expectations for the "dull" individuals in her class, and thus produced a self-fulfilling prophecy.

[55] S. Barr, "Voices of the Poor," *Trans-action*, 3 (1966), 30.

[56] E. Maccoby, P. Gibbs *et al.*, "Methods of Child Rearing in Two Social Classes," in *Readings in Child Development*, W. Martin and C. Stendler, eds. (New York: Harcourt, Brace and Company, Inc., 1954), pp. 380-396.

(i.e., love-oriented) techniques of control foster identification. [57] Lower class parents use direct physical punishment, which drives the child away from them. Lower class parents are also absent from the child's environment much of the time, which, combined with the failure to establish basic trust discussed earlier, operates against the child's use of the parents as models. In addition, the parents' interactions with their children often tend to be punitive, as demonstrated in the Hess experiment cited earlier. Finally, lower class children become children of the streets, and transfer their references to the peer group much earlier than do middle class children, again reducing the opportunities for identifying with the parents.[58] Thus the basic experience of taking over the behaviors and attitudes of another person, as the child's first extended practice at taking others' roles, is lacking or minimal, leaving the child with reduced ability to acquire and use role-playing skills easily and automatically as a means of seeing himself and the world in alternative perspectives.

Conscience. Those processes that reduce the opportunities and motivations for internalizing the parents are the same ones that, theoretically, are responsible for a low level of superego development and the capacity to experience guilt. Thus "superego lacunae" have been cited as characteristics of many disadvantaged youth.[59] It may also be suggested that the process of early desatellization from the parents before conscience-producing internalization and identification have been completed leaves the child with only the initial form of internalization: shame before one who has discovered a transgression. Thus we have the familiar trait of anxiety about being caught, but little inhibiting guilt.

Peer Influence. The frustrations of life in the home, the crowded living conditions, the unpleasant interaction with parents, all combine to make the street a more gratifying and freer place for the poor child. Thus, despite the fears and wishes of many lower class mothers, the peer group takes over much of the family's socializing role, becomes the child's source of values, and the group from which he derives his status. The conditions are thereby established for the lower class adolescent's close dependence on his peer group, a quality even more exaggerated than it is for the middle class adolescent.

[57] J. Whiting and I. Child, *Child Training and Personality* (New Haven: Yale University Press, 1953).

[58] B. Ausubel and P. Ausubel, "Ego Development Among Segregated Negro Children," in H. Passow (ed.), *Education in Depressed Areas* (New York: Teachers College, Columbia University, 1963).

[59] F. Redl and D. Wineman, *Controls from Within* (Glencoe, Ill.: The Free Press, 1952).

Sexual Identity. The lower class disadvantaged family is often headed by a female.[60] In one study of boys serving in a vocational counseling program, it was found that the natural parents were not living together in 61 per cent of the families.[61] In many ways this is a response to the conditions of life, in which unemployed men cannot support families, and in which women can only have children and obtain ADC (Aid to Dependent Children) and welfare aid when there is no male head of family; it is also a pattern for which the dynamics of the disadvantaged male suit him. The young male child growing up in a family life that includes a succession of men with only the most tenuous commitments to the other family members learns that often, when a man comes to the house, either there will be a fight between the man and his mother (in response to the man's drunkenness, or to his demand to share the woman's money), or the child will be abused in order to get rid of him. Soon enough the man goes away, leaving the mother even more resentful of men and even more disdainful, especially if she has been able to maintain employment when he has not. Thus the boy, already lacking a male model, learns that men are bad, and that, by implication, he is bad if he acts like one.

This is the background for the boy's deep ambivalence about his status as a male, and his self-hatred in response to his almost obsessive attempts to prove his masculinity in order to dispel the doubts produced by an initial identification with a female model in a female-dominated household.[62] This ambivalent sexual identity may account for the quasi-homosexual nature of his gang loyalty in a context of almost outrageous attempts by the group members to assert and demonstrate their masculinity, their *machismo* [63] to each other, again an exaggeration of middle class adolescent processes.[64] These masculinity needs thus provide further

[60] A. Cohen and H. Hodges, "Characteristics of the Lower Blue-Collar Class," *Social Problems*, 10 (1963), 303-334; A. Hollingshead and R. Redlich, *Social Class and Mental Illness* (New York: John Wiley & Sons, Inc., 1958); W. Miller, *Social Service Review*, 33.

[61] *Report of the Youth and Work Training Programs* (New York: Sloan House YMCA, October 28, 1964).

[62] W. Miller, *Journal of Social Issues*, 14.

[63] O. Lewis, *The Children of Sanchez* (New York: Random House, Inc., 1961).

[64] The picture described here is present in much of the literature on disadvantaged youth. It suggests that the flamboyant sexuality of such boys is really a product of underlying sexual uncertainties, and weakness of masculine identification. Middle class reactions to lower class sexuality range from outraged morality to romantic idealization and idolization of the sexual freedom and spontaneity of the poor, compared to the presumed sexual inhibition of the middle class. Such reactions suggest the possibility that the ascription of an underlying weakness and ambivalence in sexual identity is really only a projection by the middle class, an attempt to take away from the lower class youth that which is envied and feared (often at the same time) by the sexually anxious and conflicted middle class. James Baldwin makes this charge in much of his later writing; I suspect that it is a valid one in many cases, and that the theme of the lower class boy as latent homosexual has been much overdone. Never-

impetus to the adolescent entrancement with cars, power, and speed, with strength, with size.

The sexual identity problem of the lower class boy is further complicated by the positions of girls in his society. Especially in segregated Negro communities, mother-dominated families openly prefer girls: they do better than the boys in school, they get along better socially, and have higher aspirations (and higher academic achievements). They advance further in school; and if they drop out, it is at later grades than boys.[65] The boys therefore have reason to resent girls, to feel inferior to them, and to avoid any enduring but humiliating relationships with them. The cycle is then complete for the next generation of men to relate to women in the same fashion that produced the matriarchal family structure that gave rise to the cycle—a pattern uniquely functional to the socioeconomic conditions of the American lower class.

The sexual ambivalence also enters into the disadvantaged boy's perceptions of the work role. In his family, it was the women who worked at jobs; it was the women who urged the men to work. To the boy, therefore, work is a feminine value; and to accept the work role is to endanger his masculinity. The proper role of men is to get women to support them. These are some of the reasons behind the need for the work role to be clearly defined as a masculine one for the disadvantaged boy.

Added to the connection between work and sex role identity in the Negro boy is the fact that too often the potential male models available to him have themselves been denigrated and degraded by whites, referred to as "boys" regardless of age, treated with paternalistic belittling—in short, emasculated.[66] The Negro boy who has experienced the humiliation of his father, his father's inability to retaliate, to "be a man," has scant motivation for being that kind of male, and doing that kind of work. The consequences of this for role modeling in the boy who rejects

---

theless, one cannot ignore the findings reviewed by Rainwater (1966) which indicate that while early sexual experience is more frequent among lower class youth, it has a competitive, driven, anxious quality to it: that lower class people are more inhibited in varieties of sexual activity, express more moralistic attitudes, and report less enjoyment of sex than middle class subjects. This could be another case of lower class respondents saying what they think the authority-figure interviewer wants to hear, but I doubt if that can account for all the findings. It does seem to be a case of "smoking more and enjoying it less." Thus the data lend more support to the "latent homosexual" hypothesis than they do to the "freedom and spontaneity" position.

[65] Deutsch *et al.*, *Contributions to School Retardation;* R. Smuts, "The Negro Community and the Development of Negro Potential," *Journal of Negro Education,* **26** (1957), 456-465.

[66] A. Kardiner and L. Ovesey, *The Mark of Oppression* (New York: Harcourt, Brace and World, Inc., 1962); E. Frazier, *Negro Youth at the Crossways* (Washington, D.C.: American Council on Education, 1940).

his father as an identity model, trying to identify with the white oppressors, and for the self-hatred that such developments lead to, will be explored later in this chapter with reference to the function of counselors as models.

In families of chronic unemployment, the youth has few opportunities to learn some of the characteristics and aspects of the role of worker. This was brought home to me recently when, on a Monday morning, following a weekend during which I had been ill with a cold and thus had stayed in pajamas and bathrobe, I arrived at the breakfast table in a business suit. My four-year-old daughter asked me why I was dressed up; and I told her that I had to go to work, even though I still had a cold. Thus at an early age she began to learn that one aspect of one's role as a worker is to go to work regularly even when one does not quite feel like it—a lesson that many disadvantaged youth have never had an opportunity to learn from any steadily employed and adequate representative of the worker role.

One can only speculate on the consequences of these developments for the counseling relationship. On the one hand, there are often strong needs for the male counselor to serve as a model by the youthful counselee, but on the other there is also great difficulty in his ability to engage in imitation. The youth may also make obvious attempts to impress the counselor with his masculinity in an effort to establish his membership in a common group with the male counselor. To some counselors, the flamboyant masculinity paraded before them may then serve as both seductions and threats; some may respond by subtly and unconsciously encouraging the masculine display, or by emphasizing their own masculinity—in either case providing the client, with his fears of too close an interpersonal relation with a potentially punitive man, with a means for diverting the counseling from the work at hand, and for keeping the counselor at an emotional distance from himself.

Educational Background

It has been sufficiently indicated in preceding sections of this chapter, and in much of the available literature and rhetoric concerning the poor, that from the very beginning they are ill-prepared to cope with the demands of formal education in schools and classrooms organized around a middle class model of verbal facility, delayed gratification, impulse control, and reduced motor functioning in favor of cognitive-conceptual activity. Adding to the child's initial lack of readiness for reading and verbal development, and his unfamiliarity with the manipulanda and common concepts of American society (many, for obvious reasons, are not even sure of their last names), is the typical inferiority of the schools in slum areas and the low levels of teachers' expectations for the disadvantaged child. This low expectation becomes a self-fulfilling prophecy as the teacher thus provides fewer learning opportunities and encouragements, derives less gratification from the disadvantaged child, and is less set to perceive good performance; thus the child learns less and receives low grades even when performing adequately.[67] Daniel Katz (personal communication) describes an as yet unreported study in which an experimenter administered to school children a test purported (to the teachers) to identify the "late blooming" child. After administration of the test, children of various IQ levels were randomly selected by the experimenter and identified to the teachers as found to be "late bloomers." At the end of the term it was discovered that the children so identified actually increased in their academic achievement scores more than did control children, demonstrating the extent to which teachers' expectations become self-fulfilling prophecies.

For most disadvantaged children, the prophecy is of failure; and as failure experiences rapidly accumulate, along with resentments of the teachers and the educational process, and inability to sit still and attend to words for long hours, the disadvantaged youth is put on the road to dropping out. With a national dropout rate around 50 per cent, the rate in many ghetto areas rises to 90 per cent.[68]

Lack of home support for school achievement adds to the process. While lower class parents tend to set high values on education, they also tend to expect disappointment; and their behavior does not lend support to their verbalized values. Their children do not see them reading or writing; there are no books or magazines in the house; the parents' language is far from school-required usage; the parents do not inquire about and follow their children's school progress and activities; they move often from one apartment to another so that their children must frequently shift schools; they do not always take responsibility for getting their children to school on time; and they are not always able to provide enough nourishment to keep their children awake and alert during school.[69] Low achievement motivation leads to lowered performance, failure, and thus, further lowering of achievement striving.[70]

Hence the high dropout rate, especially among the boys. However, it should also be noted that in some studies, at least 24 per cent of the so-called dropouts were school push-outs.[71] Another unknown portion

[67] A. Wilson, "Social Stratification and Academic Achievement," in *Education in Depressed Areas*, A. Passow, ed. (New York: Teachers College Press, Columbia University).
[68] Korbin, "Sociological and Cultural Foundations."
[69] W. Boutwell, "What's Happening in Education," *PTA Magazine*, 57 (1962).
[70] J. Kagan, L. Sontag, C. Baker, and L. Nelson, "Personality and I.Q. Change," *Journal of Abnormal and Social Psychology*, 56 (1958), 261-266.
[71] Urban League of Greater New York, "Center for School Dropouts Annual Report," 1963.

were only slightly less obviously encouraged to leave at the earliest opportunity. According to Stripling:

School administrators, teachers, and counselors are threatened by the presence of the potential dropout and often encourage him to leave school. . . . The potential school dropout, in most of our schools, creates a threat to the school staff because they recognize that they cannot meet his needs. . . . Such a student threatens the faculty's sense of adequacy as professional people, since they have neither the time, the skills, nor the specialized services available to assist him. This causes the staff to become hostile toward the student or to reject him in some other fashion such as ignoring him, ridiculing him, or just leaving him alone without encouragement or help. In many cases, one or more members of the staff might suggest to the potential dropout that he would be better off outside the school program.[72]

Other research indicates that those who dropped out of school had fewer contacts with their counselors before dropping out than nondropouts. Thus the disadvantaged youth's main contacts with counselors have often been the occasions on which they were rejected by the very institutions advertised as being "for all America's youth." With his tendency to personalize his interactions with bureaucratic systems, it is understandable that the disadvantaged youth comes to the vocational counselor only reluctantly and suspiciously, prepared to see counseling as the power structure's euphemism for rejecting him while laying the blame for the rejection on shortcomings in himself, rather than on the inappropriateness of the school program to his needs and style.

Other factors also play a role in dropping out. One study indicates that dropouts tend to be far too old for their grade levels, and more physically mature.[73] It was estimated many students overage for their grades would be 21 years old when they were graduated, if they did not drop out.

Thus the disadvantaged youth has a history of educational failure, of rejection, matched with self-hatred and inferiority feelings, and little achievement motivation. He brings to the counseling situation, then, little readiness to seize opportunities made available to him or revealed to him in the course of the counseling, a lack of response that often causes counselors to conclude that the client lacks the capacity, is too passive or too unmotivated, to profit from counseling.

Many counselors, cognizant of the advantages of a high school diploma, often direct their counseling toward encouraging youth to return to school.

[72] R. Stripling, "Professional Preparation of Counselors: Implications in Regard to School Dropouts," in *Guidance and the School Dropout*, D. Schreiber, ed. (Washington, D.C.: National Education Association and the American Personnel and Guidance Association, 1964), pp. 213-226.

[73] L. Nachman, R. Getson, and J. Odgers, *Ohio Study of High School Drop-outs, 1962-1963* (Columbus, Ohio: State Department of Public Instruction, 1964).

However, this is not always appropriate or helpful. Super finds that dropouts who later obtained high school equivalency diplomas were at the same or lower occupational levels than dropouts without diplomas, and were less satisfied with their vocational careers.[74] Further, many returned dropouts are regarded with suspicion by the schools: dropout equals delinquent in the minds of many; and at the first sign of the slightest deviation, he is dropped again. Few can be expected to continue with confidence in the reality of the promised ultimate gratifications under such circumstances, and the youth may then be permanently lost to the counselor's efforts. It thus behooves the counselor to be sure that the school is prepared to accept and help the returnee before he attempts to induce him to return to school.

Interpersonal Operations

This section will consider some of the interpersonal stances, and their meanings, that arise from the kinds of socialization experiences described above.

Peer Loyalty. One of the most valued and potentially positive characteristics of the inner-city slum adolescent is his great loyalty to his peer group. It has already been pointed out that from quite early in the slum dweller's childhood, peers have been the source of values, status, learnings, and protection. The peer group provides him with many sources of gratification: it is the place and context in which his sexual ambivalence is acted out and his sexual anxieties reduced; it is the vehicle for his thrill seeking; it is the object of the solidarity and submersion of belongingness that he does not get in his family; it is his source of defense against the arbitrary power of authorities, and the support through group norms he *can* meet to replace the success he cannot achieve in school; it is the frame for the only social structure he can understand and appreciate, offering him an unambiguous code of behavior, and reliable and predictable terms for his conformity; it gratifies the dependency needs that his family has been unable to satisfy, but it does so in a way that does not violate his masculinity needs, or arouse fear. The peer group is thus the only structuring authority he can accept, understand, and with which he is motivated to comply, as it lends him some definition of himself through the status he derives from the group and earns within the group. These are powerful forces—in many ways the most powerful forces operating in the young disadvantaged adolescent male. Thus Gordon lists "capacity for meaningful and loyal personal relationships" as among the strengths of the poor youth.[75] The whole function of these relationships

[74] O. Super, "Vocational Development of High School Dropouts," in *Guidance and the School Dropout.*
[75] E. Gordon, *Counseling and Guidance.*

within the peer group may be summed up in the notion of full and implicit mutual aid.[76]

To some extent the group's source of influence lies in the other-directedness of many disadvantaged youth who, lacking the internalized conscience as a source of guidance, and subject to often arbitrary and harsh treatment by parents and by authorities, has become wary and attentive to interpersonal cues for behavioral guidance. This stance is probably also related to the tendency noted earlier to personalize events. It does indeed make the disadvantaged adolescent wary of others—attentive and sensitive to cues that will enable him to predict their behavior, and in need of interpersonal contacts to supply such cues.

The power of the gang or group is overwhelming for the disadvantaged youth, even more than it is for the middle class adolescent. But unlike the middle class boy with his strong commitment to individualism (at least in achievement situations), and his underlying acceptance of parental values and goals, the lower class boy's group membership stands in opposition to the organization of middle class life. American education, as Cohen points out, is largely individual achievement-oriented and competitive, rather than cooperative.[77] The boy who does well in school must engage in many study and work activities that he cannot share with others. Similarly, advancement in a job requires separation from the group, and individual competition. Thus the group must, in order to preserve its organization and viability, oppose school and job, even if its members had no other reasons for disaffection from those institutions.

Individual counseling by its very nature is also inconsistent with the youth's group loyalties. So great are the youth's needs to remain in and with his group that I have seen young counselees insist on being counseled together. For the youth in whom the powerful forces described above are operating, the only defense against the individualizing pressure of one-to-one counseling is to engage in it only as a delegate of his group, and to withhold personal commitment to the counseling. Thus he participates minimally, with large mental reservations. I believe that this is one of the important reasons that much individual counseling of disadvantaged young gang members is ineffective. It clearly suggests the appropriateness and advantage of group methods over individual methods; for it seems likely to me that whatever the attractions of individual counseling for such a youth, they cannot compete with the commanding and overriding gratifications made available by the group to the young

[76] W. Whyte, *Street Corner Society* (Chicago: University of Chicago Press, 1943); A. Cohen, *Delinquent Boys: The Culture of the Gang* (New York: Free Press of Glencoe, Inc., 1955).
[77] Cohen, *Ibid.*

man with little else to fall back on. It is suggested that this accounts for the superiority of group methods over individual casework in one of the most thoroughgoing experimental evaluations ever carried out of work with the disadvantaged; [78] it also accounts for the success of such programs as the Provo work with delinquents,[79] the Highfields [80] and Essexfields [81] projects. They form the background for the observation that a great many of the experimental and demonstration projects for disadvantaged youth carried out under the MDTA (Manpower Development and Training Act) and President's Committee on Juvenile Delinquency programs seems spontaneously to turn to group methods in their work.[82]

When it comes to a showdown between the claims of counseling and the claims of the counselee's peer group, the counseling is most likely to lose; the best strategy of the agency is thus to turn a liability into an asset: to bring the group into the counseling process, or to create a new group in the counseling for the youth to relate to.[83] This does not imply, of course, that no youth can profit from individual counseling, and that group methods are the methods of choice for all disadvantaged youth in all settings. But it does suggest that for those with the kinds of needs and dynamics that gangs spontaneously gratify, group methods are likely to be more productive. Despite the preference for individual counseling that occupies a somewhat credo-like status in the profession, the evidence available is either neutral or favors group methods. An insistence on individual methods so far remains little more than an act of faith, or a projection of the professional's own relationship needs.

Powerlessness. Feelings of powerlessness are also characteristic of many disadvantaged youth. Gladwin describes many disadvantaged families as feeling that their lives are subject to forces beyond their control, in which the institutions of our society—businesses, agencies, public employees—are ranged against them.[84] Of course, such a percep-

---

[78] H. Meyer, H. Borgatta, and W. P. Jones, *Girls at Vocational High* (New York: Russell Sage Foundation, 1965).

[79] L. Empey and J. Rabow, "The Provo Experiment in Delinquency Rehabilitation," *American Sociological Review*, **26** (1961), 679-695.

[80] L. McCorkle, A. Elias, and F. Bixby, *The Highfields Story* (New York: Holt, Rinehart & Winston, 1958).

[81] S. Pilnick, A. Elias, and N. Clapp, "The Essexfields Concept: A New Approach to the Social Treatment of Juvenile Delinquents," *Journal of Applied Behavioral Science,* **2** (1966), 109-125.

[82] M. Herman and S. Sadofsky, *Youth-Work Programs: Problems of Planning and Operation* (New York: Graduate School of Social Work, New York University, 1966).

[83] "Seeding" the group with more advanced boys who can establish the group norms for the newcomer would seem to be an effective device to do this.

[84] T. Gladwin, "The Anthropologist's View of Poverty," *Official Proceedings, National Conference on Social Welfare* (New York: Columbia University Press, 1961).

tion (however much it is related to the passivity that it implies) is far from false, considering the position of the poor in American society.

To some extent, these feelings of powerlessness may also function to further reduce the potentiality for feeling guilty, for guilt implies the perception of one's self as the agency of his actions and circumstances. One who feels that he is the object of forces outside his control thus does not see his own behavior as chosen by himself, but rather as provoked and explained by the behavior of others.

Dependency. In a certain sense, then, poor people are made passively dependent by their reliance on interpersonal cues as guides to action and to the status of the potentially threatening interpersonal environment, and by their powerlessness. Haggstrom describes the situation of the poor:

> ... the poor, by virtue of their situation, tend to be more dependent than other groups on a large number of powerful persons and organizations, which are often very unclear about the bases for their actions and unpredictable in their decisions, and which further render the poor helpless by condescending or hostile attitudes, explicit verbal communications which state or imply the inferiority of the poor, and callousness or actual harassment. If we divide the powerful persons affecting the poor into two groups, the benevolent in intention on the one hand, the callous or punitive on the other, we will find that the majority of both type of power figure treat the poor as inferior and reach down to relate to them. . . . The fact of being powerless, but with needs that must be met, leads the poor to be dependent on the organizations, persons, and institutions which can meet these needs. The situation of dependency and powerlessness through internal personality characteristics as well as through social position leads to apathy, hopelessness, conviction of the inability to act successfully, failure to develop skills, and so on. . . . Over the time the dependency relationship of the poor becomes institutionalized and habits, traditions, and organizations arise in both the affluent community and in the neighborhoods of poverty, maintaining the relationship between them. . . . "Lower class" delinquency does not only stem from the fact that the poor have few and drab job opportunities. There is also the perception that the conforming poor tend to remain indefinitely in low social positions. . . . The situation gives rise to the typical absence of that hope which is associated with action and which gives salience to intentions and attitudes.[85]

This powerlessness, and the situation of forced dependency of the poor, are in conflict both with the values of our society and with the early experience with independence from parents and home described above. This is the situation which leads to counterdependency and the angry rejection of "helping" persons,[86] as the conflict leads to frustration, which in turn generates aggression.[87] The aggression generates fear of reprisal,

---

[85] Haggstrom, "The Power of the Poor."

[86] A. Townsend, "The Relationship Between Parental Commitment and Certain Focus of Dependent Behavior" (doctoral dissertation, University of Michigan, 1958).

[87] J. Dollard, L. Doob, N. Miller, O. Mowrer, and R. Sears, *Frustration and Aggression* (New Haven: Yale University Press, 1939).

evokes the feelings of powerlessness in relation to reprisal, and thus begins the dependency-counterdependency cycle all over again. The outcome is often a sullen passiveness, superficial compliance, a complaint about the lack of real help, together with self-blame for the situation, and under all a burning resentment of the agencies and personnel of society.

Localization. These dynamics, together with those described earlier concerning uncertainty about the interpersonal environment and withdrawal from parts of the environment that can be avoided, result in a restricted range of geographical mobility. One study found, for example, that disadvantaged youth tended to look for jobs only in their home communities.[88] They rationalized this by saying that businessmen in their areas might know them and thus might be more inclined to hire them, or they were afraid to go through the territories of rival gangs. Many were circumscribed in their attempts to look for work because they simply did not know their way around the city in which they lived.

Poor youths have often never been beyond their ghetto areas, have never been in locales where they expect to be rejected, and which therefore stimulate the hate and fear that they know are in themselves. It is an irony of the situation, then, that the poor often participate in their own ghettoization—another example of the fineness with which characteristics of the poor are appropriate to match, to support, and feed into the socioeconomic conditions of their lives that created those characteristics. Thus there is a fear and avoidance of the outside world that, combined with gang and peer group loyalty and the search for a reduction of ambiguity, leads to a polarization of the world into "us" and "them." [89]

Aggression. Explicit in much of the foregoing, and primary in the minds of many who anticipate contact with poor adolescents, is the problem of aggressiveness and hostility. No doubt for very complex reasons, among which are probably guilt, projection, and inhibitory socialization that led to their values, middle class people are hyperaware of, and made anxious by their overwhelming expectation of free-wheeling aggression and hostility in lower class adolescents—a stance that is entirely complementary to the resentments that disadvantaged youths feel. In many ways, their aggression is a summing up of all the dynamics and personality structures described thus far: motoric style; low impulse control; the need to prove masculinity; the lack of introspection, and low levels of guilt that lead the poor youth to blame his situation on the personal agents of society; training in aggression implicit in the harsh and arbitrary

[88] Leshner and Snyderman, *Employment Review,* March, 1966.
[89] R. Hoggart, *The Uses of Literacy* (London: Chatto & Windus Ltd., 1957).

child socialization practices he has experienced; the tension and irritabil-
ity produced by unsatisfied needs, imposed failure, and powerlessness,
as well as by the internal conflicts between masculinity and feminine identifications, between feelings of failure and the need to feel that one has
identity as a self-owned agent of his own actions and experiences, between the fact of imposed dependency and independence strivings.
Finally, aggressiveness also functions as the only mode of relating to
people that is safe and acceptable to the lower class male adolescent, who
in many ways presents an exaggeration of typical middle class male
adolescent rejection of tenderness and positive sentiment—a rejection
operated through masking of positive feelings with a gruff and bantering
aggression that may turn to more desperate anger and rage at attempts
to stimulate positive feelings only tenuously repressed.

Thus the aggressive stance works to hold others off, to prevent them
from arousing uncomfortable and dangerous feelings, to resist invasion
of the self. At the same time that these functions are met, the aggressiveness permits gratification of needs for interpersonal contact, for resolving
ambiguities in a relationship, for expressing real feelings, for controlling
others and rendering them safe, for emasculating others to bolster one's
own masculinity. It is a further illustration of the classical truth that
aggressive acts represent both impulses and defenses, with the two
functions so amalgamated in the same behavior as to be inseparable in
action, though they may be conceptually isolated for heuristic purposes.
This is simply another way of saying that an aggressive act often has
many and widely varying gratifications inherent in it; that it leads to
many different sources of gratification all at once.

Self-Concept. Many of the factors so far discussed are associated with
a negative self-concept in disadvantaged people. Sharing the major
American values regarding income and status, they see themselves as
failures. They accept the social and political philosophy prevalent in a
society that prizes individual initiative and upward mobility, implying
that failure to move up can only be the result of some internal lacks and
deficiencies in themselves—a view that much of this chapter has attempted
to imply is a self-fulfilling prophecy.

The Economic Opportunity Act is an excellent example of this phenomenon. While its title refers to economic opportunity, implying the
premise that lack of opportunity in the society is the reason for poverty,
the contents of the Act are almost exclusively concerned with procedures
for transforming the behavior and personalities of the poor. Despite the
title, only one section of the Act, and that dealing with the smallest and
least implemented program (business loans to poor businesses in order to
stimulate employment), is an *economic* measure in any sense directed at

the provision of employment *opportunities.* This kind of double-think is not wasted on either the affluent or the poor; both have accepted the illogical premise and conclusion that where there are poor people who are not making economic progress, the fault lies within the poor.

For obvious reasons on the part of the affluent segments of society, and because of the tendency to personalize and concretize rather than to think in terms of systems and macroprocesses, neither the poor nor the rich give much attention to alternative possibilities: that the system contains a restriction of opportunity in which available opportunities are garnered by those who, already affluent, have the power and access to the opportunities, thus blocking the poor out; that the affluent owe much of their success to the existence of a poverty group to provide cheap labor and to pay comparatively more for goods and services than the middle class without having the power or opportunity to question or oppose those who set the prices, or to escape to other areas; that children born into the ghetto are as much victims of their circumstances as they are the agents of their fates.

Thus poor people are self-rejecting. It seems likely that their low self-concepts are also related to many of the factors already discussed: avoidance of introspection and self-analysis; difficulties in developing adequate identifications; powerlessness; avoidance of feelings; externalization of their problems, etc. The self-image of Negroes is even more severely affected as a product of the class-caste system to which they are subject. Ausubel and Ausubel point out that

In addition to suffering ego deflation through awareness of his inferior status in society, the Negro child finds it more difficult to satellize and is denied much of the self-esteem advantages of satellization. The derived status that is the principal source of children's self-esteem in all cultures is largely discounted in his case since he can only satellize in relation to superordinate individuals or groups who themselves possess an inferior and degraded status. . . . We can understand, therefore, why young Negro children resist identifying with their own racial group, why they seek to shed their identities (Deutsch et al., 1956), why they more frequently chose white than Negro playmates (Stevenson and Stewart, 1958), why they prefer the skin color of the culturally dominant caste (Clark and Clark, 1947; Goodman, 1952; Landreth and Johnson, 1953), and why they tend to assign negative roles to children of their own race (Stevenson and Stewart, 1958). These tendencies persist at least into late adolescence and early adult life, insofar as one can judge from the attitude of Negro college students. These students tend to reject ethnocentric and anti-white ideologies and to accept authoritarian and anti-Negro propositions (Steckler, 1957).[90]

To some extent, the negative identity described here may be associated with what sometimes appear to be attempts to lose consciousness

[90] Ausubel and Ausubel, "Ego Development among Segregated Negro Children."

of self, as in the quest for thrills, and self-overpowering stimulation in the use of marijuana, in the use of a transistor radio plugged into the ear for long periods of time. The complement of this is the seeking after stimulation through motor activity rather than through thought.

Defenses. Some of these reactions suggest the nature of the defenses frequently used in lower class culture. The habits of thinking and acting already described apply not only to cognitive functioning unrelated to internal conflicts; they also condition the nature of the ego's responses to anxiety. Theoretically, it is this function of cognitive styles that sets the pattern for the kind of functioning in nonconflict areas already discussed.[91] The mechanisms required in the service of anxiety reduction come to be employed in dealing with other kinds of problems, as a habit of thought, originating in conflict and utilized in both conflictful and nonconflictful situations. It is therefore appropriate to look at the nature of these defenses.

The defensive style of the lower class adolescent shows a high frequency of denial.[92] This defense is a fairly primitive one that does not make extensive use of intellectual constructs or subtlety of thought. As opposed to more sophisticated defenses—such as rationalization and sublimation—that transform anxiety-arousing stimuli into safer events, denial involves a crude blocking out of the anxiety-arousing impulse or event. Theoretically, it is a defense learned early in life, before the child is able to discover more sophisticated constructions of events. It is thus a reaction to early difficulty in dealing with impulses and an environment that is beyond the ability of the young child to manipulate or transform.

Another common defense is one that has already been discussed: acting out. There is no need to discuss it further, except to point out its defensive functions through giving expression to impulses behaviorally but not through conscious representation in direct verbalization.

In addition to the dissociation implied in the above, Bernstein also cites displacement as one of the defenses consistent with the kind of linguistic code described earlier in this chapter; it is a response that is consistent with the concreteness and personalization tendencies of many poor adolescents, as well as with the tendency to externalize problems.[93]

The fruits of these defensive styles are seen in the kinds of psychopathology that seem to be overrepresented among psychiatric patients from disadvantaged backgrounds, compared to middle class patients. The lower class patients are relatively more often diagnosed as having disorders associated with motoric symptoms: catatonic schizophrenia and

---

[91] H. Hartman, *Ego Psychology and the Problem of Adaptation* (New York: International University Press, 1958).

[92] Miller and Swanson, *Inner Conflict and Defense.*

[93] Bernstein, *Social Class, Speech Systems, and Psycho-Therapy.*

hysteria, compared with paranoid schizophrenia and obsessive-compulsive neuroses in the middle class.[94]

Limits Testing. Many of the interpersonal operations described in this section have their counseling representations in the kinds of relations that disadvantaged youth tend to develop with their counselors. These relations are often marked by extensive testing of limits, operated through shifting provocation and passively dependent compliance, almost as if the youth were trying to resolve the ambiguity of the role relations in such a way as to define the counselor as the source of anticipated failure and rejection in the counseling, and as a way of bringing that rejection about, thus preserving the defenses and adaptation the youth has developed from the invasions of dangerous feelings stimulated by the possibility of hope. Sometimes this limits testing is part of a process of trying to coopt the counselor by informalizing the relationship, feeling him out personally, seducing him into a stance that approaches personal friendship, and then making demands on the counselor (as a friend) that the counselor (as a professional worker) cannot gratify. The youth then interprets the counselor's refusal as a rejection, and the counselor as a hypocrite ultimately shown up and thus rendered impotent as a potential model for the youth.

These dynamic relations are not always manifest in the superficials of the client-counselor relation, and may never approach awareness in either party in counseling that is highly task-oriented and structured. They are, nevertheless, frequently present below the surface, and may account for the seemingly inexplicable loss of influence experienced by some counselors in the course of their work with a client, at about the point that the client begins to miss appointments.

Analysis of such problems is easy, compared to handling them. I have no suggestions to make on this score, other than that limits ought to be clearly structured and sanctions for their violation designed that will operate as sanctions, although not permanently estranging the youth from the agency or the counselor. Thus a counselor may terminate an appointment and ask the youth to leave his office; but he should also be sure to invite the youth to return, and should suggest a time for a next appointment.

To a great extent, the ability of the counseling to survive the client's testings is a function of the counselor's ability to project his commitment to and interest in the youth.[95] It would be difficult to specify the counselor

[94] Hollingshead and Redlich, *Social Class and Mental Illness.*

[95] The counselor may have to go much further in making his commitment and interest overt than he does with middle class clients, who expect to be liked and treated with respect by others. At the same time, too flamboyant a demonstration of interest will justifiably raise doubts in the suspicious disadvantaged adolescent, who has often experienced prejudice and rejection in benign garb. In one project dealing

behaviors that will accomplish this; it has usually seemed to me that counselors experience themselves as committed and interested, and that failures to project such feelings are the result of counselor actions of which the counselor is usually unaware, or whose meanings he has not adequately explored. Thus one cannot state a rule for establishing a good counseling relationship; it is the responsibility of capable supervision to help counselors expand their self-awareness. Such teaching, I suspect, must inevitably be *ad hoc* and on-going.

Many of the foregoing characteristics suggest that the counselor for disadvantaged boys is in a focal position to serve as a model. The extensive research of Bandura and Walters indicates that people are more likely to imitate a model if they are: 1) lacking in self-esteem; 2) have difficulty in meeting task requirements; 3) dependent; and/or 4) have a history of failure.[96] Thus many disadvantaged boys fit the prescription for good imitators. Those likely to be imitated, according to Bandura and Walters, are those who are perceived by the imitator as controlling important resources, as competent, and as having high status.

In the case of the Negro youth with a white counselor, the problem is complicated as indicated by the findings that Negro children have strong and frustrating identity conflicts including wishes to identify with whites, to be white; that they are resentful of their skin color, and acceptant of

---

with such youth, the counselor routinely takes a picture with a Polaroid camera of each of his counselees; he then posts the picture on his wall. His clients are sincerely flattered by this interest (for many it is the first time they have ever been photographed for other than police purposes), and impressed by the thought that the client's picture is in the office and looked at by the counselor even when the client is not there. It seems like a very good idea, although I hesitate to recommend such "gimmicks," whose success probably lies at least as much in the natural warmth and interest of the one who invents the gimmick as it does in the gimmick itself. The best of gimmicks merely imitated as a compulsive duty, or only as a trick device, by a counselor who lacks the supporting affects, would certainly be a failure, and worse, would reduce the effectiveness of the device in the hands of those for whom it is a more natural technique.

There is one counselor activity, more than any others, that cannot fail to win the support and acceptance of his disadvantaged clients: the counselor's support of and active participation in social movements within the ghetto that seek to alter the system under which the poor grow up. His reputation in the community he seeks to serve will be more firmly established in this way, and on a more solid and realistic footing than any counseling trick, technique, or device I can think of. The counselor who is known by the peer group as one who supports them in their needs, who defends them against unfair treatment, who stands up for them in court, who joins their indigenous leaders in activities designed to win improvements in the conditions of their lives and neighborhood, who demonstrates that he *cares*, not only as a part of his job, but also personally—such a counselor, almost without regard to his technical proficiency and sophistication, has at least mastered the problem of rapport.

[96] A Bandura and R. Walters, *Social Learning and Personality Development* (New York: Holt, Rinehart & Winston, 1964).

the white prejudicial view of Negroes.[97] Clark and Clark found that Negro children tend to blame themselves for their color, to add to the self-hatred described earlier in this chapter.[98] Of course, such strivings to identify with whites are doomed to failure, often leading to a reaction-formation of rejection of whites—including counselors—as models.

In this context, the study by Mooney and Polansky demonstrating that perceived similarity to an interviewer on the part of subjects increased subjects' verbal accessibility and responsiveness, becomes pertinent.[99] Their findings suggest that where the counselor's function as a model is blocked by reaction-forming rejection of the possibility of achieving an adequate identity, it would be appropriate to increase the counselor's perceived similarity by using a counselor of the same or similar race-class-caste characteristics as the resistant youth.[100]

[97] Kardiner and Ovesey, *The Mark of Oppression;* Frazier, *Negro Youth;* E. Brody, "Color and Identity Conflict in Young Boys: Observations of Negro Mothers and Sons in Urban Baltimore," *Psychiatry,* **26** (1963), 188-208; W. Adams, "The Negro Patient in Psychiatric Treatment," *American Journal of Orthopsychiatry,* **20** (1950), 308-312; J. Teicher, "Some Problems of Personality Development in Negro Children," in *Personality in Nature, Society, and Culture,* C. Kluckhohn and H. Murray, eds. (New York: Alfred A. Knopf, Inc., 1965), p. 457; B. Dai, "Some Problems of Personality Development in Negro Children," in *op. cit.*

[98] K. Clark and M. Clark, "Racial Identification and Preference in Negro Children," in *Readings in Social Psychology,* T. Newcomb and E. Hartley, eds. (New York: Holt, Rinehart & Winston, Inc., 1947), pp. 169-178.

[99] J. Mooney and N. Polansky, "The Influence of Perceived Similarity and Personality on Verbal Accessibility," *Merrill-Palmer Quarterly,* **7,** 1961.

[100] Feelings about this point run high, so it is necessary to indicate that I do not mean that all whites should have white counselors, and Negroes Negro counselors. It all depends on whether the situation is one of blocked communication and modeling.

It has sometimes been contended that when a youth demonstrates blocking because of his feelings about the race of the counselor, that is not the time to give in, but rather the time to use the opportunity to get the youth over his prejudice, so that he can relate more effectively to people of other races at work, etc. Fine if it can be done, but if the blockage is too much to permit the relation to proceed, nothing has been gained and all is lost. An employed and self-supporting prejudiced youth is better than an unemployed and dependent unprejudiced youth.

On the other hand it has also been argued that the Negro boy who works with a Negro counselor is in the best position of all to discover that there are possibilities for upward mobility for him.

The ability of the counselor to function as a model without further generating self-rejection for not being able ever to be white, the mobility, the research indicating that verbal responsiveness is higher in Negro children with Negro examiners and interviewers (see also Pasamanick and Knoblock, 1955), together with the suggestion made earlier in this chapter that the counselor be one who is familiar with the verbal and body languages of his counselees, all combine to suggest to me that, other things (including professional competence) being equal, the Negro counselor from a disadvantaged background is likely to do better with Negro disadvantaged boys than the white counselor.

Role Mastery

Two roles that disadvantaged boys are ill-prepared to play appropriately are of particular interest to the counselor. These are the role of job-seeker and worker, and the role of counseling client.

Work Roles. I have already remarked on the disadvantaged youth's lack of familiarity with occupational roles. He does not know how to look for work, how to apply for work, or how to keep a job. He may not know that he is expected to go to work every day at the same time; that he must obey orders; that he must accept a superior-subordinate relationship vis-à-vis his supervisor; that he is not being cheated when his take-home pay is less than the pay promised for the job because of deductions for FICA and withholding tax; that he is supposed to learn to do all tasks required of him, and with as little overt admission of ignorance as possible; that he should defer to the business's customers and to relatives of the boss, etc.

The sources of the ignorance of these job-role behaviors in a lack of available models (and, for many adolescents, in the presence of models who too well played these roles, only to be rewarded by a life spent in dead-end and menial jobs, without respect, status, or hope) have been described earlier. These failures of models become manifest in the approach of disadvantaged young men to work. In one study by McDonald, a survey of disadvantaged youth found that as far as the youth were concerned, the hardest thing about working was getting up in the morning (24 per cent); 10 per cent listed taking orders as the hardest thing.[101] Sixty-four per cent chose income as the thing they liked best about working, with only 16 per cent citing an intrinsic interest in the work.

Study of the job-seeking behavior of disadvantaged adolescents in another city found that such youth characteristically applied for dead-end jobs, and seemed to look for jobs by occupation, rather than by opportunity. They had little knowledge of the meaning of job titles, and had familiarity with only a narrow range of occupations—primarily those in the service, domestic, and unskilled and semiskilled classes. Their job searching was thus greatly restricted, and most could not state a second choice, after indicating their primary job preference. They tended to apply for jobs only in their neighborhoods. Few used the want ads, or public or private employment services. Many stopped seeking work, or sought it only desultorily, after the first or second failure. Many did not know why they

---

[101] R. McDonald, "Some Characteristics of the Population Served by the Youth and Work Training Projects in New York City," *Report of the Youth and Work Training Programs.*

stopped looking for work; they said that they "just stopped." Some filed applications with employers, and then simply waited to be called. Altogether, their job seeking was aimless and vague.[102]

Ignorance about work patterns and the role of employees suggests that counseling should include or be related to direct instruction in how to apply for a job, how to fill out an application, how to handle interviews, supervisors, etc. The counselor of disadvantaged youth may not assume, as he may with middle class youth, that they have command of the role elements. I once saw a poor Negro youth filling out an application for a job in a business office, along with several other applicants. At one point he went to the interviewer at the desk and asked him how to spell a word; most of his middle class contemporaries would know that one does not reveal ignorance of such a matter before the authority figure—they would be more likely to ask a fellow applicant. This is one small example of what can only be described as a lack of *savoir faire* in moving within the middle class ethos of jobs and employment; counseling ought to include direct teaching and rehearsal of the necessary role behaviors.

It may also be suggested that the very first day of work on a new job is a point at which counseling can make a great difference in whether the youth will have a successful or unsuccessful employment experience. The first day on a new job is a difficult time for anyone, including the most sophisticated of professionals. It is a day on which the new man in an organization has all his radar going in an attempt to learn the lay of the land, to discover what the interpersonal relations are, to learn the informal code of expected behavior, to recognize the authority relations in the implicit but informal structure as well as in the formal structure of the organization. How much more difficult this day is for the youth with only a limited repertoire of roles, with his restricted range of alternative constructs for understanding social situations, with all his fear and ambivalence about the job.

Not surprisingly, then, many job placements fail on the first day; the youth, anxious and uncomfortable and feeling out of place, simply fails to return for work the next day. Immediately after that first day of work would be an excellent time for counseling that would help the youth to understand the things he experienced during the day, support him in his anxiety, and suggest strategies for resolving the ambiguities he finds so uncomfortable. Counseling on this occasion is also consistent with many of the suggestions in the early pages of this chapter designed to make the counseling concrete and relevant to immediate concerns. Thus it is suggested that what used to be called follow-up interviews, and

[102] Leshner and Snyderman, *Employment Service Review,* March, 1966.

were therefore scanted as not being an intrinsic aspect of the counseling program, should really be the place where a great deal of effective counseling can proceed.

There is an alternative view: Cloward and Ontell charge that youth employment programs err by imparting nonskills.

Faced with the harsh realities of an increasingly specialized and technical occupational structure, we have retreated to teaching out-of-school, unemployed slum youth "habits of work discipline" and "positive attitudes toward work." We have decided that their difficulties in employment bear some substantial relationship to poor grooming, to their fear of leaving the familiar neighborhood, to failure to come and go at appointed times. But young people entering the labor force have always exhibited these problems. Today's slumbred youth are no different. What is remarkably different is that we have suddenly decided that these age-old problems are *the* problems with which our training programs must now deal. And so we place the young in work situations, proclaiming at the outset that the purpose is not primarily—or at least initially—to convey specific occupational skills but, rather, to ensure that they know how to conduct themselves on a job if the occasion should ever arise that one is made available to them. How young people of any earlier time ever found their way into the occupational world without these aids in grooming, without help in developing job habits, and without special attention to their attitudes toward work remains something of a mystery. Perhaps it was that, given a much simpler occupational structure, they were better prepared to go out and to do a piece of work and they knew it, and the knowing gave them pride. If that is so, then training programs which do not convey specific occupational competence will not only fail to equip young people to take a real job but will fail to prepare them psychologically for work as well.[103]

The point is well taken that role training should not replace skill training. However, for the youth who must be placed on an initial job as a precondition of counseling and skill development, because without such placement he will reject the agency for not getting him what he wants— for such a youth, moving in today's world of artificially high standards and expectations by employers, specific work role preparation, and guidance along with job placement would seem to be appropriate.

There is one further important proviso: disadvantaged youth are likely to be suspicious and resentful of an agency that allies itself with arbitrary expectations of employers, an alliance implicit in the agency's program to teach behavioral conformity under the guise of work role training, if that conformity functions only to make the youth more socially acceptable to the middle class majority without the world represented by the majority doing a service in kind. In other words, it had better be a job worth minding one's p's and q's about, or one that clearly leads to a worthwhile job, if the agency is to ask the disadvantaged youth to mind his p's and q's in

[103] R. Cloward and R. Ontell, "Our Illusions About Training," *American Child*, 47 (1965), 6-10.

connection with it. To do anything else is to play a hypocritical role vis-à-vis the youth, and will be seen as such by him. That is what dropouts from many job training programs are made of. "No decent behavior without opportunities for decent living" is a slogan not very far from "No taxation without representation"; and the youths who symbolically assert such a slogan are well within the great American tradition.[104]

Client Roles. The second role deficiency to be commented on here is the disadvantaged boy's unfamiliarity with the role of counseling client. It has already been noted that his contacts with counselors in school have tended to be occasions for rejection. Thus he does not necessarily see the counselor as a helping person. His limited experience leaves him without knowledge of the usual form of relations between counselors and clients—relations in which the client is expected to sit in the inferior position (i.e., on the other side of the desk); to act deferential; to remove his hat; to sit alertly but shyly; to not take such independent actions as moving the chair, or touching objects on the desk; to be polite and grateful to the counselor for the time spent; to assert that one has been helped, even if only "somehow"; to arrive appropriately early for appointments, and to wait for the counselor to signal the proper time to begin the conversation seriously after pleasantries have been exchanged; to voice knowledge of the proper values and adherence to them, even if one must admit transgressions, etc. We have already discussed the disadvantaged youth's difficulty in playing other parts of the client role, such as being introspective, accounting for behavior in psychological terms, expecting the counselor

---

[104] This is not the place to explore in depth the possibility that changes in the economy may be such that in fact it may be impossible for the nation to supply decent jobs for youth (decent in the sense of good income and intrinsically interesting and rewarding work). Suffice it to say that there are some writers who appear to see the present trend as irreversible, and who therefore look forward to a future so routinized and automated that only the professional-managerial positions will contain any possibilities for enjoying one's work. Certainly as things now stand, the kinds of jobs that even the best and most committed of disadvantaged youth serving agencies turn up most often are not the kinds to inspire very much motivation in the youth. As long as this is so, we cannot expect very much wholesale success in youth reclamation work. The current scene is one in which the classic goal of finding the right job for the particular youth is irrelevant: too few jobs contain any features that could be connected with a youth's interests and skills; and finding *any* job, let alone the right job, is the most many youth workers hope for. In such circumstances, a counseling program aimed at identifying and maximizing a client's unique interests and job skills is a hypocrisy, and raises false hopes in the client.

For a discussion of some possible roles for vocational counseling if the day comes when most jobs will be intrinsically ungratifying, see the interesting paper by Loughary (1965).

I would only add that I am not convinced that the system must be allowed to continue in the direction it is going—if a closing out of all but the most routine or menial factory and domestic jobs through increasing the production of civic improvements and facilities does not mean that it cannot or may not.

to be supportive of weaknesses and anxieties, and more interested in them than he is in the objective events and outcomes of behavior.

These problems of a mismatch between the client's expectations and role skills and those of the counselor may account for much of the difficulty and awkwardness in counseling disadvantaged youth. They simply do not always behave in ways that the counselor has been led to expect from his work and training with middle class clients. It has been demonstrated in research on psychotherapy that length of stay in treatment is related to the extent of the match between the patient's and the therapist's expectations.[105] Where there is a mismatch, at best neither party feels that he understands the other, and each seems just too queer, too odd to inspire the desire to continue the relationship. At worst, to quote Hollingshead and Redlich:

> . . . the therapists interviewed disapproved of the dominant behavior patterns in the class V patients. They were repelled by their crude, vulgar language, their outbursts of violence, at times by their passivity and apathy, or by their acceptance of such behavior as a husband beating his wife and the wife taking the beating for granted, and their endurance of poverty and economic insecurity. The therapists were puzzled and upset over the sexual mores of their class V patients. As a group, the psychiatrists were irritated by the patients' inability to think in their terms.[106]

The counselor who assumes that his own sensibilities have precedence over the client's, because his own are right according to the norm-defining middle class (which owns and operates the agency in which he works), does not belong in the field of working with the disadvantaged, if he belongs in the field of counseling at all.

THE COUNSELOR AS AGENT OF SOCIAL CHANGE

The characteristics of disadvantaged boys presented in this chapter comprise what Linton has described as a "status personality." [107] That is, they are the kinds of behaviors that are products of the life experience of people who occupy a particular place in the social structure. They are the responses to that social status, and function adaptively within it. In short, we are not dealing here with individual psychopathology, but rather with the intersections of sociology, social psychology, and personality development, defining a modal personality pattern that, like every other personal-

[105] D. Levinson, "The Psychotherapist's Contribution to the Patient's Treatment Career," in *Research in Psychotherapy*, II, M. H. Strupp and L. Luborsky, eds. (Washington, D.C.: American Psychological Association, 1962), 13-24.

[106] Hollingshead and Redlich, *Social Class and Mental Illness.*

[107] R. Linton, *The Cultural Background of Personality* (New York: Appleton-Century-Crofts, Inc., 1945).

ity, is uniquely integrated into the conditions that created it and maintain it, and that it in turn maintains. The traits I have described are, in my judgment, necessary and lawful responses to the conditions of life, to the status of the poor young man in present American society and indeed in any society that tends toward rigidity of class structure and restriction of economic opportunity, and in which maturity and status are dependent on the individual's direct contribution to the productive economic life of the community. Unlike neuroses and maladjustments, these traits are not pathologies arising from individual and unfortunate accidents of traumatic experience or of birth to atypical parents. Rather, they are functional and adaptive responses to the socioeconomic facts of life. Indeed, a good deal of cross-cultural evidence suggests that almost wherever there are poor people, the kinds of personality attributes described in this chapter arise.[108] For where there is lack of money with which to purchase decent housing, to buy adequate food, to pay for medical care, almost all the rest follows: powerlessness, ghettoization, inferior schooling and thus inability to compete for jobs, apathy, illness, lack of energy, absence of hope, broken families and matriarchy, etc.

However much they are adapted to the conditions of poverty, jobless-ness, dependency, and powerlessness, the characteristics described are unfortunately ill-suited to the demands and needs of middle class life. And as the behavioral styles described in this chapter have created a "problem" for the middle class (welfare expenditures, labor shortage, aggression, crime and delinquency) there is pressure to change the lower class. But if lower class behaviors are responses to the conditions of lower class life, it would appear that middle class behaviors are likely to be elicited only as responses to the conditions of middle class life. If the poor are not suited to that life, it is because they have not had the opportunity to de-velop adaptations to it, for it has not been a life that was available to them. To provide the poor with the living conditions of middle class life, even if they are not adapted to it beforehand, is no more illogical than expecting an adaptation to middle class life *before* the conditions of that life are encountered as realities.

[108] Hoggart, *Uses of Literacy;* R. Redfield, "Peasant Society and Culture," in *Little Community and Peasant Society and Culture* (Chicago: University of Chicago Press, 1960), pp. 36-39; Lewis, *Children of Sanchez;* J. Mogey, *Family and Neigh-borhood* (London: Oxford University Press, 1956); E. Bott, *Family and Social Network* (London: Tavistock Publications Ltd., 1957); E. Padilla, *Up From Puerto Rico* (New York: Columbia University Press, 1958); M. Young and P. Willmott, *Family and Kinship in London* (London: Routledge & Kegan, Paul, Ltd., 1957); M. Kerr, *The People of Ship Street* (London: Routledge & Kegan, Paul, Ltd., 1958); D. Lerner, *The Passing of Traditional Society* (New York: The Free Press of Glencoe, Inc., 1958); R. Smith, *The Negro Family in British Guiana* (London: Routledge & Kegan, Paul, Ltd., 1956); Gans, *The Urban Villagers.*

However, counseling generally assumes that the locus of problems is in the individual client, rather than in the conditions to which he has adapted. This kind of counseling, as an instrument for changing lower class boys, will at best have an up-hill battle because it seeks to make them maladapted to the conditions of their lives while those conditions remain unchanged. At worst, such counseling will simply temporize by "taking the edge off" obstreperous behavior and directing it back at the individual as the locus of his problems, without revising the causes or conditions of his discontent. Most benignly, such counseling may be a palliative, helping a few individuals to move a little; but if there is no enduring structural change in the factors creating an infinite future supply of clients needing counseling, there will be no end to the counseling, and no possibility of anything but limited success. And what success is achieved will be at the price of deepening the self-blame for failure, already so deeply enmeshed in the problems of the poor, by agreeing with the premise that the causes lie in the individual and his responses, rather than in the conditions to which he is responding.

Thus my position is that though counseling is necessary for those who are already the products of the forces indicated, the more important task is structural socioeconomic change to end the production of disadvantage-ment, and that this goal represents a better and more productive use of the resources of counselors than a continued palliative effort to patch up the mistakes of the past without preventing the mistakes from recurring. If counselors are to be seriously concerned with the plight of the disad-vantaged, they should bend their efforts toward changing the societies in which boys grow up disadvantaged. Indeed, it seems to me that the most exciting and dramatically successful programs for working with disadvan-taged boys tend to be those that do just this; they in effect create a new social structure for the disadvantaged boy (Provo, Highfields, Essexfields, National Training School for Boys) in which behavioral change occurs in response to new conditions of life more consonant with productive work and achievement as a way of life. The task that faces all of us, then, is to make all of America the kind of supporting, rewarding environment in which effort and achievement are reliably crowned with success regard-less of the class, caste, or color of the worker, as has been achieved in the miniature societies built in Provo, Highfields, Essexfields, and Washington.

The vocational counselor stands at the crucial intersection of indi-vidual behavior and the structure of opportunities available to the indi-vidual. If he sees his job as primarily working with the individual, so that he is presumably better able to take advantage of the limited opportunities that are available, he will be doing only half his job, and that the easier half, since it manipulates the weak and the powerless while leaving the dominant majority safe, unchanged, and protected in its preservation of the better opportunities for itself and its own children. Thus it seems to me that only if the counselor sees himself as an agent of social change in the wider community of which he is a part can he take pride in carrying out the mandate of his profession. For it is only then that he will be stimulating natural and adaptive change in his clients, instead of engaging in psychological manipulation of them; it is thus the precondition of honesty in his profession.

SELECTED READINGS

1. Bandura, A., and R. Walters, *Social Learning and Personality Development*. New York: Holt, Rinehart & Winston, Inc., 1964.

2. Berger, B., *Working Class-Suburb*. Berkeley, California: University of California Press, 1960.

3. Clark, J., and E. Winniger, "Goal Orientations and Illegal Behavior Among Juveniles," *Social Forces*, 42, 1963.

4. Cloward, R., and L. Ohlin, *Delinquency and Opportunity: A Theory of Delinquent Gangs*. New York: The Free Press of Glencoe, Inc., 1960.

5. ————, and R. Ontell, "Our Illusions About Training," *American Child*, 47 (1965), 6-10.

6. Cohen, A., and H. Hodges, "Characteristics of the Lower Blue-Collar Class," *Social Problems*, 10 (1963), 303-334.

7. Gans, H., *The Urban Villagers*. New York: The Free Press of Glencoe, Inc., 1962.

8. Gordon, E., "Counseling and Guidance for Disadvantaged Youth," in *Guidance and the School Drop-out*, ed. D. Schreiber. Washington, D.C.: National Education Association and the American Personnel and Guidance Association, 1964, pp. 173-208.

9. Gordon, J., *Personality and Behavior*. New York: The Macmillan Company, 1963.

10. Leshner, S., and G. Snyderman, "Preparing Disadvantaged Youth for Work V: The Failure Cases in a Vocational Development Program," *Employment Service Review*, March, 1966.

11. ———— and ————, "Preparing Disadvantaged Youth for Work III: Work Adjustment Training," *Employment Service Review*, January, 1966.

12. Lewis, O., *The Children of Sanchez*. New York: Random House, Inc., 1961.

13. McDonald, R., "Some Characteristics of the Population Served by the Youth and Work Training Projects in New York City," *Report of the Youth and Work Training Programs*, 1964.

14. Miller, S. M., and G. Riessman, "The Working Class Subculture: A New View," *Social Problems,* **9** (1963), 86-97.

15. Riessman, F., *The Culturally Deprived Child.* New York: Harper & Row, Publishers, 1962.

16. Smuts, R., "The Negro Community and the Development of Negro Potential," *Journal of Negro Education,* **26** (1957), 456-465.

17. Urban League of Greater New York, "Center for School Dropouts Annual Report," 1963.

8

COUNSELING

THE DISADVANTAGED GIRL

BENNETTA B. WASHINGTON

Introduction

... Mary was an illegitimate child who grew up with a series of stepfathers. None of her mother's marriages worked, and she and her mother have "lived on welfare for as long as I can remember." She has lived in a number of foster homes, and admitted to being unhappy in most of them. In the eleventh grade, she became pregnant, and was unable to return to school after her child's birth. Because she put her child up for adoption, her mother will no longer have anything to do with her.

... In the eleventh grade, Jean left school because her mother had a nervous breakdown and needed a daughter at home to help out. She liked school and felt she would have remained if it had not been for her mother's condition. Some of her friends have been in jail, and have turned against her because she would not join them in their unlawful pursuits.

... Sally is an only child. Her parents are separated, and she has no idea where her father is. She dropped out of high school because she was bored, never went to classes anyway, and can't understand how she managed to reach her junior year before leaving. "I guess I was looking for somebody to put his foot down and tell me what I could and couldn't do. I never got that, so I just pushed my way out of school."

... Barbara decided to leave school when her mother received notice that, as soon as her daughter became 17 and eligible to work, their welfare payments would be terminated. She liked school while she was there. It had been difficult for her because she had attended schools in so many different cities. The only objection she had was to the rough boys in her classes—police were needed to guard classrooms, and she felt she wasn't learning anything.

. . . Grace was 17 years old and in the ninth grade. Her difficulty: poor knowledge of English. (She came here from Puerto Rico four years ago.) All her friends asked her how old she was, and she was ashamed to say. So, she quit school before they found out. Even if she had stayed in school, it would have taken her too many years to graduate.

The names of the above are fictitious; the cases are real. They serve to highlight the conditions of some of our young women, aged 16 to 21, living in poverty. Mary, Jean, Sally, Barbara, and Grace turned to Job Corps Centers for Women to acquire job skills, to escape permanently from their poverty-permeated environments. If they have found avenues for hope, for change, and for growth, their backgrounds exemplify those of 500,000 young women in their age and economic brackets—500,000 who continue to live on the fringes of the Great Society—untouched, unapproached by forces that carry the potential for economic and personal stimulation. But what about the millions of women across the nation who continue to lead marginal lives, hidden by the vastness of impersonal cities, *unseen, and unappreciated* by the multitudes around them?

Fourteen million women 16 and over—more than one fifth of all the women in the United States—are today among the 35 million people living in poverty. This is greater than both the numbers of impoverished men (10.5 million) and of impoverished children under 16 (also 10.5 million).

Women head 10 per cent of all families, but they head 25 per cent of poor families, and most significantly, 75 per cent of nonwhite poor families.

Many of the 14 million impoverished women work, but their levels of education and work skills are so low that their wages yield only bare subsistence. Others who need and want to work stay home because there is no one else to care for their children. And still others cannot find jobs because they are unskilled and untrained for the jobs available, or because they live in depressed areas where jobs are scarce, or are faced with multiple job discrimination because of race and sex.

Economic distress frequently occurs in families headed by a woman, regardless of whether she works or not. It is possible that one fourth of all nonwhite children are in a family with a woman at the head, and 86 per cent of these families are poor. Of all mothers under age 25, both white and nonwhite, listed as a family head, 80 per cent have insufficient income to care for themselves and their children. Clearly, one of the most pressing problems of our time is the young woman living in poverty.[1]

[1] Bureau of the Census, U.S. Department of Commerce, *Income of Families and Persons in the United States:* Series P-60, No. 41 (Washington, D.C.: Government Printing Office, 1962).

The question before the communities of America is, Shall we leave our young girls to develop under substandard conditions, with little or no constructive involvement? Or, shall we develop programs and attempt to deal with the problems of the impoverished girl and the children she will bear?

The questions before the counseling profession are: Can a counseling relationship help the impoverished girl better to understand herself? Can it help the counselor to understand the needs of the girl? Can it help the girl to begin to cope with the complexities of life; to begin to break the poverty-linked characteristics of poor education, lack of a job skill, poor health, and inability to mother a stable family?

The problems to be faced are: inadequate education, lack of job skills, disorganized family life, isolated community contacts, deprecation of self. Though these problems confront many women, they are intensified for the girl who has difficulty communicating verbally, cannot read, has failed in school, has found school boring and irrelevant, has been unable to hold a job, has major health defects, has been forced to move frequently, has lived under intensified overcrowded conditions, has few, if any, positive relations with adults, and, above all, has a poor estimate of her ability to cope with these problems.

The counselor working with such girls in a residential center, an employment service center, in a school, or in a community agency, must recognize the importance of decision points in the life of the counselee. He must recognize the importance of these critical points of decision from the counselee's perceptions of herself, rather than from his own. Thus, his major function may be that of a facilitator, of helping the girl to reach a stage of self-responsibility and maturity in decision making. In counseling the disadvantaged young woman, the problems of her previous life experiences, her motivation, her attitude toward new opportunities, her attitude toward herself, and her attitude toward authority figures, must be seen as major components of her total behavior pattern.

Thus the counselor must be conscious that the life experiences—the circumstances under which the individual lives, and has lived—cannot be isolated from the individual's concept of herself.

The counselor must view the girl as an individual, not as a member of a group, though her complex and differing moods, her tensions and frustrations are common to the more advantaged youth as well as to those sharing her general social condition.

As the segment of our society labeled youth is broken down into subgroups, by socioeconomic background, by sex, etc., the criteria used in defining the group, the general postulates developed about behavior, become more specific and more applicable to the individual. But membership in a group, no matter what its size or composition, necessitates sub-ordination of some part of the individual's personality.

As a recent advertisement for teenage apparel notes about girls:

> They dress alike
> eat like, dance alike
> act alike, walk alike
> talk alike, shriek alike
> sigh alike, giggle alike
> but underneath
> it all, no two girls are
> really alike.

Each individual is affected differently, and to a differing degree, by the same set of stimuli. Within the whole range of possible influences, distinctive combinations affect each individual. The result is that outlooks based on unique combinations form personalities of which these "conditional sets" are an integral part, and remain unique for each girl.

Who the Girl Is: Poverty Perspectives

Poverty stricken girls come from homes with few of the experiences that indicate readiness for learning, either intellectually or attitudinally. In most cases, the girl's view of society has been limited by her family and neighborhood where the struggle for day-to-day survival has been the primary concern. Most of the girls are school dropouts and have been unable to cope with the verbal, mathematical, and generally abstract components of the regular school program. Their failures in school, in work, in life, have contributed to their negative self-image. They do not know who they are, what they can do, or what they want to be. They are young but dying spirits—struggling, grasping, fighting to hold on to a life they know exists, but which they cannot reach without the support and guidance that fate and circumstances have denied them. Peculiarly, the only central link or pattern in these cases is a mangled family relationship, complicated by the condition of poverty.

Consider the backgrounds from which these girls come—the severely overcrowded homes; the unsanitary, often rodent-infested environment; the total lack of privacy. Consider the problems imposed by urban ghetto or rural isolation. Consider the problems where the other world and its other people are beyond comprehension and certainly beyond trust or relevance.

The economically deprived home produces vicious rivalry and dissatisfaction. Within many of these homes competition rages, the usual sibling rivalries intensified by too many sharing too little. The dress, the underwear, the second helping, the bit of personal attention and affection—all become the proverbial bone to be growled over and fought for. In homes such as these, girls learn as quickly as boys to cope with their insecurities and anxieties by exhibiting tremendous hostility and aggression.

In this atmosphere of emotional and material deprivation, the girl is given little respite in which to undergo the complex process of developing a healthy ego. She has little chance to learn mature methods of resolving conflict, and her personality remains unstructured and impulsive. Her impulsive behavior is strengthened by the fact that, in an environment where survival is precarious, temper tantrums, irrational hate, and anger become assets.

Girls born into geographic or ethnic isolation lack the knowledge, skill, and sophistication that would make them personally and socially adequate to meet the demands of a highly competitive world. Often they react with hostility toward their parents because they find them wanting and unhelpful in many respects. The school climate is alien to the girl's out-of-school environment and is therefore threatening to her. The world of work is unfriendly and often demeaning.

Moreover, in many instances, the girl's identification process is greatly complicated because there is no father in the home, or because the father is brutal. A girl who remembers her father as the man who beat her pregnant mother, or as the man who "dropped in" only once every month or two, and whom her mother educated her to resent and hate, will find it difficult to establish a healthy, constructive relationship with any man. Girls who have had unpleasant relationships with men feel threatened or disgusted by any further relationships with the male; *and when they have sons, what can one predict?*

In the poor homes where there is no father, it is the mother or grandmother who most often represents and maintains stability in the family. The girl must, inevitably, know consciously or subconsciously that her role is not only that of creator, but of preserver as well. Some girls from disadvantaged homes need the counselor's help in clarifying this role, since they do not believe that men can be responsible husbands. Such girls will need help in finding a way to wholesome family life.

In almost all cases, the disadvantaged girl cries out for affection, for love. This desire is not unlike that of any normal girl, but the concerted pressures resulting from deprivation tend to deepen the need. In an effort to meet her need for friendship, she gets involved early in highly emotional, introspective, and romantic relationships. Her image of these relationships contains little reality. At the same time, she is sensitive enough to perceive the "phony" among adults, realistic enough to recognize that these adults say one thing but do another. Resentment of such adults, added to defeat in the home, in school, and in the world of work, weakens the girl's desire to succeed and confirms her belief that a different life for her will never be possible. Therefore, she continues to search for the activity that will lead to immediate gratification or resorts to a world of fantasy, in which she romantically views herself as a movie queen. In many instances, when she comes to the counselor, she has been completely barred from social membership in a group that values learning, work, and the idea of a broader society; she may, however, be a valued member of a subgroup with very contrary values.

As does any woman, the disadvantaged girl has difficulty in connecting her earlier childhood role with the new roles she must assume: mother, housewife, worker, citizen. She feels there are too many lives to live, but she does not know which is good. And so she hesitates to choose a lasting model for her final identity. An adolescent girl, more often than a male contemporary, has difficulty in choosing occupational roles and committing herself to specific ideals. She is too confused by the contradictory models she sees in her home, her community, her school, her leisure-time contacts, her church, and in the mass media by which she is surrounded.

The effective counselor must use the general postulates derived from group behavior as a basis for getting closer to the individual.

A counseling approach that is effective for suburban white, Anglo-Saxon youth will not be appropriate for a minority group youth who has grown up in an urban ghetto. The disadvantaged young woman is an individual *and* disadvantaged—both aspects of her personality must be understood.

LIKE A MICROCOSM: THE MINORITY GIRL

Women around the world may be classified as disadvantaged. They are often relegated to inferior professional positions, due to their sex. Tradition has frequently limited them to specific spheres of endeavor; and these time-honored precepts have remained largely intact in the face of new conditions, new outlooks on life, and with full awareness that women are prepared, and aspire to become full participants in the events that shape their lives. The Report of the Committee on Women, prepared for the White House Conference on International Cooperation, clearly states the priorities for attention, the worldwide desires of women.

1. Education freely available to all, directed to the full development of the human personality including technical and professional training with access to counseling and guidance.
2. The elimination of poverty; free choice of employment with just and favorable remuneration; provision of a standard of living adequate for health and well-being, including food, clothing, housing, medical care, necessary social services, and social security.
3. The assurance of life of human dignity, with security of person, protection of the family. . . .

4. The right to participate in community life, and to take part in the government of her country, either directly or through freely chosen representatives.
5. The creation of a world in which understanding, tolerance and friendship exist among nations, racial and religious groups. . . .[2]

The above goals have direct applicability to the disadvantaged women in America, as well as to women throughout world society. For while all poor women need to be freed from their personal deprivations and sub-sistence-centered lives, women from minorities struggle under conditions of greater inequality than are common to women in general. Minority groups of women, with behavior and attitudes based on differing cultural traditions and heritages, need to be seen and assisted differently, so that they may strive to attain their goals on an equal footing with all women. To begin with, their economic status is lower than that of women in general, including white women classified as living in conditions of poverty.

The tradition of the Negro matriarchy has been often chronicled with direct reference to historical causes and to the changing role of the Negro male. But it is also necessary to understand how such a background affects the young Negro girl, whose cultural patterns are influenced by her family makeup. Her resulting attitudes and aspirations must be taken into consideration with cognizance of their environmental antecedents. Desire for personal and social achievement may appear nonexistent to the counselor; it is entirely likely that many of these young women have come from generations of deprivation, and know no alternatives. Hostility may be directed toward the counselor, if the girl feels he can't understand her and if she feels the latter is talking about unreachable goals; it may be directed toward society that has rejected her. But the evidence of hostility may in fact be a manifestation of rebellion against the circumstances which she feels set the boundaries of her life, but which she is unwilling to accept.

For the Negro girl, as well as for other individuals from other minorities who display hostility or apathy, it is necessary to concentrate initially on reachables, the attainment of which may facilitate further growth, and the strength to make greater strides.

Forty-six per cent of all nonwhite women work, compared to 36 per cent of white women; the nonwhite female earns only 64 per cent of what her white counterpart earns. While the recent emphasis on equality of employment and salary for all races should help to insure that nonwhite women's salaries are commensurate with those of white women, for equal work performed, the heart of the problem remains untouched. For the Negro female is engaged in occupations that have been relegated largely to members of her race. Legislation does not erase the fact that poor

[2] Report of Committee on Women, White House Conference on International Cooperation. Unpublished. October, 1965.

nonwhite women are paid low wages for unskilled work. The largest single category of employment for Negro women is that which is titled "service occupation." A full 56 per cent of Negro women are engaged in this work, the majority being hired for factory and household occupations.

The Negro girl cautiously seeks to enter fields where she sees Negro women already employed. Since there are still relatively few Negroes of either sex in professional jobs, and only 8 per cent of the adult female Negro population are currently in the professional and skilled occupations, a conscious effort must be made to help the girl become aware of opportunities that she may not know exist.

The counselor has a responsibility to increase his awareness of the presence of members of the girl's group in professional positions, and to emphasize the practicality of further education. The girl may also need to be prepared to better handle the rebuffs she has been conditioned to encounter.

She may need the help of the counselor also in interpreting her aspirations to her family, who often expect every child to contribute earnings to the household as soon as possible.

It is particularly important for the counselor of girls to be cognizant of existing public and private programs of occupational training, to be knowledgeable about continuing education, and to be aware of such undertakings as the work-study program, which may mean both a paycheck and the acquisition of education or training.

But most important, within all this, is the necessity for the counselor to be able to relate to the girl, to find avenues that will allow expectations to rise, and additional changes to follow. Only within a trusting relationship can hope develop; if the girl feels that the counselor cares about her, and believes in her as an individual, then the potential for personal development is greatly augmented.

WHERE SHE HAS TO GO: TOWARD A REALIZATION OF HER GOALS

Question: Who is the person you'd most like to be?
Answer: My philosophy, maybe it's wrong, is that I should build my own abilities instead of copying others. I just want to try to be myself.

The young lady in the above interview at a Job Corps Center for Women has achieved a major victory for herself. She has acknowledged her own worth. She is striving for personal development.

Toward what is the counselor striving, and to what end does he serve the disadvantaged girl? Thus far, the basic purpose has been to set forth the nature of the problem, and to suggest general frameworks for consideration. It has been mentioned that the girl needs to be encouraged to strive toward personal, social, and economic advancement; that these attainments are not mutually exclusive, but must build upon each other, and become integrated within the individual's frame of reference. But what will the attainment of these advances procure, and how will such achievement affect the girl's response and sensibilities to a broadened environment?

A counseling relationship, as it evolves, may enable the girl to see urban society more realistically than was previously possible. If the individual envisions herself as a functioning member of that society, she is more likely to view it favorably; but more significantly, she will be more interested in seeing herself within its structure, and will be more open to investigating how its complexities affect her, one of its members.

It is important that the girl acknowledge the multiple roles of women in America. The disadvantaged girl is likely to have come from isolated circumstances, where limited responsibilities and relationships have been the rule. The counselor can be a central figure for the successful confrontation of doubts and fears that, if considered by the girl in solitude, may be overwhelming.

What are the multiple roles she is likely to discover? Broadly speaking, she will find that women are actively engaged in three fundamental components of society: the family, the work world, and a local community—this last as a participating citizen, a member of a democratic society.

Each of these phases of a woman's life, so common and taken for granted by most, may reveal unthought of and unknown concepts for the individual who has been living on the fringes of society, rather than in its midst. Attitudes and actions that result from an indifferent societal upbringing may appear quite foreign to the poverty-ridden girl. Yet the counselor can facilitate comprehension of these phenomena, and therefore ease the transition from being a member of a neglected subculture to becoming a participant in the greater American society.

The disadvantaged girl, living in a family whose whole life is centered around the conditions of poverty, may see herself as a member of a unit whose sole existence appears to be that of staving off the next tragedy, stalling the landlord another week, or doling out food so that it can be stretched to serve as one more meal. Her concept of her role as a future mother is greatly influenced by her knowledge of and experience with her own mother. Her hopes for marriage may come from direct observations; or if she is quite horrified by the associations she has witnessed, she may revert to fantasies that, reinforced by the popular arts, create unrealizable idealizations.

It is important for the counselor to help girls to realize that marriage can and should be a positive institution, where love and respect do exist, where the father comes home, and is sober, and is instrumental in the governing of the household. She can be helped to understand the pressures and circumstances contributing to her parents' seeming failure, and encouraged to consider how her attitudes and efforts may make her own life different in a society where some changes are occurring. She needs to discard the notion that marriage and motherhood are just the next inevitable steps in life, neither desirable nor undesirable, but inescapable.

As the level of aspiration rises with the level of understanding and faith in the self, the young woman will find that she can have certain expectations; that all does not have to be simply accepted or endured. Developing a positive attitude toward the self, and hence toward life, will bring many revelations to the young girl who was once fearful of anything outside her realm of experience. These discoveries will help in the formulation of positive goals.

As the disadvantaged girl's self-esteem rises—as she begins to see herself as an individual of worth, possessing potential and individual and unique talents—she may find that work takes on new meaning. Hopefully, she will come to realize that she doesn't have to go out and look for just any available job; hopefully, she will learn that work is not performed solely for monetary return, without relation to interests and talents. She may find that certain tasks are particularly well-suited to her, and that she is actually capable of enjoying employment. Acquiring the feeling of pride in a task well done is an important step, and is a concomitant to the rise in self-esteem and aspiration.

Concurrently with the above is the realization that society can be a positive phenomenon. One does not have to fight all of life, nor come prepared to meet it with ready defenses and hostilities. As the self becomes important and positive, so will society be seen as a unit in which one is a participant, in many senses a partner. While all of society's dictates may not be desirable, the girl may nevertheless come to see its purpose as one that is enabling, rather than disabling to the individual. Her life within it can then be viewed as contributory, rather than solely dependent. She can accept its edicts, because she is an active participant.

The goal for the girl is actually one of integration of roles, within a positive conceptualization. It is also the ability to accept new experiences in a complex and rapidly changing world.

The counselor can be a mirror in which she is helped to see a reflection of herself as one respected, with the confidence and strength to permit her to adapt to whatever the future holds.

How She Gets There: Transitional Approaches

The transitions to be faced by the girl existing in the culture of poverty can be traumatic and fateful; the result may be that she is doomed to remain a victim of her environmental circumstances.

After the young girl has left school, with or without a diploma or degree in hand, with fond or embittered remembrances, she is subjected to a harsh and unceremonious rejection by the outside world. In all probability she sees no one to turn to, no opportunities to lead her to the kind of life she has every right to expect, but little actual hope of achieving.

It is within this setting that innovative programs have developed, and must continue to develop. There is no one answer; every avenue needs to be explored; there is room for an infinite number of approaches.

An emerging role for the school counselor is that of preparing the young individual for the transition from school to community before it has occurred. In this way the transference of roles of the girl may go more smoothly, and with less emotional upheaval and turmoil. What are some of these programs, and what new approaches do they offer?

The Job Corps Centers for Women have developed out of the belief that a residential program for young women can offer unique opportunities; that removal to a totally new environment can help to bring forth potentials that have lain dormant for a lifetime. The departure of the young woman from her circumstances of poverty, from a ghetto of fear, frustration, and hostility, is one means of freeing the individual of bonds and associations that have served to restrict horizons, determine behavior, and press the cycle of deprivation and hopelessness upon her.

Within a residential environment, where the young woman is allowed to pursue knowledge of herself and to acquire skills and abilities, a new life can be opened. The crowding oppressions of family and environment are not present to hamper growth; a well-structured program is designed to suit the needs of each individual, and serves to bring order to a previously disordered existence. While there is a degree of freedom and self-reliance heretofore unexperienced, the institutional structure does place limits on the girl—perhaps the first restrictions of her life. This enables her to see that expectations can be realized; that she is cared for, that others are concerned about her health and general well-being. Adults demonstrate that they believe in her, and are eager to assist her in all possible ways. She may see herself as central to their lives; perhaps for the first time in her life she is the one for whom others are working. Within this type of setting, the counselor is central to the program, as a coordinator of the various levels of learning, and as an aide to the girl who is attempting to find an order and logic in the events and experiences she is undergoing.

Counselors working in community agencies have invaluable opportunities for reaching out and meeting youths whose needs have not yet been met. Here the counselor can seek out youth; there is no need to wait for them to come to professional doors.

For too long the traditional approach to counseling has reigned; the counselor encased in his professional structure, serving only those who come to him. Individuals from depressed circumstances, in particular, are unlikely to be the aggressors in a counseling situation. Even when initially approached by the counselor, they are likely to shy away, to remain unimpressed, and display an attitude of "being above it all." The counselor must win the trust and respect of the youth of the streets before he is able to approach a counseling relationship of any depth. If the counselor remains at his desk, waiting for disheartened, dispirited individuals to come to him, he will never meet, far less influence, the youth he proclaims he is sincerely attempting to help. Counselors must take to the streets, to the ghettos, to the playgrounds; they must see the conditions of the deprived. The counselor hidden behind his mahogany paneling will never know the young women in our disadvantaged population, nor the environment that has been instrumental in forming their outlooks and personalities.

Each and every counselor, regardless of his professional milieu, has the potential for making a real contribution to the population of young women living on the outside of society. But it is mandatory that he shed his preconceptions; it is mandatory that he step down from the confines and the security of his office, view the lives of his counselees, and interact with them under actual stimuli, rather than responding to fabrications. Counselor and girl; they are to view themselves and each other as living bodies, as humans sharing life's disappointments and hopes, challenges and realities.

How We Counsel Her: New Perspectives

The problem of the counselor is not whether to imbue the young women with middle class values, or even whether to strengthen the many "positive aspects" of their own unique cultural backgrounds. Rather, the problem is finding and implementing ways to provide these young women with the skill and knowledge that will enable them to choose their own future direction, to make decisions meaningful to them, to change goals as horizons expand, and to break away from a life of isolation.

How can the counseling relation shift the disadvantaged girl's attitude from one of failure, hostility, and impotence, to one of success?

As indicated above, the starting point must be respect. Nothing that the counselor does will help the young woman understand herself if counseling and advice are offered with a contemptuous or patronizing attitude. The counselor must accept the girl's assets and liabilities without making moral judgments. Such acceptance will help the girl to recognize the traits that prevent her from achieving her highest potential; and, recognition achieved, the girl herself will be able to change those traits. The counselor's acceptance of the girl enables *her* to accept the counselor. This is the basis for the rapport that is essential in the counseling experience. Counselors of the disadvantaged must be perceptive, and must understand the nature and needs of the young women with whom they work.

The counselor does help to instill values. He has an important, and still developing role in this area. But he must prevent himself from attempting a direct transference of his values to his counselee. Rather, he should be concerned with instilling criteria, with providing information that will help the counselee to develop her own values, rather than to succumb to wholesale acceptance of another's values that may be dysfunctional for her. The goal is for the individual to see that the examined life is far more worth living than the unexamined life. She also needs assurance that she is capable of determining responsible attitudes for herself. The counselor is the tool whereby questions and answers may be discovered and investigated; he is not the answer.

We must search out the girls' strengths as well as their weaknesses. Many, for instance, communicate in a language that is not grammatical but is often rich, vivid, and expressive.[3] But, if the counselor feels that the girl's speech, her dress, her manner, and her background place her forever in the realm of inferior life—the girl will know it, and her damaging negative self-image will be reinforced. "What can you expect of a girl from a shabby background?" I once heard a counselor ask. The answer is, If you expect little, you will get even less.

On the other hand, the counselor who truly believes it possible to offer support and guidance to disadvantaged young women may achieve unbelievable results. If he is able to establish a climate of mutual trust, he may find an extraordinary determination on the part of the girl to change herself.

Each girl has a picture of herself as a person. The counselor must be concerned with understanding the depth of the girl's dissatisfaction with her present situation. Does she feel hopeless, helpless, unloved, worthless? Where is the balance between the desire for change and the will to change? Is her motivation to change her thought and behavior sufficiently strong to overcome her reservations about herself; strong enough to overcome the forces in her environment that work against change?

What a girl thinks of herself is one of the essential determinants of her behavior. The way she sees herself is perhaps her most important frame of reference. In order for behavioral changes to take place, self-concepts must be altered. Hope must be developed. A rehabilitative and therapeutic program must provide an accepting climate, free from threat and the necessity for defense. Praise for small accomplishments, plus the coun-

[3] Gisela Konopka, *The Adolescent Girl in Conflict* (Englewood Cliffs, N.J.: Prentice-Hall, Inc., 1966), p. 5.

selor's faith that the girl can succeed, are essential if the latter is to develop a better self-image.

One of the problems with which the counselor of deprived girls must cope is apathy. Withdrawal from the world is understandable when one's world is not good; but the greatest hope for such girls will come when they see possibilities for a good life. The counselor must, therefore, be a person who enables the girl to find new experiences, and to feel success in an environment in which she realizes the greatest satisfaction and sense of self-fulfillment. Most people can develop when given the right stimulus. Sometimes group recreational activities are used to help socially deprived girls develop a sense of accomplishment: they may feel more comfortable in what seems a play situation that develops the confidence needed in other more important activities.

Innumerable opportunities can be opened to the young woman to promote emotional growth; to develop a sense of involvement; to help her discover that following instructions, reading, working, and completing a task are actually pleasurable experiences.

In providing all this variety for successful experience, the counselor must be constantly on guard that he does not contribute to the psychological burdens of the disadvantaged girl. At no time should a status that may be construed as inferior be assigned to any task, for such a status may reinforce her negative image of self. At no time should a task be regarded as a segregated one for any particular racial or ethnic group of girls. The effect would be to isolate the girls from those they consider to be the more privileged members of society. At all times, the task assigned should be so developed that the dignity of the girl is respected and protected. One goal should always be the raising of each girl's personal ambitions, and her image of herself as a productive human being.

The urge to learn is basic in every individual. Deprived girls have learned to distrust the hostile, careless, unstable people they were forced to depend on. They have learned that rage and monetary power could be used to clothe fear and cover helplessness and despair. Adults could be made to flinch; other children could be frightened and made to run away. They learned invective instead of ordinary speech to convey feelings, and an unreasonable anger to communicate basic needs, frustration, and fear. They learned, with considerable skill, that with twisted methods and techniques they could enrage adults and render these adults as helpless in dealing with them as they themselves had been in dealing with privation.

The task of the counselor, then, is the difficult one of re-education—of helping the girl to unlearn the hateful lessons of her unfortunate youth. The promotion of ego development, needed to reinforce the girl's positive but arrested skills, is a formidable task. The atmosphere must be nonthreatening and there must be consistency in relationships. She is preparing to enter a social world that she will not recognize, having never known it. Limits must be clearly defined, yet freedom must exist to explore many points of view and to attach personal meaning to new insights. Self-direction and the inner controls that are essential to learning may then develop.

Some girls need specific help in planning for training and learning how to get a job after a baby comes. One survey indicated that three out of five preschool children of mothers working full-time were cared for by relatives or the other parent. There are facilities for the preschool child and counselors who interview disadvantaged girls should know these "day care" and other resources for the working woman.[4]

It is not easy for young people handicapped by economic and social disadvantages to evaluate their assets and liabilities. The disadvantaged girl may face the compound obstacle of poverty and prejudice. She finds herself in a rapidly changing society that, while demanding personal responsibility and growth, does not provide equal opportunity for the self-discovery and self-realization essential to maturity and growth.

Purposeful and intelligently directed action can be effective in helping the girl to escape from the perpetual deprivation and helplessness associated with the absence of work-related skills and personal insight.

Certainly, study after study has shown that it is during the adolescent stage more than any other that we find the individual seeking acceptance —that it is here that she wants most to become what those she respects want her to become. From this point of view, the counselor must recognize that the young woman, fearing one more rejection, experiences difficulty in letting the counselor know what she feels and thinks about herself. Therefore, the counselor must establish a nonthreatening relationship, rather than one in which the young girl fights to determine whether she should present herself as she senses herself to be, or as she thinks the counselor would like her to be. And yet, the counselor must necessarily see his role as contributing to the girl's growing understanding of herself so that the girl can cope with the multiplicity of roles she must play.

What the counselee is finding out about herself must then be related to the environment in which she experiences the greatest satisfaction and sense of self-fulfillment. This means that the counselor must not only perceive the characteristics of the girl, but must know the many kinds of growth experiences that might be made available to her.

In working with disadvantaged youngsters, the emphasis should be on the choices that will contribute to the greatest possible growth of the individual, and will help to prepare the individual for the rapidly changing

---

[4] Marguerite Zapoleon, *Occupational Planning for Women* (New York: Harper & Row, Publishers, 1961), pp. 5, 17, 21, 22, 28, 37.

kind of society in which she must function. In other words, the counselor is helping the girl to chart a voyage of self-discovery by finding out many ways in which she can function as a valuable and a unique person.

The counselor must also know where others can function in the counseling experience: where peer groups can be utilized to help in developing self-understanding; where group experiences may yield the most insights for the young person in terms of self-understanding.

Very often the disadvantaged girl has a desperate need to work through her relations with adults, but finds she cannot do this alone with one person in authority. She must talk, but she talks more readily and more easily with other girls. Therefore, it is necessary to provide her with the opportunity to talk with other girls in the presence of an adult who will listen and sympathize, but not direct. In this setting, the girl can discuss problems openly and relate closely to others, and at the same time know that someone is there to protect her if she should need support. Group counseling provides one means of achieving our objectives.

Given the probability that nine out of ten women will have to work outside the home, we also recognize the increasing importance of the unified family in breaking the cycle of deprivation, the role of the female as central to the family, and the necessity for an intelligent citizenry in our democratic way of life. We must recognize, too, that counseling is as necessary and critical for disadvantaged young girls as it is for members of any other underdeveloped segment of our society. The counselor of the disadvantaged girl must be supportive in helping these young women find the self-respect and self-confidence to function in their multiple roles. He can help young people build on even the most unrealistic ideas, helping them turn their interests to more practical channels.

The counselor must be respectful of the talents of these girls, even if these talents differ from those he had regarded as standard, even if they differ from the kind of talents he has. We are all aware of the tendency to be threatened by the unknown, and by the talent that someone may possess that we do not possess, or have not been familiar with.

The counselor must recognize that his personal problems can interfere with his effectiveness as a counselor. The situation becomes more difficult when the counselor has a personal need for power. Under no circumstances must the counselor let his own values interfere with his acceptance of the counselee. If either party to the relationship does not get some satisfaction, the situation will develop unsatisfactorily. Energy that goes into the power conflict is not productive energy for purposes of guidance and counseling success.

The counselor must be aware of the fact that every individual has his own bias. However, biases can and must be dealt with. Personnel who work with disadvantaged girls should be warm and generous adults who have worked through their own conflicts and can expect the confusion of adolescents who have different value standards.

VOCATIONAL GUIDANCE

Vocational guidance may be incorporated into professional counseling and serve in a complementary and enriching manner. Consideration or acquisition of vocational goals may be invaluable in raising the self-esteem and the aspirations of the individual. As the counselee becomes aware of herself as a unique person, exploration of job potentials may help to reinforce her emerging view of self, and help her to view channels through which she can contribute. As the girl gains a positive self-image, she will become more interested, and more hopeful for her future. She will be more likely to be interested in joining society as an active participant. With the aid of the counselor, concurrently with, or near the termination of her self-analysis, she may begin to look for avenues that will allow her to live as she sees, or would like to see, herself.

The usual vocational guidance approach of helping youth to make long range plans is not suitable for most girls from families where there is no security—and little hope. The development of long range plans and a "vocational choice" for a girl who hasn't finished elementary school is usually impractical at best. The needs of the moment loom too large in her thinking to permit the type of vocational choice that many counselors have been trained to try to develop. Young girls who have lived with hunger and all the other ills of poverty do not easily think far into the future. They are not aware of the horizons available to them. If their awareness of possibilities is not developed, then they will continue to think in terms of the jobs they know about—those that their impoverished circumstances have brought to their attention. Such jobs, needless to say, generally provide little opportunity for escape from the poverty syndrome, little challenge or relation to the perhaps latent interests and inclinations of the individual.

The girls cannot be expected to think in terms of long range plans and goals when short range needs are pressing. Counseling, therefore, must often be for short range goals: the next step, good general direction. This is not to say that the disadvantaged girl may not be ambitious and go far. She may be very ambitious and highly motivated, but her counseling needs may initially be in terms of next achievable steps rather than toward a definite vocational choice.

The counselor accustomed to meeting the problem of the sometimes unrealistically high job aspirations of the suburban youth may discover that the girl afflicted with poverty has adjusted her sights far too low in terms of her potential.[5] She tends to seek the kinds of jobs that women in her milieu have been doing.

In a group of 291 girl dropouts (mostly Negro) from the slums of Philadelphia in a special program for "Hard-To-Place" youth, 31 said they wanted "Clerical Work," most said they wanted "Factory Work," floor work, nurse's aide jobs, sales, sewing machine operating, waiting on tables, and counter work.[6] The only professional ambition mentioned was "artist" by two girls. Five girls said they wanted to be models.

The report of a work conditioning project for dropout youth conducted by the Philadelphia Jewish Employment and Vocational Service provides interesting information concerning placement of girls by the Pennsylvania Bureau of Employment Security. The percentage of girls placed in unskilled jobs was higher than for boys—61 per cent as compared to 21 per cent. The percentage of girls and boys placed in trainee jobs was the same (32 per cent). This included work assembling, bookbinding, pressing, sewing machine and other operating jobs.[7] Usually, however, there would be a higher percentage of placements in the service industries for similar applicants.

For some girls, vocational plans are for limited periods before marriage and childbearing. Career patterns for girls represent a combination of school, work, and marriage. Havighurst [8] reports than an analysis of the career patterns of girls 15 to 20 years of age in which school dropouts comprised 34 per cent of the sample revealed that more than half the dropout girls were waiting for marriage. Approximately 3 per cent planned work to the exclusion of marriage, and approximately 14 per cent of the girls planned a combination of marriage and work.

It has been estimated that a woman may have as much as 40 years of life remaining after she places her last child in school. Thus, some of those girls who did not plan to work will eventually need and seek employment; but any long range vocational counseling they may have received during adolescence will undoubtedly have been forgotten during the interim.

Women are more handicapped than men because of the greater unpredictability of what roles they will play, and the timing of those roles.

[5] *Consultation on the Occupational Preparation of Women.* Department of Labour, Canada, 1962.

[6] George Snyderman, "Experimental Program for Hard-to-Place Youth." Unpublished. (Philadelphia: Pennsylvania Bureau of Employment Security, 1960).

[7] Joseph Messick, "The Employment Service Cooperates," in *Preparing Disadvantaged Youth for Work* (Washington, D.C.: U.S. Department of Labor, 1966), p. 12.

[8] R. J. Havighurst, "Counseling Adolescent Girls in the 1960's," *The National Vocational Guidance Quarterly,* Spring, 1965, pp. 153-160.

The effects upon a woman of such unpredictable hazards as illness in the home, the death of her husband, or of divorce or separation all have to be taken into account in her work plans.

When girls with limited education are referred to or placed in jobs that do not utilize their full potential, they should be encouraged to take advantage of opportunities to complete their general education while working.

Counseling after placement as well as before may be crucial, particularly if the girl is entering an occupation formerly closed to one of her group. In this connection, it should be recognized that knowledge of the kinds of jobs held by nonwhite women in the past gives only a general indication for future planning since hiring patterns for nonwhites are changing.

VOCATIONAL INTERESTS

While surveys and testing program results are often interesting, and may be very helpful to the counselor, they often refer to a general population, or are based on tests not yet completely validated for use with young people who have grown up outside the mainstream of American life.

Most vocational guidance literature does not differentiate between boys and girls in citing the information to be given youth, nor does it distinguish between methods of dealing with girls and with boys. However, research has indicated there are some sex differences in vocational interests. Strong found that feminine leanings are toward musical, artistic, and literary interests; people, especially those needing help; clerical work; teaching; and social work.

A large majority of women and girls responding to the Strong Vocational Interest Blank for Women achieve their highest interest scores on three occupational scales: Housewife, Stenographer-Secretary, and Office Worker. The "general factor" underlying these scales has been variously labeled "generally feminine interests," "interest in male association," or "nonprofessional interests." There is a clear-cut sex difference in the shapes of profiles shown on the Strong scales of men's and women's interests.[9]

The counselor needs to realize that if the potential of the disadvantaged girl is to be realized, she needs to step higher and higher. This is true of those who come to the counselor with vocational goals, as well as those that develop vocational interests through their relation with the counselor. It does not suffice to say, Mary has a definite job goal in mind.

[9] Wilbur L. Layton, *Counseling Use of the Strong Vocational Interest Blank,* Minnesota Studies in Student Personnel Work, No. 8 (Minneapolis: University of Minnesota Press, 1958), p. 40.

She wants to be a waitress, or a typist. Evidence of a goal does not imply suitability or contentment if and when the goal is reached. Often those who do have vocational goals in mind adhere to the motion that women become only office workers, waitresses, or receptionists. The individual's horizon of knowledge determines her awareness of available opportunities from which to choose. It will then be to her advantage to postpone making a vocational choice until she is more fully aware of the actual situation.

Nine out of ten women work at some time in their lives. But not until individual girls perceive this fact as reality can they be expected to be receptive to long range vocational planning. Some who need vocational counseling, but are not receptive to it, will respond to interest in their general future and welfare. Because more than many girls, she will face the necessity of work as well as homemaking, the disadvantaged girl should be stimulated and guided into thinking in terms of preparing for marriage and work.

Her vocational choice may be seen as an ever-evolving process. The disadvantaged young woman should be exposed to a series of vocational experiences so that she may become increasingly realistic about her strengths and handicaps. The counselor must stay open-minded to the discovery of hidden and underdeveloped talents. In the residential setting, in the school setting, in the employment service setting, in the setting of the community agency, the counselor does not operate in a vacuum; rather, he works with a counselee whose perceptions of self are being continuously modified by the kind of experiences she is undergoing. The counselor's emphasis must be on helping the young woman to develop her individuality, to personally discover and accept a value system, to develop skill in making personal decisions in a highly complicated world.

As the counseling profession increases its role in assisting the disadvantaged, and heightens its sensitivities to their problem, it is to be hoped that many more of our young will have the opportunities they deserve. A Job Corps enrollee has stated, quite simply, what these opportunities mean to her. We need to take heed, and provide similar experiences for the thousands like her, who remain outside our grasp, isolated from our thoughts.

... I am learning and accomplishing a lot of things I never knew before. The Job Corps gave me this opportunity to come to a large city, a new environment with more hopeful surroundings, meet a lot of people, continue my education, and train for the kind of job I want in the future. It really gives me the opportunity to make something of myself. It is also going to help me reach a new goal in life. It gave me this chance to come to a new environment where the situations are better and where the doors of opportunity are open wide. Not only for me, but for a lot of others who want hope, opportunity, education, and a better job.

SELECTED READINGS

1. Bureau of the Census, U.S. Department of Commerce, *Household and Family Characteristics*, Series P-20, No. 125 (March, 1962).

2. Bureau of the Census, U.S. Department of Commerce, *Income of Families and Persons in the United States*, Series P-60, No. 41 (1962).

3. Bureau of Labor Statistics, U.S. Department of Labor, *Employment and Earnings* (February, 1964).

4. Bureau of Labor Statistics, U.S. Department of Labor, *Labor Force and Employment in 1963*. Special Labor Force Report No. 43.

5. Bureau of Labor Statistics, U.S. Department of Labor, *Marital and Family Characteristics of Workers*. Special Labor Force Report No. 40.

6. Committee on Women, White House Conference on International Cooperation, unpublished report (October, 1965).

7. Davidson, Helen H., and Gerhard Lang, "Children's Perception of Their Teachers' Feelings Toward Them Related to Self-perception, School Achievements, and Behavior," *Journal of Experimental Education*, December, 1960.

8. Department of Labour, Canada, *Consultation on the Occupational Preparation of Women* (1962).

9. Havighurst, R. J., "Counseling Adolescent Girls in the 1960's," *The National Vocational Guidance Quarterly*, Spring, 1965, pp. 153-160.

10. House Committee on Education and Labor, *Poverty in the United States* (1964).

11. Konopka, Gisela, *The Adolescent Girl in Conflict*. Englewood Cliffs, N. J.: Prentice-Hall, Inc., 1966.

12. Layton, Wilbur L., *Counseling Use of the Strong Vocational Interest Blank*, Minnesota Studies in Student Personnel Work, No. 8. Minneapolis: University of Minnesota Press, 1958.

13. Pollack, Jackson, "Girl Dropouts—A Neglected National Tragedy," *Parade Magazine*, September 26, 1965.

14. Riessman, Frank, "The Helper Therapy Principle," Mobilization for Youth, Inc., New York, mimeographed report.

15. Snyderman, George, "Experimental Program for Hard-to-Place Youth," Pennsylvania Bureau of Employment Security, unpublished report, 1960.

16. Washington, Bennetta B., "Books to Make Them Proud," *National Educational Association Journal*, May, 1966.

17. Zapoleon, Marguerite, *Occupational Planning for Women*. New York: Harper & Row, Publishers, 1961.

9

COUNSELING
THE SCHOOL DROPOUT

WILLIAM C. COTTLE

Introduction

In a period when youth unemployment is three times that for other workers; when unemployment for nonwhite youth is almost double that for white youth; when high school graduates have much less unemployment than nongraduates; when the availability of fewer farm jobs causes more youths to move to urban areas where fewer jobs are available, something more than the traditional approach to the dropout problem is needed.

The person who drops out of school before high school graduation faces steadily increasing problems of employment, and consequent increases in problems of earning a living in an automated society. The *Manpower Report of the President* points out:

Though the proportion of young people graduating from high school is rising, 3 million, or 45 per cent, of the 16- to 21-year-old youth out of school in February 1963 had not completed high school. . . . Of the nonwhite out-of-school youth, 3 out of every 5 lacked high school diplomas. This is not the whole story. Nearly a fourth of the dropouts had completed no more than the 8th grade, and 2 out of 3 had left school before completing the 10th grade. Over 1 million (of the total of 3 million) had dropped out before they were 16, and 400,000 when they were 14 or under. And around 40 per cent were below the normal grade for students of their age when they left school. Clearly, an effective "back to school" program must recognize the need to repair major educational deficiencies and, often, to use new educational tools and techniques for this purpose.

Dropouts typically leave school too early to obtain a significant amount of vocational education and their lack of general education—in many cases, even of basic verbal and arithmetic skills—makes it very difficult to get such training later on. Thus the gap widens—only 10 per cent of the dropouts in the February 1963 survey had received formal training since leaving school, compared with 30 per cent of the high school graduates.[1]

It is obvious from these facts that older approaches to the problem of the school dropout have not been successful. The traditional approach to the dropout problem has been to carry on research that describes students who have left school before graduation (Eckert and Marshall, 1938; Dillon, 1949; Isaacs, 1953; Summerskill, 1964; Cervantes, 1965), and try to get such students to return to school. The description of actual dropouts is a necessary preliminary to further research in identifying *potential* dropouts before they leave school.

The second part of the approach, urging dropouts to return to school, is highly unrealistic. Many of them left because the school failed to meet their needs. Merely putting on a campaign to urge them to return is useless. They need counseling help to explore all the possible alternatives open to them; and then they *should* be permitted to make *their own* choice. A school diploma for these individuals is not the sacred cow that the school, parents, employers, and others in the community have tried to make it. It is much more important that they be helped to an effective job placement in work they can do, perhaps for the rest of their lives. If added training is needed before they can do such work, they should be helped through counseling toward choices that will make such training effective and possible.

Definitely, a fresh approach is needed. The 1966 *Manpower Report of the President* states that, while unemployment in the United States was less than four per cent, unemployment of youth aged 16-21 was 12.5 per cent and that for nonwhite youth was 21 per cent. These figures include both graduates and nongraduates. This suggests that a new approach to the education and counseling of potential and actual dropouts should be developed. All groups in the community must become involved in helping dropouts: the school, parents, government and voluntary agencies, service organizations; and particularly, efforts must be made to tap the tremendous resources possessed by labor, and by business and industry.

It is questionable, however, that the community's interest in helping the dropout should result in some other agency's taking over the functions

[1] *Manpower Report of the President* (Washington, D.C.: Government Printing Office, 1966).

that should be performed by the schools. Preparation for the world of work, like preparation for higher education, is a function properly delegated to the schools. Until everyone in the community has made a sincere and thorough effort to help the schools achieve this, the responsibility of providing education for a profit should not be delegated to private enterprise. This should be a last resort. The immediate objective should be to improve the schools by joint community effort, not to replace the schools by some other organization. In question also is the *psychological* effect involved in transporting youth great distances from their homes to some isolated spot where they have to depend on some strange, hastily organized, self-contained unit for every need during rehabilitation.

The first step in any new approach to the effective preparation of the potential dropout for the world of work is to identify him so that a counselor can work with him. One of the obstacles to such identification and counseling has been the lack of joint effort by schools and other organized groups in the community that are equipped to contribute to the solution of this problem. If the potential dropout can be identified before he leaves school, the resources of the school and of the rest of the local community can be mobilized to help him achieve a maximum placement, either in school or in the community at large. The school has a twofold responsibility in this case. It must mobilize its own resources, and request additional help from other organizations—public and private, local and national—in areas where those others are better prepared to cope with the needs of a given dropout while he is still in school, or when he leaves. The school must also bear the responsibility and obligation of giving to other agencies in the community the information it has collected about the longitudinal behavior of a given dropout so that the other organizations may take over the attempt to help him accomplish best his own purposes, and society's expectations for him.

Monthly lists of dropouts should be given by the school to the other agencies cited. If one such individual has a physical or mental handicap, his name should be given to the local representatives of the state vocational rehabilitation services, preferably before he leaves school. Names of nonhandicapped dropouts should be given to the state employment service so that its resources can be brought to bear to call them in for placement, counseling, job development, or training. The school should expand its cooperation with the counselors of the state employment service. This latter service provides specialized personnel for employment testing to help school pupils make more appropriate job choices when they leave school, and for employment counseling either at school or in the employment service office.

In addition to making the above services available in the school, the state employment services have recently developed Youth Opportunity Centers, and have worked out cooperative programs with government agencies also providing services to youth in need of training or work. Other government agencies are the Job Corps and the Community Action Programs of the Office of Economic Opportunity; the Neighborhood Youth Corps; training under the Manpower Development and Training Act; training provided under the Area Redevelopment Act; and the training provided under the various education acts, from Project Head Start to the Higher Education Act.

In like manner, if service organizations, such as Kiwanis or Rotary, are in a position to help a given dropout, the school should inform them. Labor organizations or private industry should be asked to mobilize their resources when they most effectively contribute to a dropout's plans after he leaves school. It is the responsibility of the school to show how they can do this. Insufficient use has been made of the tremendous sources of help that labor and business and industry can be to the effective placement of individuals who drop out of school.

For example, business and industry could undertake specific activities intended to encourage pupils to remain in school, or to undertake further training if they leave school before graduation. Such activities could include:

1. Making the school aware of the common needs of most employers so that the curriculum could be revised to help pupils prepare themselves for such needs.

2. Earmarking entry jobs for dropouts who could not remain in school, and tying these in with training programs.

3. Revising or developing business and industrial training programs open to school dropouts to supplement, but not duplicate, the offerings of the school.

4. Providing *temporary* summer work for school pupils so that they can learn about the many job skills they will need to earn a living. This should be coupled with an orientation to most jobs in the participating plant or business, particularly the beginning ones.

5. Providing part-time jobs (similar to the Neighborhood Youth Corps Program) labeled "Earn for Education" during the school year, to help pupils earn enough to remain in school until graduation.

6. Bringing in more school personnel for the summer and showing them differences in the jobs dropouts and high school graduates would get. Then the school people would be in a position to discuss these differences with their pupils.

Similarly, labor organizations could provide valuable help in the total community attack on the dropout problem. Some of their efforts could involve:

1. Developing a program aimed specifically at selecting and training dropouts with potential for a given trade or industry.
2. Realistically expanding the number of apprentices and *really* eliminating all barriers to acceptance of qualified youth in training programs.
3. Accepting the challenge of making a competent worker of the non-white youth.
4. Encouraging continuance in school by awards and scholarships for children of parents below the professional and semiprofessional occupational levels.

As all these community organizations bring their resources to bear on an attempt to decrease the number of school dropouts, or to prepare them most effectively for appropriate jobs if they must leave school, the school should be the central agency in all efforts toward helping the *potential* dropout before he leaves. After he has decided to leave school, the public employment service is usually in a key position to help him through placement in a job, employment counseling, or referral to the organization best able to provide the help he needs. This does not mean that either of these agencies should monopolize this function. However, they are usually in the best position to coordinate such activities, and to assume the obligation of passing on data about a specific individual when it is obviously the task of some other organization to help him adjust or adapt to a nonschool setting.

IDENTIFYING THE DROPOUT

We are only beginning to develop techniques of identifying the school dropout *before* he leaves school. As indicated above, until quite recently the research on the school dropout has centered upon identification and description of dropout characteristics. Such identification has consisted of seeking out pupils who have left school prior to graduation and have not returned. Some studies have been of such short duration that they have included and described as dropouts pupils who later returned to school. Some of the most recent research on *college* dropouts has indicated that some of them return later and are graduated over a period extending as long as ten years.[2] A similar situation may exist with dropouts at the junior and senior high school levels; but, because of other community

---

[2] J. Summerskill, "Dropouts from College," in *The American College: A Psychological and Social Interpretation of the Higher Learning*, ed. N. Sanford (New York: John Wiley & Sons, Inc., 1964), pp. 627-657.

pressures, this is not as likely. Our present school populations are so mobile that it is hard to know whether such a situation exists. Because of poor pupil accounting processes, it may never be known whether a pupil classed as a dropout by one school enters (perhaps ultimately graduating from) another school.

In addition, in our larger cities (where the bulk of the dropouts occur), the pupil accounting systems have not been adapted to identify a dropout. Conducting research on dropouts as recently as 1962, this author was told by representatives of the New York City school system that it would be too involved to find out what junior high school pupils had failed to attend senior high school and, therefore, that research on potential dropouts involving these two school levels in New York City was not practical. For similar reasons, the Boston city schools also refused to participate in such research.

Another facet of the identification problem is that many local school authorities have been more concerned with concealing than with exploring the dropout situation in their schools. Perhaps because the dropout demonstrates undesirable characteristics, or needs the school cannot meet, it is easier to heave a sigh of relief when he leaves school and becomes someone else's problem. Federal and local projects to encourage dropouts to return to school, while highly worthwhile in their objectives, have also contributed to the difficulty of identifying the real school dropout from those who remain in school or those who return to school after dropping out. All of these factors have made identification of the potential school dropout a difficult process. However, once the dropout has been identified, research studies have proceeded to describe his attributes.

Usually, the listing of characteristics of those who have left school has constituted such descriptions of dropouts. Cervantes states that the twenty characteristics listed below are common among potential or actual dropouts:

School

1. Two years behind in reading or arithmetic at seventh grade level. Majority of grades are below average.

2. Failure of one or more school years (1st, 2nd, 8th, 9th grades most commonly failed; 85 per cent of dropouts behind one year; 53 per cent two or more years).

3. Irregular attendance and frequent tardiness. Ill-defined sickness given as reason.

4. Performance consistently below potential.

5. No participation in extracurricular activities.

6. Frequent change of schools.

7. Behavior problems requiring disciplinary measures.

8. Feeling of "not belonging" (because of size, speech, personality development, nationality, social class, family disgrace, retardation in school, dress, lack of friends among schoolmates or staff, etc.).

Family

9. More children than parents can readily control (e.g., only child for divorced and working mother; five or more for nondivorced and working mother of blue and lower white-collar class).

10. Parents inconsistent in affection and discipline.

11. Unhappy family situation (common acceptance, communication, and pleasurable experiences lacking; family solidarity minimal).

12. Father weak or absent.

13. Education of parents at eighth grade level.

14. Few family friends; among these few many problem units (divorced, deserted, delinquents, dropouts).

Peers

15. Friends not approved by parents.

16. Friends not school oriented.

17. Friends much older or much younger.

TAT (*Psychological orientation*)

18. Resentful of all authority (home, school, police, job, church).

19. Deferred gratification pattern weak.

20. Weak self-image.[3]

Cervantes also presents case data on dropouts, and verbal self-descriptions supporting the conclusions listed above, and providing an intimate and realistic picture that contrasts the behavior of dropouts and matching stayins.

If the approach to the dropout problem is based on the above data, it is well to remember that some dropouts return to school, voluntarily or with help from others. In addition, those who leave school permanently make up at least two distinct kinds of dropouts.

One kind of dropout is the person whose behavior is unstable or inconsistent for various reasons, and whose dropping out of school is difficult or impossible to predict. This dropout may be somewhat emotionally disturbed; and because he drops out of school as a result of a whim, or because of momentary pressures, it is difficult to predict that he will do

---

[3] Rev. L. F. Cervantes, S.J., *The Dropout: Causes and Cures* (Ann Arbor: University of Michigan Press, 1965).

this, or when he may do it. Another impossible-to-predict case is that of the girl who becomes pregnant and cannot continue school, whether she marries or not. It is also difficult to predict what will happen to the father, if he is in school.

Ferrer discusses this in a newspaper article concerning the confused rules over the United States about married or unmarried pupils and their continuance in school. He says:

There is no question that the number of student marriages has risen dramatically. Almost half of all girls in the country are married before they are 20, according to the nonprofit population reference bureau in Washington, against a 1963 figure of 44 per cent. Two years ago, the U.S. Office of Education asked Lawrence W. Knowles, associate professor at the University of Louisville's law school, to study the constitutional implications of school administration. Knowles has completed his research on 350 school districts and how they deal with the problem of the married student. The constitutional issue is whether the 14th Amendment is violated when married pupils are denied an education through expulsion or suspension. . . .

In many states a child is required to attend school until 16 years of age, whether married or not. Only four cases have considered whether a married child can be compelled to attend school. The answer was no in all cases. . . .

Knowles found few districts require married pupils to attend school; to the contrary, board policies tend to discourage them from coming. . . .

Some schools simply suspend married students for half a year, which usually means they never return to school. They are damaged in terms of earning power for a lifetime.

When a girl becomes pregnant, Knowles found, all 350 school districts suspend her, but at varying times of her pregnancy, from early discovery of pregnancy to the eighth month. Knowles feels there is "no justification for dismissing pregnant girls before the pregnancy is clearly apparent." [4]

The closer individuals in this category come to graduating, the more they resemble school graduates. Fewer differences exist between these dropouts and graduates; therefore it is less possible to predict they will leave school. If possible at all, prediction of these dropouts would require an intimate knowledge of their self-psychology that only a professional counselor or a trusted teacher is apt to possess. Such knowledge is often the result of establishing a relation with the dropout of the sort that will cause him to come to talk about his intention to leave school. It might be possible to predict some of these dropouts in some other manner not widely used at present, such as the self-report instruments discussed below.

A more predictable kind of dropout is the person whose behavior over a long period, as shown in cumulative school records, includes indications that he is retarded in school; weak in essential academic skill areas;

[4] T. Ferrer, "Married Student Dilemma Revealed" (New York: Herald Tribune News Service, April 17, 1966).

strongest in skill areas not covered by his particular school, or motivated toward activities other than those the school offers to him. This person can be identified and helped, if the school has kept adequate records, and if it has personnel who have the time and skill to use these records.

Two recent research approaches have given evidence that school personnel can identify the would-be dropout before he leaves school, so that it is possible to work with him to achieve a maximum use of his *potential*, and the most effective placement possible for him. However, as indicated earlier, it is a definite mistake to undertake this task with the objective of keeping *all* potential dropouts in school. Rather, the objective should be the most appropriate placement for each individual in terms of his knowledge and his choices: in school, when this is indicated by the individual's situation and choices, and where the school still meets his needs; or out of school, when exploration of the situation causes the individual to choose some other training or job placement as more appropriate for him. A counselor, teacher, parent, or person other than the potential dropout cannot make these choices for him.

One of the methods for identifying the potential dropout before he leaves school is that proposed by the Illinois Department of Public Instruction.[5] Here school data about a given pupil are used in a system similar to a mathematical equation to find those pupils most apt to leave school prior to graduation. When the school records are complete enough, a high percentage of school dropouts can be predicted by this method. The two drawbacks in using this method are the fact that many pupil records are incomplete, and the considerable amount of in-service training of school personnel needed to insure that records *are* complete and accurate enough to be useful. Considerable in-service training is also necessary before school personnel are prepared to *use* these records effectively. In addition, much staff time and effort are required to assemble data from records to accomplish this purpose. Advanced preparation is necessary if the data are to be coded on cards to be used in a computer system.

Another recent approach to the identification of the potential dropout entails the use of self-report instruments or self-inventories, such as *The School Interest Inventory*.[6] These instruments attempt to combine items covering the factors included in school records with items about the individual's attitude toward school, work, home, and other known causes of leaving school. The inventories represent an attempt to quantify the self-psychology of the potential dropout with particular reference to motiva-

[5] Illinois Department of Public Instruction, *Procedures for the Identification of Potential High School Dropouts* (Springfield, Ill.: Office of the Superintendent of Public Instruction, 1962).

[6] William C. Cottle, *Manual for the School Interest Inventory* (Boston: Houghton Mifflin Company, 1966).

tional factors involved in his approach or attitudes toward school. Research contrasting responses to the items of such an inventory made by those who remain in school, and those who drop out can produce a scoring key by which responses of those most resembling dropouts, i.e., potential dropouts, can be identified for counseling purposes. Such a process is dependent on reaching these individuals before they leave school (in grades six through ten), the candor of the individual completing the inventory, and in the way confidentiality of the responses is preserved. Competent professional counselors can adequately control these variables. The process of using self-inventories is probably no more expensive than the time of personnel using a system like the Illinois Plan, and can furnish data about various attitudes and other motivational factors not found in school files.

Before either of these promising approaches to the problem of identifying the potential school dropout can be utilized fully, it is vital to overcome attitudes (among public officials and private groups) that create two deterrents to research in this area. There has been substantial opposition to establishing the control groups essential for comparison with experimental groups of potential or actual school dropouts. Whereas varying kinds of help are offered to the students in the experimental groups, the control groups, obviously, can receive no help. Only in this way is it possible to show what value the processes carried out with the experimental groups may have. Only in this way is it possible to show whether there is any advantage in trying to identify and counsel dropouts, or whether it produces no change in dropout behavior and is thus a waste of public and private funds. Objectors actually contribute to the waste of research funds, and through misdirected zeal prevent dropouts from being helped effectively.

A second deterrent to research to alleviate the school dropout problem is the furor over the use of self-inventories or personal records. This is mistakenly looked on as an invasion of the individual's privacy under any circumstances. This may or may not be true. It depends on how these data are used and who uses them. The professional counselor using self-inventories with a client is concerned with helping that client to enhance his knowledge and feelings about himself. Professional behavior requires the counselor to offer the client a choice of taking or not taking the inventory. The counselor further considers only the scores a scoring stencil or scoring machine produces. Except in rare instances, usually at the request of the client, or when he suspects an error in scoring, he does not look at specific or particular client responses to given items of the inventory. In these two ways—client choice about taking the inventory, and the use of cumulative item scores instead of inspection of specific client answers to items—client privacy is maintained and protected by the counselor except when court action forces disclosure of counseling records. In like manner, the professional counselor is required by professional ethics to maintain personal records in a way that preserves the confidentiality and privacy of such records.

Research and professional use of self-inventories conducted under these circumstances should have the support of everyone, in public or private positions, who is interested in helping youth. However, these persons, especially parents, should recognize that if confidential information a pupil discusses with a counselor is revealed to anyone—even parents—without permission of the pupil, the effectiveness of the counseling process is destroyed.

Until recently, the counselor has been forced by pressure from varied groups in the community to devote his efforts to individuals in upper socioeconomic levels, particularly those bound for college, with special emphasis on the academically talented and the "creative" person. Now, with increasing emphasis on the counseling of individuals in the lower income groups, the counselor is aided to broaden his work to cover all who need the help he can provide. Now he needs the professional skill and the time to do the job. Most counselors have or can acquire the professional skills; the crucial element is the increased number of counselors needed so that sufficient counseling time is available for *every* pupil in school, and for *every* individual who needs the help of a professional counselor in a nonschool agency. This increase in professional staff and broadened professional preparation is vital, if school dropouts are to be decreased, or helped effectively.

Another recent focus of attention has been the preventive aspects of guidance in the elementary school. Gradually the number of elementary school guidance workers has been increasing as their impact on pupil behavior has become apparent. Also apparent has been evidence that the elementary guidance worker is a blend of school psychologist, school social worker, and school counselor. His primary function appears to be working with teachers and parents to identify and transfer to appropriate referral sources any boy or girl who exhibits symptoms that could later produce academic, occupational, or community problems.

For example, early identification can bring about corrective measures that reduce the number of potential dropouts long before they have a chance to leave school. Lambert points to a study by Bower and Larsen that clearly indicates that the emotionally disturbed child can be identified by teachers and elementary school guidance workers in the early school years.[7] She also reports a followup study of Bower and Larsen's group and, in this connection, discusses other problems in the identifica-

[7] Daniel Schreiber, ed., *Guidance and the School Dropout* (Washington, D.C.: National Education Association, 1964).

tion and treatment, in the elementary school, of the potential dropout. She presents data gathered in the elementary school that, she claims, will distinguish among pupils who later graduate, drop out, or become delinquent. Many of her data resemble those described by Cervantes (reported previously). Lambert's material does, however, emphasize that identification of potential dropouts can begin early in the elementary school; it emphasizes that preventive aspects of counseling and guidance require that the dropout be identified as early as possible in his school years.

Scattered through his article on dropouts, Sullivan has some sensible suggestions on how the school and the counselor should cope with the dropout problem.[8] He says that more emphasis should be placed on working with parents to help them accept their child's need for training before he tries to earn a living. (Perhaps this goal should really be to help them realize their child's need to acquire work skills before he leaves school to undertake his first job.) Sullivan suggests that work-study programs organized by the school, and community programs to pay for clothing and food so that a pupil can attend school with the strength and self-confidence needed to perform adequately there, are absolute necessities. (Perhaps we need local CARE programs as well as international ones.) He also points out that one person in the school should undertake the responsibility for making the potential dropout feel wanted as a human being. This in itself can be a vital factor in encouraging the potential dropout to seek the school activities, in classes or extracurricularly, that will enhance his self-respect. These are ways other than those listed previously that the counselor can utilize to help the person identified as a potential dropout to remain in school.

Some school dropouts can be "prevented," or assisted most effectively, at the junior or senior high school level by helping them to perceive alternatives to leaving school. For example:

1. A boy may feel he needs more money than his parents can furnish in order to meet some of the "hidden costs" of going to school or being a member of a given group.

2. A girl may want money to buy clothing and other material things that support her as an individual.

3. A boy or girl may feel the need, or may be asked by parents, to contribute to support of the rest of the family.

4. A young couple who have to get married may need help in completing her education.

5. A pregnant, unmarried girl may need help in completing her education.

8 N. V. Sullivan, "The School Dropout Problem," in *Poverty in America,* ed. Margaret Gordon (San Francisco: Chandler Publishing Co., 1965).

6. An emotionally disturbed pupil may need psychological help in order to remain in school.

7. A minority group member may need help in resolving a conflict between his values as a member of such a group and continued school attendance.

8. A school leaver may need help in developing a plan to earn while he completes some added training that will place him in something better than an unskilled job.

When the school counselor is able to help any such individual to work out a plan that ultimately permits him to complete his education, the latter does not become a statistic indicating one more dropout; and, if he does leave school, he becomes a more effective and satisfied adult in the world of work. Other potential school dropouts need other kinds of help in making an effective placement without completing school graduation.

Before the counselor is to work with school dropouts, he should have special preparation in the knowledges and skills needed to be an effective counselor with this group. He must know about:

1. Research that has been done on school dropouts, such as:
   a. *NEA Project School Dropouts.*[9]
   b. *The Dropout.*[10]
   c. *Dropouts: Selected References.*[11]

2. Processes that have been developed for identifying the potential dropout.
   a. The Illinois Plan.
   b. The School Interest Inventory.

3. Special tests and other counseling tools or procedures that have been developed for use with potential or actual dropouts.
   a. The School Interest Inventory.
   b. United States Employment Service tests.
   c. The Wide Range Achievement Tests.

4. Community resources currently available or possible for counseling and placement of dropouts, such as the following:
   a. Amendments to the Manpower Development and Training Act (MDTA) in 1963 have made it possible to expand the coverage of youth in both institutional and on-the-job training (OJT) programs. Youths may enter at age 16, but may not receive training allowances until age 17. Twenty-five per cent of all trainees receiv-

[9] Schreiber, *Guidance and the School Dropout,* p. 7.
[10] Cervantes, *The Dropout,* p. 3.
[11] Office of Education, U.S. Department of Health, Education, and Welfare, *Dropouts: Selected References* (Washington, D.C.: Government Printing Office, 1963).

ing allowances can be under age 22. These allowances can be paid for 104 weeks; they cover basic education needed as a preliminary to regular occupational preparation, as well as the vocational preparation itself. Allowances can be used for more highly skilled training (upgrading) for persons possessing necessary preliminary education and training. In 1966 there were 60,000 youths aged 16-21 enrolled in MDTA institutional training and about 20,000 in OJT programs. In addition to vocational training, other services available to MDTA trainees are: testing and counseling; referral to health, social, or psychological services; basic education; placement and job development services; and followup services after training and placement.

b. The state employment services have developed Youth Opportunity Centers (YOC) as separate offices devoted to job needs of the young worker. Special youth workers go into slum areas in "outreach" activities to find young people who need and will accept help. The employability of these youths is then increased through counseling, training, job development, or needed services from outside the employment service.

c. The Neighborhood Youth Corps (NYC) and the Job Corps. These programs are discussed in detail in Chapter 11.

d. The Community Action Program (CAP) is a federally financed series of projects in 50 of the largest cities, and scattered smaller communities. It is designed to be operated by local persons for specific needs of a given community such as: service to a given age group, specialized training in a given field, or as a "holding agency" or framework within which the programs of other agencies operate. This program is designed to focus attacks on current problems of disadvantaged persons in a given community, and varies considerably from place to place.

e. State vocational rehabilitation agencies, including services to the blind, are a source of help to youths who need physical or psychological treatment before they can be employable. Training, even at the graduate level in college, is available to persons who can qualify as handicapped and who need added training before they can gain suitable employment. Some who may not be eligible for training allowances may be eligible for other kinds of help from these agencies.

f. Varied agencies operating under local United Fund auspices also provide services for youth that are available to dropouts. These vary with the community, but usually the United Fund publishes material describing the services, and the persons eligible for them.

g. See also, "A Counselor's Guide to Federal Aid Programs." *Occupational Outlook Quarterly*, December, 1965.

h. The various employment, training, and educational programs that private industry may provide for disadvantaged youth in a specific area.

CONCLUSION

The counselor needs to modify his approach to the dropout, using appropriate material and processes he was taught in academic courses in general counseling, and those he has learned in his practice with other clients. The dropout poses a peculiar challenge. Because he usually comes from a background of personal failures, he has learned to distrust his own judgments, tending to rely on the judgments of others. At the same time, he has learned to resent and to oppose authority; so the counselor cannot be successful in counseling if the dropout sees him as an authority figure. Like the mentally disturbed youth, the dropout has more need for security than the average person his age. His ego, however, cannot accept obvious protections that the counselor provides for him. Somehow the counselor needs to steer a course that offers more support to the dropout client without the possible implications of direction and authority that such support could produce. It is the delicate job of helping the dropout to grow in self-realization and in self-confidence by reinforcing the beginning of real autonomy without the inference that "father knows best." This means that the counselor must develop an approach to counseling somewhat different than he has used with other clients; but most of all it means, as emphasized above, that the counselor cannot leave the development of this frame of reference to chance.

It is the opinion of this author, based on twenty years of experience as a counseling psychologist whose major responsibility increasingly tended toward counselor education, that the counselor in training should encounter formal or specifically planned situations in which he is forced to delineate his frame of reference for counseling. This cognitive and affective integration of personal experience and professional experience makes the counselor a more consistent and effective person, and tends to lessen the chance effects in counseling and the unwitting biases the counselor produces when he is less aware of his professional procedures or of his personal foibles.

If the counselor of dropouts has been able to accomplish these objectives, he is ready to identify the potential dropout and to offer him counseling help. He should bear in mind, however, that the help he offers may be refused, in which case he must devote his efforts to seeing that some of the community groups mentioned above are aware that a specific dropout can use help they are in a position to provide.

A cooperative effort by all groups to provide help to the dropout can be effective only to the extent that the dropout wishes. He cannot and should not be forced to accept counseling and placement. He should be helped to decide what he wants to do, *but the choice should be his.*

SELECTED READINGS

1. Abraham, Willard, *The Slow Learner*. New York: The Center for Applied Research in Education, Inc., 1964.

2. Amos, William E., and Marilyn A. Southwell, "Dropouts: What Can Be Done?" Federal Probation, **28** (1964), 30-35.

3. ———, *et al.*, *Action Programs for Delinquency Prevention*. Springfield, Ill.: Charles C Thomas, Publisher, 1965.

4. Bienstock, Herbert, *Factbook on the School Dropout in the World of Work*. U.S. Department of Labor, Bureau of Labor Statistics, 1963.

5. Burchill, George W., *Work-Study Programs for Alienated Youth*. Chicago: Science Research Association, Inc., 1962.

6. Byrne, Richard Hill, "Beware the Stay-in-School Bandwagon," *Personnel and Guidance Journal*, **36** (March, 1958), 493-496.

7. Cervantes, L. F., *The Dropout: Causes and Cure*. Ann Arbor, Mich.: University of Michigan Press, 1965.

8. Cohen, Eli, and Marsha Freedman, *Getting Hired, Getting Trained*. New York: National Committee on Employment of Youth, 1964.

9. Cottle, William C., *Manual for the School Interest Inventory*. Boston: Houghton Mifflin Company, 1966.

10. ———, and N. S. Dournie, *Procedures and Preparation for Counseling*. Englewood Cliffs, N.J.: Prentice-Hall, Inc., 1960.

11. Gordon, Margaret, ed., *Poverty in America*. San Francisco: Chandler Publishing Company, 1965.

12. Illinois Department of Public Instruction, *Procedures for the Identification of Potential High School Dropouts*. Springfield, Ill.: Office of the Superintendent of Public Instruction, 1962.

13. Schreiber, Daniel, ed., *Guidance and the School Dropout*. Washington, D.C.: National Education Association, 1964.

14. ———, ed., *The School Dropout*. Washington, D.C.: National Education Association, 1964.

15. U.S. Department of Labor, *The Challenge of Jobless Youth*. Washington, D.C.: Government Printing Office, 1963.

I O

EMPLOYMENT OPPORTUNITIES

FOR DISADVANTAGED YOUTH

CLYDE W. GLEASON

Introduction

Speaking in the mid-Sixties, the Secretary of Labor warned this country that about a quarter of a million young boys and girls are ending up on a human slag heap every year. Thus he estimated an annual accretion to the hard core of a malignant growth in the American economy, and his estimate is conservative. Surrounding that hard core are far larger numbers of youth who avoid the slag heap in its most desolate forms, but find themselves in the wastelands, bound to stultifying blind alley jobs or moving restlessly and aimlessly from one unrewarding task to another. They, as well as the youthful unemployables, are "disadvantaged" in seeking employment fitted to their potentials and their needs. Individually they bear the burdens of their failures (and ours); collectively they retard our national progress. They, and their chances for suitable employment, are the concern of this chapter.

The disadvantaged youth of this generation are being ground between the upper and nether millstones of an industrial mechanism that has not recognized its need for them, and has been perilously close to rejecting them permanently. The upper millstone is comprised of employment opportunities for youngsters with "acceptable" cultural and ethnic backgrounds, skin colors, and other assets. The nether stone is comprised of

206

what purport to be opportunities for youth, but which too often are more in the nature of opportunities for some employers to get cheap labor. In the narrow space between the unattainable and the intolerable, the young people with whom we are concerned in this chapter must find their opportunities.

For those who counsel such youth there are two contrasting approaches: 1) to accept the hard facts of their personal liabilities and help them find jobs that tolerate them; 2) to help them develop vocational assets to meet the equally hard facts of existing job demand.

The only practicable course, sometimes, is to accept the youth's deficiencies and help him find work that is tolerant of them. But the second alternative becomes more feasible and profitable for all concerned, as we develop better resources for remedial education, prevocational and vocational training, and other modes of self-improvement; and as more employers, recognizing their responsibilities, alter unnecessarily rigid job requirements and abandon discriminatory hiring practices.

Whatever the compromises between these two approaches, the fact remains that job opportunities are inevitably related to the personal qualities and circumstances of the individual. Opportunities for many disadvantaged youth must be found among the simplest, least demanding types of work; but there is no upper limit for those who have it in them to rise above their initial handicaps. There is no moral or practical justification for assuming that in the world of work there must be a ghetto of low-level occupations called suitable for the disadvantaged.

Another reason that neat classifications and listings of employment opportunities for disadvantaged youth are unrealistic is the difficulty of defining employment opportunity. A common stereotype is that of a declared job opening in competitive (as opposed to sheltered) employment, offering the prospective worker a more or less permanent job with an established wage large enough to meet his legitimate living needs. For the typical underprivileged youth, such an opportunity is something at the end of the rainbow, and an attempt to limit this chapter to a discussion of so narrow a category would be futile. For one reason, we must deal in contingencies. An employer's willingness to give a boy or girl a chance to learn on-the-job, with regular employment later IF the training is successful, can be a more substantial opportunity than many an immediate opening that does not call for such preparation and trial. What line then, should be drawn between a training and an employment opportunity?

Another kind of contingent opportunity, defying clear definition, is the scheme for self-employment in some small enterprise, while it is little more than a "gleam in a young man's eye." Far from being an established job opening, it still is in the realm of ideas; potentially, however, it may be far more valuable than the open-and-shut offer of a job.

One also may wonder what kinds of openings should be considered as employment opportunities, and what kinds should not. Which, for example, of the following: An offer of work for "board, keep and pin-money" in domestic service, on a farm, or in an institution? A chance to sharecrop in cotton or tobacco? A street-corner location for selling newspapers? A sheltered workshop assignment? An invitation to become a numbers runner or dope peddler? A standing offer to buy one's blood by the pint? A draft notice or call for volunteers for military service? An unfilled Job Corps quota? From the most dubious to the most promising, and regardless of anything else these may be, they are ways that disadvantaged youth can and often do get at least some part of a living.

Such examples suggest another obstacle to the development of meaningful classifications of job opportunity for the youth with whom we are concerned. It should be clear to both counselor and client, in the practical situation, whether the opportunity to be sought is a temporary stopgap job, or something preparatory to a long term objective, or the career objective itself. These distinctions are well understood by middle class youth. For them it is not difficult to fit various types of work into one or another of the three categories. But for the disadvantaged youth, common labor can itself *be* a career; and work that is only a steppingstone for the more favored youth may be the highest level attainable for the less favored.

Still another difficulty in identifying opportunities for such youth is that, as often as not, jobs for them must be *developed* rather than *found*. Because so many opportunities at higher levels of employment take the forms of recognizable openings, there is an understandable tendency to think of employment opportunity in general as being something "out there," awaiting discovery. This premise underlies most of the formal surveys of employer need, and most of the order-filling activities of employment agencies. Employers are, however, far less likely to have ready-made openings for young people who lack job knowledge, skills, or established work habits, or whose ethnic characteristics differ sharply from those of other employees.

Some sympathetic employers create special niches for disadvantaged young people, but more often the youths themselves, or those counseling or otherwise aiding them, must take the initiative. For example, an employment service interviewer receiving an order for a more or less experienced worker may invite the employer's attention to the possible advantages of relaxing certain age, experience, or educational requirements, and suggest hiring some particular youngster whom he could train in his own methods.

Ranging outward from such modest job development efforts, interviewers and counselors may go on to bolder proposals tailored to their understandings of employers' possible needs. One of these might be to split a certain job between two youths, so that each can give half of his time to education or training; another, to add some new service (delivery, packaging, repair, or any of a hundred others); another, to provide certain present higher-paid employees with youthful helpers, cutting the time the established now spend in the simpler, routine aspects of their jobs, and at the same time giving the youngsters a chance to observe and learn. Such creativity is limited only by one's familiarity with the industries and establishments of his area, and by one's imagination, ingenuity, and persuasiveness.

Guidelines for the Search for Opportunity

Thus for disadvantaged youth the world of work is an amorphous mixture of job and training possibilities; schemes for self-employment; casual, permanent, and in-between types of employment whether public or private, sheltered or competitive, respectable or on the fringes of legitimacy. How can one search for opportunities in it? As we review the early experiences of experimental and demonstrational youth training and placement programs that have been organized in recent years under Federal, state and local public auspices, we might be tempted to conclude that the search must be mainly a matter of trial and error. And yet, as the workers in such programs have continued to develop training and placement opportunities, they have found certain industries and parts of industry, certain types and sizes of establishment, certain kinds of employers, and certain kinds of job situations and arrangements to be more promising than others. There is reason to believe that an assessment of the collective experiences of such projects can give us useful guidelines for the benefit of permanent programs established more recently.

The same is true for cooperative programs in the private sector, such as Plans for Progress which seeks to mobilize the efforts of the nation's industries in expanding employment opportunity for minorities. Considerable attention will be given, later in the chapter, to a number of these programs.

SOME EMPLOYMENT TRENDS AND THEIR IMPLICATIONS

Before discussing such recent experiences in seeking job opportunities for disadvantaged youth, it should be useful to examine some basic employment trends in the American economy, and discuss certain of their implications.[1]

[1] Employment and Earnings Statistics for the U.S., 1909-64; Bull. 1312-2; Bureau of Labor Statistics, U.S. Department of Labor (Washington, D.C.: U.S. Government Printing Office).

Back in 1948, a little after World War II, the total number of people employed in this country in the so-called *production* industries—mainly agriculture, mining, construction, and manufacturing—was about 26 million. That same year, there also were about 26 million people employed in what are just as loosely classified as *service* industries, including trade, transport, public utilities, finance, insurance, real estate, government (outside the military establishment), and a few others. By 1960, the *production* industries thus broadly grouped were still employing roughly the same numbers of workers. Modest increases in some of them (notably manufacturing), were offset by heavy decreases in others, mainly mining and agriculture. In vivid contrast, employment in the *service* sector had grown by 1960 to about 32 million, and since then through the Sixties it has continued to soar, leaving *production* far behind, in spite of recent increases in war production. Activities of the public employment service system in placing its applicants reflect the status of employment opportunity. During the mid-Sixties and on, there have been roughly two and one half job placements in *nonproduction* establishments for each placement in goods-producing establishments.

Such figures tell only part of the story. For example, within manufacturing itself, there have been heavy reductions in the proportions of factory operatives and others engaged directly in goods production, and proportionate increases in administrative, research, development, sales, clerical, and other ancillary nonproduction services.

The Trek to the Cities

One of the most obvious effects of this fundamental change in the nature of American employment is that the nation's farms, forests, fisheries, mines, and other outdoor production industries no longer offer anything approaching the wealth of opportunities that they provided unskilled and semiskilled workers not many years ago. Although technological change is commonly associated in our thinking with manufacturing and other typically urban activities, actually its effects on employment in the essentially rural outdoor industries have been far more radical. In agriculture for example, so many of the small farms are disappearing, and technical innovations on the larger farms are eliminating so many workers that, at a fairly conservative estimate, fewer than 10 per cent of the youth living on farms during the early Sixties may be expected to remain as farmers. During that period, some eight million children and youth were living in rural families whose total incomes were at or below the subsistence level, and their numbers have been growing. The futures of these children will be dim unless they leave home, or unless timid, tardy actions being taken to rebuild the socioeconomic foundations of American rural life are heavily reinforced.

About the only alternative open to most disadvantaged rural youth has been to move to town. The first port of call may be some village, town, or city nearby, where they may or may not be welcome. From there (or bypassing such places entirely), many go on to larger metropolitan centers where an alarming proportion of them have clustered in the alien environments of inner-city and suburban slums. The consequences have been unhappy and often tragic. The Urban League estimated that during 1965, the half million Negro population of Los Angeles was being augmented by in-migrants, most of them leaving Mississippi and Alabama (lesser numbers from Louisiana and Texas), at the rate of a thousand a month. The Los Angeles ghetto of Watts, reduced that year to a shambles by one of the most destructive race riots in our history, has been described as a dumping ground for the problems that the community has failed to solve. The study found an extremely high level of functional illiteracy among the in-migrants from the deep South, and it was estimated that very nearly half of the area's out-of-school youth were without jobs of any kind. The situation in Watts has been paralleled by festering sores near the hearts of most of our large cities.

The Spread of Urban Uniformity

A second pervasive effect of the massive shift toward service and related work is the development of extremely complex but increasingly uniform patterns of employment in large urban communities throughout the country. This has an interesting history, and some ambivalent implications. Physical geography has always been a major factor in locating production industries, with their traditionally unique occupational patterns. Mining must be carried on where ore is to be found; agriculture, on fertile plains and valleys floors; manufacturing, where there are favorable combinations of raw materials, power resources, and transport routes. Always of course, there are the workers, but usually they are more mobile than the other factors in the process of goods production, and the production industries are traditionally oriented more to places than people. The earlier patterns for most of our cities were fairly simple—one or more production industries, each with its special job composition, and at first a thin, then a thicker overlay of services to the industries and the workers in them, as citizens and consumers.

More recently, however, as the manufacturing industries in the larger cities have developed automated processes calling for fewer operatives, urban workers have turned toward service and other nonproduction jobs. New kinds of services, and complications and refinements of older services, bring a host of new occupations into being. They have a tendency to fall into patterns that are increasingly similar from city to city. Thanks to advertising and other means of stimulating and controlling mass desire, the service demands of urban populations are highly conventional and standardized. What the people of New York and Chicago have, the people of Houston, Detroit, Atlanta, and Seattle must have too. To some of us at least, it is more ominous than comforting to find ourselves, after flying two or three thousand miles from home, not in strange cities, but surrounded by virtual duplicates of familiar institutions, establishments, and facilities. And the workers in them seem almost to be the ones we thought we had left behind a few hours before.

Whether they are themselves natives or in-migrants, the disadvantaged youth who live in large urban centers are affected in many ways by this universally repeated complex of service and related occupations within which, for better or worse, they must find most of their employment opportunities. The numbers and varieties of jobs (nearly all of them already filled), make the picture confusing to all of us, but impossibly so for youngsters who have only a worm's-eye view of the economic underworld. What kinds of work, other than the obvious ones, are to be had? Where in the urban maze are they to be found? What (or who) does one have to be, or know, to get one? How does one go about it? Is there any use looking?

If the local situation seems hopeless, might it be better somewhere else? Thumbing one's way from city to city, one will discover sooner or later that unless one has something special to offer, the chances are little better in St. Louis than Kansas City or Philadelphia. It is all much the same: the same thankless jobs in hash-joint kitchens and the like. The industry that many a city has been noted for—steel in Pittsburgh or Birmingham, meatpacking in Omaha or Chicago, auto manufacturing in Detroit, shipping in Baltimore or San Francisco—may be taking on little or no green, casual labor. More generally, the jobs to be had in any of those cities are like those of cities back in the home area; and there at least, one was in familiar territory.

Some aspects of this endlessly repeated complex sameness are more hopeful. When a youth acquires skill in an occupation that has lost its former unique and local character, he is less likely to be bound for a lifetime to one employer, or to the vicissitudes of employment in a single community, but can become a true "journeyman," reasonably free to live and work anywhere that his skill may be needed. This can be a source of limited comfort to the counselor who has nothing better to suggest to his youthful counselee than to take some dubious local job "for the experience"—provided, of course, that the counselor follows through and sees him out of it some day.

The growing uniformity in urban employment patterns has another increasingly important consequence for the counseling profession: namely, that much of the knowledge and understanding that an urban counselor can acquire through assiduous study of the service and related industries and occupations of his own community, is valid for most other urban communities. The difficult and involved process of collecting and organizing reliable and reasonably current information about the occupation compositions of services and related industries, and details about requirements, rewards, employment outlook, and other characteristics of the many occupations in them, need not be very different for each locality. The development of a common center for the collection, organization, and distribution of such information can therefore become a public service at the Federal level, and is becoming one.

The third edition of the *Dictionary of Occupational Titles* provides the basic pattern, identifying and defining the occupations and their industrial designations, and grouping them according to schemes of comprehensive classification calculated to relate them to pertinent characteristics of the workers in them. These resources of the new Dictionary are complemented by a less comprehensive but still broad coverage of employment and outlook information published in successive editions of the *Occupational Outlook Handbook,* and by the *Occupational Outlook Quarterly.*

These and other special purpose publications essentially based on them, may or may not take account of regional, area, or local variations in the characteristics of occupations or employment patterns and trends. To meet the need for such information, still taking full advantage of the organization and comprehensiveness of the national publications, the Employment Security agencies of most of the states conduct periodic surveys covering the employment and/or training needs of employers in particular areas, sometimes including particular industries or types of occupation. Ordinarily these skill and other surveys use the nomenclature and classification systems of DOT; they probably anticipate what before long may become a widely ramified but integrated system covering all of American industry, through which information about manpower needs is collected and disseminated through data processing and instant communication methods. Through the nationwide operation of this system, the nation's youth—disadvantaged and otherwise—might receive invaluable aid threading the intricate and now baffling maze of industry in our urban economy.

The Revolution in Job Demand

A third important result of the high concentration of job opportunities in the service and related sector of the American economy is a major change in the demands of work on the abilities and capabilities of the worker. Whether a product is grown in fields, dug from mines, made in factories, or assembled on building sites, the production worker devotes most of his attention and effort to *things*, rather than to *people*, or to what we may loosely call *data*. Culturally deprived youth, however, usually relate more effectively to *things* than to either *people* or *data*. Even the more elemental service occupations tend to involve interpersonal relations that make heavier demands on the worker's social intelligence, and his verbal and numerical abilities than do most farm or factory jobs. Almost any farm boy can learn to do a fine job hoeing corn alone in the field. He, and almost any city boy, can soon learn to do just as well on a factory assembly line. But in the typical service occupation, the worker must relate well, not only to his fellow workers, but to customers or others in a "public" to be mingled with, adjusted to, satisfied, persuaded, or even controlled. Social crudities that are acceptable in a logging camp, mine, fishery, factory, or farm, and which might be the norm in an inner-city slum, are not tolerated in service work that demands cleanliness, neatness, courtesy, articulate speech, and other social sensitivities and skills. Unless youth have been reared outside the slum (rural or urban), or have been exposed to powerful disciplines in family or ethnic groups that have held the line against the corrosive influences of slum life, this consequence of cultural deprivation may be one of the most serious of vocational handicaps.

It is also essential that workers in most nonproduction occupations be able to deal with *data*. Nursing the sick, protecting the public, transporting people from here to there, fixing their domestic appliances, preparing and serving their food, cleaning clothing, selling merchandise, pumping gasoline, delivering milk or mail—all these call for some facility with such media for data as signs, printed instructions, blueprints, charts, wiring diagrams, maps, directories, sales slips, statements, menus, laundry lists, and inventory sheets. Workers must make change, complete applications, write reports, calculate fares and other charges, give fairly intelligent directions, make estimates, interpret measuring devices, et cetera. They need appropriate vocabularies and other language skills, and certain competencies in mathematics. The deficiencies of educationally and culturally deprived youth keep vast numbers of them virtually unemployable in any but the most elemental kinds of work.

To keep the record straight, however, it must be observed that the effects of slum life, and life in depressed rural areas, are not all negative. During the long history of the American city slums and the American frontier, rigorous conditions have sifted and winnowed human strengths and weaknesses. It is a fact of life in our economy that not all of the vocationally useful traits are on the side of middle class virtues and economic behaviors. Struggle in the lower strata nurtures in many a youth a keen, incisive intelligence that can recognize and seize upon opportunity, know the angles, size up the prospective customer (or victim), evade complications, and otherwise make its way in the hard environment. In urban slums in particular, youths often show a sophistication well beyond that of their middle class contemporaries, and surprising insights into the dynamics and mechanics of the slum economy. Much of this relates to approaches and methods in moneymaking activities such as street-vending; buying and selling used cars, furniture, and other commodities; salvaging parts from auto dumps; operating amusement concessions, pawnshops, bail bond and small loan establishments, horse parlors, flophouses, parking lots, and other enterprises, some of which are not mentioned in polite society but nevertheless are integral parts of the culture of poverty. The counselors of such youth must be alert to these evidences of their counselees' knowledges, skills, and interests, not only because they suggest certain kinds of ability and motivation, but also because future careers may be built on such foundations.

Thus far in this chapter, we have considered some of the factors that underlie employment opportunity for disadvantged youth, noting the almost infinite variety, and the elusiveness, of what may be called "opportunities," and their essential relativity to the individual. We have taken a quick but comprehensive look at a national economy that has mounted the steep slopes of goods production to the high point at which a basic, revolutionary, and irreversible change has occurred, with the consequence that—barring major war or other catastrophe—the energies of most of our workers must be directed into channels of service to themselves and others. This fact, as we have seen, has tremendously important implications for disadvantaged youth. In large measure indeed, it is responsible for their *being* disadvantaged. It has forced a mass migration of rural young people to the cities. It has created a growing uniformity in the bewilderingly complex employment patterns of urban communities. It imposes increasingly heavy social and intellectual demands on the worker.

All this may sharpen one's sense of the irony of a situation in which many if not most of our nation's underprivileged youth, themselves denied the educational, medical, social, and other services they have needed so badly while growing up, are now being required, if they are to work at all, to earn their livings by serving others.

RECENT EXPERIENCE IN THE SEARCH FOR OPPORTUNITY

Through the years, the rates of unemployment among youth who are seriously disadvantaged by reason of race, nationality, interrupted education, and cultural deprivation have continued to be stubbornly, persistently, and markedly higher than those for other youth. Nevertheless it is being demonstrated that opportunity can be created for the disadvantaged through skillfully executed processes of accommodating youth and jobs to one another.

The public employment service system, with nearly two thousand offices located in every state and territory, has for years been instrumental in such arrangements. Its Youth Opportunity Centers in the larger cities, and extensions of specialized service facilities for youth in smaller cities and rural communities, are progressing rapidly in their effectiveness. The state rehabilitation agencies have been notably successful in their intensive services to the disabled; and other agencies and institutions have been bringing their experience to bear on the problem. These ongoing services have profited much from earlier and still continuing operations of the experimental and demonstrational projects already mentioned, particularly those financed through funds provided under the Manpower Development and Training Act, and administered by the U. S. Department of Labor.

No two projects have been alike. Some have been rural, some urban, some both. In various combinations, they have served youth ranging from ages 16 to 21, male and female, Negro, white, and of Spanish-American and other national backgrounds. Some of the projects have been large and complex, and some small, with simple missions. Some of them have provided prevocational training and other disciplines, others vocational training; some of them, both. Some have concentrated on institutional training; others principally on on-the-job training arrangements with employers. Some have provided no training at all, but have counseled and referred their clientele to local training facilities. Some have found jobs for them while others have tried only to help them prepare for employment, leaving placement to the employment service. All of them, however, have had employment as their ultimate goal, and the mark of their success; and in varying degrees their programs have been determined by the actual or presumed employment opportunities in their respective areas.

As this is written, a few of the projects to be mentioned below are discontinued or superseded, and others will be.[2] Still others seem more durable, but all of them are experimental: their findings and achievements cannot be evaluated with confidence or finality. Failures of yesterday are today's successes, as purposes have been clarified, resources developed, methods changed, and relations with employers and the public improved.

---

[2] The project descriptions and comments in the next several pages are based on information from a variety of sources, including progress reports received by the U.S. Department of Labor's Office of Manpower Planning, Employment and Research (OMPER), and its predecessor, OMAT (Office of Manpower, Automation and Training). Persons or organizations having a special interest in particular projects might direct their inquiries either to the Employment Service Office, or to the school authorities in the locality served by the project, or to OMPER in Washington, D.C.

But we need to learn what we can from them for the guidance of the more massive programs of the future.

They are arrayed along an axis from rural to metropolitan.

Keeping Them Down on the Farm

The axis along which one might plot the ways that disadvantaged rural youth try to meet their employment needs has, at one pole, a continuance of the hard-scrabble existence of their parents, and at the other, a move to the city and a search for urban employment. Vast numbers of them have made the leap from farm, timberland, fishing village, or mining community to the city, with no intermediate steps and little or no assistance, or even moral support, from anyone. Many have failed, and some have succeeded. In either case ". . . after they've seen Paree" (or even Watts), it is hard to keep them down on the farm or elsewhere in rural life. There is pride and, if nothing else, there is a change in the mode of misery and frustration.

The prevention of the tragedies of Watts and its successors in other cities, is far better and may be easier than the cure. So think the sponsors and supporters of certain projects that, in one way or another, undertake to make rural life more tolerable and practicable, and even more attractive for youth, than the move to the city.

In California's San Joaquin Valley, the American Friends Service Committee has set up, under contract, a Year Round Farm Worker project, to explore ways to help itinerant and casual farm workers (ages 16 and up), mostly of Spanish-American ancestry, who normally follow the Valley harvests from fruit picking and haying to "stoop labor" in the vegetable fields, and who spend the times between in enforced idleness. The theory is that systematic instruction in "nonpicking" skills can be phased into slack periods in the seasonal crop progression, and that with these skills, the youth (and some older workers as well) can keep usefully occupied in agricultural and related work the year round, at better wages than they now are getting. The job opportunities include farm maintenance work, tractor operating and repairing, pruning, and nursery work. These are supplemented by training for other vocational skills, but also in arithmetic, work disciplines, job-seeking methods, and in the improvement of English. The results are encouraging. Trainee and employer reactions are favorable; youth completing the program are being well placed, and some of the dropouts are leaving because of job opportunities for which their partial training seems adequate.

The State of Vermont, with federal support, approaches the problem quite differently. It has undertaken a Farm Family Development Project, intended to help rural families who face failure or who need support to strengthen their farming operations, and lift them above the subsistence level. Quite a few of the beneficiaries are Vermont rural youth who in some cases are family heads and inheritors of family farms. The help given is in informal Vermont style, with staff workers who know local conditions intimately giving counsel and arranging for aid, financial and otherwise, of many types. The employment opportunities thus preserved or created are mainly on the farm, though progress reports indicate that many are being helped to get supplementary employment in activities such as Vermont's growing summer and winter recreation industry.

A program centered on the campus of Tennessee A & M, in Nashville, provides institutional trade experience to white and Negro residents of Upper Cumberland and other Tennessee regions. Males predominate, ages ranging from eighteen to sixty-five. All must have family incomes below $1200 a year to qualify. The mean educational level is seventh grade. The races study and work in close association. The employment goals are mainly farm, park, and small town jobs. There are courses in livestock maintenance (feeding, medication, and other aspects of animal care), meat processing (preparatory to employment with feed distributors and retailers), park service and maintenance (looking toward jobs in state and national parks, and involving masonry and other construction skills, machine maintenance, road building and repair, etc.), and electronic equipment repairing. Results are encouraging, and are so regarded by the local press and others who are watching the progress of this demonstration.

COMET (Citizens' Organization for Manpower Extension Training), under the joint sponsorship of higher educational and resource development organizations in the Tennessee Valley area, operates several centers offering basic education and work experience to rural heads of families both Negro and white, including a considerable number of youth in their early twenties. The purpose is to give the trainees skills they can use in work similar to that covered by the Tennessee A & M project, but including also numbers of specific objectives such as motorboat repairing and car upholstering. It is characteristic of programs involving on-the-job training that the individual arrangements with prospective employers admit of a wide variety of job goals, each for only one or a few persons, in contrast with institutional courses that usually train considerable numbers for the same objective.

Another southern area project at Tuskegee, Alabama, is limited to Negro males, the training being in brick masonry, carpentry, farm machinery repairing, and meat processing.

What we are learning from these and other projects for training in rural occupations is that there are unmet needs for skilled workers in some of the very areas that are losing most of their more active and promising youth to the cities. Multiplied a hundredfold, such programs might make a real contribution to the national welfare by slowing the present demoralizing movement into the city slums. Not only Los Angeles, but large southern cities such as Houston, New Orleans, Dallas, Birmingham, and Atlanta might well afford to give full support and assistance to such programs for reducing the in-migration of rural youth at the source. The northern cities might wisely do the same, rather than spend all of their energies in a less promising effort to fight, figuratively and literally, the fires already burning.

However, such programs of local training and job development can be only one aspect of the total effort to improve job opportunities for disadvantaged rural and small town youth. Whether or not the rural segment of American society will be able to muster enough internal strength to slow down the present exodus to the cities, will depend more heavily on prompt and massive legislative and other measures. Some of these would more fully support the incomes of small farmers and small town business people. Others would protect American farm laborers, not only from the wage-depressing competition of foreign imported workers, but also from the demoralizing conditions of so much of their work. Still others would further expand present national and regional programs for the protection of forests, farmlands, wildlife and water supply, and the development of parklands and recreation facilities for the future generations of Americans. In the context of such a comprehensive program, we might reasonably hope to develop a nationwide network of educational, training, and employment service facilities to help rural and small town youth find satisfying work near their homes.

One approach to the development of comprehensive programs for the rehabilitation of depressed rural areas is getting underway as this is written. The program of Concerted Services in Training and Education is sponsored by federal department and agency heads who constitute the President's Rural Development Committee. Its statement of objectives calls for the concentration of all available resources on the occupational education problems, and as necessary, on the health, welfare, socioeconomic and related problems of those residing in three communities. The communities referred to are selected counties in New Mexico, Arkansas, and Minnesota. By concentrating funds, technical assistance, and other federal resources in a closely coordinated, locally controlled countywide program, it is hoped to get results that would be unattainable through the piecemeal efforts of various agencies, or by unaided local effort. It is expected that no small part of the total effort will focus on the needs of area youth, and the program may provide a valuable test of a widely held conviction that rural youth can best be helped through a comprehensive attack on the problems and needs of the areas in which they live.

Between Farm and Metropolis

Given the foresight and sense of responsibility required, leading citizens of debilitated rural areas might well seek the cooperation of nearby middle sized cities. Des Moines and Montgomery, Portland and San Antonio, Columbus, Salt Lake City, Milwaukee, and New Haven are or should be much more than halfway stations betwen rural communities and large population centers. If all such middle sized cities were to honor their obligations to the areas surrounding them from which, in the past, they have gained so much of their wealth, they might help save themselves from the blight of creeping depression in the countryside, and from the encroachments of sick metropolises on the other side. They might begin by

1. Lending a helping hand to the many disadvantaged rural youth who might be trained for work, and guided into employment back in their own rural areas;
2. Absorbing others into their own economies; and
3. Helping the remainder, as they pass through en route to the metropolis, to orient themselves to urban life.

This responsibility has been accepted by the prime movers in a number of programs initiated in middle sized cities. The following projects exemplify their purposes and methods.

Eugene, Oregon and surrounding Lane County have been among the first to organize to help what they have called the "invisible" youth of the county's more remote cutover timberlands, and other depressed rural areas. The Lane County Youth Project is designed to serve unemployed, out-of-school rural and small town youth. The stated purpose is to orient them to future urban employment, although some of the participants are being helped to find work in their home communities. A key element in the project has been a center in Eugene where, depending on their individual needs, the young "invisibles" are given diagnostic and therapeutic counseling, prevocational exploration, opportunities for vocational training and (through the employment service) for placement with local employers. The project staff have arranged with numbers of commercial, industrial, and other establishments, and public and private institutions, to admit individual youth for brief periods of work experience in which they observe work being done, get the feel of the work situation, and sometimes take a hand in the work itself. Some of these experiences extend into arrangements for on-the-job training, or even employment, though their purpose is exploratory. Some of the youth then enter formal institutional training with or without remedial education. Since the project's emphasis is on the earlier stages of transition from the rural setting into urban life and work, it is difficult to define the job opportunities being found or created; it seems evident, however, that they are well distributed among the production as well as the nonproduction establishments of the city and county.

In Charleston, West Virginia, the federally supported project KEY (Kanawha Employment for Youth), is sponsored by Action for Appalachian Youth, Inc. Its intent is to provide a program of selection, testing, evaluation, counseling, work orientation, and referral for training and placement of disadvantaged youth of Kanawha County. It seeks to demonstrate, among other things, that disadvantaged Appalachian youth can function in an urban area. The project has drawn considerable numbers of youth from the West Virginia back country into a program of prevocational work experience similar to that of the Lane County project; it is followed for some by vocational training courses, and for others by on-the-job training with Charleston employers. The opportunities provided thus far include service station and other auto service jobs, machine tool operating, custodial work, cook helper, nurse's aide, sales cashier, and other types of clerical and related work.

The Arizona Migrant and Indian Ministry developed a project with federal support, near Phoenix, Arizona. Its objective was to find, recruit, and counsel itinerant field workers for a program of basic literacy and occupational training. Most of the trainees were Mexican-American; and most of these were once itinerant farm workers who were "mechanized" out of employment. The challenging task of aiding these people in their transition from agricultural labor to urban employment has included helping them change deeply traditional attitudes and habits, learning English and other educational rudiments, mastering vocational skills, and overcoming serious postemployment job adjustment problems, many of which require repeated placements. Combinations of social service, educational, and training methods have been used, including both institutional and on-the-job training. Placements have usually been in service jobs, including among others, laundry, restaurant and hotel services, automotive services, yard work, truck driving, janitorial and custodial jobs, pest extermination, landscaping, nurse's aide, and certain forms of clerical work. A few are reported to have been placed in small craft-type manufacturing. Employers are reported to be generally sympathetic and helpful, but one of the project's most time-consuming and troublesome activities has been to find people who can and will fit the openings developed.

In Tallahassee, Florida A & M has conducted an all-Negro project serving predominantly rural youth and older persons in about equal numbers. All participants must be unemployed, or in households with incomes of less than $1200 a year, and presently unqualified, due to poor educational achievement, for conventional retraining or jobs. Training and placement is provided for an array of typically urban service and related occupations which include modest types of clerical and sales work, service station attending, electrical appliance repairing, upholstering, tailoring, cooking, and domestic service.

These are only a few of the middle sized and smaller city projects that have concentrated on the transition problems of rural and small town youth. A considerably larger number of projects, located in cities of comparable size, combine services to their own disadvantaged youth with assistance to those from the countryside. Space permits reference to only one of them: the system of Neighborhood Employment Centers maintained in New Haven, Connecticut, by Community Progress, Inc. (CPI).

CPI is an excellent example of a program principally financed through federal funds and strongly supported by the employers, institutions, and agencies of the community. Cooperating closely with the schools, the employment service, and other organizations, CPI engages in a variety of counseling, placement, and related activities in six New Haven neighborhoods euphemistically called "gray areas," in which most of its Negro and Puerto Rican population live. It is significant that such special services are only a part of what is termed the "CPI mandate"—the improvement of living, working, housing, recreational, and educational conditions of people in the community. This comprehensive approach is an integral part of New Haven's urban renewal program, which has attracted the attention of the nation.

Roughly half of the disadvantaged population receiving employment-related assistance are youth; approximately three fourths are male; over half are Negro. Although some of the job finding is the outcome of immediate job development and order-filling activities, most of those eventually finding suitable work through the Neighborhood Employment Centers have had the benefit of intensive counseling and various combinations of remedial education, prevocational training, and vocational training—institutional or on-the-job. One of the most valuable of these services has been prevocational work experience as member of a small work crew, in which the boy or girl works half-time for a small stipend, on a useful project of some kind, stimulated by his peers and by a foreman (or lady) who can be role-model as well as supervisor, and who can help the youth develop good work habits and attitudes.

Work crew experience may or may not provide usable vocational skills. The program's on-the-job training activities, closely supervised during the training period, continue the process of orienting the youth to the disciplines of employment, giving him the chance to develop particular job skills with a good prospect of regular employment after completing the training.

However, no mere recital of the many kinds of training or employment opportunities uncovered or created in a given community can be as significant as an understanding of how an enterprise such as CPI creates employment opportunity for youth by bringing the area's employers into effective working relations with the institutions and agencies that work with the community's disadvantaged youth. This process cannot be easily summarized, though it is close to the heart of the problem of creating employment opportunity. CPI feels that it is the building of a bridge of common need between employer and worker. The bridge, in New Haven, is the working committee. This committee brings the employer, trade unions, educators, employment service placement specialists, and CPI staff together to preplan for recruitment, counseling, selection, training and placement of hard-core unemployed. The employer specifies the jobs he wants filled, states his *real* (as opposed to paper) entry qualifications, and the precise skill level he requires. He approves the curriculum tailor-made for his firm; he guides the development of aptitude tests directly related to his jobs; and he accepts the job candidates before training begins, acceptance being conditional on performance in the training.

Perhaps this is a large part of the secret of the success of CPI's comprehensive approach to the problem. It is, perhaps, something that the counselors of disadvantaged youth in hundreds of other middle sized communities throughout the land might help convert from wish to reality.

Metropolitan Prospect

It already has been said, but will bear repeating, that every youth kept suitably employed outside the metropolitan stew is one less victim of it. The best means of giving opportunity to many a metropolitan slum youth would have been to help him avoid becoming one. A prime way to approach the solution to a difficult problem is to reduce its dimensions. Therefore, much of the foregoing material in this chapter has a definite bearing on employment opportunity for metropolitan youth.

However, until they are abolished, large city slums create an urgent problem, since their youth must live and work, and opportunities for them must be found or made. It should be useful to report some of the experiences of pioneers in the more recent nationwide effort to develop urban programs for such youth, viewing their experiences against the backdrop of two pertinent facts of metropolitan life, namely:

1. The depressed levels of job opportunity in some of our largest cities; and

2. The social and economic isolation of the ghetto.

Levels of Opportunity: The physical crowding and growing obsolescence of the typical inner-city slum tends to discourage the expansion of established industry, or the entry of new enterprises; and this relative stagnation is reflected in general hiring levels. New York City is an outstanding example.[3] During the five-year period 1958-63, well before the atypical years of stepped-up defense activity of the mid-Sixties, non-farm employment throughout the nation rose by about 11 per cent. The corresponding increase in the New York metropolitan area was only 6 per cent. Much worse, the net increase in jobs in New York City itself was only 1.6 per cent. Furthermore, employment in goods production of all types (generally a favorable area for the unskilled and semiskilled) did not increase at all during the period; and there was, in fact, a net decrease of some 23,000 jobs in New York's manufacturing industries, as against a nationwide increase of 6 per cent in manufacturing employment. During the five years, blue collar employment dropped off about 12 per cent, while white collar employment increased by 14 per cent.

Given such facts, which should not be obscured by more recent statistics reflecting the abnormalities of defense production, some difficult long term alternatives must be faced. The youthful populations of the slums continue to grow. What to do? Let cold economics force an eventual mass exodus from the city? Somehow discourage immigration from major sources such as, presently, Puerto Rico? Degrade still more of New York's industry to the level of its sweated components, to accommodate the present work capabilities of her slum youth? Or, perhaps, greatly extend and intensify the effort to prepare New York youth for the kinds and levels of work for which there is a legitimate growing demand? New York is not alone in facing such choices.

Isolation of the Ghetto: Watts, the Los Angeles slum that exploded in the heat of summer, 1965, is a place apart, though surrounded incongruously by places such as the campus of the University of Southern California with which Watts has few economic, and no social relations. Most of the jobs that might be even remotely possible for Watts youth are miles away, and inaccessible for many reasons—the lack of decent clothing, carfare, and knowledge of possible job locations being only a few, and not the most fundamental.

Los Angeles and other sprawling metropolitan centers have numbers of such ghettos, and invisible walls have risen around them all. One of the higher and more durable of these walls would seem to have cut off the vision of much of the national Congress from the Washington slums

---

[3] The following statistics are taken from Regional Report No. 3, "Jobs in the New York-Northeastern New Jersey Area," published by the Middle Atlantic Regional Office, Bureau of Labor Statistics, U.S. Department of Labor, New York.

lying physically so near the Capital. Much has been researched and written about the unhappy effects of slum isolation on the employability of its residents; so it may be enough to say here that, short of abolishing the slums themselves, there is no more difficult, or more rewarding task than salvaging the masses of slum youth through helping them find useful, remunerative, and reasonably satisfying work. All of the principal approaches to this task are being tried, though with limited success, in our large cities. Three of them call for special mention: 1) to remove youth from the slum, temporarily at least, freeing them from its worst influences; rehabilitate them in new environments where they can work usefully, remedy deficiencies, and develop sound habits and attitudes. Such, for example, is the mission of the Job Corps, and the military services have this as a possible and not infrequent byproduct; 2) to put youth to work in their own slum neighborhoods, contributing to community programs of service to the most needy, and for the improvement of the environment; 3) to help young people to prepare for and find private employment, and through it to contribute to the economy and improve their own modes and standards of living.

It may be most useful to discuss these three approaches, with special attention to their employment in the Youth Opportunity Centers that have been established by the public employment service system, in all of our large cities. Although YOC services are readily available to all youth in need of them, most of the Centers are located in, or not far from inner-city slums, accessible to their youth.

The Approach Through New Environment

Collectively, the YOC's and other ES facilities screen and refer nine tenths of the Job Corps enrollment. As this is written, it is too early to know the numbers and proportions of urban slum youth who are finding suitable employment, or who are progressing in vocational training directed toward such employment, either in their home communities or elsewhere. One might speculate that the radical stimulus of living in a Job Corps camp, with its relatively clean break from old associations; its balance of work, study, and recreation; and its facilities for orienting its enrollees to work activities having some utility in outside employment, will be a valuable aid to growing numbers of such youth. On the other hand, part of the Job Corps's mission is to give what help it can to certain youth having very serious personal problems; and some of these troubled young people are gaining little from their experience, and leave about as unemployable as they were on arrival. Of the large majority who respond favorably, some few find continuing employment in the Corps's own installations. Much larger numbers enter military service, mainly in response to draft calls, and of these it must be presumed that considerable numbers are making careers in the armed services. Most of the remainder leave the camps for civilian employment, quite often preceded by courses of vocational training. As this is written, there are no reliable statistics covering the activities of Corpsmen after separation.

A meaningful assessment of the effects on the later employability of slum youth of military service in distant places is even more difficult. In spite of some thirteen years of administering veteran rehabilitation programs, the writer cannot venture more than a general opinion that, while there is a strong tendency for them to return from service to their slum homes, those who return physically and mentally intact tend to be broadened in outlook, better disciplined, more conscious of the need to find suitable work, and experienced in types of work that have at least some transfer values to civilian employment.

Public Service

The public service gateway to employment opportunity can be found or developed in any inner city. Temporary or part-time public service assignments, carefully fitted to the nature and needs of the individual disadvantaged urban youth, can go far toward preparing him for adult employment. A brief discussion of the Neighborhood Youth Corps in Chapter 11 reveals something of the practical scope of such assignments, and of their contributions to opportunities for adult employment.

The NYC, together with various other programs of a similar nature established under state, community, or other auspices, participates in comprehensive programs that are analogous in principle to Operation Bootstrap which, over a period of more than thirty years, has transformed Puerto Rico's economy. Whether it is applied to an insular commonwealth or an inner-city slum, the purpose is to rehabilitate the area as a whole, initially through introducing liberal amounts of financial aid; but this aid is directed so that the community, rebuilding from within and relying mainly on the constructive efforts of its citizens, can improve the lives of its people, increase its productivity, and carry its own weight economically.

In this general connection it should be noted that the immanent heavy demand for helping services to supplement hopelessly inadequate professional medical and trained nursing staffs—accompanied as it is by money to pay for the treatment and care received—must exert an upward pressure on wages. It will be impossible to attract even moderately competent persons at the very low pay levels now prevailing. The NYC, among other organizations, will surely continue its stand against exploiting its enrollees; and Department of Labor policy will give across-the-board encouragement and support only to programs of training and employment providing adequate assurance that the avenues to promotion to reasonably well-paid jobs are kept open for those trained and placed at public expense. The ultimate consequence should be the opening of an area of employment opportunity for many young men and women whose backgrounds give them practical knowledges and skills that they can use, after training, in satisfying and remunerative services to the people of their own communities.

This brief treatment of community service can be concluded after a reference to prospects for training and employment opportunities for inner-city youth in the physical renovation of the slums. Too often in the past, slum clearance programs have only pushed the residents out into other already overcrowded slums, adding insult to injury by denying them anything better than common labor on the building projects. There now seems to be good prospect for serious consideration of a massive, nationwide renovating and rebuilding program that would not only leave the residents in their own home areas, but would train and employ in the task of rebuilding those able and willing to participate. According to one proposal, worth watching partly because of the strong bipartisan support it is getting, the job would be done through creating privately financed, federally insured development corporations that would engage in and manage the physical reconstruction of the urban ghettos.[4] The proposal further suggests that slum residents employed on the reconstruction projects receive part of their wages in the form of stock in the development corporation, thus increasing their stakes in the enterprise. However it is accomplished, it may reasonably be expected that the youth of our urban slums will find public services in their own neighborhoods to be viable gateways to employment opportunity.

Employment in Private Industry

Change of environment has its undisputed value, and public service in the home neighborhood, its high promise. It is likely, however, that for some time to come most youth who do not leave their inner-city slum homes (or who, having left, return), must find their employment, if any, in nearby industrial, commercial, and other private establishments. The main thrust of YOC activity has been toward helping them prepare for, find, and enter such employment. As this is written, few of the Centers have been operating long enough to have established close relations with most of the employers in their respective areas, or to have developed special programs specifically directed toward the vocational preparation and selective placement of disadvantaged applicants. As the YOC's augment their staffs and add to their technical facilities and community resources, they should be able to profit from the experiences of some of the successful pioneering E&D (Experimental and Demonstration) projects serving metropolitan slum youth. Numbers of such projects have been discon-

---

[4] The proposal is that of Senator Robert Kennedy. Similar proposals have been made by Senator Jacob Javits and Mayor John Lindsay of New York City.

tinued with the coming of the YOC's, but others are continuing. Although several of these are making notable contributions to our store of knowledges and skills in this difficult area of service, only two will be described in this chapter: Chicago's JOBS (Job Opportunities for Better Skills), currently supported through OEO funds; and the work-evaluation and adjustment program of the Jewish Employment and Vocational Service in Philadelphia, some significant projects of which are also federally supported.

JOBS: JOBS concentrates almost exclusively on Negro youth of the Chicago slums, providing a wide variety of preparatory services, leading in most instances to jobs with Chicago's private employers. Only certain aspects of the JOBS experience will be mentioned. One of these relates to the matter of employer acceptance of the youth. This glimpse of the JOBS experience in its beginnings should be of interest to metropolitan programs still in their earlier stages:

To insure a citywide feeling of cooperation in the sincere desire to aid the culturally different, the federal government asked that in addition to the lip service heretofore rendered at the banquet table or cocktail party by major industrialists, they sign 400 declarations of intent for employment. . . . Out of these possible 400 jobs some 10–15 per cent materialized. The reasons for not hiring were numerous and familiar . . . no present openings; am planning to hire in the future; would rather wait until I see how other companies fare with the trainees; I'm in favor, but will have to clear with my supervisor; I don't mind helping the underprivileged, but we cannot afford to take a chance on a youngster with a record. . . . These were the kinds of reasons given for NOT employing. . . . Employers that initially hired JOBS trainees insisted on the cream of our crop. . . . The reason given was that they had to insure success among the first hired. . . . We did find some employers who saw our trainees as a good source of cheap labor. No agreements, however, were made with companies that did not pay the minimum starting wage for the particular industry.[5]

Another stubborn fact learned during that first year was that the youth must fit employers' established standards and specifications, whether or not they were realistic:

The employment screening devices used by Chicago industry were, in the main, prepared by middle or upper-middle class psychologists whose cultural perspectives and realities differed greatly from those of our trainees. Rather than argue the cultural bias of these tests (for they will not change substantially in the next few years), we propose to acquaint the trainees with them as much as possible.[6]

[5] *Job Opportunities Through Better Skills,* Final Report, 1963-64 (Chicago, 1965), pp. 115-124.
[6] *Op. cit.,* p. 122.

Although the JOBS training program involved a variety of contents and methods, including remedial education, prevocational training, institutional training courses and on-the-job training, it was the last of these that emerged as a particularly promising means of developing employment opportunity, and of actually getting the youngster on the job.

This reference to on-the-job training, and earlier references to such training in the New Haven CPI program and a number of others, call for special comment. On-the-job training, and other modes of training as such, are the central concern of another chapter in this book. On-the-job training viewed as a highly important gateway to employment deserves more attention than some programs for disadvantaged youth have given it to date. Its limitations are well known. They include among others, the propensity of some employers to use subsidized OJT programs as a source of cheap labor; and the sometimes poor quality of the training, due in part to the ineptitude of some employers as teachers, and in part to the narrowness of the training, with its focus on knowledges and skills peculiar to the particular establishment. Moreover, the development of OJT openings takes considerable time and effort, and familiarity with employers and their needs; also, in spite of a streamlining of procedures, the steps involved, and requirements to be met for federal financing limit their numbers and scope. It may be hoped, however, that the very favorable experiences of those E&D projects that have relied heavily on OJT will encourage the YOC's and other organizations serving disadvantaged youth, to recognize the basic importance of this time-tested means of entry into employment for those who learn best by doing.

As JOBS has found a place for itself in the Chicago "jungle," it has succeeded in preparing its clientele for an ever-widening range of jobs, a simple listing of which (inappropriate in this chapter), would indicate what can be done with time, good will, and devoted effort. It might also be said as a footnote to the first of the above quotations from the JOBS report (concerning the reluctance of Chicago employers to "buy the product"), that JOBS has subsequently established excellent working relations with some of Chicago's leading employers—witness International Harvester, which has become one of several to take on a sizeable number of young Negro clients as one step toward meeting its obligations under "Plans for Progress."

Plans for Progress

In Chicago, as in any metropolitan area, the prevailing attitudes of the larger employers toward the hiring of minority youth are important, and sometimes decisive to the success of programs for the disadvantaged. The several hundred large commercial and industrial firms and other organizations that have joined the nationwide voluntary program, Plans for Progress, collectively employ, as this is written, nearly nine million workers. Much of their hiring is in or near metropolitan centers such as Chicago, where great masses of minority youth are in critical need of jobs. A firm joining the program pledges to take effective steps to end hiring discrimination against ethnic minorities, and to extend and improve employment opportunities for members of these groups. The organizations identified with Plans for Progress vary widely as to actual depth of commitments, extent to which they make special arrangements to meet commitments, and magnitude of the actual hiring needs that might be met through the employment of disadvantaged minority youth. Nevertheless, it may be assumed that most of the member firms willingly explore their hiring needs with a view to giving a fair trial to those youth who show reasonable promise of fitting into their organizations. On the whole, the many branch establishments of such firms are favorable prospects for locating training and placement opportunities for minority youth. It also may be expected that if most of the youth brought to their attention by service organizations are found by them to be productive, dependable employees, more referrals will be welcomed, and ultimately, that other employers will follow their examples. Thus the road to opportunity may be widened and smoothed through wise collaboration between employers and youth services.

Preparation, Key to Opportunity: The Philadelphia Story

The writer has sought to make the point in this chapter that, for disadvantaged youth, job opportunity is more a creation than a discovery. It is made through meetings of the minds of those who employ, those who need employment, and those who mediate between them. The most difficult aspect of the role of the mediator is to stimulate and direct vocationally useful changes in youths themselves. Nowhere has this been demonstrated more clearly than in Philadelphia, in 1964.

Chicago has its Northside, and North Philadelphia has its "jungle." The story concerns three hundred and thirty-one youths living in it, all of them out of school and out of work as the story begins.

They represented a population which is culturally alienated from the mainstream of middle class aspirations and vocational values. They viewed work as a punitive, and not as a rewarding activity. For them, work was arduous and menial and offered neither wages above minimal subsistence needs (which were already met by public assistance sources), nor the opportunity to move up the occupational ladder.[7]

---

[7] U.S. Employment Service, U.S. Department of Labor, *Preparing Disadvantaged Youth for Work* (Washington, D.C.: Government Printing Office), p. 4.

Most of the youths were further described as having dropped out of school during the tenth or eleventh grades, but with average reading ability at the fourth grade level, and arithmetic achievement still lower. More than half had been classified as functionally retarded. About half were known to the police, and a third had been adjudicated delinquent by the courts.

The Pennsylvania State Employment Service had interviewed all of them, but had been unable to place them in either employment or training. Thus they were considered good candidates for a special program of evaluation and work adjustment services in which the Employment Service was cooperating with the Jewish Employment and Vocational Service.[8]

The 331 youths were referred to the JEVS Work Adjustment Center where they entered individualized programs for the evaluation of their vocational potentials and job readiness, and for subsequent work adjustment training. One hundred sixty-five (almost exactly half) completed their programs, spending periods ranging from a few weeks to a few months; the other half quit or were terminated for reasons themselves enlightening as to the young people's natures, problems, and needs.

It is highly significant that *every* youth who completed his or her program of evaluation and work adjustment, and was referred back to the Employment Service for placement, was placed, either in a job or in some type of vocational training—this in spite of the fact that none of them had formerly been considered employable, or ready to profit from job training. It is also significant that most of the 165 were placed in much the same kinds of jobs and training courses that had formerly been available —though not to them. About half of their placements were in unskilled jobs; about a third were in established training courses; semiskilled jobs and a few apprenticeships comprised the remainder. Several months after the project ended, 142 were found to be still employed or in training.

It seems reasonable to draw the conclusion that for metropolitan slum youth such as those described, the true locus of opportunity for competitive employment lies more within the youth himself than in the establishments where he may or may not ultimately find work. The object of the most careful search must be the youth's hidden personal assets, and the main object of the pre-employment services must be their cultivation.

The Philadelphia outcome also suggests that *work* is itself the most effective means of revealing those hidden personal assets, and the most effective means of cultivating them. This is no new discovery, but the needed reaffirmation of an ancient experience of the race. Our metropolitan jungles are compelling us to re-examine the crude fundamentals under-

[8] The project was funded through OMAT, U.S. Department of Labor; coordinated by the Philadelphia Council for Community Advancement.

lying human development and adjustment, getting behind and beneath the overlay of verbalism that only obscures the problems and the progress of the culturally deprived. This applies to counseling. The description of the project's methods and findings says:

> There is no point in talking about feelings with a youth who is accustomed to ignoring his feelings. It is meaningless to discuss vocational plans with a youth who cannot project his ideas beyond the present. . . .[9]

Thus, rather than extensive interviewing, testing and other essentially verbal exercises, the approach was to set the youth to *work*. The general procedure used throughout the course of the project, and subsequently with many other disadvantaged youth, has been to start by evaluating work readiness and potentials through the administration of a series of samples of tasks representing or associated with various fields of work. The samples for each field are graded in difficulty, and can be administered in any number and sequence that the counselor believes will best capture and hold the youth's interest. The samples give the youth what usually is his first opportunity to explore, and get some of the "feel" of types of work found in the area. They give his counselor the opportunity to see his client approach such work; to note his reactions to novelty, tedium, obstacles, and his own error or ineptitude; to get badly needed evidence of his tolerances and preferences. The samples do not have the forbidding formality of most conventional tests, with their stereotyped instructions, time limits, and resemblance to unhappy experiences in school. An unobtrusive tally of errors, and a record of time required to complete the tasks, gives the counselor some objective evidence to support observations of behavior, and conclusions based not only on such observations, but also the expressed reactions of the youth in subsequent counseling interviews. It is an arresting fact, and one of special significance to counselors of disadvantaged youth with limited ability or desire to communicate, that discussions of their work sampling experiences can convert otherwise sterile, unproductive interviews into meaningful explorations into parts of the world of work possibly available to the youth; and equally meaningful, such discussions facilitate cooperative evaluations of the youth's personal qualities as they relate to his future employment.

The work sample evaluation procedure in JEVS is valuably supplemented by providing the youth with at least a limited period of paid, productive work experience in a sheltered workshop environment, described in the project report as equipped with the usual

> . . . work benches, fixtures, tools, time clocks and belt line. . . . Work obtained by contract from private industry at competitive prices and in accordance with

[9] *Preparing Disadvantaged Youth for Work,* p. 5.

federal wage and hour standards, was typically simple or repetitive. . . . The young people were exposed to a variety of job tasks and situations. The pressures of the contracts were used to teach what to expect, accept, and deal with in industry. . . .[10]

It will be of professional interest to counselors to note this statement in the report:

The function of counseling in the work adjustment process was a supporting and reinforcing one. As the youth developed suitable attitudes and coping behaviors, counseling enabled him to bring to awareness the changes that were occurring within him. Periodic counseling interviews crystallized his feelings and provided a mental image of his new worker identity. He was helped to verbalize the positive and negative feelings he experienced, to express in words the values and purposes of working that he felt were satisfying. Thus, counseling helped him to develop a worker self-concept which clearly reflected personal status and vocational goals and the ways to achieve those goals.[11]

CONCLUSIONS

Three general approaches to the creation of employment opportunity for metropolitan slum youth have been discussed. They are not mutually exclusive, and this part of the chapter could have been otherwise organized. But whatever may be our patterns of thinking about this critical area of national concern, certain conclusions seem inescapable.

The first is that no marked progress can be made toward freeing such youth from the vicious circle of cultural and economic deprivation in which so many of them are now imprisoned, unless substantial progress is made in slowing the drainage of deprived youth from the countryside, into inner-city septic tanks. Part of the chapter has been addressed to an overview of this problem, and a survey of some of the more exemplary efforts to solve it through creating rural job opportunities for rural youth, and through aiding those who migrate, in the earlier stages of their rural-urban transitions.

A second conclusion is that many youths who are born in, or enter inner-city slums, can enhance their opportunities for useful and rewarding employment and better lives thereafter, by changing—even temporarily—to special civilian or military environments that give them new perspectives, knowledges, and vocationally usable skills.

A third conclusion is that, although its directions, magnitudes, and timetables are not predictable, there is high promise for a really determined effort to convert the ghetto—rather than merely to disperse its people into other ghettos; that much of this can be done by its own youth;

[10] *Preparing Disadvantaged Youth for Work,* p. 7.
[11] *Op. cit.,* p. 5.

and that developing this area of opportunity may do more ultimately for slum youth and, through them, the nation, than any other course of action.

A fourth conclusion is that while these several modes of attack on the central problem are gathering momentum, employment in the private sector must continue to be the objective of most disadvantaged youth. Although there can be a certain amount of accommodation by private employers to the special needs and limitations of the youth, and some imaginative searches for kinds of work that are tolerant of their limitations, the main thrust must be toward preparing them to meet the normal demands of employment.

This leads to a final, fifth conclusion. It is, that whether such preparation takes the form of prevocational work disciplines in the Job Corps or the armed services, or of work crews on the CPI model, or job explorations and tryouts, or work sampling and sheltered workshop programs modeled on the Philadelphia pattern, *work itself* must be the salient, common element in all of the various modes of preparation, if they are to lead reliably to job opportunity. This conclusion has its special significance for counselors of the disadvantaged. It recalls their attention to the fact that their best hope for success is to subordinate words about work to work itself, and that they and their organizations must somehow bring monitored work intimately into the process of their counseling.

Within the broad range of these several conclusions there is room for qualification and even dissent; and the writer hopes that these and the other observations offered in this chapter will lead its readers to such reflections.

SELECTED READINGS

1. Amos, William E., and Jane Perry, "Negro Youth and Employment Opportunities," *Journal of Negro Education.* (Fall, 1963).

2. Briggs, William A., and Dean L. Hummel, *Counseling Minority Group Youth: Developing the Experience of Equality Through Education.* Columbus, Ohio: The Ohio Civil Rights Commission, 1962.

3. Gordon, Margaret S., ed., *Poverty in America,* San Francisco: Chandler Publishing Co., 1965.

4. Kvaraceus, William C., "Poverty and Undereducation: What School and Community Can Do," *Occupational Outlook Quarterly,* VIII, No. 3 (1964).

5. Morgan, James N., *et al., Income and Welfare in the United States.* New York: McGraw-Hill Book Company, 1962.

6. National Committee For Children and Youth, *Rural Youth in Crisis.* Washington, D.C.: U.S. Department of Health, Education, and Welfare, 1965.

7. Northup, Herbert R., and Richard L. Rowan, eds., *The Negro and Employment Opportunity.* Ann Arbor, Mich.: Bureau of Industrial Relations, University of Michigan, 1965.

8. Riessman, Frank, "Overlooked Positives of Disadvantaged Groups," *Journal of Negro Education,* **33** (Summer, 1964), 225-231.

9. Shostak, Arthur B., and William Gomberg, eds., *New Perspectives on Poverty.* Englewood Cliffs, N.J.: Prentice-Hall, Inc., 1965.

10. U.S. Congress, *Manpower Development and Training Act of 1962 As Amended (42 U.S.C. 2751-2620).* Washington D.C.: Government Printing Office, 1965.

11. U.S. Department of Agriculture, Economic Research Division, "Employment, Unemployment, and Low Incomes in Appalachia," *Agricultural Economic Report No. 73.* Washington, D.C.: Government Printing Office, 1965.

12. U.S. Department of Health, Education, and Welfare, *Education and Training: The Bridge Between Man and His Work.* Washington, D.C.: Government Printing Office, 1965.

13. U.S. Department of Labor, Office of Manpower, Automation and Training, *Occupational Training: Pathway to Employment.* Washington, D.C.: Government Printing Office, 1964.

14. U.S. Senate Subcommittee on Employment and Manpower of the Committee on Labor and Public Welfare, *Toward Full Employment: Proposals for a Comprehensive Employment and Manpower Policy for the U.S.: A Report.* Washington, D.C.: Government Printing Office, 1964.

I I

TRAINING OPPORTUNITIES
FOR DISADVANTAGED YOUTH

EDWARD C. ROEBER

The number of young men and women who have been able to rise above impoverished environments has been relatively small, however spectacular their accomplishments may have been. Causes for this encapsulation within subcultures are many, and some of them have been discussed in prior chapters. Until very recent years, the product of this encapsulation—disadvantaged youth—has been a consistent "loser" in the educational enterprise of this country.

From the time youths of impoverished environments entered formal school situations, they were subjected to curricula, out-of-class activities, and even so-called special pupil personnel services, that persistently reinforced disruptive attitudes, such as those associated with failure, disappointment, lack of trust, and inadequacy. In one way or another, most of them were encouraged to leave school. As school dropouts, and under the influence of these debilitating attitudes, they seldom had much more success in finding or holding jobs than they had had in formal school environments. Thus disadvantaged youth generally became adults with serious educational handicaps, no marketable job skills, and even worse, little hope of attaining such skills. And even if they could find less formal training opportunities, such as those in vocational schools, apprenticeships, adult education classes, and on-the-job training, these were not adapted to the needs and deficiencies of disadvantaged youth. If one was able to

236

be a "winner," he did so in spite of his environment, discouragements in training situations, and probably with some "scars" to show for his efforts.

Except for a few transitory attempts to correct the problem, such as the CCC's and NYA in the early Thirties, there was formerly little concern for youth and adults who were trapped in noneducational, under-employed subcultures. Recently, however, a sudden awakening to the needs of people in these subcultures has triggered the beginnings of experimentation that can ultimately provide adequate educational and training opportunities for all children, youth, and adults. And thus this discussion is hopefully a prelude to an enlightened era when this nation realizes one of its older ideals, i.e., educational and training opportunities for *all* children, youth, and adults, to the limit of their capacities to profit from them, with no one denied such opportunities on economic, social, racial, religious, or other grounds.

Issues Associated with Training Opportunities

In any consideration of training for the disadvantaged youth, we are faced with several issues, some of them very critical to the development and evaluation of training opportunities. It would be simple to say that all issues can be traced to characteristics of disadvantaged youth, to their familial patterns, and to weaknesses inherent in their subcultures. But such a form of rationalizing away issues and problems has developed several generations of disadvantaged adults who contribute minimally to national manpower needs and to their own sense of well-being. Apparently, ways must be found to break subcultural bondages that produce successive disadvantaged generations. The following issues, although not intended to be all-inclusive, are associated with training opportunities and indicate the dimensions of the task facing our society.

Training and Education

Disadvantaged youth are generally lacking in marketable skills, and also in basic education so necessary to developing marketable skills. In addition, they are or have been "losers" in school. They have strong drives, therefore, away from further educational endeavors and toward immediate economic gratifications, honest or otherwise; thus, and understandably, they are not willing to endure long periods of basic education before they enter programs of training for jobs.

At the same time, some concern should be expressed for *training* programs that, while preparing a disadvantaged youth to perform a routine task, do not require much basic education. Products of such training programs are not able to transfer their narrow band of skills to performing other tasks, however similar the latter may be to the original task. Basic education, providing, for example, minimal skills in reading, communication, and number concepts, may yield a readiness to train and retrain efficiently. Without such basic education, moreover, a disadvantaged youth who has been given training may, in a short period of time, find that he has no marketable skill. How much disappointment can a disadvantaged youth tolerate when narrow training does not yield relatively stable employment?

Fundamentally, then, the issue remains how to provide a balanced program of preparation that includes tolerable amounts of basic education, a re-education of attitudes toward and an orientation for work and education, and skill training for jobs. Perhaps the most pressing need in the development of training programs for disadvantaged youth is experimentation that seeks to ascertain the necessary ingredients, and the proper balance of these ingredients in various types of training programs.

Evaluations of Training Programs

Concomitant with much needed experimentation is concern for ways in which to study outcomes of training programs. If we have learned a few things from past experiences with disadvantaged youth, we might incorporate these lessons into a set of researchable concepts. Kranz feels that we have already learned a few lessons:

In the first place, the young person who needs the training most is too often ruled out of competitive examinations or because he fails to apply at all. . . . There should be a program of work experience activities to determine, more exactly than by testing, whether the job is suitable.

. . . once the hard-to-reach youth is enrolled in a program, new techniques must be used to retain his interest while his employability is increased.

It has also become evident that we will need counselors to deal with the problems that fall outside strictly vocational lines. . . . The youth with multiple problems must have a flexible, multi-faceted program. Counseling is, of course, the key, but it must be flexible enough to match the youth's responses to the various training situations.

Equally important, of course, is the follow-up after placement. Getting a job is of utmost importance to the young person who has been on the ragged edge of economic desperation. The follow-up process—with its attendant encouragement, display of interest, and meaningful praise—is of inestimable value.[1]

Assuming that jobs can be made available and also adaptable for youth with basic education and skill training, we can study the effects of various training programs, hopefully adjusting the balance among program ingredients as our knowledge increases. Without active attempts at evalua-

[1] Harry Kranz, "Washington Charts a Course," *American Child*, January, 1965, pp. 4-5.

tion, training programs can become ritualistic and lose touch with the needs of disadvantaged youth.

EXPERIMENTATIONS WITH TRAINING OPPORTUNITIES

Traditional forms of vocational and technical education have been notoriously lacking in experimentation, particularly when it comes to meeting the needs of disadvantaged youth. In public education, it is not uncommon to hear vocational educators complain, for example, that vocational education is the "dumping grounds" in schools. In this so-called dumping grounds would be numbered potential dropouts and many who have been poor achievers. And vocational education has ordinarily found it difficult to adapt goals, shops, and methods to the needs of these youth. Furthermore, vocational education has been receiving some criticism because its programs do not appear to satisfy the needs for skills in a modern economy.[2] It obviously will require considerable experimentation for vocational education to link the needs of disadvantaged youth with the needs of a modern economy.

Private vocational schools have catered to youth who possess some motivation for further education, have the financial resources to pay tuition, and have sufficient basic education to succeed in training programs —disadvantaged youth would not generally seek, or be able to benefit from traditional programs of such schools.

Because traditional training opportunities have not been adapted to the needs of disadvantaged youth, it has been necessary to develop new forms of training opportunities. The number of new forms has steadily increased, supported by federal legislation such as the Manpower Development and Training Act of 1962, the Vocational Act of 1963, and Economic Opportunity Act of 1964. Training opportunities for disadvantaged youth are now at an experimental, developmental stage and thus cannot be cataloged by any rational process. It has, therefore, been necessary to group rather roughly some experiments that illustrate the breadth of opportunities, but must await results of follow-up and other types of research before we have assurance that they do in fact provide training *opportunities* for disadvantaged youth.

Training Opportunities under MDTA

One of the first legislative steps toward training disadvantaged youth was the Manpower Development and Training Act of 1962 (MDTA), intended to provide institutional and on-the-job training (OJT) for young

[2] Office of Manpower, Automation, and Training, *Young Workers: Their Special Training Needs,* Manpower Research Bulletin Number 3 (Washington, D.C.: U.S. Department of Labor, May, 1963), p. 17.

men and women 16 years old and older. Experiences with programs under this act indicated several shortcomings that were subsequently overcome with amendments to the act. As changed, programs could pay training allowances to youth 17 years of age and older (lowered from 19 to 17); could pay allowances to 25 per cent of the trainees (up from 5 per cent of total allowances) between 17 and 22 years of age; and could pay allowances for as long as 108 weeks (double the original limit). These modifications in MDTA meant that programs could reach larger numbers of disadvantaged youth at a critical age, provide some source of income while in training, and make possible a longer training period for basic education or training for higher level, technical occupations. Provisions for disadvantaged youth under MDTA (particularly special youth projects) provide relatively flexible, individualized plans for vocational development, including counseling, job development, placement, follow-up, and supporting services.

Altogether about 60,000 young people 16 to 21 years of age were enrolled in MDTA institutional programs during 1966; nearly 165,000 from August 1962, to December 1966.[3] Programs for OJT enrolled nearly 21,000 in 1966 with a cumulative total from 1962-1966 of nearly 40,000.[4] Not all trainees completed their training—and apparently no data are available regarding the dropout rate for disadvantaged trainees.[5] Initial job placement for trainees who completed training has been 85 per cent or higher for both institutional and OJT training; and a later survey indicated that approximately 70 per cent were still employed.[6]

An important feature, one that will assume increasing significance for training disadvantaged youth, is the experimental and demonstration (E & D) program under MDTA. This program, representing contracts with private and public agencies, provides opportunities to experiment with training disadvantaged youth who cannot be reached, motivated, or prepared in regular training programs. The *Manpower Report of the President* lists five types of such training approaches: [7]

a. *Sheltered Workshops.* These projects which produce marketable goods simulate as realistically as possible industrial conditions and, under supervision, trainees are introduced to basic job requirements, such as regular attendance, cooperation with fellow workers, acceptance of supervision,

[3] Information supplied by the Branch of Training Operations Reports Analysis, U.S. Employment Service, U.S. Department of Labor, Washington, D.C.

[4] Information provided by the Division of Reports and Analysis, U.S. Department of Labor.

[5] *Manpower Report of the President and a Report on Manpower Requirements, Resources, Utilization, and Training* (Washington, D.C.: Government Printing Office, 1966), p. 99.

[6] *Ibid.,* p. 100.

[7] *Ibid.,* pp. 100-101.

a standard work pace, and the relation between work performance and pay. Sheltered workshops generally operate on the basis of contracts with businesses and industries for their work projects. These projects involve assembling, packaging, sorting, and similar activities. A workshop may contract, for example, with a variety store to assemble Easter baskets, with a manufacturing concern to assemble into a packet a manual of directions, a warranty, and descriptive materials for some product, with another manufacturing firm to assemble a relatively simple product, or with a manufacturer to file burrs from metal parts. There are several goals behind such a sheltered workshop type of program. In a sense, it provides a trainee with an opportunity to test himself in more than one worklike situation. He may find he is able to do some tasks better than others, or he may discover what is expected of an employee in terms of attitudes, habits, skills, and performance—all within a relatively protected environment where he is not fired or severely penalized for substandard work performance. Also such workshops include counseling and other special services as an integral part of their operation so that trainees can be assisted in their adaptation to work situations as well as in their discovery of work situations that best meet their particular needs.

b. *Skill Centers.* These projects also simulate many aspects of a work setting, but the goods and services are not marketable. In many respects, skill centers have attributes in common with some aspects of vocational education in school settings and in workshop settings. Trainees may be taught how to perform certain tasks with the expectation that the development of skills is paramount and not necessarily the goods or services produced. These centers develop a wide variety of skills depending upon the resources and the ingenuity of those who plan such centers. Basically, though, they are concerned with skills that have a direct application in the labor market, such as repairing electrical appliances, and performing simple machine operations with wood, metal, or plastics. It is the purpose of these centers to give trainees an opportunity to test themselves in a work setting and, at the same time, discover and develop skills having direct applications to jobs in the labor market—skills that can be put to use as quickly as trainees reach acceptable levels of performance. Accompanied by counseling and other special services, skill testing and skill development follow the usual pattern of a multifaceted approach to the eventual employability of disadvantaged youth.

c. *Vestibule Training.* This type of training combines on-the-job training for specific entry jobs and classroom instruction; however on-the-job training is not necessarily in the business or industry which will eventually employ trainees. Typically these programs, along with classroom instruction, have been sponsored by city governments where trainees have secured training in city government agencies, such as in clerical, hospital, maintenance, and other jobs. After reaching acceptable levels of performance, trainees are placed in entry, training-related jobs, and usually not in government agencies. This approach to training provides each trainee with an exposure to work and with an opportunity to develop job-related skills along with attitudes and habits that are desirable in most work settings.

d. *On-the-Job Training.* Job training is provided by a private employer at wages substantially higher than MDTA youth allowances. Project sponsors furnish counseling and supporting services, while the employer furnishes the on-the-job training. If all goes well, there probably is no better experience than actual training on-the-job; however disadvantaged youth, without significant changes in attitudes and habits, are not necessarily the type of individuals tolerated by many employers. So perhaps the greatest deterrent to this type of training-on-the-job program is the availability of training stations. Placement of disadvantaged youth in this type of training is by no means as high as for graduates of the regular OJT projects. Whether or not on-the-job training proves successful in the long-run may depend upon entry-job-development activities, i.e., the modification of existing entry jobs and the development of new entry jobs. Disadvantaged youth in the very beginnings of their work experience may require some modifications in standard work tasks until they are able to develop higher level skills, and until they develop acceptable work attitudes and habits. Unless industries can accommodate some changes in their entry jobs and their expectations from neophyte workers, the dropout rate among disadvantaged youth from this type of program is likely to be high—and could reinforce attitudes of defeatism so common among disadvantaged youth.

e. *Pre-Apprenticeship Training.* These projects furnish higher level knowledge and the skills to dropouts for the purpose of meeting entrance requirements for apprenticeship programs. Increasingly, apprenticeship programs have sought high school graduates or individuals with the equivalence of a high school education. Assuming that the trades will accept disadvantaged youth if the latter can reach acceptable levels of basic education and pre-job skills, this type of training program will meet the needs of a limited number of disadvantaged youth; however the time necessary to acquire acceptable levels of education and skills, and then to complete apprenticeships, is not apt to attract large numbers of disadvantaged youth. "The results, though not uniformly favorable, demonstrate that school dropouts who would never otherwise have an opportunity for apprenticeship may, by successfully completing a year of coupled OJT and classroom instruction, gain admittance to formal apprenticeships in the construction and metalworking trades." [8]

These efforts to experiment and demonstrate with many approaches to training disadvantaged youth may, in time, pay greater dividends than efforts with more traditional programs. Experimental programs may discover ways in which disadvantaged youth may be motivated and assisted toward the development of healthy attitudes toward training and work, the antecedent to developing job skills. Furthermore, they may help foster a new way of life, one associated with regular employment rather than unemployment, and dependency upon society.

TRAINING OPPORTUNITIES UNDER
THE ECONOMIC OPPORTUNITY ACT OF 1964

This piece of legislation was directed toward ways in which to bring economic well-being within reach of subcultures whose needs have generally been ignored throughout the history of man. Some of the experi-

[8] *Ibid.,* p. 101.

ments growing out of this legislation have been aimed at some level of training for disadvantaged youth: they still have not touched the lives of all disadvantaged youth. They must be regarded as experiments and, hopefully, as forerunners of more comprehensive, pervasive training programs that will meet the unique needs of all disadvantaged youth. Two prototypes of training programs, the Neighborhood Youth Corps and the Job Corps, are still in their early developmental stage; however they illustrate programs designed to reach the hard core of disadvantaged youth.

Neighborhood Youth Corps

The Neighborhood Youth Corps (NYC) is designed for disadvantaged youth 16 to 21 years of age. Highest priorities are given to youth from poor families with poor achievement in school, poor attitudes toward work, physical and mental disabilities, etc. "Altogether, 1,658 projects providing 577,500 jobs for enrollees were approved during calendar year 1966. . . . The total number of jobs for youth from fiscal 1967 appropriations was about 356,000." [9]

The federal government contracts with local and state governments and with private nonprofit agencies. All work performed by disadvantaged youth does not displace present workers; rather, it is expected to satisfy some of the unmet public needs in five major fields—health, education, welfare, recreation, and conservation.

The possible range of jobs is illustrated by a single city government project, which lists the following: School ground beautification aides, landscaping aides, janitor aides, library aides, clerical aides, teacher aides, street beautification and street repair aides, conservation workers, cafeteria aides, recreation aides, warehouse aides, television and audiovisual aides, and beautification aides at the city hall, water plant, fire department building, parks, and housing projects.[10]

NYC's expressed purposes are to keep disadvantaged youth in school, to help them return to school if they are dropouts, and to give them work experience. For youth who are in school and who might drop out of school, the NYC's provide financial assistance and, hopefully, motivate them to stay in school. Full-time students are limited to 15 hours' participation per week (20 hours for part-time students). In-school projects can enroll youth for the full school year as well as for the summer months. Students receive the regular project rate of $1.25 an hour. This program apparently has helped reduce the dropout rate. "In one Detroit school, for example, the dropout rate for NYC enrollees was only 4.2 per cent, compared with 9.7 per cent for all students. This is the more impressive

[9] Information provided by the Office of Program Development, Neighborhood Youth Corps, U.S. Department of Labor.
[10] *Manpower Report of the President, op. cit.*, p. 102.

because the students selected for the NYC were, in general, those most likely to leave school." [11]

For youth who have left school, enrollees in NYC's may work up to 32 hours per week and earn up to $40 a week. They are limited to 26 weeks unless they participate at least six hours a week in an after-work educational program, in which case the 26-week period can be extended. Special services for many of these youth include remedial education, instruction in basic skills, counseling, and medical assistance. This out-of-school program concentrates on developing healthy attitudes toward work, and on enabling enrollees to return to school, to undertake skill training and, eventually, to hold regular jobs.

Summer projects for youth who normally attend school have also been developed and resulted in the employment of nearly 255,000 youth in July 1966.[12]

Selection of youth for NYC's has been the responsibility of project sponsors, aided typically by state Employment Services and Youth Opportunity Centers. As a group, enrollees had the following characteristics: 1) In-school project enrollees were typically eleventh and twelfth grade males, 17 years of age, those whose unemployment rates were highest. About one third were nonwhite. Work in the NYC was the first job experience for over three fourths of the young people. There were substantial numbers of young women, with the proportion higher among nonwhite than white enrollees. 2) Out-of-school project enrollees averaged 18 years of age, and a majority of them were nonwhites. Nearly half of them had dropped from school after the ninth grade. For more than half of these enrollees, NYC supplied the first work experience in their lives. As in the case of in-school enrollees, there were more nonwhite than white young women.[13]

Outcomes of the NYC have as yet not been assessed. It is already apparent, though, that certain features require further study and strengthening:[14] improved on-the-job supervision, more planning time, and more emphasis on developing good work-experience arrangements, including, for some enrollees, more emphasis on basic work attitudes and habits, and for other enrollees more challenging work assignments.

Job Corps

Disadvantaged youth generally come from environments that offer them very little stimulation to become productive citizens; thus the Job

[11] *Ibid.*, p. 103.

[12] Information provided by the Office of Program Development, Neighborhood Youth Corps, U.S. Department of Labor.

[13] *Manpower Report of the President, op. cit.*, p. 103.

[14] *Ibid.*, p. 104.

Corps is especially adapted to meet their needs. The first center began operations in early 1965. By mid-January 1966, the Job Corps had 73 conservation centers, with over 8000 enrollees; 8 urban centers for men, with another 8000 enrollees; and 6 urban centers for women, with 1500 enrollees. Plans call for an increase in the total enrollment in all centers to 30,000 by the end of fiscal year 1966 and to 45,000 by the end of fiscal 1967.[15]

Typically, the Job Corps, both in conservation and urban centers, has attempted to recognize needs associated with disadvantaged youth and, consequently, the program and its management have offered the following experiences to enrollees:

A. A basic education program
  1. A goal of reading up to seventh or eighth grade level
  2. Basic mathematical skills necessary for many present-day jobs
  3. Understanding the world of work, including types of jobs available, how to apply for jobs, and how to hold jobs

B. Physical training, health education, and recreation of many types

C. Motor vehicle operation

D. Training in use of hand tools, and general employability skills

E. Counseling, individually and in groups

In conservation centers, which are located on public lands, young men spend half their time in needed conservation work, such as building trails and shelters, digging ditches, planting seedlings, pruning trees, and fighting fires, in addition to time spent in remedial instruction and special services described earlier.

Urban centers give specific job skill training. The sponsor of each center determines the nature of job training offered; therefore no two men's centers are likely to have identical training programs. (If a young person demonstrates interest and aptitude for a particular skill not offered in one center, he can be transferred to another one that has the training.) A rough tabulation of the types of training offered in urban centers is as follows: (The number in parentheses indicates the number of centers offering that particular type of training.)

automotive repair and maintenance (7)
food service (5)
business (clerical and retail) (6)
electrical and electronics repair (5)

[15] *Ibid.*

building maintenance (4)

industrial and commercial occupations (welding, machine tool operation, residential heating, etc.) (4)

household appliances (installation, repair, and service) (3)

refrigeration (installation, repair, and service) (2)

landscape and nursery occupations (2)

heavy and light equipment operators' course (2)

heating equipment (installation, repair, and service) (1)

dry cleaning and laundry (1)

tailoring (1)

drafting (1)

medical services (1)

building trades (1)

office machine repair (1)

boating industry trades (1)

recreation assistant (1) [16]

Screening for the Job Corps has been handled by public employment offices; they accept youth between the ages of 16 and 21, poor, uneducated, and jobless. In addition, special attention has been given to the need for taking youth out of their present environment, hoping that a new one will give them a "fresh start." Enrollees were also chosen for lack of motivation, and on the basis of other handicapping circumstances. Two categories of youth—those who had committed crimes of violence and those who were drug addicts—were not accepted as enrollees. (These two groups have persistently experienced few opportunities for training or for employment, a condition requiring special rehabilitation services and re-education of the public and employers. This need has not been resolved through participation in existing programs.)

Enrollees in the Job Corps have typically been between 17 and 18 years of age, and slightly below the ninth grade level educationally. One quarter of them have been out of school more than two years and nearly three fourths for more than six months. More than half the enrollees had lived in substandard, overcrowded housing, and about the same proportion had a deficient and disruptive home environment. About 37 per cent came from families on public assistance, and 34 per cent from a home where a parent was seriously ill. In 55 per cent of the families, the primary wage earner was unemployed. More than one fourth of the corpsmen had tried to enter the armed forces and been found disqualified.[17]

[16] Office of Economic Opportunity, *Job Corps Urban Centers*, Circular Memorandum 66-48 (Washington, D.C.: March 21, 1966).

[17] *Manpower Report of the President, op. cit.*, p. 106.

As yet, the results of the crucial test of Job Corps—eventual employment, and usefulness as a citizen—have not been ascertained because the program has not operated long enough. "Despite their previous record of failure, between two thirds and three fourths of the enrollees have stayed with the Corps. This record is a real measure of success. About half of those who have left quit during the first month; this may indicate either that their commitment to the Corps was limited, or perhaps that they lapsed into the pattern of failure which had pursued them." [18]

Some needed improvements in Job Corps have already become evident: more attention to selection and placement of enrollees in programs where the needs of disadvantaged youth can best be met; the recruitment of adequate numbers of well-trained staff, such as remedial teachers, group workers, guidance and counseling personnel, and other specialized workers; and improved public relations as various centers experiment with different approaches. [19]

TRAINING OPPORTUNITIES UNDER THE
VOCATIONAL EDUCATION ACT OF 1963

Emphases of the Vocational Education Act of 1963 were significantly different from the Smith-Hughes Act after World War I, and the George-Barden Act after World War II. Vocational education curricula, in the new act, are directed at meeting current needs for complex skills in a modern labor force. In addition, substantial sums of money are appropriated to experiment with programs and services designed to meet the needs of disadvantaged youth. In fiscal year 1966, about 58,000 youths were enrolled in special needs projects. It is projected that over 700,000 youths will be served in similar projects in fiscal year 1967. [20]

Of the various provisions in the act, two may prove especially valuable to disadvantaged youth. Area vocational schools and work-study programs hold considerable promise for reaching substantial numbers of disadvantaged youth.

Area Vocational Schools

On the theory that small independent school districts do not have adequate financial resources, provisions in the act encourage the construction of area vocational technical schools. These schools can offer curricula that are readily adapted to the needs of disadvantaged youth (as well as others in the region, including adults) and that are sensitive to the demands for skills in the labor market. "Some 125 area schools in 41 states

[18] *Ibid.*
[19] *Ibid.*
[20] Information supplied by the U.S. Office of Education, U.S. Department of Health, Education and Welfare.

were authorized in fiscal year 1965, and the states' projected programs indicate the need for 1,333 more by 1975." [21]

Although there is no complete list of curricula covered by all area vocational technical schools, a sample from *Vocational and Technical Education* [22] indicates a greater variety than that existing in vocational education programs in traditional secondary schools, e.g., data processing, restaurant-hotel services, hospital services, industrial chemistry, industrial electronics, engineering aide, commercial sewing, institutional cooking, tool and die design, and building services.

Work-Study Programs

Work-study programs are not an altogether new approach in educational institutions. Provisions for cooperative education, as well as distributive education, were a part of the George-Barden and George-Dean Acts after World War II. These programs catered to the needs of students 16 years old or older who were probably not going to attend college and who could easily become employable while they were still in school. Because of the high selectivity exercised for these formal work-study programs, very few disadvantaged youth were included in them.

The Vocational Education Act of 1963 included financial aid and work experience for 15-year-olds who were enrolled full-time in vocational educational courses. These students could receive up to $350 a year to begin or continue in a vocational training program while working up to 15 hours a week *in a public agency*. It was anticipated that financial aid and work experience at an earlier age than that provided in traditional school work-experience programs and the Neighborhood Youth Corps would help to reduce the number of boys and girls who drop from school on reaching the age of sixteen. It is anticipated that the number of students served will increase significantly from the 15,000 in fiscal 1965, and that potential dropouts (including disadvantaged youth) will be encouraged to stay in school, and complete a vocational education program.

TRAINING OPPORTUNITIES UNDER THE HIGHER EDUCATION ACT OF 1965

Many of the provisions of the Higher Education Act of 1965 are not specifically directed at meeting the needs of disadvantaged youth. If some of these youth have sufficient motivation and potentialities to succeed in institutions of higher education, provisions of the act (e.g., scholarships, loans, and work-study programs), can obviously help them to secure such an education. But for some time to come, such provisions are not apt to

[21] *Manpower Report of the President, op. cit.,* p. 112.
[22] U.S. Department of Health, Education and Welfare, *Vocational and Technical Education,* OE-80008-63 (Washington, D.C.: Government Printing Office, 1963), pp. 23-33.

meet the needs of many youths from disadvantaged environments. The act also provides for indirect assistance to disadvantaged youth through such programs as the National Teacher Corps which is composed of experienced teachers and teacher-interns who are employed in schools having a heavy population of disadvantaged children.

Eventually efforts of the Teacher Corps may improve the possibilities that youth from these schools can profit from higher level training opportunities. Monies are also available for students expecting to become teachers, and for the improvement of teacher training programs in colleges and universities. The net side effects of such provisions of the act are likely to improve training opportunities for all youth, including those who are disadvantaged. Certainly, in summary, there are long term potentialities in the Higher Education Act that may at least indirectly improve training potentials of disadvantaged youth.

TRAINING OPPORTUNITIES UNDER STATE AND
LOCAL PUBLIC SPONSORSHIPS

Federal legislation promises training for substantial numbers of disadvantaged youth in all states and territories. In addition, units of state and local governments must also be recognized for their efforts in developing special training programs and special services. In most cases, these latter programs have been experimental and sporadic; however the lessons learned from such geographically scattered experiments can become increasingly useful as state and local governments utilize federal monies for expanded training programs and services.

State and local governments have attempted in many ways to deal with the educational and training needs of juvenile delinquents, minority groups, dropouts, and other groups that are sources of disadvantaged youth. Generally speaking, these approaches to training and special services cannot be grouped in any meaningful manner, so a few examples are presented to show the dimensions of state and local programs:

Pre-Employment Training and Guidance in Junior High Schools
(New York City, Board of Education)

. . . school work is organized so as to have an occupational emphasis and to serve as a pre-employment program for potential dropouts. Those pupils who show a decided change of attitude for the better and express a desire to remain in school are returned to regular classes, provided that reading has been raised to the expected grade level. Schools have occupational emphasis in English and social studies (the core curriculum), and at least one has its total instructional program organized around the needle trades. Students who stay in school go on to a regular high school program.[23]

23 Mary Conway Kohler and Marcia K. Freedman, *Youth in the World of Work* (New York: Taconic Foundation, 1962), pp. 11-12.

Occupational Training in Junior High Schools   (Baltimore, Maryland, Public Schools)

The educational program in these schools is organized along usual vocational school lines with one half time spent in the trade major, a quarter time in trade technical subjects and a quarter in general education subjects. It is designed primarily as a terminal educational experience for nonacademic students, although graduates may go on to the vocational technical high schools. There is a try-out program in seventh grade, after which choice of a shop major is made. Courses are designed to develop skills in broad fields of employment such as tailoring, upholstery, furniture refinishing, food service, etc. Some of these schools conduct occupational training classes for the retarded. Both retarded and regular students are provided with work experience where possible.[24]

Occupational Training   (Indianapolis, Indiana, Public Schools)

Graduates of the eighth grade, regardless of their age, may take courses in auto-body repair, commercial foods preparation, cleaning and pressing, and shoe rebuilding, together with academic work in regular subjects. Other courses which require age or grade qualifications, including barbering, beauty culture, dental assistance, and practical nursing, are open to those qualified. All occupational training is job-oriented. Work experience is accepted for credit. When the young person reaches a state of employability, the school attempts to place him.[25]

Education for Out-of-School Youth   (Milwaukee, Wisconsin, Board of Vocational and Adult Education)

The average IQ on group tests of those in the program is about 86, and reading and arithmetic scores are three years retarded (corrected for mental age). School personnel characterize the students as hostile and more anxious than ordinary students, as well as being culturally deprived. About one half of the students are on probation or parole (but it should be understood that habitual truancy is equated as delinquency in Milwaukee, and delinquents are in court for this offense more than in other localities). Because of the assessment of the school personnel, the program is heavily weighted to counseling and other therapeutic techniques. Occupationally speaking, the program is geared to a pre-employment job conditioning with some occupational training being given in such areas as food trades. There is great emphasis on the inability of such boys to learn a trade in the accepted sense of the word "trade." The stress is on work habits that will enable the student to adjust to unskilled employment opportunities.[26]

Training Opportunities under Private Sponsorships

Private sponsorship of training opportunities has also been widespread, but lacking in availability to disadvantaged youth in all parts of

[24] *Ibid.,* p. 29.
[25] *Ibid.,* p. 38.
[26] *Ibid.,* pp. 58-59.

the country. Until federal legislation was expanded to meet the needs of these youth, private sponsorship of training opportunities had been valuable from an experimental point of view; but such programs were "only a drop in the bucket" in terms of numbers of youth needing unique forms of training. (Subsequent discussions do not include certain contractual arrangements made by industries with the federal government to provide training for youth in the Job Corps.)

The rapid expansion of private vocational and trade schools after World War II did little to provide opportunities for disadvantaged youth. Even had they been aware of the existence of such schools, disadvantaged youth would have been turned away by tuition costs, and inhibited by their lack of motivation and inadequate fundamental learning skills, from enrollment in these private schools. Whatever the private sector of our culture has provided has been developed specifically for disadvantaged youth, recognizing that any effective program for these youth must be tailored both to their individual differences and to their communalities (lack of financial resources, disinterest in "book learning," and inadequate learning skills). The following examples indicate only a few dimensions of training opportunities and are not intended to describe all possibilities.

Counseling for Occupational Aspiration (Detroit, Michigan, Urban League)

Sixteen workshop sessions were held for about 55 students. The sessions were divided into two parts. One part of the program presented "successful" individuals who related their personal experience in overcoming economic and other handicaps. Success and failure were discussed candidly. In addition, community speakers spoke and tried to give the students "votes of confidence." A second part of the program consisted of small discussion groups with an adult leader in which students were encouraged to raise questions regarding their chances of succeeding. School counselors gave the students added counseling services, while welfare workers gave the families added counseling. Community leaders and agencies tried to help the students when they showed that they (the students) believed "that somebody cared" about them and their futures.[27]

Pre-Employment and Occupational Training (Neighborhood House, North Richmond, California)

This program has three aspects—the Study Hall, the Job Upgrading and the Janitorial Service.

Study Halls were provided initially for junior high school students (now include fifth and sixth graders) in a community where junior high school students tended not to bring books home from school. By providing the students with a place in which to study and qualified people to help them, the main

[27] *Ibid.*, p. 7.

aim was to change the value systems of the teenage peer group in the direction of making education acceptable and desirable.

Job Upgrading is a program for boys 16 to 22, currently all Negroes, who have dropped out of school and are unemployed. The object is to encourage them to return to school or enter vocational training or to prepare them for work through personal counseling, coaching as to job application, grooming and remedial instruction. . . . Some training takes place on the job where public spirited persons in the community take the youths for training by employing and paying them from funds which the Neighborhood House provides.

Janitorial Service training is given to those youngsters in the Job Upgrading class who are found to be too great a risk to send to jobs except under extremely tolerant supervision. The object is to help them acquire good personal work habits and such stability as is necessary to make them employable. Neighborhood House provides first-rate janitorial training, first in a class situation and then by having the student observe good janitorial work in a local public building and, finally, by work experience.[28]

SUPPORTING SPECIAL SERVICES

In addition to training opportunities, disadvantaged youth typically need counseling, testing, and other special services in order to profit from formal instruction and on-the-job training. These services have become an integral part of some training programs and, in other cases, they have been centered in a public or private agency. Some of these services, such as Youth Opportunity Centers, were designed specifically for meeting the needs of disadvantaged youth.

Youth Opportunity Centers (YOC) are special youth employment offices, under the auspices of state Employment Offices, designed to increase the employability of youth through counseling, and to help them to get training and/or jobs. At the beginning of 1967, there were 166 YOC's functioning in 127 urban areas throughout the country. These offices are located where they are easily accessible to disadvantaged youth; they also employ specially trained workers who locate such youth in slum areas, and explain services that are available to them. These outreach services are designed to allay suspicions, fears, apathy, and hostility —characteristics not uncommon to disadvantaged youth. These are the characteristics that could inhibit disadvantaged youth from making use of any counseling and placement services.

A FINAL CONCERN

This review of training opportunities has revealed quite a variety of educational programs and special services available to disadvantaged

[28] *Ibid.*, pp. 21-22.

youth. Inherent dangers, however, in a multifaceted approach to training opportunities are threefold: lack of, or breakdowns in cooperation, communication, and coordination among programs and services. Because numerous private industries, foundations, private or community organizations, and so many levels of government, take an interest—indeed an active role—in the attempts to alleviate problems associated with disadvantaged youth, serious problems that can easily occur are more a function of duplication, vested interests, and competition among program sponsors than a function of the quantity and quality of programs.

One of the older approaches to community cooperation and coordination is the Community Action Program (CAP). Although not primarily concerned with youth, CAP as a plan for community action necessarily includes youth. More than ten years ago, communities concerned with poor housing, lack of education, unemployment, poverty, family disorganization, crime and delinquency, and the decaying inner cities, developed action programs with the aid of monies from foundations, local contributors, and local, state, and federal sources. In the early stages, federal funds came from many and quite diverse pieces of federal legislation. More recently, the Economic Opportunity Act of 1964 has specifically encouraged the development of CAP.

CAP serves as a coordinating program for all youth services and programs. "The thrust of the programs, whatever their financing, has been to strengthen community resources for service to youth, to improve staffing and coordination within and among youth serving agencies, and to offer a more effective network of related services.[29] If *all* disadvantaged youth are to reach satisfactory levels of employability, and find employment, they must be able to locate appropriate training opportunities and services with a minimum of delay and frustrations. Glaring deficiencies in training programs and services, ignorance about training opportunities and special services, duplication and competition among private and public programs, in addition to a multiplicity of sterile referrals, could drastically multiply the frustrations and discouragements of disadvantaged youth. If not CAP, then some other local or regional body will have to exercise leadership in program planning, program coordination, and evaluation of program outcomes.

CONCLUSIONS

Until the recent passage of federal legislation, training opportunities for disadvantaged youth were quite scarce. Even in the foreseeable future it is unlikely that all problems related to such training can be

---

[29] *Manpower Report of the President, op. cit.,* p. 107.

resolved without considerable planning, and an extension of efforts to date. Although there is no way to determine all exigencies, there are at least three conditions that seem highly related to effectively training all disadvantaged youth:

1. It is necessary to develop a wide range of training opportunities related to occupational goals consonant with skills needed in the contemporary domestic labor market.
2. In addition, it is essential that this wide range of training opportunities be distributed throughout the country in such a manner that, if training programs are not readily available to disadvantaged youth, financial and psychological arrangements make it feasible for disadvantaged youth to go to the training stations or schools.
3. Accompanying all training opportunities, either on the premises or in some affiliated setting, it is necessary to expand multiple services such as counseling; job development; placement; followup; programs of orientation or re-education of attitudes toward work, education, and retraining; and programs to develop higher level learning skills.

Whatever efforts are made to develop adequate training programs, they cannot succeed unless there are employment opportunities for disadvantaged youth at the time they are ready for employment. Frustrations caused by persisting unemployment after completion of training programs would undoubtedly be greater than frustrations youth would have had without any training. Furthermore, such unemployment after training would wipe out progress made through training programs and special services in removing scars left by a disadvantaged environment—the resulting disillusionment could mean that these disadvantaged youths would make no further attempt to improve their economic status. It is, therefore, essential that all sectors of the economy foster the creation of new jobs, and the redevelopment of old ones, that can absorb skills developed by disadvantaged youth. Social policies, too, must promote such expansion of job opportunities. Furthermore, employers must institute flexible policies in hiring disadvantaged youth who may be physically handicapped, those who have police records, and those whose pasts indicate other characteristics that distinguish them from typical employees. Without a persistent campaign to hire these young people, the best training programs and special services can be disastrous for youth and society as a whole.

SELECTED READINGS

1. Bureau of Employment Security, *The Development of Occupational Training Programs*. Washington, D.C.: U.S. Department of Labor, 1965.

2. Cloward, Richard A., and Robert Ontell, "Our Illusions about Training," *American Child*, **47**, No. 1 (January 1965), 6-10.

3. Ginzberg, Eli, "Needed: A New Perspective," *American Child*, **47**, No. 1 (January 1965), 19-23.

4. Kohler, M. C., and M. K. Freedman, *Youth in the World of Work*. New York: Taconic Foundation, 1962.

5. Kranz, Harry, "Washington Charts a Course," *American Child*, **47**, No. 1 (January 1965), 1-5.

6. Lynton, Edith, "Will They Be Hired?" *American Child*, **47**, No. 1 (January 1965), 11-14.

7. Manpower Administration, *Manpower and Automation Research Sponsored by the Office of Manpower, Automation and Training*. Washington, D.C.: U.S. Department of Labor, 1965.

8. *Manpower Report of the President and a Report on Manpower Requirements, Resources, Utilization, and Training*. Washington, D.C.: Government Printing Office, 1966.

9. Office of Economic Opportunity, *Job Corps Urban Centers*. Circular Memorandum 66-48. Washington, D.C.: Government Printing Office, 1966.

10. Office of Manpower, Automation and Training, *Young Workers: Their Special Training Needs*. Manpower Research Bulletin Number 3. Washington, D.C.: U.S. Department of Labor, 1963.

11. Office of Manpower, Automation and Training, *Training Facts*. Report No. 14. Washington, D.C.: U.S. Department of Labor, 1964.

12. Smith, Harold T., *Education and Training for the World of Work, Studies in Employment and Unemployment*. Kalamazoo, Michigan: The W. E. Upjohn Institute for Employment Research, 1963.

13. U.S. Department of Health, Education and Welfare, *Education and Training: Passport to Opportunity*. Washington, D.C.: Government Printing Office, 1966.

14. U.S. Department of Health, Education and Welfare, *Vocational and Technical Education*, OE-80008-63. Washington, D.C.: Government Printing Office, 1963.

12

PRESENTING EDUCATIONAL AND OCCUPATIONAL INFORMATION TO THE DISADVANTAGED

S. NORMAN FEINGOLD

Many guidance counselors believe that career development is a lifelong process. It is a constant process of experiencing new ideas, new events, and new processes. One evaluates these experiences. Theories of career development are being developed by Ginzberg,[1] Holland,[2] Super,[3] and Tiedeman.[4] The acquisition of educational and vocational information is part of a guidance process that begins in early childhood and continues throughout life. From their earliest days, youngsters in childhood fantasies or in play, are testing educational and work roles without necessarily being aware of it.

It is important to expose children to educational and work roles of our society because these life experiences are an integral part of each young person's orientation to our culture. This does not mean that we

[1] E. Ginzberg, S. W. Ginsburg, S. Axelrad, and J. L. Herma, *Occupational Choice: An Approach to a General Theory* (New York: Columbia University Press, 1951).

[2] J. L. Holland, "Some Explorations of a Theory of Vocational Choice: I. One and Two-Year Longitudinal Studies," *Psychological Monographs, 76*, No. 26 (1962), (whole No. 254).

[3] D. E. Super, J. O. Crites, R. C. Hummel, H. P. Moser, P. I. Overstreet, and C. C. Warnath, *Vocational Development: A Framework for Research* (New York: Teachers College, Columbia University, 1957).

[4] D. V. Tiedeman, R. P. O'Hara, and R. W. Baruch, *Career Development: Choice and Adjustment* (Princeton, N.J.: College Entrance Examination Board, 1963).

are trying to interest children in a particular skilled trade or a profession. However, when young people are introduced to the world of work, they gain a better impression and appreciation of work; they learn what people contribute to the welfare of our society. More guidance counselors are now recognizing that broad educational and occupational experiences are a part of one's general education. It must be kept in mind that culturally deprived youth literally have not seen many hundreds of occupations in our economy. Indeed, they have not even heard about a large proportion of them. It therefore follows that their vocational choice is far more limited than it is for youth who are exposed to a greater extent to over-all community resources and facilities.

The individual must never lose contact with occupational reality. By having a better understanding and appreciation of the world of work, an individual gains a better perception of not only his environment but, even more significant, of himself. For youth, and particularly the disadvantaged, work is a chance to discover, Who am I?

In this chapter, we are focusing primarily on boys and girls from low socioeconomic groups. This is done with the assumption that through various guidance methods the children from these families can realize their potential. The disadvantaged are often those for whom the opportunity to work is either nonexistent or at "last to be hired and first to be fired" expectation level. The forward thrust of this chapter is to suggest ways in which educational and occupational information may be presented to the disadvantaged so that their work expectation level rises to that of mainstream America. We must discover talent when it is only potential ability. A favorable educational climate can facilitate its full development.

Educational and occupational information, important as it is in counseling, should not be isolated from the broader and even more dynamic concepts of occupational experiences. Occupational experiences comprise information about careers and occupations, and the manner in which individuals react to what is presented to them. It also includes direct experiences that a person may have as a worker in any occupation or career.

In a changing technological society, with changing occupational structures and increasing job mobility for men and women, career development must be viewed as a lifetime process. The U.S. Department of Labor estimates that young people in school today will eventually have five or six different jobs.

The endless possibilities that exist for distorting information make career development an extremely complex process. The occupational experiences of any one individual are the total exposure and reaction and interaction with work and education. Occupational experiences may be deliberate and systematic, or accidental and erratic. These experiences start early in life. There may be success and/or failure in school experiences, extracurricular activities, leisure time, and personal relationships. These experiences help develop for each individual an understanding of the educational and occupational roles necessary for career planning and career development. The career development of any one individual is influenced by many variables and determinants.

In a changing, automated society, the counselor must recognize that, no matter where a person lives, there are multiple factors in career development. At the same time, there is a constant stream of factors influencing the development of any person. Understanding of this sort receives strong support in recent theories of career development. Some of these factors, for example, are biological.

BIOLOGICAL FACTORS

Individuals have little control over the physical structure inherited from their parents. Genes help determine such things as body build, color blindness, sex, and even some aptitudes. Biological structure does set certain limits to occupational experiences and behavior. Biological deficiencies of one sort or another may be compensated for during career growth and development. We know that occupations requiring certain strict physical or mental standards, at least at present, make it impossible for some people to attempt certain careers—not everyone, for instance, can be a deep sea diver, a jet pilot, or a sand hog.

PSYCHOLOGICAL FACTORS

Interests and abilities, for many years, have been associated with the concept of career development. This association has been fostered because of a continued interest in how interests and abilities may be measured, rather than concern about their part in career development itself. In recent years, professional counselors and psychologists have increasingly seen the importance of feelings, values, and attitudes in the growth and career development of each person. *The Psychology of Careers* by D. Super is an indication of the importance of psychological factors in any discussion of careers.

SOCIOLOGICAL FACTORS

Groups play an important role in youth and adult career development. The family often plays a critical role in career growth and development since youngsters spend so much prime time in the family setting. As part of a family, individuals are exposed to feelings, a certain emotional and physical climate, relationships, emotional experiences, values, and a way of life. Other groups that may be designated as social institutions are youth groups, the church, unions, etc. All have a bearing on career development. Groups such as trade and professional associations, government, and others, also play a role in the growth and development of many individuals' careers. As these groups have grown in strength and power, their influence has come to have a bearing on how an individual feels and thinks about his environment.

POLITICAL FACTORS

Political factors perhaps play a more important role today than ever before. Legislation such as the Economic Opportunity Act of 1964, directly affects hundreds of thousands of members of various groups as they seek employment. The G. I. Bill after World War II changed the lives of hundreds of thousands of veterans and their families. Totalitarian forms of government provide educational and work opportunities best in line with the needs of the state. In a democracy, however, every effort is made to see that people have the opportunity of finding work that is consonant with their interests, abilities, and potentialities. In developing countries, political factors play a major role in career development.

CHANCE FACTORS

Chance factors have had influence not only on average people but also on individuals who have made large contributions over the course of centuries. One example is provided by James McNeill Whistler, who had dreamed of being an Army officer but, unable to measure up to the physical standards, became instead a renowned artist. Then, too, war brought rural youths into the armed forces where they learned a trade or, subsequently, started their professional training through the G. I. Bill. Counseling, over an extended period of time, may provide some planned answers, not chance or a gambler's choice.

In spite of all these factors affecting career development, the counselor may be in the center of the arena. In his work, he can help develop in each counselee creative endeavors that may lead to career growth and development. Enriching occupational experiences contribute to the growth process.

Planning for career development involves a consideration in depth of how education and work roles can satisfy an individual's basic needs.

Donald Super's concept of career development is that of vocational life stages paralleling the life stages of Buehler. He stresses the importance of concepts such as occupational choice as a means of developing and implementing a self-concept. Occupational choice is viewed as a developing synthesis of an individual's needs and resources, and cultural demands. Super's approach—one that is widely accepted today—emphasizes our need for successful occupational experiences beginning in childhood and continuing throughout our lifetime. Enriching occupational experiences, particularly in the early years, are of great significance for later development. It is evident, however, that the career growth and development of many disadvantaged youths has been handicapped.

Counseling the culturally deprived or socially disadvantaged, and providing educational and occupational information, either in individual counseling or in group sessions, is a complex process. Children respond differently to educational and occupational material. The same material that produces insight for some children will only baffle others. Research on socialization, child rearing, or enculturation (local and cross-cultural) shows that the manner of social acculturation may enhance or inhibit the actualization of human potentialities. Research by Hoppock and others, showing the benefits of educational and vocational information, has dealt primarily with middle class young people. Counselors themselves, for the most part, come from the middle class, and have middle class values. Counselors, with the stimulation of writings of Samler and others, have discovered that the counselor's values cannot be removed from the counseling process. The values, language, and life experiences of many of the disadvantaged are worlds apart from those of many professionals who counsel them. The world of ADC, AFDC, food tickets, mollygrub, public baths, an arrest record, dunning letters, chitterlings, brownstone chippies, and sight of a cop on the beat, does not evoke the same emotions or thinking process in counselors and counselees. Youths from culturally deprived families are often unfamiliar with firm assignments, fast deadlines, time limits, or scheduling. This is not surprising considering the absence of career or other planning in the home, and the little experience with comparable situations.

Disadvantaged youth have had a long time to make adjustments to a fundamentally hostile environment. Indeed, many opportunities that did exist were closed: they had not been utilized because of lack of knowledge. The culturally disadvantaged knew too little of what was available to nearly everyone else. Nearly all social relationships depend on the ability to spend some money. Thus even the educated disadvantaged person often found that he still could not raise himself up by the bootstraps. Bewilderment and loneliness and no place to go were a way of life. This writer has found similar patterns with severely handicapped individuàls. Because of their deprivation, they too were unaccustomed to, and had little experience with available community resources.

Continued mention of opportunities for the handicapped led to the growth of numerous community activities that helped in education, training, and selective job placement. It is important that little scraps of information be utilized effectively in the total growth process of an individual. For many years, culturally deprived youth have not been stimulated to use available resources; their deep discouragement is readily apparent. It was not so many years ago that Negroes in the South were not allowed to use public libraries.

In most instances, youths from lower socioeconomic backgrounds cannot readily look for help from their parents or other adults in their own neighborhoods. Therefore, the burden of responsibility on counselors, administrators, and teachers for influencing these students' career growth and development is far greater.

Counselors, teachers, and others working with youth, particularly the disadvantaged, have to understand a multidisciplinary description of the world of work. Some counselors and teachers and parents who are familiar with the economics of work understand little about the psycho-social dynamics of the world of work. The disadvantaged differ in many ways. Many factors, based primarily on the geographic area from which they come, the ethnic groups of which they are members, presence of severe physical handicaps, etc., influence work opportunities.

Unemployment has been heavily concentrated in some 1000 economically distressed regions designated as redevelopment areas. Unemployment has remained relatively high through periods of prosperity and periods of recession. The unemployed include railroad workers in Pennsylvania, sheet metal workers in West Virginia, bituminous coal miners in the Appalachian highlands, farm workers in the South and Southwest, iron miners in the once ore-rich Mesabi Range, lumberjacks in the Pacific Northwest, production workers in Michigan, textile workers in New England, cannery workers in California, and Indians on various reservations. Some of the poor have sunk into poverty slowly, victims, perhaps, of dwindling job opportunities, as were many in West Virginia. For some, as time went on, a complete erosion of self-respect took place. We see today more and more families in America whose members, born in poverty, remain there until they die. They do not die because of starvation—government and private welfare agencies see that this does not take place. On the other hand, poor diets, inadequate housing, and inferior sanitation facilities have made for a disadvantaged group who are no longer part of the greater affluent society. The educational and occupational information perceived by the culturally disadvantaged is significantly different than that viewed by the affluent society. Too often the poor behold misery and self-hatred and inferiority as they look into cracked mirrors in slum sections of our large cities.

More and more professional workers in the War on Poverty have come to realize that perhaps only the poor really know poverty. The economist who defines it with statistics, or the social worker or psychologist working by day with disadvantaged youth in an urban slum section and returning home nightly to an extra-dry martini and a New York cut sirloin steak, may not understand. He may find it difficult, in a one-to-one relationship, to do any counseling with disadvantaged youths whose experiences are so different from his. All of us in the helping professions, and all of us involved in the dissemination of educational and occupational information —we somehow inject into such relationships ourselves, our backgrounds, and our biases. Our continual recognition of this obstacle can, however, lessen its possible harmful effects. Until the counselor is liked and trusted, learning cannot take place. Poverty in the 1960's is unlike the poverty of even a few decades ago. On the other hand, poverty has many faces and ramifications and, of course, there are subgroups among the poor.

From a total educational point of view, the slum environments of Harlem or West Virginia handicap a child from the times of conception and birth. Too often the culturally deprived youngster has, quite realistically, felt that school was irrelevant to his immediate needs and any possible future career goals. For the most part, schools are inadequate for the disadvantaged. One can well recall that up to the time of emancipation, a white person who taught a Negro how to read was guilty of a crime.

The youngster brought up in a culturally deprived area, too often stultified by shame, and afraid to trust his own intelligence, frequently has undeveloped abilities. He has a negative concept of himself. The stark terror of rejection blocks the maturation of many of the poor and the disadvantaged. Such an individual, for example, may be unable to distinguish subtle nuances in sound. The reasons for this are many. The hearing handicap is what he pays for living in crowded conditions—the helter-skelter of the city noises, all sorts of regional dialects and language —together with his own restricted vocabulary. One can easily be fooled by the brownstone house fronts that belie the crowded and unsanitary conditions inside where many more people (a sort of extended family) than can possibly make for good physical and psychological health, are living. Sharing information, communicating concepts, or initiating even a single family task, are seldom byproducts of disadvantaged family life. The extended family lives together as cheaply as possible in order to provide for other expenses. Behavior is formed that benefits the group rather than the individual: listening rather than talking, conformity rather than self-expression. Crowding and lack of privacy are not conducive to individual growth and development. The self-concept needs to be upgraded. Time and samples of success appear essential.

The child from suburbia plays with educational toys and electric trains from an early age. He learns to learn. The slum child is at a technical disadvantage. Living conditions and handicaps of the sort just described make learning exceedingly difficult for him; often, too, he has a poor attention span. With his untrained memory, he has trouble following instructions or directions. His perception is limited, his motivation dulled. He displays a constant physical restlessness that perhaps stems primarily from having lived too closely with too many people. Frequently he enters the vocational course in school.

Traditionally, the worst schools have been maintained in our slums. Here are overcrowded classes with dilapidated buildings; teachers, overworked and underpaid, saddled with textbooks outdated long before they are used for the first time. Here are dropouts, inaccuracy in keeping records, vandalism in schools, and a climate conducive to anything but learning. Too often, the school in the slums has been a "blackboard jungle." It is little wonder that certain school systems, such as that in New York City, have had to pay higher salaries in order to obtain teachers to teach in certain metropolitan sections. These students' values are different from those the teachers know or may even understand, intellectually or emotionally. Obviously, an atmosphere conducive to learning is more difficult to achieve in such a school.

Let us first look briefly at what may be done initially to improve the education of the disadvantaged. It seems to this writer that the nation's public schools must begin admitting children at a much earlier age. There is research evidence to suggest that this idea is worth much further exploration. Many more nursery schools may be developed in an effort to reverse the effects of a poor environment. This goal appears possible if we can provide the necessary stimuli in the earliest years, and there are sufficient healthy models for children to follow. The need for counselors in the elementary school is a pressing one, and many school systems are adding such personnel to their staffs. We can help youngsters and their parents so that teaching at more advanced levels will "take."

Many schools must be changed from a physical point of view. Dilapidated schools in poor areas do not offer the impetus for learning that we find in beautiful suburban schools; and a well-conceived physical plant can be helpful in presenting a new vision of school to the disadvantaged. Improvement of school facilities should be accompanied by upgrading of the teaching staff. Furthermore, utmost use should be made of presently underused facilities.

WORK-STUDY PROGRAMS

The thrust of an accent on work for school youth has been included in a number of communities. The Kansas City, Missouri, Work-Study Program, for example, is sponsored by the Ford Foundation, the Kansas City Public Schools, and the Kansas City Association of Trusts and Foundations. This is a six-year controlled experiment, begun in 1961 to test the hypothesis "... that boys vulnerable to delinquency will become less delinquent if they are given a systematic work experience...." [5] In most programs of this sort, work experience and selective job guidance are continued. (The Vocational Advisory Service of New York, for example, is a private nonprofit agency offering counseling to youth from ages 16 to 25, as well as the handicapped of all ages. This agency works very closely with the New York State Employment Service and has been an official counseling agency for the New York City Youth Board.)

A number of compensatory educational programs have been initiated during the past few years. School systems in Boston, New York, New Haven, Philadelphia, Baltimore, and Oakland, California, for example, have developed pre-school enrichment programs. The goal is to bring the culturally deprived child into an enriched learning situation at an age as early as three or four years. Curricula are also being developed to aid these children in meeting more effectively the learning tasks of school in the early and middle grades. Special schools in many areas, based and organized on experience, are set up expressly to help overcome the many handicaps that are commonly noted among young children and youths who have grown up in subcultures of poverty throughout the land. There are, of course, many important compensatory educational programs that are not based in the schools. However, many of the techniques and procedures seem to follow along similar lines.

In speaking on broad terms of education, we are also speaking of additional changes needed in vocational education. There is a need for new equipment. New courses must be instituted. What the school teaches should not be too far removed from what is taking place in the world of work. There must be courses of value to the future television repairman, laboratory technician, data processing specialist, etc. The school and the world of work must work together, and not move in divergent directions.

Lower class and middle class citizens alike should be drawn closer to the schools their youngsters attend. The local man who performs successfully on the job has much to offer the student in terms of comprehensibility. This may be so even if he is not as articulate as educators would wish. The articulate teacher, unfamiliar with actual conditions on the

[5] G. W. Burchell, *Work-Study Program for Alienated Youth* (Chicago: Science Research Associates, Inc., 1962), p. 135.

job, is often a poor substitute to bridge the gaps between school and industry. The poor and underprivileged need to know samples of success if we are to win the current War on Poverty. Career planning and its concomitants offer many possibilities if we start early enough.

Slum schools and their personnel, including counselors, must become an intimate part of their community by actually becoming involved in school and community affairs. The underprivileged child and the under-privileged family will not move ahead unless there is community concern for the entire family. If a contribution is not made to the total com-munity, the bright youngster may view action taken as an attempt to separate him from those with whom he has been brought up. Hardening of attitudes toward school takes place as early as the second and third grades.

Educational and occupational information may be presented to the disadvantaged in many ways that relate the student's daily experiences to mainstream America, and the work expectations of the majority. The techniques are the same as those used for middle and upper class youth. The difference is in content. Language, customs, and illustrations must relate to the world the disadvantaged know. The teacher and counselor must have some understanding of the differences in value systems and upbringing that exist between him and his students. If teachers and coun-selors expect to motivate disadvantaged youngsters toward the main-stream, middle class values, they must in turn attempt to understand the milieu of these students. Having survived the pushes and pulls of their environment, the culturally deprived have an uncanny grasp of what will or will not take in a slum community. They may not, however, under-stand the texture of middle class values and customs. But only when they do understand will school experiences be meaningful, and will there be communication.

Communication of educational and vocational information, in any me-dium, is a most complex process. Merely telling people about educa-tional and vocational opportunities is not a panacea. These young peo-ple must know that there are expanding opportunities for all youth. This is particularly true for the hard-core unemployed, and youngsters who come from families with a long record of cultural deprivation. Some counselors are trying desperately to communicate, but just don't know how.

It was interesting to note that, at a recent annual convention of the NAACP in Denver, one of the top government officials, a Negro, told a joke "pointing up" why a white judge did not understand the Negro. Ap-preciation of the punchline necessitated understanding of current Negro slang, and most of the Negroes present laughed, thoroughly enjoying the story. Although there were not many white people present, all who were there were interested and active on behalf of minority groups, and particularly that of the Negro. Yet none of them understood the story or, perhaps, the Negro. Stories often illuminate in a few minutes the heart of a problem.

Negro and white professional workers may not really speak to each other in mutually comprehensible terms. Superficial strategy and meaningless statistics flourish, but not intimate working knowledge. The personality characteristics of the Negro poor and culturally disadvantaged may be different from those reported in texts. Much of the scientific literature is based on things said or done by poor in the presence of researchers, usually of middle class or a higher status. The researchers are much higher in the power structure than those who are being studied.

The crux of the communication problem, to this author, is not only to develop occupational and educational materials that are meaningful to the disadvantaged student but, perhaps more important, to provide these students with teachers and counselors who understand the psychological and sociological backgrounds of the underprivileged—Negro, Indian or Mexican. As we understand the complexities, values, backgrounds, and needs of underprivileged groups, it gives us a broader perspective that will enable us to be helpful to them as individuals. The counselor who experiences greater knowledge and depth of understanding of the groups with whom he counsels can fulfill his function more successfully.

Vocational guidance institutes have been initiated by Plans for Progress, in Washington, D.C. This is a voluntary program under a President's Committee headed by a group of "dollar-a-year" industrial executives who are given policy guidance by an advisory council. Companies who join the program commit their management and employees to take an affirmative approach to resolve the economic problems of the nation's minorities.

The purpose of the program is to help close the communication gap between education and industry. It is hoped that these programs will make it possible for school programs to adequately serve students to prepare themselves for opportunities available in industry.

The employee seminars are being sponsored and underwritten by Plans for Progress companies and civic organizations in collaboration with local universities. Programs are conducted for a period of from one to six weeks.

The writer has noted over the years that disadvantaged youths often do not receive the recognition, affection, rewards, and security of a psychological nature accorded to middle class children for performing at approximately the same levels of ability. If teachers and counselors have low expectations for disadvantaged youth, this stands as an obstacle to their identification of talented youth. Too many of the disadvantaged were told over and over again about their weaknesses, and accepted them. They expected little from life and demonstrated little academic drive. Their assets were too often overlooked. The stereotyped approach of some counselors to minority groups has been changed in recent years by the changing times, and greater contact at all levels between both diverse groups.

Teachers and counselors must be cognizant that there are different methods of rearing children. Knowing what patterns of behavior take place in the home, the counselor, the teacher, and the school may help to provide understanding. Curricula and extracurricular activities of an educational and vocational nature that are most appropriate for the growth and development of each child may be applied. We know, for example, through the studies of Bernard Rosen, that groups place varying emphasis upon independence. David McClelland has pointed out that families that stress independence and competition tend to produce children with high achievement motivations. Studies with Greeks, Jews and white Protestants indicate that achievement motivation is more characteristic of these groups than of Negroes and Italians.[6] With occupational and social change, these patterns too can change. We must not freeze the results of these studies into stereotypes.[7]

Occupational Information

For purposes of communicating occupational information, the author has grouped methods into categories.

The Printed Word

Most of the career and educational information published commercially tends to be skewed toward professional jobs and those careers on the higher rung of the ladder relative to education and salary. Most of these publications are far too difficult for disadvantaged youths to read. Up to now, very little written career information has been pre-tested with minority and disadvantaged youth. Written by members of the middle and upper middle classes it has little or no relevance to experiences with which the disadvantaged are familiar, or to the opportunities now available to them. Career material must be adapted to youth who have different backgrounds, different life experiences, and different ways of looking at the printed word. A great deal of career information merely rests on

---

[6] David McClelland *et al.*, *The Achievement Motive* (New York: Appleton-Century-Crofts, Inc., 1953).

[7] F. L. Strodtbeck *et al.*, "Evaluation of Occupations—A Reflection of Jewish and Italian Mobility Differences," *American Sociological Review*, October, 1957, pp. 546-553.

the shelves of counselors and teachers. It is rarely used: the disadvantaged often do not even know that it exists. In any event, the reading level is primarily at the high school and college level. Printed resources are beyond the reading ability and attention span of many who come from disadvantaged groups. Even the *Occupational Outlook Handbook*, the standard reference guide for material about occupations, is written in a style that students, particularly from disadvantaged groups, cannot readily understand.

New educational and vocational materials are now being prepared for disadvantaged youth. One government-sponsored project [8] in the Wilmington, Delaware, school system involved culturally deprived students and counselors in developing occupational material that "makes sense" to those who will use it. There seems to be a trend in the direction of larger type, more sophisticated art work, and a better grade of paper. At the same time, educational and occupational information is viewed not as a separate entity, but very much as a part of the total counseling process. Career reading material aimed at the elementary and junior high school levels is being written.

Some new projects written up for the Job Corps of the Office of Economic Opportunity may offer new guidelines. New materials will also emanate from industry, now actively engaged in the education business as it relates to disadvantaged youth. SCOPE, the scholastic magazine for urban youth, contains resource material of value. It is possible to present career information to disadvantaged youth so that it appeals to them and stimulates action. However, unless the poor are more actively involved in all ramifications of the War on Poverty, materials of a career content will probably lack a necessary ingredient.

The question remains, What can the teacher or counselor do until educational and vocational materials are available? For one thing, they can interest parents in furnishing help. Use a tape recorder. Ask questions the parents can answer. Either use the questions and replies in classes, or have them transcribed and mimeographed for use in school until more suitable material is available from commercial publishers, or local, state, and federal governments. Students in the earlier grades can work up occupational information themselves, with the help of counselors and teachers. This has been done with disadvantaged youth in preparing materials for a résumé, filling out application blanks, and learning how to present one's self during a job interview.

[8] School of Education, University of Delaware, Reading Study Center, *A Teachers Institute to Prepare Teachers and Materials for the Education of Rural Low-Achieving, Disadvantaged Junior High School Students for Entry into Vocational-Technical Programs.* U.S. Office of Education, Contract No. 5-85-086 (Washington, D.C.).

When and how educational and occupational information is to be introduced requires great sensitivity and understanding. Educational and occupational information can be given too soon, too late, or at inappropriate times. The book, *Teacher's Guide to Group Vocational Guidance*,[9] contains guidelines and lesson plans, already tried in some areas, that may well be adapted for use with disadvantaged youth. These guidelines may be helpful in group counseling and in individual counseling sessions. Many of the suggestions, however, need to be implemented with other techniques. The use of material, pre-tested with culturally deprived groups, would appear to be worth greater exploration. In New York City, various MDTA projects are changing regular printed educational and occupational material to make it more appropriate for the particular group with which a counselor is working.

The Spoken Word

Communication of educational and occupational information, orally or in writing, formally or informally, may be offered in diverse and subtle ways. Ordinary ways of disseminating educational and occupational information that work reasonably well with middle class youngsters of average ability may work poorly when they are used with the culturally disadvantaged. For example, a teacher or counselor who recommends for the culturally deprived two or three hours of quiet study time each evening at home is asking for the impossible. For the child from affluent suburbia, of course, the suggestion is by no means unfeasible.

Announcement of the availability of scholarships or other forms of student aid to a middle class group of students, or their parents, is enough for many of those who need help to get started. A letter follow-up of the initial student aid announcement noticeably increases the number of qualified applicants.

Communicating the availability of scholarships to a disadvantaged group, however, requires an entirely different approach. Unless the counselor is aware of the differences in experience between his students and himself, he draws the wrong conclusions and communication ceases. Too often he also asks the wrong questions—How much do you need to earn at college? The counselor may not realize that the student may have to contribute to the support of his parents in addition to his college expenses.

A scholarship program for members of a local Hodcarriers Union in the Washington, D.C. area, and their children, failed for a long time to take partial hold. At first, very few candidates applied. Some took a few steps in asking some questions. Some wrote preliminary requests for applications. The matter took them no further. The sense of futility that

---

9 Bruce Shertzer and Richard T. Knowles, *Teacher's Guide to Group Vocational Guidance* (Cambridge, Mass.: Bellman Publishing Co., 1964).

constantly comes with failure smothered out even slight samples of success. It took a great deal of effort by a scholarship committee and the union officials to let members know that the union now offered opportunities to help members in their educational and vocational training, no strings attached. Regular methods of dissemination of educational and vocational information were not enough. Information was passed via the Afro-American press, the mass-circulation press, word of mouth, and constant repetition at union meetings: here were constructive activities that both members and their children could accomplish in order to further their education and training.

In spite of concerted efforts during the past six years, however, many members have yet to "get the word" that student aid is available through the union. All the techniques combined did not generate the results accomplished with one technique used for middle class youngsters.

There are obviously no easy answers—only complex questions. An educative job and a multiplicity of techniques used in trying to reach the Washington youngsters gradually paid dividends. One of the best methods was having youngsters who were helped tell another youth of the help they received. Parents of children who were helped also were a referral source.

Thus the word got around, although letters announcing the program, at its inception, went unanswered. When we glance behind the "lack of motivation," though, we realize that letters may not be answered because much mail contains dunning bills, because the addressees can't read, or because addresses are incorrect. The simple fact that something is being done for the poor is open to question. Trust is not always easily achieved. There is behavior behind behavior.

TV, Radio, Film, Film Strips, Recordings

Audiovisual methods are playing an increasingly important role in most schools. Their impact will continue to grow. Radio at times carries programs that detail educational and occupational roles of people at work. The Chicago B'nai B'rith Vocational Service and Mundelein College in Chicago jointly sponsored a thirteen-week guidance program that evoked noticeable interest in listeners, including disadvantaged youth and their parents.

Film strips, although they do not appeal as easily to youth as motion pictures, have some advantages. Here the counselor or teacher can add locally relevant commentary; this can make for creative group discussion. The potentialities of the film strip or 8 mm single concept film are becoming more apparent. For more than 15 years Northeastern University has had unusual success with this technique in presenting information about careers, student aid, and various occupations to high school assemblies in the Roxbury, Dorchester and Mattapan, Massachusetts area.

Tape recordings have career development possibilities. They are utilized to a greater extent at the college level than at the high school level. A well qualified person can tape an address on the opportunities available in a certain career. The tape may be used over and over again with large student bodies or small groups. Some colleges have developed extensive tape libraries on a wide variety of careers. The B'nai B'rith Vocational Service has had career tapes recorded by B'nai B'rith Vocational Service adult advisers who are successful in their chosen life's work. The organization's experience reveals, however, that unless the recorder or a guidance counselor is present, meetings held with youth groups may evoke only a limited interest.

Tape recordings have proven most successful when the leader who presents the tape recording is knowledgeable in the field. Speakers who understand group techniques have the know-how to provoke lively discussion afterward. *Educator's Guide to Free Films and Film Strips* [10] is a standard reference source to these materials. It should be noted that much of the material must be adapted or revised if it is to be used successfully with disadvantaged groups.

Film Festivals

Various vocational counseling organizations have made extensive use of the film festival. Certain career films are chosen, based on the interests of young people who are members, or regularly attend activities of a community center. The dates, hours, and series of the films to be shown are published in newsletters and newpapers weeks in advance. The program is prominently displayed on bulletin boards and in the community center newspaper. A news release may also be prepared for the daily papers. The film festival may be combined with a dance or other youth event so as to attract still more young people.

Written evaluations by young people who have attended these film festivals mention that the programs have stimulated them to do further reading, and to explore specific career areas in greater depth. In a number of communities where there has been a successful film festival, a number of young people, some from lower socioeconomic groups, have come to Vocational Service offices for individual counseling. This series technique, with carefully chosen career movies, might well be used to a greater extent with the disadvantaged. Efforts along these lines have already begun.

[10] Educator's Progress Service, *Educator's Guide to Free Films and Film Strips* (Randolph, Wis.: The Service, 1965).

Phonograph Records

One of the new methods for presenting educational and vocational information is using phonograph records. Record topics range from how to get scholarship aid to accurate information about certain careers. At this particular stage of development, many of the records, although informative, are not stimulating enough by themselves for many young people and adults; many records may hold the continued attention only of students already motivated for the topic at hand. Without the use of a knowledgeable guidance staffer who has some expertise in group sessions, these records fall far short of their goals. The technique, however, seems to be worth further exploration. Critical information about education and careers can be thus presented by knowledgeable people who would not otherwise be available to the youngster who is isolated. This procedure can be particularly helpful in small towns and where counseling services are often limited.

The possibilities for using recordings in guidance seem endless. The curious fact is that up to the present time this particular educational thrust has been limited. Although popular records are sold in the millions, records with an educational and vocational theme have met with only a limited market. But the records tend to be expensive; and they have not been used aggressively by many counselors. Nor has this technique been used to any great extent with disadvantaged youth. Though the culturally deprived could obviously benefit from this method, records now available have, for the most part, proved disappointing when used with disadvantaged youth. New creative endeavors with records seem indicated.

Television and Radio

Television and radio can be used more extensively with the disadvantaged than has thus far been the case. England, for example, uses this technique with youth to a far greater extent than does the United States. One U.S. nationwide television program early in 1965 attracted a great deal of publicity, although some of it unfavorable, from adults. The fact remains that a jazz program oriented to teens, and particularly to disadvantaged youths eligible for training opportunities in the War on Poverty, evoked active results. Youngsters who watched the program accepted facts and ideas that they had previously ignored.

Educational television, which has come of age only in recent years, has made modest beginnings in helping youth with career development. More than 90 communities in the U.S. now have nonprofit educational TV. Efforts for the disadvantaged in educational television have been conspicuous by their absence. Far too many television and radio programs for youth are aimed at the college level. These programs, for the most part, relate only superficially to careers. Those at the high school level highlight almost exclusively higher educational level jobs. Heavier use of mass media to disseminate information about process and content seems to be indicated.

Portable Video-Tape Recorders

The portable video-tape recorder has opened up new horizons for teaching and learning. We now have sound and picture recordings, and immediate playback. This technique has obviously broad implications, and may provide new breakthroughs with the disadvantaged. This kind of tape recorder catches the distinct flavor and essence of what is taking place, an especially valuable attribute since films of an educational and occupational nature too often appear artificial. The silent, unobtrusive camera does not require special lighting or other precautions. Relationships and career activities are recorded as they happen.

Video tapes appear to hold great promise in introducing new teaching techniques for the study of careers and occupations, although the equipment is still expensive. The surface has yet to be scratched.

Career Conferences

The career conference, throughout the years, has had its ups and downs in popularity. With the recent publication by the B'nai B'rith Vocational Service of *A Career Conference for Your Community*,[11] there has again been an upswing in the number of career conferences carried out in a professional manner throughout the United States and Canada. In Canada, some career conferences have been taped and recorded; the resulting video tapes have been used at other career conferences. A career conference is a technique that may introduce the disadvantaged to the reality of the world of work from a long-range point of view and not as a one-time panacea.

Too often a career conference shows a skewed, work-a-day world far different than the one that participants will face as adults. In some career conference programs held in schools and community centers, one may well wonder, Where is the bus driver, the barber, the letter carrier, the assembly line worker? Career conferences must include types of work that youngsters in various communities will actually enter. A wide variety of

[11] S. Norman Feingold, *A Career Conference For Your Community* (Washington, D.C.: B'nai B'rith Vocational Service, 1964). Outlines various educational and vocational projects that have taken place, including career conferences specifically for the disadvantaged.

types of work can be presented in a career conference. Careers included should be based on interest of the participants. The dignity and importance of each job and each person's contribution is important.

Occupations already known to the underprivileged youth must be placed in proper perspective in any career conference. It is too easy for young people from disadvantaged surroundings to look forward to being another Joe Louis, or another Lena Horne. It takes just a short period of time for them to realize how much self-discipline, not to mention natural ability, was a necessary part of these glamourous careers.

Many leaders of underprivileged groups (and the members themselves, but probably not to the same extent), want to move up the occupational ladder as fast as possible. The career conference, as part of a total counseling process, has much to offer. This is particularly so if qualified adult participants can continue as advisers to youth. This does not negate the necessity for counseling by a professionally trained person. The realities of educational and vocational achievement can be realistically demonstrated by participants who are life models. They have known the thorns of poverty and have been able to rise above it. If the live model is at too high a level, however, minority groups may question the speaker's sincerity, and feel that the model has probably "sold out" to get where he did.

Human Resources Directory

A Human Resources Directory that includes minority group members who have made good may be particularly stimulating to minority youth who need a hero to emulate. This is particularly so for young boys whose father figure may be a weak one.

In recent years, many B'nai B'rith lodges with the professional help and direction of the B'nai B'rith Vocational Service, have compiled Vocational Resources Directories. These directories contain a list of lodge and chapter members interested in talking at regular intervals with young people considering similar work and careers. Those listed have been particularly helpful as resource persons, prior, during and after career conferences.

These adult advisers, selected with care, represent a wide variety of careers. They include knowledgeable people engaged in professional, managerial, clerical, technical, and trade work. The advisers have expressed strong interest in working with youth, as well as willingness to participate in various career projects. Advisers take part in group settings such as career conferences; they also discuss possible careers informally, on individual bases, with interested boys and girls. They are given as much orientation as possible regarding their role, so that there is no confusion between professional guidance counselors and these dedicated volunteers.

A young boy interested in becoming a mail carrier may go on rounds, on occasion, with a postman. A boy interested in bricklaying, or any one of dozens of different occupations, may have a chance to spend time with an interested adult actively involved in the day-to-day operations of a particular job. These friendly discussions between adults and young people follow guidelines established by professional B'nai B'rith Vocational Service personnel. The program provides new dimensions to imparting educational and occupational information to young people.

This project usually is initiated by a Vocational Guidance Chairman of a local BBVS committee of a particular B'nai B'rith lodge. A number of B'nai B'rith lodges may combine efforts to compile a Directory. A BBVS committee or subcommittee is responsible for compiling and distributing a Vocational Resources Directory. The first Directory may be mimeographed; later editions may be printed.

The BBVS Vocational Resources Directory is more than a listing of names. It is a workable guide for using the talents and abilities of adults who are concerned for and interested in the leaders of tomorrow—the youth who are with us today. Outlines to follow in discussing careers and various other professional matters are discussed with the B'nai B'rith Vocational Service. Data needed in the Directory include: name of the adult career adviser; his address, telephone number, and occupation, including job title. In some Directories, *Dictionary of Occupational Titles* definitions accompany listings to provide a concise description of the occupation of each resource person.

Efforts are made to tell the community about the project, and how it operates. In this way the Directory becomes a handy working tool for counselors and other guidance personnel in helping meet the career needs of youth in a rapidly changing world.

In some areas the B'nai B'rith Vocational Service Resources Directory has grown into a Directory for the entire community. It alerts adults to the important role they may have in meeting career needs of boys and girls. The resource personnel comprising a BBVS Resources Directory can be the foundation for a successful career conference.

Peers

Youth often listens to youth. Thus the use in career conferences of peers who are on the way and adjusting in their jobs, education, or training, may also be another illustration of students teaching students. This method, although not yet used as extensively as adult youth advisers, merits much further exploration. The influence of peer groups on adolescents from a culturally deprived group appears to be a particularly strong one.

Career conferences have been one small step in showing youth and adults expanding educational and vocational horizons. This verbal method, for increased success, must often be combined with the printed word, visual and audio media, various other communication combinations, and the use of carefully chosen models to provide heroes for adolescent youth to emulate. Youths from culturally deprived groups listen to and learn from both peers and adults who have themselves known poverty. Models are more effective if they remember their poverty. At the same time, they may set goals and examples for the youngsters to follow.

Members of minority groups often do not know the contributions of their own group. The contributions of some minority groups often are unknown by other minority groups, or even by the majority. Albert Z. Maisel's *They All Chose America*,[12] points up the ignorance and lack of understanding of too many of us with respect to the contributions of American minority groups. This unawareness is even more noticeable in the case of Negroes, the vast majority of whom have only recently become cognizant of and comfortable with their own heritage.

Field Visits

The use of field visits to schools and colleges, as well as to industry, has lately received new impetus and recognition as a professional guidance approach. Prior preparation, adequate attention to significant details, and discussion during the trip, as well as careful evaluation afterward is essential. One can find the field trip an additional method of presenting educational and vocational information, capable of expanding the horizons of many young people. Field trips enable disadvantaged youth to understand, appreciate, and use more effectively the available community resources. Such expeditions are particularly valuable if students see members of their own group in the various environments.

Educational bus tours may be organized when lay leaders and vocational guidance counselors accompany young people on visits to colleges. Preparation takes place beforehand, group discussions are held during the bus trip itself, and experiences are evaluated afterward. Some of these bus trips start as early as six o'clock in the morning. They return late the same evening, having visited as many as three different colleges.

At the college they have the opportunity of eating in the dining room, meeting the director of admissions, and chatting with key college personnel; they also visit dormitories, library facilities, etc. These visits made to representative types of colleges available to youth in a given area are part of a total counseling process. Youths learn what to look for when visiting a college so that they may later make meaningful visits on their

[12] Albert Z. Maisel, *They All Chose America* (Camden, N.J.: Thomas Nelson & Sons, 1957).

own. In dozens of communities in various parts of the United States, more young people have signed up for these educational trips than could be accommodated. Such trips can be particularly helpful to disadvantaged youth who often have not traveled more than a few miles from their home. Further trips of this sort are well worth further exploration.

Learning how to visit a college or an industrial plant may present educational and occupational information to youth in an exciting and meaningful way. The knowledge can act as a stimulus to constructive action. Unless there is adequate preparation ahead of time, however, field visits often do not result in a positive learning experience.

Counselors themselves find that field trips give them a deeper understanding and knowledge of community resources for counseling and referral. Many counselors today have only a superficial understanding of the world of work in their own community. Field visits can provide up-to-date information of an educational and vocational nature. Fortunately, many facts of life relating to selective job placement in industry are also a byproduct of industrial visits, for the culturally deprived may not fully understand the methods of selection employed by various industries, nor the qualifications necessary for placement.

In many communities, the Red Feather Agency lists community educational and occupational resources in a printed or mimeographed booklet. Accurate and timely information of this nature can help all youth—especially disadvantaged youth—move up the educational and vocational ladder. In some areas, field trips are conducted by student groups, occupational classes, or by subject matter classes. In some instances, visits are made without the presence of a teacher or counselor. As noted above, much preparation must be taken if field visits are to have professional validity. This appears to hold true no matter who initiates and conducts the visit.

School Conferences

A number of schools have meetings in which the staff of the school meet with students, counselors, parents, and teachers. Some schools call such a conference a "College Day." School conferences should attempt to meet the needs of all students, not just those who are going on to acquire a higher education. Some school conferences are patterned along lines similar to a career conference. One-day school conferences are extremely limited in long-range value. A series of developmental school conferences held over a period of time may accomplish a great deal. Participating students and parents must have an opportunity to ask pertinent questions. They must be involved in the dynamics of the conference itself.

The usual format for a school conference is the initiation of a general session or assembly dealing with such topics as "How to Select a Creative Career," "The Importance of Marks," "Advantages of a Large or Small School," "Admission Policies," etc. Some schools include conference time for face-to-face questions between school personnel and their students. This procedure provides new opportunities for school personnel to show disadvantaged youth that they care for *all* their students; it may dissipate the negative attitude of some of the disadvantaged toward school and their teachers.

Assemblies

Nearly all schools have regular assemblies at which all students are presented with the same information. Such assemblies may be conducted in a sequential series that may be particularly helpful in providing current educational and vocational information.

One of the programs that especially interests youth is the report of what happened to "alumni"—dropouts or graduates—of their own school. The world of education and the world of work can be brought more closely together with well-planned and creative assemblies.

Career assemblies may be divided into topics suitable for students at pertinent high school levels. More and more schools are using employers and other knowledgeable community people to present career messages to the students. Service groups in particular have an important role to play along these lines. Service organizations, such as Kiwanis, Rotary, and B'nai B'rith have made member participation in career assemblies part of their programs. This allows adults to help provide meaningful occupational experiences, in a school setting, to youth.

Panel Discussions by Adults

Many employers, particularly those active in service organizations, are willing to serve on five- or ten-minute panel discussions of the highlights and advantages of the type of work they do. Successful employers representing minority or disadvantaged groups will be listened to and questioned closely. Counselors should be aware of this factor in selecting employers or resource personnel. Obviously, minority group adults who discuss their jobs, present to adolescents from culturally deprived areas an image to strive for in their own careers. Discussions of this sort, in the experience of the writer, have led young people to look for further information in depth about a type of work, or to otherwise pursue more active career planning. More schools are using assemblies, and stimulating, articulate employers who are interested in youth and successful in their work.

There is a constant need to bridge the gap between school and the world of work. As industry enters more and more into the field of education and training, the use of employers and supervisors as teachers will be further enhanced. It seems to this writer that more along these lines can be done with disadvantaged youth.

Use of Peer Groups in Presenting Educational and Vocational Information

With both middle class and underprivileged youngsters, peer groups are being used more frequently by counselors. Youth who have had certain educational and vocational experiences, and are doing well, are often listened and looked up to by youngsters of approximately their own age. Enthusiastic and articulate, these young men and women speak the same language as their listeners, who are, chronologically, somewhat younger. Discussion is particularly helpful to young people who are seeking answers and find it difficult to relate career planning to adults.

In a number of instances, a luncheon or a breakfast has featured youths who have been to college and have returned, or are on their first job, speaking to a group of youths who are considering various types of work. It is important that diverse types of work and education be presented. This technique has been used too often with only college youngsters, or those who are in types of work high in the occupational ladder. The vast majority of people, however, work at jobs that do not require a college education. Participation of people at all levels of the occupational ladder adds a firm base of reality to the participant's occupational experiences.

Clubs such as the Future Teachers of America, Future Farmers of America, Future Nurses, Future Business and Clerical, as well as others, may provide a rich experience in the career development of culturally deprived boys and girls.

Buzz Sessions

The writer has found the buzz session a particularly helpful and rewarding technique with both middle class youngsters and disadvantaged groups. Young people are divided into various groups, depending on the numbers present. Every effort is made to keep the groups small—not more than five to ten youths. The instructions are very brief: There will be a ten-minute buzz session to talk about a particular item, for example, scholarships or student aids; one member of each group should be selected as soon as possible as the chairman, who will survey the questions of his group. The groups then get together to discuss various problems, and agree on three or four basic questions in the area of student aid that they would like the leader of the meeting to answer. Questions are summarized by each group chairman.

This technique usually evokes a great deal of discussion. There is dynamic involvement and, when the sessions are skillfully handled, involvement of nearly all members of every group. The chairman of the meeting can observe behavior and note some of the discussion of the groups as it takes place, perhaps recording it for future reference. The chairman of the meeting can vary the technique by dividing the participants into special groups and giving, first, a short discussion of a particular topic.

The technique makes for interesting meetings and subsequent discussion. A formal talk by an experienced speaker can also pertain to items of particular interest to the buzz session group—part-time jobs, summer jobs, temporary jobs, and career opportunities, for example. There is a great deal of educational and vocational information that may be helpful and stimulating to young people in planning their careers.

At a recent NAACP annual convention in Denver, the writer, acting as a consultant, had approximately 300 young people complete a guidance questionnaire relating to their educational and vocational needs. Those who expressed an interest in receiving financial counseling in order to continue their education or training were brought together in one large room, where a speaker talked for about fifteen minutes about how young people might seek student aid. Search techniques were spelled out. Important background knowledge and principles about student aid were presented. The large group was then divided up for buzz sessions, following the procedure set forth above.

The ten to twelve buzz group sessions were exceedingly lively ones. The questions asked by the youngsters showed a great deal of thought. It appeared that a good deal of learning had taken place. Here are a few examples of the questions: Can a "C" student receive a scholarship? Are culturally deprived youngsters penalized on college board examinations? Are scholarships for a liberal arts education as frequently obtained as those granted for the pursuit of a specific career or vocational goal?

The questions were answered by the speaker in the form of discussion. This, in turn, led to a few more specific questions which were also answered. Youngsters expressed their opinions and told of their experiences. Those who felt that further help or individual attention was necessary were given the opportunity for individual counseling while the counselor was in Denver. Many young people expressed an interest and need for further financial aid counseling in order to continue their career.

This was an experimental and pilot project. Almost one hundred youth who requested individual help could not be accommodated while the counselor was in Denver because of a time limitation. All youngsters, however, were sent a free student aid reading kit. This student aid resource kit was first used with considerable success at the annual NAACP convention held in Washington, D.C., in 1964. In addition, preliminary plans were set up in Denver, and later on in New York and Washington, D.C., to formulate long-range plans for professional counseling for NAACP youth. The initial plans emphasize the need for dissemination of educational and vocational career material.

Psychodrama (Sociodrama) Approach: What's My Line— I've Got a Secret

The school counselor, or any counselor, may work with different and special population groups. Disadvantaged groups have certain basic needs. Processes and techniques utilized professionally in counseling any group are basically the same. Nevertheless, the thrust of counseling can be and is affected by the needs of a particular group, such as the culturally deprived. Acting and sociodrama have been shown to be helpful in getting the story across to minority groups. These means have been used and particularly accepted by Jewish groups, both youth and adult.

Words and feelings may be disguised. The most up-to-date facts about educational and occupational information can often be meaningless. Recently Negro leaders working with Negro youth have used both song and sociodrama to induce the young people to highlight to one another in drama and song positive thinking and action; for example, "I'm not going to act dumb no more, no more. I'm not going to act dumb no more." The net effect on young children may well make for significant behavioral changes.

One may expect noticeable changes in the behavior of young children in comparison with that of older siblings brought up in an atmosphere of inferiority and submission. Adequate educational and occupational information is perhaps even more important for minority youth who have a long way to go in order to catch up. Career reality must be introduced in such a way that it can motivate young people toward action, not toward defeat, and "It doesn't matter" attitudes, or the statement, "With his setup, he has it made." More minority youth, indeed, all youth, must know that there are increasing numbers of new career opportunities for educated talent. Psychodrama can be an effective way of involving students in conceptualizing these new horizons. Acting may alert them to what is expected in the world of work, and the expanding opportunities available to effectively trained and educated personnel.

Matters such as what it means to fill out an application form, prepare for an interview, obtain a job, be on time, perform successfully on the job, relate effectively to employer and supervisor, and save part of one's earnings, mean different things for many disadvantaged groups and for youth from middle class families. The behavior of culturally deprived youngsters becomes more meaningful when there is greater understanding of the causal components. C.P.T. (Colored People's Time) or other behavioral reactions (Do only what you are told to do—Spend what you earn), to the world of work may be disconcerting to the counselor who brings his own biases and values. Tendencies toward acting dumb on the job, or not showing initiative, or being submissive, or volunteering only when requested, can be deeply ingrained. Years of conditioning may have shown combinations of these techniques to be the best way to adjust to a hostile environment. The psychodrama is a means through which counselors become exposed to the underlying causes of behavior of minority groups; it also reveals to the student why new behavior may be required of him. Behavior modification with the culturally deprived is being accomplished to a greater extent than ever before.

Career Information Centers and Exhibits

Another guidance process that has been used only to a limited extent appears to have possibilities: the career information center. Here, creative booths are set up with printed materials on a wide variety of careers. Thousands of Los Angeles school children recently had the opportunity of visiting a large career exhibit hall where they became acquainted with various types of written information about many hundreds of different careers. Industry and service groups had played an active role; and the exhibits were most attractive. Knowledgeable people manned the various career booths. A great deal was done in order to stimulate young people in acquiring new educational and vocational information.

It is relatively easy to interest industry in career information centers. The possibilities of disseminating interesting and accurate educational and vocational information to thousands of high school youth were demonstrated by the Los Angeles project. Occupational experiences of this sort may be repeated in other communities. A few efforts along these lines with the handicapped have proved successful.

Bulletin Boards

Use of the bulletin board may be a valuable technique in seeing that elementary and high school students read potentially helpful information of an educational and vocational nature. Many schools now have attractive bulletin boards, kept up-to-date with accurate career or student aid information. Magazines such as *Ebony* and *The Crisis* have up-to-date materials on careers of Negroes, and can be posted appropriately. The bulletin board has been helpful in presenting information about student aid resources, on both local and national levels. The writer has noticed that some youth have been introduced to the widening student aid opportunities through reading material on an attractive school or community center bulletin board.

Exhibits

Various industrial and educational organizations have traveling bulletin board types of exhibits. These are sent to various youth conferences. Free career material is available during the exhibit. The B'nai B'rith Vocational Service has found that unusual interest is generated with an electrically operated guidance quiz board. This device challenges the viewer to predict the abilities and interests basic to several careers shown on the board. Correct selection is indicated by the sound of a buzzer. Silence greets the person who inserts the plug into the wrong outlets. The quiz board has traveled more than 50,000 miles. It has been exhibited at hundreds of meetings and conferences. It has stimulated both young people and adults to try out their skill with the machine, and also to gather career materials near the exhibit.

The Use of Trade and Professional Journals and Magazines

This technique has not been extensively used, but it appears to have many educational possibilities. Many trade journals contain a great deal of the latest information about a specific trade, including educational and vocational opportunities and job openings. In a number of vocational offices, interested businessmen who have served on boards of directors or on advisory committees have presented complimentary copies of their trade journals to a community or agency library. Then, in group settings or in individual counseling, youth and adults have had the opportunity to peruse a wide variety of trade journals. In a number of instances young people have applied to and received jobs listed in the trade journals. For many, these publications provide types of information that they are unable to obtain in books, booklets, or other periodicals.

Trade journals and trade associations are a rich, accurate source of educational and vocational information for youth and adults. Trade associations have grown considerably in recent years. Many of them have begun to publish career opportunities in their respective fields. Staff people are knowledgeable in their own areas. Many association executives contribute to trade journals in the form of articles and other information. Schools, libraries, and community centers should try to have more trade journals available for the asking where young people gather. Members of service organizations can be easily interested in contributing their trade journals to the local or school library. An excellent library of trade journals can easily be established.

The trade journal provides types of educational and vocational information that can be particularly helpful to young people. The youngster who reads an article in an automotive trade journal about the automotive parts helper may quickly understand why it is important to maintain accurate records. He can see how important arithmetic is if one is to maintain an accurate inventory, and determine what new items are to be ordered. There are many illustrations of the practicality of trade journals. They can reveal facets of the world of work not seen by visiting, chatting with people in the field, or reading in career books or pamphlets.

The B'nai B'rith Vocational Service has found that having a well-stocked shelf of trade journals can be particularly helpful in small communities where educational and vocational guidance libraries tend to be inadequate.

Information Specialists

There appears to be a need for some sort of personnel that may be called Information Specialists. This might be a subprofessional group primarily interested in the field of information storage and retrieval. It may be that the guidance movement needs to use well-trained counseling information aides in order to be helpful in the total counseling process. The counseling aide may well have as his major area of specialty the maintenance and dissemination of up-to-date educational and occupational information. The counseling aide may make it possible for guidance counselors to have a constant stream of new, accurate career information available for use in the counseling of youth and adults. Much information has been neither as accurate nor up-to-date as is necessary if young people and adults are to make viable decisions in a rapidly changing society. Youth are at times making decisions on yesterday's facts and figures. There is a need for large-scale educational and career information retrieval systems on the order of the literature-searching service now available in medicine.

Hobbies

Extracurricular activities involving, for example, music or dramatics, often evolve into hobbies. For many youth and adults, hobbies provide a continuous, rich source of occupational experiences. Sometimes a hobby, such as stamp and coin collecting, working with cars, photography, craft work, or ham radio operation, becomes a life work.

Hobbies can communicate in an enjoyable way realistic information about activities in which people earn their daily living. For most youths, a hobby does not extend into a full-time job. For others, it may offer part-time work in critical periods during their lives. For most, a hobby offers educational and vocational experience, and evaluation of certain abilities and interests that may be enriching ones. A hobby may indicate to the counselor many aspects of an individual's personality, such as conscientiousness, creativity, and other personality variables that have a bearing on work attitudes and achievement.

Although the role of hobbies for youth from middle class families has been researched, this is not the case for the disadvantaged. Nor have hobbies been used with the culturally deprived to any noticeable extent as a means of disseminating meaningful educational and vocational experiences. As opportunities for the culturally deprived expand, hobbies, with their affects and effects on career growth and development, seem well worth further exploration.

Many hundreds of thousands belong to youth organizations with various immediate goals and long-range objectives. Many of these organizations provide a worthwhile hobby for some young people, and at the same time are a source of rich educational and occupational experiences. When Boy and Girl Scouts attain Merit Badges, the relation of this achievement to the world of work, and its manifest and latent ramifications, tends to be obvious. Other national and local groups with widely diversified programs directly and indirectly relate to the world of work. These programs offer diverse educational and occupational experiences that can affect youths' motivation and creativity as well as stimulate positive career growth and development.

Minority groups are now participating to a far greater extent in activities in various youth organizations. Their exposure to such activities and hobbies may provide occupational experience that past generations have not enjoyed as part of their growing up.

Role of Parents

The parents' primary role in educational and vocational guidance is perhaps greater than both parents and counselors, until now, have realized. Counseling at the high school level is often carried on in a vacuum when the parents are not involved. At the elementary school and preschool levels, parents also must be actively involved. The involvement of parents of the culturally deprived demonstrates that someone does care.

Studies have shown the importance of parents in determining whether or not a youngster continues for further education and training. Education and training obviously are related to one's job and career. Further facts on this subject were recently brought out in a study of 6600 affiliated Jewish high school youth in 40 states and the District of Columbia by the B'nai B'rith Vocational Service. Exploration in much greater depth of the role of parents in providing educational and occupational information to young people at home appears to be indicated. Parents have an important task in providing an educational home atmosphere that leads to realistic information about the world of work. This may make for more realistic counseling by professionally trained guidance personnel.

The B'nai B'rith Vocational Service over the years has maintained guidance courses for parents. Once a week, for as many as ten two-hour sessions, parents get together in a neighbor's home. One of the professional guidance staff discusses youth and their careers with parents. The guidance workers help to interpret the active role that a parent plays, knowingly or not, in a youngster's career choice. The B'nai B'rith Vocational Service will soon publish a book by Professor Daniel Sinick of San Francisco State College: *You and Your Child's Career—A Guidance Handbook for Parents, Teachers and Counselors.* Information provided will make it easier for parents to create a climate of growth. The stimulus for learning to learn is essential for the culturally deprived. This appears necessary if young people are to obtain the amount of educational and vocational information necessary for adequate career choices.

A Parents' Course in Vocational Guidance

The parents' role in presenting occupational and educational information to their children should not be minimized. Various institutions may offer parents' courses in vocational guidance designed to assist parents in being as helpful as possible in career planning for their sons and daughters. The objectives of these courses are as follows: 1) to give parents information about the process of choosing and preparing for a career; 2) to give them information about their possible roles, and their importance in this process; 3) to enable them to discuss these roles through a group process of exchanging information and ideas, and sharing experiences.

Courses are conducted in participants' homes, mainly during the morning and afternoon. Hours are arranged to permit parents to attend while their school-age children are in school, and to be at home when children return. The sessions may be varied depending on the particular needs of the local group. The curriculum has ranged from five to fifteen sessions of two hours each. The general concepts emphasized have been the importance of educational and vocational adjustment in modern life, parental recognition of individual differences in children, psychological testing, sources of educational and occupational information, the importance of community resources, and the responsibilities of parents.

Here is a brief summary of the contents of one course offered at a B'nai B'rith Vocational Service office. Session One: *Why vocational guidance?* A presentation of the current needs for educational and vocational guidance. Session Two: *What is educational and vocational guidance?* An introduction to some of the basic concepts of educational and vocational guidance (and their implications for parents), such as the theory of individual differences, theories of the changing family, etc. Session Three: *Psychological testing.* A discussion of the role of testing and guidance.

Session Four: *Adolescent personality and vocational choice.* An exploration of the behavioral background often significant in adolescent vocational selection. Session Five: *High school and college.* A presentation of various factors that are considered in helping young people in the proper selection of high school, preparatory school, and college. Session Six: *The parent's role.* A discussion of the various aspects of parental influence on career selection. Session Seven: *Educational and occupational information.* A comparison of inadequate methods used by some youth in choosing a career with methods based on counseling, professional use of educational and vocational information, and occupational experiences. Session Eight: *You and your child's career.* Presentations of typical vocational situations in the home, with parents encouraged to explain how they would handle a particular situation. Session Nine: *A brief summary of the course, and ideas the parents may act upon in the future.*

Questionnaires and other techniques have been used to evaluate these parents' courses. In many groups, a majority of the parents found that their course had been helpful in the following ways:

1. it helped the majority of the parents to identify and clarify many of their children's educational and vocational problems;

2. it helped them to recognize their children's strengths and accept their weaknesses;

3. it developed greater understanding of their role in a child's career planning as related to suggesting, informing, encouraging, supporting, and assisting rather than being directive, authoritative, or steering;

4. it developed more parental expertise in applying themselves in the role;

5. it lead parents to feel that they had gained more information about community resources and their proper utilization for the children's benefit;

6. it permitted them to better understand the values and limits of educational and vocational guidance, and increased their realization of need to refer children for individual counseling where it appeared indicated.

In approximately 80 to 90 per cent of these courses, only mothers have been present. Plans are in the making, however, for using this technique with more fathers present; in any event, there appears to have been a carry-over into the family. Much discussion of course material took place at family dinner tables, and there were further comments long after the course was completed.

A new active role for parents with the disadvantaged, in relation to their careers, has been initiated in a few pilot projects. Further efforts along these lines may bring about a more active and positive role for parents of disadvantaged youth in career development of their children.

Part-Time, Temporary, and Summer Work Experience

Work experiences can provide educational values if they are appropriately supervised and if they occur in settings satisfying to a young person. More and more schools are finding that work and study programs for disadvantaged youth are exceedingly productive in motivating young people to stay in school. School systems in Denver, and Warren, Ohio, have recently noted publicly some of the success of their programs with the disadvantaged. It also helps provide the disadvantaged with the skills they require to meet a changing technological society.[13]

Group Project Methods of Finding Part-Time Jobs

Teenage groups looking for a project have adopted group methods both for fun and profit, making surveys of part-time jobs available in their local areas. Here is how the plan works.

Group members are assigned to cover a certain territory, such as all of the stores on one street. Coverage consists of finding the answers to questions like those on the sample questionnaire opposite. Each member of the group fills out a copy for each employer he has interviewed and brings the data to the next group meeting, where all the information is shared.

SELECTED READINGS

1. American Educational Research Association, "Education for Socially Disadvantaged Children," *Review of Educational Research*, XXXV, No. 5 (December, 1965).

2. Ames, William C., *et al.*, *The Negro Struggle for Equality in the Twentieth Century*. Boston: D. C. Heath & Company, 1965.

3. Bloom, Benjamin S., *et al.*, *Compensatory Education for Cultural Deprivation*. New York: Holt, Rinehart & Winston, Inc., 1965.

4. Clark, Kenneth B., and Lawrence Plotkin, *The Negro Student and Integrated Colleges*. New York: National Scholarship Service and Fund for Negro Students, 1963.

5. Gottlieb, David, "The First Thirty," *Corpsman Report No. 1*. Washington, D.C.: Office of Economic Opportunity, January, 1965.

[13] S. Norman Feingold and Harold List, *Finding Part-Time Jobs* (Chicago: Science Research Associates, Inc., 1962). An indoctrination to the adult world of work; indicates some of the values of youth exploring the world of work.

LOCAL PART-TIME JOB QUESTIONNAIRE

_____
Name of business or employer

_____   _____
Address   Phone

_____   _____
Type of business   Name of person answering questions

Do they employ part-time help? ____   ____   _____
                               Yes   No   Don't know

If yes, when? _____
                        Month   Year

Can they recommend any other local business that may need part-time or
temporary workers?_____
                  _____

If they do employ part-time or temporary help, what are the names of the
positions they need?   _____   _____
_____   _____   _____
_____   _____
                           How many?_____

These jobs are for ____ ____
                    Boys Girls
What educational background is required? _____

What work experience, if any, is required? _____

What ages do they prefer? _____

What are the daily working hours? _____ _____ How many days
                                  From   To
per week? _____

Is the job permanent? ____ ____   How long will it last?_____
                       Yes   No

How soon is the part-time help needed? _____

What is the starting hourly wage? _____

What is the estimated maximum hourly wage? _____

Any other special qualifications? _____

Is a return visit advisable? _____ When? _____ _____
                                                    Time   Date
Suggestions by employers for finding part-time or temporary jobs in your
neighborhood._____
_____

                              _____
                              Signature of person obtaining job order

6. Harrington, Michael, *The Other America: Poverty in the United States*. New York: Crowell-Collier & Macmillan, Inc., 1962.

7. Howard, Jack, "Neighborhood Youth Corps," *Occupational Outlook Quarterly*, **12**, No. 4 (December, 1964).

8. *Job Guide for Future Workers*. Michigan State University Cooperative Extension Service and U.S. Department of Agriculture.

9. McGrath, Earl J., *The Predominantly Negro Colleges and Universities in Transition*. New York: Teachers College, Columbia University, 1965.

10. Miller, Herman P., *Income of the American People*. New York: John Wiley & Sons, Inc., 1955.

11. National Employment Counseling Association, "Appraisal Measures Needed for the Educationally and Culturally Deprived, *Journal of Employment Counseling*, **2**, No. 2 (1965).

12. President's Task Force on Manpower Conservation. *One-Third of a Nation*. Washington, D.C.: Government Printing Office, 1964.

13. Shostak, Arthur B., and William Gomberg, eds., *New Perspectives on Poverty*. Englewood Cliffs, N.J.: Prentice-Hall, Inc., 1965.

14. Turner, B. A., *Occupational Choices of High School Seniors in the Space Age*. Houston, Texas: Texas Southern University Press, 1964.

15. U.S. Department of Labor, Office of Policy Planning and Research, *The Case for National Action: The Negro Family*. Washington, D.C.: Government Printing Office, 1965.

16. U.S. Department of Labor, Women's Bureau, *Negro Women Workers in 1960*. Bulletin 287. Washington, D.C.: Government Printing Office, 1964.

17. Welsch, Erwin K., *The Negro in the United States: A Research Guide*. Bloomington, Ind.: Indiana University Press, 1965.

13

THE ROLE OF THE

NONPROFESSIONAL IN THE

MANPOWER DEVELOPMENT

PROGRAMS*

CHARLES GROSSER

Nonprofessionals have for many years been employed in program positions by service organizations. Recently there has been a great increase in the number of such workers and in the attention devoted to various aspects of their employment.

The term nonprofessional refers to many disparate kinds of worker: holders of Bachelor of Arts degrees who provide services ordinarily dispensed by Masters of Arts or Ph.D's; persons with some college training who hold jobs ordinarily requiring a B.A.; students, and local residents of the target neighborhood who may not have finished high school, and whose income may be under the poverty level—to mention just a few. In this chapter, "nonprofessional" is used in·its broadest sense, to cover all untrained personnel (middle class, indigenous, etc.) and all ranks of nonprofessional activity (ancillary, substitute, assistant, aide). A major focus of attention will be on the "indigenous" worker, i.e., a resident of the target area, comparable to the service population in such respects as race or ethnicity, income and educational level, etc.

MDTA-sponsored youth training programs have frequently been part

* The research reported or referred to in this chapter prepared by Dr. Charles Grosser was financed through the programs of the Office of Manpower Policy, Evaluation and Research, U.S. Department of Labor, under the authority of the Manpower Development and Training Act.

of comprehensive projects encompassing many services. Most of these comprehensive programs were funded by a variety of public and voluntary sources and are centrally administered. Under the auspices of other sponsors, these projects have utilized nonprofessionals in various program divisions. Although this chapter is concerned primarily with youth employment programs, it will make reference to uses of nonprofessionals in other divisions, in the belief that the experience of the nonprofessional in the project as a whole is relevant to the manpower program in particular.

This paper is based on a comprehensive review of reports and other documents prepared by various MDTA-sponsored youth training programs and on numerous other materials collected by OMPER. From among the many projects, five were chosen for site visits. These five are not meant to represent the typical experience of OMAT youth projects. They were chosen, rather, because they appeared, on the basis of their written material, to be using nonprofessional staff in innovative or significant ways. The five programs are geographically disparate. Although all are located in large cities, no city represents a "typical" urban setting.

Interviews on project sites were conducted with agency administrators and practitioners as well as with certain community residents.[1] The conclusions reported here are those of the author; they do not necessarily represent project or community consensus or the position of the Department of Labor. Estimates of the frequency of phenomena described in this report are based on impressions gleaned from the site visits and on written reports, not on systematic enumeration.

OBJECTIVES IN USING NONPROFESSIONALS

Filling Manpower Needs

Since the historic social legislation enacted in the Thirties, the number of agencies providing health, education, and welfare services has greatly increased. The past three decades have seen the creation of what is virtually a new industry, designed to meet the service demand of an increasingly urban, industrial, highly organized, technical nation. The complexity and specialization of our contemporary society has required public programs to provide for such contingencies as retirement, unemployment, illness, and disability, as well as for the recreational, educational, and vocational needs of the populace. The personnel re-

[1] The author is grateful to the staff of the five projects visited for their gracious assistance, and to Mr. Joseph Seiler of OMPER for providing written materials, arranging project contacts, facilitating administrative matters, and being otherwise helpful.

quirements of this industry comprise a major portion of the nation's job market.

The development of the highly industrial American economic system has tended to direct available manpower to manufacturing and commercial enterprises rather than to service. As a result, the manpower needs of the welfare-service complex have never been adequately filled. Even as new sources of personnel are developed, constantly increasing demand has maintained a state of continuous shortage.

Within the last five or six years, this crisis in personnel has been intensified by the expansion of existing programs, such as services provided under the Social Security Act, as well as by community mental health programs, urban renewal programs, and others. In addition, the early demonstration projects funded under the Manpower Development and Training Act and the Juvenile Delinquency and Youth Offenses Control Act [2] have evolved into an all-out "war on poverty," based essentially on the provision of additional services to the millions of poor. The manpower needs of this vast mandate impose impossible demands on the service professions as presently constituted, and thus have stimulated much of the current activity regarding the use of nonprofessionals.

Bridging the Gap Between Institutions and Clients

Accompanying the increase in welfare and service institutions over the last several decades has been an expansion in the range of the persons served by these institutions. This reflects a public policy objective: to provide service to a full spectrum of the nation's population. Services originally limited to those who were most amenable to treatment and whose prognosis was most positive have been extended to those whose problems are numerous, acute, and unlikely to be solved rapidly.[3] Thus ethnic minorities, the unemployed, the undereducated, migrant workers, and matriarchal families, among other groups, have become the concern of employment bureaus, vocational-rehabilitation and guidance agencies, social security and welfare bureaus, and voluntary agencies as well as poverty programs. This interest in serving the total community reflects both the developing welfare-state philosophy and a growing sensitivity to practical politics. The trend to urbanization (three fourths of the nation's population is located in urban centers) has awarded the city enormous influence in national politics. The elective process—in the reapportionment and one-man, one-vote issues—acknowledges this new power.

---

[2] These laws were administered through the Office of Manpower Automation and Training (OMAT) and the Office of Juvenile Delinquency and Youth Development, respectively.

[3] Cf. E. Burns, "Social Security in Evolution Toward What?" *Social Service Review*, XXIX, No. 2 (January 1965).

In an earlier day, welfare agencies denied service to persons who they judged to be unemployable, uneducable, unmotivated, immoral, or incorrigible. But the same factors that have led welfare agencies to serve new deprived groups today keep them from abandoning these clients when it appears that the programs they offer are unsuited to the clients' needs.

Agency programs have generally been offered in a style very different from that of the target population, and have been staffed by professionals who tend to differ from the clients in ethnicity, education, and other indices of social class. Agency programs and policies have usually been created by central decision making bodies far removed from the service neighborhood. These factors have produced a gap between the service institution and the target population. The nonprofessional worker, indigenous to the population served, is seen as a bridge between the institution and the lower class community. The expansion of staff to include some members of this class as dispensers of service does not require the service agency to alter its program, replace its present staff, or revise the legislative or corporate mandate under which it operates. The use of local persons is perhaps the least threatening way of developing rapport with the new client.

The indigenous nonprofessional is seen as having mutual interests and common cause with program participants; moreover, he is able to communicate freely with the participants because, like them, he is poor, resides in the neighborhood, and shares minority group status, common background, and language. It is assumed that nonprofessional staff, being of the community, will not render clinical or moral judgments about client behavior.

Local nonprofessionals are often hired because they have succeeded in mastering the intricacies of urban slum life and can teach program participants how to do likewise. The service they offer is very different from that provided by the more clinically oriented professional. It is direct, immediate, and pragmatic. The nonprofessional may, for example, help a work trainee to succeed in a job culture by teaching him not to be a rate buster, how to show proper deference to a foreman, and the like. He may provide a welfare client with knowledge, inadvertently or deliberately withheld by the department, that enables her to obtain larger benefits. In both instances, techniques will be both informal and unofficial. The nonprofessional may suggest stretching or bending rules and regulations on behalf of the client. This should cause no alarm, for it is apparent that professionals and administrators similarly stretch rules on behalf of agency, or for expedience, or economy.

In all these ways, local nonprofessionals provide the institution with sufficient flexibility to remain in contact with program participants who otherwise would be excluded from service. Yet considerable oppositions to the use of such personnel has been generated. Even in agencies operating under directives that indigenous nonprofessionals be employed, compliance is often reluctant, and every effort is made to insure that the service program remains intact.

Providing Jobs for the Unemployed

The fact that, in the midst of great national prosperity, chronic unemployment and widespread poverty persist among certain segments of the population was forcibly brought to public attention by Michael Harrington [4] and others in the early 1960's. Many proposals have been offered to remedy this situation. As a solution to the presence of poverty in plenty, for example, Robert Theobald [5] has proposed that a minimum income level be established below which no family would be permitted to drop. Pearl and Riessman [6] seek the solution in the creation of a million welfare service jobs for the poor. They claim that the bulk of professional time is spent in activity that could be handled no less effectively by the nonprofessional, and suggest that their approach will not only provide jobs for the technologically unemployed, but will reduce estrangement between service agency and disadvantaged client, and fill a chronic manpower need.

Fulfilling Democratic Ideology

The democratic egalitarian traditions of our nation are based on the idea that all citizens must participate actively in governmental and decision making processes. Numerous studies indicate, however, that by such indices as membership in voluntary associations and voting behavior, the lower classes are significantly less active than the middle and upper classes. In fact, by any absolute measure of activism, they do not exercise their franchise or participate in the affairs of community life. Without voice, power, and influence the poor thus belie our democratic image.

Among the many sociopolitical strategies put forward to rectify this situation are programs designed for the "maximum feasible participation" of the poor, such as the community action projects established under Title II of the Economic Opportunity Act.[7] The involvement of the poor in the development and the administration of these programs, as called

[4] Michael Harrington, *The Other America* (New York: The Macmillan Company, 1963).

[5] Robert Theobald, *Free Men and Free Markets* (New York: Clarkson N. Potter, Inc., 1963).

[6] Arthur Pearl and Frank Riessman, eds., *New Careers for the Poor* (New York: Free Press of Glencoe, Inc., 1965).

[7] Public Law 88-452, August 20, 1964, Title II, Section 202, a3. "The term community action program means a program which is developed, conducted and administered with the maximum feasible participation of residents of the areas and members of the groups served; . . . ."

for in the Act, has aroused considerable controversy. Participation of the poor on a policy making level has been opposed by such diverse critics as the Bureau of the Budget, a southern governor's office, and various councils of social agencies. It is for this reason that the majority of anti-poverty programs meet their mandate to involve the poor by employing local residents in the "conducting" function, or the dispensation of anti-poverty largesse. The employment of local persons is often made a requirement of the project, without which it could not exist. Some service programs therefore employ nonprofessionals without regard for how they might best be used, but simply as a means of bringing a program into existence.

The "Helper Therapy" Principle

Observers have been struck by the fact that programs which use people in trouble to help others with similar difficulties often help the provider of service as much as they help the recipient.[8]

Such programs as Synanon and Parents Without Partners appear to have regularized this phenomenon to the point where the roles of patient and therapist become indistinguishable; the course of treatment is for the patient to devote his energies to the rehabilitation of others. One of the projects under review which employed adolescents as tutors of younger children illustrates this phenomenon most dramatically. Local high school students were assigned to tutor fourth and fifth grade pupils who were severely retarded in reading development. Many of the tutors themselves were below grade in their school work, and their educational and employment future was bleak. Over a study period of several months, the youngsters who were tutored as much as four hours a week showed significant improvement when compared to a control group. Even more striking—and unexpected—was the improvement made by the tutors, which exceeded the gains made by pupils.[9]

The ultimate objective of many nonprofessional approaches is to channel some of the forces within the deprived community itself into rehabilitative and restorative efforts so that the client becomes able to help himself. Complementing the service component in such efforts are attempts to break the cycle of pessimism and defeat that plagues low income persons. In a society in which the highest value is placed on success in the world of work, there is no more potent device for enhancing self-esteem than meaningful, productive employment. The employment of nonprofessionals may therefore produce therapeutic results simply by

8 Cf. Frank Riessman, "The 'Helper Therapy' Principle," *Social Work*, X, No. 2 (April 1965).

9 Robert Cloward, *Studies in Tutoring* (New York: Columbia University School of Social Work, 1966. Mimeographed).

awarding these workers status, regardless of the benefits derived in the helping process.

THE NONPROFESSIONALS AND THEIR ASSIGNMENTS

Background of the Workers

Nonprofessionals associated with the various youth projects have been drawn from diverse backgrounds. They include local residents and clients, middle class volunteers, graduate and undergraduate college students (both as volunteers and on field training assignments), VISTA volunteers and Peace Corps trainees. Both youth and adults have been utilized as nonprofessional program personnel. In one single large-scale project, virtually all these categories of nonprofessionals have been used concurrently, as follows:

1. Student Project Assistants: Graduates of the youth employment counseling program were given general ancillary responsibilities; they became drivers, assistant receptionists, interpreters of the youth training program to the community, etc.

2. Interns: Part-time (30 hours per week) college students were assigned tutoring, counseling, job development, and other professional responsibilities.

3. VISTA Volunteers: Full-time volunteers were assigned to tutoring and community work.

4. Neighborhood Youth Corps Trainees: Youngsters enrolled in the Neighborhood Youth Corps and placed in project programs were assigned ancillary responsibilities as clerical, research, and custodial assistants.

5. Neighborhood Adult-Participation Project Aides: Full-time employees in the project's community development program. NAPPA's carried many responsibilities among which were assignments to the youth training program as work crew foremen.

6. Volunteers (students, professionals, and housewives): Middle class residents offered a variety of services, both professional (e.g., psychotherapy, tattoo removal, legal services) and nonprofessional (tutoring assistant).

7. Work-Study Students: College students from low income families being assisted under Title IC of the Economic Opportunity Act were assigned to assist in job development, counseling, tutoring, etc.

8. Vocational Rehabilitation and Social Work Trainees: These trainees were assigned appropriately to programs that would facilitate their professional training.

Nonprofessionals may be categorized as indigenous to the target community, or as separate from it. Indigenous workers are those who reside in the target area, engage in social, economic, and political processes similar to those of the program participants, and are matched with them in such characteristics as social class, ethnicity, race, religion, language, culture, and mores. Many projects have recruited such nonprofessional staff from the broader community beyond the target area, but we shall continue to call these workers indigenous if they are matched with clients on general face-sheet characteristics.

In attempting to fill crew chief positions, for example, projects have frequently had difficulty in finding local residents with the necessary work skills. The search for such persons in the broader community was often futile as well, since for many crafts the candidates' racial and ethnic characteristics, which provide the indigenous match, preclude the acquisition of work skill qualifications. In projects that attempted to prepare youth for work through training in carpentry, masonry, plumbing, and other building trades, the crew chief often matched the client on certain working class attributes only, not on residential, racial, or cultural characteristics. In the same project, other divisions that did not require the work-related skills were able to employ nonprofessionals who were native to the target area and representative of its population. In general, the projects appear to have been most successful in hiring indigenous nonprofessionals for assignments that did not require a high degree of formal technical skill.

Nonprofessional staff that was separate from the target population and community sometimes became associated with the program, almost accidentally. This was particularly true of volunteers. The experiences of the projects with volunteers are so disparate as to defy classification. Some of these nonprofessionals were typical social agency volunteers, members of the middle and upper classes offering their services in their leisure as a gesture of *noblesse oblige*. At the opposite end of the scale were young radicals who settled in ghettos as a matter of personal choice, virtually as missionaries or colonizers, who offered their services as part of their political ideological commitment. In a number of instances, volunteers were arbitrarily thrust upon the projects and were accepted with resentment and misgivings. In these cases relations with the project tended to become pro forma, and were usually short lived.

In their early attempts to reach unemployed youth, training projects located in Spanish-speaking ghettos were faced with language barriers. In order to provide counseling as well as other services, it was necessary to find Spanish-speaking professionals. The search soon revealed that Spanish-speaking minority group members had been systematically excluded from the professions.

Because of the need to establish a relationship as a functional thera-peutic device, there is an inordinate dependence on the spoken word in counseling, tutoring, social work, and other rehabilitation services. For this reason, the use of translators with English-speaking professionals is impractical. Projects therefore recruited Spanish-speaking persons with some college or a college degree to provide such services. These workers were sometimes called aides or intake workers to distinguish them from their fully trained counterparts; but these distinctions tended to fade rather quickly. Recruitment of nonindigenous Negro staff took place for similar reasons, in the belief that Negro clients would communicate more fully with Negro workers than with white personnel.[10] Many projects also recruited Negro and Spanish personnel in an attempt to meet political pressure for integration exerted by civil rights and other activist and community groups.

Often such nonprofessional personnel were selected instead of indige-nous lower class persons. One project describes an extensive screening process that eliminated 30 or 40 indigenous applicants because they were deficient in communication skills and lacked preprofessional experience. The positions in question were ultimately filled by Negro and Puerto Rican workers, all of whom had had at least three years of college. These applicants had work backgrounds in teaching in the rural South, recrea-tion work in a large city, and work in a research assistant capacity.

Most projects employed nonprofessionals on a full-time, paid basis, and most employed nonprofessionals were adults. With few exceptions—Youth Opportunities Board, Los Angeles; Mobilization for Youth, New York—use of youth in service positions have consisted of assigning of Neighborhood Youth Corps trainees to various projects for work experi-ence. In these instances, of course, the project is not the employer of the nonprofessional youth, nor does it assume direct responsibility for su-pervising him.

Types of Assignments

The wide variety of tasks to which nonprofessionals have been assigned may be subsumed under four categories: direct service responsibilities, responsibilities ancillary to the professional service, responsibilities es-tablishing "bridges" or ties to the target community, and assignments totally apart from the professional services of the project. This last cate-gory, which simply needs to be acknowledged rather than discussed, con-sists in the main of clerical and custodial assignments often given to trainees in the NYC, Peace Corps, and other programs. The project is forced to accept these workers, who are often volunteers. Although this

[10] Cf. John Martin, "Social-Cultural Differences: Barriers in Casework with De-linquents," *Social Work*, II, No. 3 (July, 1957).

pattern is not uncommon, it does not characterize every assignment made to such nonprofessionals.

Direct service responsibilities—the least common of the four categories —refer to services usually transmitted to the client through the professional worker, e.g., counseling, remediation, job development, tutoring, and teaching. In the projects reviewed, there were examples of nonprofessionals providing each of these services directly to the client. Such assignments make best use of the qualities peculiar to the nonprofessional, for example, his enthusiasm and spontaneity.

Direct assignment also tends to utilize such nonprofessional qualities as the ability to communicate with clients, through common language or style; empathy with the client through shared life experience; and the ability to help clients negotiate the complexities of the ghetto.

Assignment to responsibilities ancillary to the provision of professional service is the most common way of using nonprofessionals. Some of these assignments are rather remote from the professional services being offered; they are, however, located within the program and are related to the client group. Ancillary responsibilities may consist of clerical, administrative, transport, and comparable duties that help to bring the client and the service into productive contact. Further along the continuum toward direct assignment are tasks frequently assigned to nonprofessional personnel that are instrumental in preparing the client for the professional service, e.g., reception, intake, and vestibule services.

Such assignments as recruitment and follow-up involve a large measure of independent service. Nonprofessionals on these assignments generally operate directly in the neighborhood, away from the supports and structure of the project agency. They are called upon to exercise considerable imagination and ingenuity, particularly when they deal with youth whom the agency has failed to induct, or for whom service has been ineffective. Although successful recruitment or follow-up ultimately entails turning the client over to a professional for service, the nonprofessional's task is perhaps more accurately viewed as contiguous rather than ancillary. Within the ancillary assignment, as one moves from the remote to the contiguous, the opportunities for exploiting indigenous qualities appear to increase.

To some degree, recruitment and follow-up serve a bridge function. However, the assignments we classify as bridge have more to do with project community relations on an institutional basis. In speaking engagements, door-to-door canvassing, leaflet distribution, and visiting youth groups and P.T.A.'s, the nonprofessional acts as agency spokesman to the target community and the community at large. The use of nonprofessionals in these capacities is often a viable device for persuading the target community that services are being offered by a congenial institution. (It can, however, become a public relations gimmick, an attempt to represent the agency as ethnically or culturally indigenous when in fact it may not be. It is something of an anomaly that the employment of nonprofessionals can be offered as tokenism to avoid the actual reordering of a public institution along congenial indigenous lines.)

Work training projects tend to discriminate between indigenous nonprofessionals and their more formally trained middle class counterparts. The former group gets assignments that are more irrelevant and less direct. The ancillary tasks assigned them tend to be remote rather than contiguous. Middle class nonprofessionals are utilized more frequently in direct assignment, often in ways indistinguishable from the professional. Agency representatives indicated that they would be willing to promote such nonprofessionals into professional positions, although few actually did. Where youth employment projects were part of comprehensive programs, this tendency was not so pronounced in other program divisions. Although indigenous nonprofessionals in employment projects were not assigned to provide counseling or remediation, they did provide social work services (casework, group work, and especially community organization) and educational services (tutoring, citizenship, and consumer) in other divisions of the same project. The failure to use indigenous nonprofessionals in employment was more pronounced in the counseling than in work readiness programs. Crew chiefs and on-the-job training personnel were often selected from among the indigenous.

SUBSTANTIVE ISSUES

The Nonprofessional and the Agency

The use of nonprofessionals in MDTA youth programs was in large part the result of influence exerted by the federal funding agencies. Federal agencies not only provided the service agencies with funds for the employment of nonprofessionals, but threatened to set up parallel organizations if these monies were not used for that purpose. A number of respondents were convinced that, without this threat, the agencies and projects would not have hired nonprofessionals and that, should federal supports be removed, they would stop using nonprofessionals. It is significant that this opinion appears to apply primarily to nonprofessional employees who are indigenous to the service community.

In part this reluctance reflects the resentment felt by many project administrators and agency executives at being compelled to employ large numbers of minority group indigenous persons. According to one respondent, the project was "paying the price for one hundred years of discrimination by the entire community." Although others expressed the conviction that nonprofessionals were vital to successful project programs, they frequently felt inhibited with regard to reassigning or dismissing these indigenous personnel because of fear of community reprisals. When the administrative head of one project dismissed the director of a neighborhood program that employed many indigenous nonprofessionals, these workers picketed project headquarters and eventually involved the local congressman and the regional OEO office. Largely as a result of the public turmoil the workers were able to raise, the professional director was rehired with considerable loss of face for the project administration. Among professionals associated with the project, this incident resulted in widespread enmity regarding this program in particular, and indigenous workers in general. The potential for a re-enactment of this situation exists in all projects, programs, and agencies that employ local residents.

The attitude of various state employment service offices illustrates that they perceive a threat inherent in the use of local personnel stemming from the fact that the employment of such persons forces the agency to a degree of accountability to the client community. This is contrary to the traditional pattern in all service agencies—professional self-regulation and accountability to the total community,[11] and to the employment service's views of its responsibility to the employer.

The district manager of a state employment service office employing nonprofessional staff complained that the nonprofessional doesn't play by the rules. The persistence with which such workers undertake job development, he claimed, often alienates employers: they tend to demand, rather than ask for job placements. In addition, these workers are not content to stay within the perimeters of their assigned tasks; they want to "take over the entire agency."

A demonstration project staff member observed that turnover among nonprofessional provisional workers in the Bureau of Employment Security was inordinately high. "The best provisionals end up being the ones who fail the tests and get fired." According to the respondent, this phenomenon cannot be explained in terms of the workers' failure to meet state job standards, since the employment service could train provisionals to take tests just as the project prepares trainees to take tests. The phenomenon illustrates the reluctance of the employment service to hire and to retain local nonprofessionals. Once hired, these staff members are generally abrasive to the operation of the office as conceived by its executive hierarchy, and a high turnover rate ensues. According to project informants, further evidence could be found in the high turnover rate of cause-oriented counselors in the employment service.

A nonprofessional who served as a neighborhood extension (outreach)

---

[11] "Total community" generally means the formal organizations and representative groups of the community. It apparently never includes the unaffiliated poor.

worker for the employment service office voiced a number of griev-
ances regarding lack of employment service cooperation. She charged
that supportive counseling services were not provided, that only certain
kinds of jobs were made available to her people, and, most particularly,
that the employment service did not take her word for anything. What
was the use, she asked, of a neighborhood extension program if all the
information gathered through that program was verified independently
by the downtown office? The employment service office felt that nonprofessionals were useful in pre-employment and intake functions, but
lacked the skill and training to operate effectively beyond this point; professional counselors therefore had to take over. This view reflected in
part an ideological disparity between the professional and the nonprofessional. The nonprofessional apparently feels that the most important
thing to be done for the client is to get him a job, while the professional
feels the need to "correct the root of the unemployment problem through
programs of counseling, training, and education that will make the person
employable." The professional also tends to select the most amenable
candidates, excluding "drifters, gamblers, and hustlers," while the nonprofessional believes that the service should be available to all on a first
come, first served basis. It is clear that there are both merits and problems
in each of these points of view. Despite the strains, the employment
service has managed to contain both elements. Its administration describes
the nonprofessional in program as a "must."

The use of nonprofessionals in the projects, and in the public welfare
service agencies in particular, must be seen in terms of institutional
change, as well as service objectives. The introduction of a program
device as innovative as this one, even if the original intention is only to
improve service, must soon produce strains leading to alterations in patterns of agency function. A somewhat anomalous circumstance surrounds
this social change objective in that it is articulated by the staff of the
CAP agency that administers the federal funds, but not by the public
agencies that are the targets of the change. Thus the antipoverty administrators conceive of the nonprofessionals as change agents while the
welfare agency sees them as facilitating existing services. It would appear
that the stress inherent in this situation is exacerbated by this dual
perception.[12]

The experience of one neighborhood employment office nonprofessional illustrates the way in which alterations in service impinge on general
agency functions. Because of this worker's roots in the community, she

[12] It may very well be that this disparity is essential if the nonprofessional is to
be accepted by the service agency at all. If this is the case, there is little that can be
done about this complication beyond recognizing its genesis and some of its consequences.

is contacted on matters pertaining to all programs offered by the local community action program. On one not atypical occasion, she received a call from a local resident, greatly agitated because her welfare worker was investigating a report that she was receiving income for babysitting. The information had been given to the welfare worker by the Head Start coordinator, who was working with the family for which the babysitting was said to have taken place. After hearing from the client, the employment aide called the Head Start worker, the welfare worker, and the neighborhood family to ascertain the facts. She then explained to the welfare worker that no payment had been made for sitting, that funds were not being diverted from the regular family food budget for this purpose, and that this was, after all, the kind of neighborliness to be encouraged in building community pride and spirit.

The indigenous worker then explained to the Head Start worker, politely but firmly, that babysitting arrangements on the part of the Head Start family were none of the professional worker's business. If the latter were to inadvertently become privy to such information, she should keep it to herself. Later, describing her own work, the respondent said that if she succeeds in helping a person on public assistance to get a job, she does not share this fact with the welfare department. She points out to the client that he is required to inform the department and that she hopes he will do so. However, she can understand that need may drive the client to withhold information, and she will not interfere with this.

In this instance, the worker remains loyal to indigenous rather than professional values and behavior patterns. The community's acceptance of this worker as interpreter, confidante, and advocate is undoubtedly a response to this loyalty. Her professional associates in the CAP agency regard her with some fear and suspicion. The employment service people look upon her as a troublemaker, and top agency administrators tend to see her as a model of what the indigenous nonprofessional ought to be. The question of whether the indigenous worker is loyal to the neighborhood from which he is drawn or to the agency is not always resolved in so clear-cut a manner.

In another project, another nonprofessional indigenous worker faced with the same dilemma indicated that she would share information with her agency, but not with the Department of Welfare, if the client refused to do so. This worker expressed a sense of alienation from her own community. Regarding her relations with her neighbors after becoming employed by the youth project, she indicated that "The people do stand off, they feel that you are not the same." It appears that nonprofessionals who feel this alienation tend to seek acceptance from the agency staff group, in whose milieu they are likely to take on additional values, attitudes, and norms of behavior alien to the neighborhood.

Another factor that appears to have a bearing on where the indigenous nonprofessional will build continuing loyalties is the nature of the job assignment. In the first instance described above, the worker was employed in a direct service capacity; the responsibilities of the second worker were ancillary. Primary identification with the community seems to be enhanced if the nonprofessional is engaged in activity that can stand on its own. Where the nonprofessional's successful performance was tied to a client's amenability to service to be provided by a professional colleague, high professional identification and orientation ensued. Where performance was independent, and community participation by heretofore unserved persons was esteemed, identification with community was primary. In the project in which the professionally oriented ancillary worker is located, there is a division in which nonprofessionals are used in direct service capacities. These workers, drawn from the same community, of identical class and racial background and employed under the same project executive, are militantly identified with community.

Issues of Recruitment and Selection

Although professional and nonprogram staff are systematically and regularly recruited through conventional channels (employment services, ads, etc.), nonprofessionals are apparently recruited on an *ad hoc* basis. Community informants, particularly such influentials as local welfare agency executives, clergymen, political leaders, and school officials, are often asked to refer local persons for employment. Sometimes "outstanding" residents are specified. Even when this is not explicitly done, the persons referred tend to be those who have assumed some leadership in the organization with which the referrer is affiliated. (As will be noted later, there is reason to believe that relying on local institutional leaders as a source of candidates screens the applicants in light of the qualities that the recruiter deems desirable. In addition, unrelated factors may influence selection; for example, positions may be seen by referrants as rewards for service, as political patronage, or as largesse for the deserving poor.)

In most cases, neither the local institutions doing the recruiting, nor the projects, have formally specified the qualities they seek in nonprofessional staff. One informant indicated, however, that his project sought "a quickness of mind and a capacity for growth," along with "a public capability to lead and organize." Nonprofessionals in this project appear to have a good measure of the qualities sought. In a project in another city, staff have indicated that they seek nonprofessionals with white collar experience. High priority has been placed on the ability to prepare written reports and to participate easily in staff meetings and conferences. This project expressly attempts to avoid nonprofessionals who are "overidentified with the client." (It is interesting to note that the white collar experience that this project seeks apparently successfully screens out those who tend to be "overidentified.") In still another city, the project staff sought persons with a strong personality and a strong positive commitment to the agency; "do-gooders" were not welcome in staff positions.

Still another agency at its inception developed differential recruitment practices and standards for its various categories of nonprofessional staff, depending on the function each individual was intended to fill. One group, which helped local residents with household management, was selected from a list of women recommended by local settlements and churches. The qualities sought were homemaking skills, demonstrated mastery of the intricacies of urban slum living, and good feeling toward people. Members of another group, hired to teach a craft or work skills to young people, were recruited directly from industry. They were not local residents or affiliated with local welfare or religious institutions. Community workers were recruited from among the local unaffiliated residents. The quality sought was leadership, which was measured in terms of following; thus, influential community persons who were not involved in community institutions were selected. As is apparent, very different kinds of nonprofessionals were hired in each of these job categories.

The Neighborhood House Project in Richmond, California developed written specifications describing job qualifications and requirements (as well as responsibilities and benefits).[13] Requirements included local residence, prior work experience, and participation in the P.T.A., the Scouts, a union, a fraternal group, or some similar organization. Personal characteristics sought were maturity, the ability to work with people, agency loyalty participation in some form of personal upgrading, and willingness to undertake training, if necessary. Educational requirements are listed as high school, G.E.D., or strong potential for G.E.D. The specifications noted that the position for which the nonprofessional was to be hired was regarded, not as an end in itself, but as a means of helping him find a permanent place in the labor force, or encouraging him to seek additional training. Although many of the requirements and conditions listed in these documents are the same as those of other projects, the fact that they are available to candidates and recruiters makes for a consistency in the selection of nonprofessionals that is too often lacking in practice.

In two of the projects surveyed in connection with this report, candidates who had been trained under an OMAT grant to the National Committee for the Employment of Youth had been interviewed for nonprofes-

[13] It is of interest, with regard to possible replication of MDTA experience, that this community subsequently developed a highly sophisticated community action program that included specifications for each distinctive nonprofessional position.

sional employment. One project found none of these candidates suitable for employment as counseling and job development aides. The other project employed seven of these trainees in such direct assignments as recruiters, work readiness evaluators, and assistant crew chiefs. Apparently a project's ability to make effective use of nonprofessionals depends more on its willingness to surrender areas of professional discretion to them than on issues of training, or the availability of trained applicants. Competence is judged differently by different projects, and it is likely that each sees the nonprofessional as serving a different organizational purpose.

Nonprofessional staff have also been drawn from among local people who were active in the project as volunteers. Recruits of this kind pose problems for local residents who continue to serve as volunteers, particularly for those who are engaged in activities similar to those of the employed worker.

A number of projects reported that the target community was involved in choosing nonprofessional personnel through the participation of residents in selection committees. In some instances these committees see all candidates; others see candidates who have been screened by the project's administration. Some committees make specific recommendations for hiring; others designate the acceptable candidates, from among whom the administration can then make their choice. Professional employees are not screened by selection committees, although in some cases their application forms are reviewed by these bodies. In these cases, local community residents are not a part of the personnel committee.

Issues of Identification

Recruitment practices are not unrelated to the question of whether the nonprofessional, particularly the indigenous nonprofessional, will identify with the project that employs him or the community from which he was recruited. When recruitment patterns select the upwardly mobile, and job assignments encourage agency dependency, one can be reasonably certain that the project and the professionals will become the basic reference groups for these staff members. This is especially true with respect to those whose desire for job security is strong.

The projects' experience confirms the numerous studies that describe the tendency of the less skilled and lower class worker to favor security over a risky but real opportunity for advancement. Patterns of employment tenure among nonprofessionals indicate virtually no turnover, in contrast to the very high turnover rate among professionals in the same agency. The nonprofessional's general experience in the job market leads him to be conservative in his approach to employment. Realizing that his opportunities for employment are restricted, he will eschew conflict with the agency and seek rapport, both deliberately and unconsciously, by internalizing agency professional norms.[14]

The experience of several projects with nonprofessional staff illustrates both their tendency to avoid certain nonprofessional, community-based activities, and their tendency to emulate professional practice. In one of the projects, nonprofessionals assigned to a service provision program demanded to be supervised by means of regularly scheduled weekly conferences; to be assigned offices equipped with desks, blotters, and lamps; and to utilize appointment books and office hours. These workers wished to avoid home visits to deteriorated buildings, babysitting, and homemaking assignments. However, nonprofessionals in the same agency who were assigned to community organization tasks did not pursue a similar pattern. The success of the latter group depended on viable community ties. Thus they frequented the streets and the tenements, preferred storefront locations, dressed casually, and avoided any distinctions that would separate them from the neighborhood residents. This supports our earlier conclusion that the choice of reference group is strongly influenced by job assignment, in part because job assignment may influence the pattern by which employment security is best established.

The role of the professional in the community organization program offers yet another affirmation of the potency of job assignment in this respect. In a number of ways the professionals in this division were more community-identified than the nonprofessionals in the other service divisions. They dressed casually, without tie or jacket, spoke the neighborhood argot, and did without desks, appointment books, and formal conferences.

Issues of Upward Mobility

Although some thought has been given to the problem of creating a career line through which the nonprofessional may be promoted and increase his earnings, no such plans are currently operational. Two patterns of advancement are discernible. The first brings the nonprofessional into common cause with professional, clerical, and maintenance personnel in a trade union organization. Advancement takes place collectively rather than individually, through negotiated agreements that include incremental salary increases and improved fringe benefits. One project makes it a policy that current staff be given first option on all new job openings. This provision occasionally affords upward mobility for the nonprofessional.

In the second pattern, which is much more widespread, the individual

---

[14] Cf. Charles Grosser, "Perceptions of Professionals, Indigenous Workers, and Lower Class Clients" (Doctoral dissertation, Columbia University School of Social Work, 1965).

advances by moving from one program in the community to another, seeking a higher rate of pay; or he may move to a more demanding, better paying position within the project in which he is employed. As a nonprofessional worker gains white collar experience in a project job, he not only learns the skills that are required to do the work, but also becomes aware of employment possibilities in other CAP and OEO programs. Thus he might move from an ancillary or unrelated assignment to a direct service assignment either within the same project or across several antipoverty programs.

Issues of Professional-Nonprofessional Relations

Generally the professional worker accepts his untrained, noncredentialed colleague in ancillary, bridge, or unrelated assignments within the project. Although there are a few professionals who feel that even in these areas the nonprofessional is inappropriately involved, in the main the professional views the untrained worker (particularly the indigenous worker), positively. In fact, the reaction of the professional is often somewhat romanticized. The vaunted virtues of the nonprofessional—spontaneity, ability to communicate, informality, style, and identification with clients—often perceived in idealized fashion, are frequently belied by performance. The tendency of nonprofessionals to exhibit quite different characteristics under certain circumstances is infrequently acknowledged. In addition to romanticizing the virtues of the untrained, the professional tends to assume—often erroneously—that he himself wholly lacks these qualities.

A survey conducted by one of the projects indicated that the attitudes and beliefs of nonprofessional staff tend to be highly judgmental and moralistic regarding the behavior of local target area residents. They often regard illegitimacy, unemployment, drinking, and even boisterous asocial behavior as evidence of moral turpitude. They also tend to be somewhat fatalistic about a person's ability to affect his life. These observations indicate that the services of the nonprofessional might be utilized best if assignments were made selectively. The professional's objectivity and dispassion might be more functional in serving low income clients in certain circumstances than the nonprofessional's congeniality and judgmentalness. However, it appears that little discretion in assignment was exercised consciously. When the project's view of the use of the nonprofessional was positive, their attitude was, "You can't have too much of a good thing"; when their set was negative, they tended to feel that it didn't matter anyway. Either view resulted in indiscriminately awarded assignments.

Even in the area of advocacy, it was found that, under certain circumstances, nonprofessionals constituted an impediment to effective service.

This was most striking where project staff had to negotiate on behalf of a trainee with a hostile community institution. Such institutions tend to be more favorably disposed when approached by a professional whose "style, language, and affect" are familiar. If what is being sought is immediate service for the trainee, the professional is obviously the best bridge between project and formal community institution. Several projects identified this phenomenon in its negative aspect, describing how staff members with Spanish accents were summarily brushed aside when they phoned certain institutions for assistance, whereas these same institutions responded favorably when called by (English-speaking) staff with no accent.

The reactions of nonprofessionals to professional staff tend to follow the patterns of identification described earlier. Those who are project-identified tend to be less critical than those who are community-identified. The community-oriented group shares the residents' perception of the professional as an outsider, something of a cold fish, too formal, bureaucratic, and not sufficiently sympathetic to the neighborhood. One is struck, however, by the clear-cut distinction made by virtually all community residents as well as by the nonprofessional staff between project professionals and professionals employed in other community service organizations. The former group is accepted and viewed critically in the light of this acceptance; from the latter group, however, there is virtually complete estrangement. In assaying the consequences of the use of nonprofessionals below, we shall suggest that not the least of them is the effect they have on total project staff.

Strain between the formally certified and untrained staffs is most likely to appear when nonprofessionals are assigned to direct service responsibilities. In virtually every instance, responses indicated that the professional group reacted defensively, at least at first. They were unwilling to concede that there were significant portions of their jobs that could be given over to nonprofessionals. As a result, administrators were reluctant to experiment with direct assignments, anticipating that professional staff would object sharply.

Clearly, the professional in these instances saw the direct service assignment of the nonprofessional as an encroachment on his designated area of practice. It appears that this resistance owed more to the feeling that the use of untrained persons denigrated professional training than to any actual threat to job security. The problem was much more formidable in anticipation than in practice. Where nonprofessionals were actually given direct service assignments, accommodation soon resulted. Unfortunately, the timidity of administrators appears to have precluded many such assignments.

Personnel practices have proved to be a source of dissonance in the relation between these two groups. As indicated, the problem of dismissing workers, particularly when the nonprofessionals call on community support, has created enmity between the staff groups, exacerbating feelings that may already have been present as a result of differential hiring practices, salaries, and working conditions. Personnel practices for nonprofessionals in a number of agencies are the same as those for maintenance and clerical staff, rather than the more generous arrangements made with the professionals.

In some projects, direct assignments have evolved to the point where staff members from both groups are engaged in identical activities. In many cases, the only difference between them is a year or two of formal training, or training in a different area, with the result that the members of one group have professional certification. Yet the salary differential between such workers might be as much as 40 or 50 per cent. Typically it is in the neighborhood of 25 per cent, which still may amount to several thousand dollars a year.

TRAINING PROGRAMS FOR NONPROFESSIONALS

Before referring to problems of training relating specifically to nonprofessional personnel, we would do well to consider a few of the generic issues that underlie this area. In a war, untrained troops are often forced into situations they are unprepared to face. This happens because the time, resources, or necessary personnel to conduct proper training programs are lacking. It appears that in the current effort to socialize welfare and other services, which we have euphemistically dubbed a war, the same situation prevails. Funds are generally not forthcoming for training. Legislators, funding agencies, administrators, and beneficiaries prefer that funds be utilized to produce tangible service programs with visible results. Statistics of persons served do not result from training programs, nor are the qualitative differences produced sufficiently visible to meet the pressures being exerted. As a result, available resources are allocated to programs that produce quantitative results; training is not among these programs.

Some respondents indicated that the training programs for project nonprofessionals were generally a part of the training program offered the total project program staff. This means that there was no formal orientation period and that in-service training consisted of staff meetings, in some instances regularly scheduled, in others, sporadic. Administrators feel some discomfort with this situation though it is clear that they have resigned themselves to it. Only one project administrator was candid enough to acknowledge, without prodding, that he had no training program worth mentioning.

What separate programs exist for nonprofessional staff sometimes have a strong doctrinaire character. They are designed to encourage agency loyalty and to interpret agency programs and policy. One respondent suggested that training served as a vehicle to handle the nonprofessionals' strong negative feelings toward such public agencies as the Department of Welfare.

New Careers Programs

Nonprofessionals who had participated in new careers programs as client or project beneficiaries did receive extensive training. This may be because in this case the training itself is service that can be statistically cited. One such program (Neighborhood House, Richmond, California) was quite imaginative and creative. The training was distinct from that offered to any other staff group; and unlike the conventional forms of presenting job orientation and administrative information, it focused on correcting deficiencies in basic education skills, and exposing the careerist nonprofessional to new experiences. Trips around the state, attendance at meetings, participation in conferences and conventions, and visits to legislative bodies were part of the program. Attention was also focused on developing organizational, job-related, and general social skills.

Substantive training often took place at the inception of the earliest E & D projects (usually amalgams in which OMAT, OJD, and municipal and private funding sources participated). Here the training of both professional and nonprofessional staff was given much attention. Because these projects were charged to produce knowledge rather than substantial services, they were permitted the luxury of substantial training investments. One such program, which devoted 6 per cent (some $300,000) of its budget to training, was able to assign three staff members in addition to outside resource personnel to a full-time training program for one group of local nonprofessionals. Once the total program was in full swing, such an arrangement was not possible; as nonprofessionals were added they were placed in their jobs with little orientation or training.

Centralized Training Programs

In two of the projects observed, the MDTA project had turned over its training function to another agency. In both these cases, nonprofessional staff received high qualitative training experiences. In one case (Action Housing, Inc., Pittsburgh) a citywide agency had undertaken responsibility for training nonprofessionals for all public programs in the city, and the project reluctantly complied. The administrator of the training program complained that she was hard-pressed by the groups she was serving to push trainees through quickly and avoid wasting time on nonessentials. The agencies made it clear that they regarded themselves as the proper training agents. They resented the central system, and participated in it only to comply with the demands of the local CAP. In other cities, proposals to centralize training or negotiate training contracts with local academic institutions encountered similar resistance.

The centralized training program itself is quite comprehensive. Under the direction of a full-time training supervisor, a functional syllabus outlining the goals and methods of the training unit has been prepared. The training is directed to building a broad knowledge base encompassing the rationale behind the program as well as preparation for specific tasks. Relations between nonprofessionals and professionals, clients and the community at large, are explored. The presentation of material takes into account educational, cultural, and ethnic differentials. Local historical and traditional materials, as well as such topics as the culture of poverty, the role of the family, and economic and educational theories and institutions are covered in the syllabus. It appeared, on the basis of a brief site visit, that this material was effectively presented to the trainees.

There is much to commend this training arrangement. It relieves the service program of the burden of training, and greatly increases the likelihood that training will take place. It raises the content level of training from concern with narrow operational issues to more creative exploitation of personnel and program.

In the second instance, the training function was assumed by the National Committee for the Employment of Youth. In a sense this instance is a variant on the new careers model, except that it is specifically geared to meet the needs of manpower projects. In this regard it stands as perhaps the most effective and most relevant training device. Substantively, this program is the most sophisticated one reviewed. It consists of twelve weeks of on-the-job and classroom training combined with discussion and field trips. Program content is geared to the general and the specific, attempting to elucidate the conditions underlying the problems that the nonprofessionals will be coping with, as well as their own functions in the projects. The program is staffed by three full-time professionals and operated under independent funding from OMAT.[15] Apart from the substantive knowledge it generates, this program also serves as a training institution for other projects that hire graduates. It represents a most viable approach to training, combining the advantages of locating this function outside the service agency with the resources of an experienced, highly sophisticated staff. Local academic institutions will also lend themselves to this approach.

[15] See: National Committee on the Employment of Youth, *A Demonstration On-The-Job Training Program for Semi-Professional Personnel in Youth Employment Programs.* Mimeographed, 1965.

SUMMARY AND CONCLUSIONS

The employment of nonprofessionals in manpower projects has important consequences for a project's program, its target population, the nonprofessionals themselves, and the professional staff. Nonprofessionals have no influence on the substance of a manpower training program. In their capacity as project employees, they are directed to limit themselves to furthering organizational purpose. Although a nonprofessional may offer program in a unique style, he is discouraged from trying to alter its substance, nor could he do so if he were encouraged to. Projects see professionals and nonprofessionals in light of their own organizational needs; as solutions to problems of service provision, not as vehicles of institutional change or program innovation.

Issues of job security support these tendencies. Programs in training projects become locked in place, much as they do in continuing institutions. Issues of funding, politics, organizational self-interest, and the like are among the operational imperatives determining program. Neither professional nor nonprofessional staff can alter this pattern through programmatic strategies. The actual substance of program will be altered by strategies that are economic, political, or organizational.

In visiting projects, particularly in the community itself, where many nonprofessionals pursue their assignments, the observer is impressed with the extent to which the target population has been engaged. The presence of the nonprofessionals is very much felt. Often they are regarded as "the agency" by the neighborhood population. Professionals are less well-known and their presence is not felt to the same degree.

In areas like Hunters Point in San Francisco, Hough in Cleveland, and East Los Angeles, all of which reflect severe deprivation and urban blight, nonprofessional staff were among the few social welfare personnel who remained engaged with these communities through their recent crises. A stated goal of antipoverty program in the use of nonprofessionals is to relieve tensions. To this end, local persons of influence as well as residents of a troubled area are sought out for nonprofessional assignments. One program effectively emasculated a militant local civil rights organization by hiring virtually all its leadership as nonprofessional staff. However, the militant mantle of the first organization was promptly seized by another group.

Another project placed former activists ("hell raisers") in program positions, where they were quickly immersed in diverse complex procedures that inhibited their ability to perform as previously. These nonprofessionals then found themselves in the position of having to explain to their neighbors that their demands could not be met for reasons having to do with funding, legislation, jurisdiction, etc.

In another context, the function of the local untrained nonprofessional was described as keeping the clients from "conning the professionals." It is being suggested here that the target communities join the projects in an interacting continuum. At the point of juncture, nonprofessional positions provide a number of residents with channels for upward mobility; however, the essential issues of discord (unemployment, inadequate housing and education, etc.) remain.

In this regard, it can be noted that project employment has profound consequences for the nonprofessionals themselves. Most striking, and not at all atypical, is the high school tutor group mentioned earlier. Welfare recipients, school dropouts, unwed mothers, and the chronically unemployed have also utilized the opportunities afforded through project employment to enormous personal advantage. In such instances, standards of living have risen, with debts cleared, permanent employment maintained, school continued, etc. for the nonprofessional employee and his family. These results are perhaps the clearest and least ambiguous positive consequence of nonprofessional employment.

Professional staff has probably been affected more than is generally acknowledged by the employment of nonprofessionals. For one thing, they find in the office—on their own side of the desk, as it were—attitudes, life styles, and points of view that heretofore they had seen only in clients, and then usually characterized as pathology. They are forced by their nonprofessional colleagues to justify their practice in client-related terms. The effect on the provision of services seems to be salutary, for professionals in these projects are markedly more effective with the poor than are their counterparts in other agencies.

Experience in the use of nonprofessionals has suggested that some professional services can be effectively performed by untrained personnel. Although this issue has by no means been resolved, the fact that it has been clearly stated is of no small consequence.

It appears that the advantages (particularly bridging gaps and fulfilling democratic ideology) sought through the utilization of nonprofessionals will stem from three separate sources, one of which is nonprofessional indigenous status. Locating of the nonprofessional in a decentralized, neighborhood-based, comprehensive setting appears to be required to enable his contribution to come forth. In addition, the organization (i.e., E & D project or state employment service) within which this program is located will determine the extent to which those qualities inherent in the worker that are facilitated by the decentralized setting are utilized. Nonprofessional status is essentially instrumental; organizational policies and structural forms determine in large measure the direction of this instrumentation. Perhaps the greatest source of disappointment in using this staff group has resulted from the expectation that their nonprofessional status in itself contained sufficient magic to transcend the limitations that plagued the rest of the project. We have tried to suggest that this is not the case.

Implications for Manpower Training

Certain trends that may cause some concern are discernible in the use of nonprofessionals. The patterns of service provision seem to cast the nonprofessional staff member with the lower class, minority group client while the professional serves the middle class, more highly motivated client. The former provides direct, concrete service while the latter provides therapeutic and rehabilitative services. Clients of employment service administered programs ordinarily find no occasion to have contact with the nonprofessional. Such contact is reserved for clients of the special training, antipoverty, or E & D project, which deal with the most disadvantaged segment of the population.

A similar pattern is apparent in other service programs as well. Nonprofessional teachers and medical aides tend to be utilized in the slum school and hospital ward. The use of nonprofessionals in this way reinforces the dual standard that already characterizes the participation of the poor in society. It may also be offered as a substitute for more schools, reorganized employment services, or higher salaries for nurses.

Problems of training nonprofessional staff are related to the issue of making the most efficacious use of them in broad social terms rather than narrow organizational terms. To achieve such ends, it is necessary to resist premature pressures to produce visible results. Adequate training takes time and resources that have rarely been available. Succumbing to the blandishments and threats of the poverty war's armchair generals, professionals and administrators have too often utilized nonprofessionals as the shock troops. As a result, administrators have squandered the potential of this vast resource of service personnel for a quick increase in the gross statistics of clients served. Perhaps the most striking aspect of this waste is the widespread failure to make the nonprofessional an integral part of the service offered. As we have suggested, this failure is particularly noticeable in manpower programs. That it is not an inevitable consequence, implicit in the nature of employment training, is demonstrated by the several outstanding experiences cited.

Generally, the problem of replicating experience in using nonprofessionals is formidable. Local programs administered through such continuing agencies as state employment services and the Bureau of Apprenticeship Training are notably unresponsive to the potentials available to them. This lack of receptivity is a matter of public policy to be resolved in quarters other than the nonprofessional utilization programs.

We cited negative factors first in the belief that the experience of manpower and other service programs has established the value and viability of using nonprofessional staff. The potential of this approach on all levels—meeting manpower needs, bridging the gap between service agency and the very poor, and creating new careers to alleviate chronic unemployment—has been demonstrated by the broad range of programs undertaken by the Department of Labor, sponsored by the Office of Manpower Training.

Implications for the Service Professions

Although it may not be politically expedient to join the issue, there are few who would seriously dispute the contention that this nation is a highly developed welfare state. The provision of welfare services is becoming an increasingly accepted function of government, serving millions of citizens. In contrast to the notion that welfare services should be provided as a matter of *noblesse oblige* to a select group of deserving poor, the welfare state model strives to make its benefits available to the entire citizenry as a matter of right.

The provision of service by means of a small, specially trained professional elite is viable for limited programs. But this method cannot possibly be effective in programs providing massive benefits. The future of the service professions in the welfare state is therefore inevitably linked to the utilization of the nonprofessional. Narrow professional issues will eventually be set aside to meet the more significant national welfare issues that impinge upon us. The programs reviewed have indicated many possibilities. Policy makers and social planners will have to provide the contexts within which these possibilities can be fully exploited.

RECAPITULATION AND SPECIAL SOURCE MATERIALS

This paper has highlighted several issues in the experience of a handful of projects funded by the Department of Labor under the Manpower Development and Training Act. Because of the nature of these programs, considerable attention has been focused on the new careers—antipoverty models. The point has already been made that the use of nonprofessionals transcends this model; however, it bears reiteration. The many projects demonstrating the usefulness of working and middle class nonprofessionals in educational, health, therapeutic, recreational, child-care and other roles, comprise a substantial part of the literature on the subject. Generalizations, which go beyond the observations of this paper, regarding manpower social policy issues need reflect these experiences, as well as those cited in this report.

This report has presented a number of issues judged to be both salient and useful to agencies engaged in the kind of manpower antipoverty programs typical of much recent activity. The provisions of the Scheuer Amendment have insured that such areas of nonprofessional usage will continue and expand. We would suggest that the following are priority considerations for agencies participating in programs of this general type.

Some Conditions

Nonprofessional employment is a complex, differentially useful strategy. It is not a panacea that will solve problems of chronic unemployment, or make up for the inadequacies of the service professions.

Problems such as organizational malfunction and inadequacy of service or benefit stemming from administrative or legislative policy will not be altered by the employment of nonprofessionals.

Justification of the nonprofessional in the labor force will ultimately be made on the basis of production, as it is for other workers. There is no particular "magic" associated with their employment.

Some Virtues

The manpower shortages in the service professions have been chronic and pervasive. The only foreseeable solution to these shortages is in the vast resources of the nonprofessional.

Differential usage of nonprofessionals acknowledges the unique contributions they can make in such distinctive roles as bridge, helper-therapist, and the like.

Some Issues

The training function, central to all productive employment, has been neglected in nonprofessional employment. As nonprofessionals move from special training and E & D projects into continuing public departments and institutions, as well as private industry, establishing suitable training programs becomes critical.

To be effective, nonprofessional positions will have to be located in a job continuum that provides open career lines. Any strategy restricting the nonprofessional to entry level positions will frustrate all benefits—those accruing to the nonprofessional, the service recipient, the agency and the community.

The relation between professional and the nonprofessional ought to be supporting and complementary. However, strains between the two groups often develop out of explicit issues. Such issues, particularly those that make invidious or marked distinctions between the two groups, need be anticipated and avoided.

If the generic benefits of nonprofessional personnel are to be realized, their services cannot be restricted to the less influential or less affluent.

Complementary nonprofessional services have their place in the schools, hospitals, welfare departments, family agencies and service industries serving the entire community. Manpower plans ought to be predicated, if anything, on redressing the professional shortages in the less affluent community. Plans for the use of nonprofessionals ought certainly to avoid aggravating such shortages by providing nonprofessional substitutes.

By way of a final comment, we wish to make explicit what we believe to be the implicit conclusion of this chapter. We believe that recent programs using nonprofessionals have demonstrated the manpower resource they represent, the enrichment that this resource can provide the program, and the spate of direct and indirect benefits that may accrue to the total community. We do not believe that present programs have yet realized the potentials inherent in this new manpower source. The conviction that the nonprofessional not be exploited for short-range, superficial, relatively insignificant goals is what moves us to some of the critical suggestions presented here. Diligent appraisal of past experience, and utilization of whatever insight such appraisal produces, may provide us with clues as to how the use of nonprofessionals may ultimately solve substantial problems and meet fairly significant long-range goals.

SELECTED READINGS

1. Barr, Sherman, "Some Observations on the Practice of Indigenous Nonprofessional Workers." Paper presented at the 14th Annual Program Meeting of the Council on Social Work Education, January, 1966.

2. Benjamin, Judith, et al., Pros and Cons: New Roles for Nonprofessionals in Corrections. U.S. Department of Health, Education, and Welfare. Washington, D.C.: Government Printing Office, 1966.

3. Brager, George, "The Indigenous Worker: A New Approach to the Social Work Techniques," Social Work, 10 (April, 1965), 33-40.

4. Brager, George, and Francis Purcell, eds., Community Action against Poverty. New Haven: Yale University Press, 1967.

5. Decisions of the Arden House Conference on Manpower and Training for Corrections: June 24-26, 1964. New York: National Association of Social Workers, 1964.

6. Epstein, Laura, "Differential Use of Staff: A Method to Expand Social Services," Social Work, 7 (October, 1962), 66-72.

7. Fishman et al., eds., "New Careers: Ways Out of Poverty for Disadvantaged Youth." Conference report, Howard University Center for Youth and Community Studies, 1965.

320   *The Role of the Nonprofessional*

8. Grant, J. Douglas, *et al.*, "Job and Career Development for the Poor." Report prepared for the California Office of Economic Opportunities, 1965.

9. Grosser, Charles, "Local Residents as Mediators Between Middle-Class Professional Workers and Lower-Class Clients," *Social Service Review,* **40** (March, 1966), 56-63.

10. Haber, William, *et al., Manpower in the United States: Problems and Policies.* New York: Harper & Row, Publishers, 1954.

11. Klein, William, L., *et al., Training Nonprofessional Workers for Human Services: A Manual of Organization and Process.* Howard University Center for Community Studies, 1966.

12. MacLennan, Beryce W., *et al., The Implications of the Nonprofessional in Community Mental Health.* Howard University Institute for Youth Studies, 1966.

13. Pearl, Arthur, and Frank Riessman, eds., *New Careers for the Poor: The Nonprofessional in Human Service.* New York: The Free Press of Glencoe, Inc., 1965.

14. Richan, Willard C., "A Theoretical Scheme for Determining Roles of Professional and Nonprofessional Personnel," *Social Work,* **6** (October, 1961), 22-28.

15. Shaffer, Anatole, and Harry Specht, "Training the Poor for New Careers." Monograph No. 5. Richmond, Calif.: Contra Costa Council of Community Services, 1966.

I4

THE STATE

OF RESEARCH

HARRY SMALLENBURG AND CAROL J. SMALLENBURG

INTRODUCTION

Research on counseling the culturally disadvantaged is meager. A few reports deal directly with research on the disadvantaged. Other studies concern related topics such as intellectual performance, social class, ethnic groups, aspirations, testing, etc. Research from related disciplines adds to the awareness of the milieu, group life and family patterns, language and communication styles of deprived. It is the purpose of this chapter to (a) point out difficulties in conducting research on and evaluating the effectiveness of counseling, (b) identify additional problems inherent in research on culturally disadvantaged, (c) present studies illustrating a research approach to counseling the disadvantaged, (d) present studies illustrating a research approach to problems intrinsic to counseling the culturally disadvantaged, and (e) present suggested guidelines for needed research studies.

DIFFICULTIES IN CONDUCTING RESEARCH ABOUT,
AND EVALUATING COUNSELING

A number of writers have pointed out the difficulties in evaluating the effects of counseling. Stefflre [1] states that an evaluation of the state of

---

[1] Buford Stefflre, ed., *Theories of Counseling* (New York: McGraw-Hill Book Company, Inc., 1965).

counseling research, particularly as it applies to educational settings, indicates that we are far from definitive answers. Sprague[2] continues the thought, "Carefully designed studies which support the efficacy of counseling or guidance programs are rare." The inadequacy of research in the area of counseling has been stressed in successive issues of the *Review of Educational Research*. Patterson[3] points out that the importance of and necessity for evaluation of guidance and counseling programs and services have been repeatedly stressed. Rothney and Farwell[4] note little evidence that much was being done in the area. Cottle[5] has also commented on the paucity of research relating to evaluation of counseling.

A researcher who attacks problems of design and execution of studies about counseling for a special group faces not only the general hazards attributable to research (and to research about counseling as a general field), but also some additional problems that that particular population may involve. Most frequently cited difficulties or problems besetting research about, or evaluation of effectiveness of counseling are:

1. Inadequate statement of goals or objectives for the counseling program;

2. Difficulty in defining the goals of counseling in behavioral and measurable terms;

3. Uncertainty as to the criteria to serve as indicators of having achieved —or not having achieved—the objective defined;

4. Unavailability or inappropriateness of instruments used to measure the defined criteria;

5. Failure to design experiment in clear-cut terms: the sample and its selection, the experimental or statistical controls, administration or identification of the treatment or independent variable, and the application of the criterion measure;

6. Difficulties in statistical handling of the data in such a way as to determine the effectiveness of the program in achieving its objectives;

7. Failure to design long-term and longitudinal studies in assessing achievement of objectives;

[2] Douglas G. Sprague, "Evaluating Counseling Effectiveness," *Newsletter* (California Counseling and Guidance Association, December, 1966), p. 1.

[3] Cecil H. Patterson, "Methodological Problems in Evaluation," *Personnel and Guidance Journal*, 39 (December, 1960), 270-274.

[4] John W. Rothney and Gail Farwell, "The Evaluation of Guidance and Personnel Services," *Review of Educational Research, Guidance, Counseling and Personnel Services*, 30, No. 2. April, 1960.

[5] William Cottle, *Review of Educational Research, Guidance, Counseling and Personnel Services*, 27, No. 2. April, 1957.

8. Variability of input factors in counseling that handicaps the interpretation of research findings. (Descriptions of counseling situations may differ widely, for what is meant by "counseling" can vary from person to person, experiment to experiment, and perhaps even from event to event for any one counselor. Thus, generalizing from data derived from divergent situations but expressed primarily in modal terms may not be warranted.)

DIFFICULTIES IN CONDUCTING RESEARCH
ABOUT COUNSELING THE DISADVANTAGED

When the researcher conducts studies about counseling the disadvantaged, the problems just discussed are intensified and additional problems must be faced.

1. Definition of the nature of cultural disadvantage or deprivation. Reports in current literature use a variety of designations for the population to be described: "deprived," "disadvantaged," "alienated," or "differentiated." Further effort at description is made by attaching to these names a modifier such as "economically," "socially," "culturally," or "educationally." Some writers point out that the pupil populations to which the above terms frequently refer are not distinct, either from each other or from subgroups sometimes called "pre-delinquent," "dropout," "push-out," "underachievers," "ghetto children," "urban-centered school children," or "visible minority group children." The research criterion of a clearly defined population is hard to meet under such conditions of variability and overlap.

Sanborn and Wasson [6] point out that the term culturally deprived is not so restrictive as to imply economic deprivation alone. The comment, "Any pattern of social, ethnic, familial, economic or geographic factors which combine so as to interfere seriously with educational and vocational fulfillment of individuals may be thought of as cultural deprivation. Their definition is a broad one, and the outcome, "educational and vocational fulfillment," is nonspecific to say the least. Such a statement can emphasize the complex nature of deprivation but, for the purpose of designing research or focusing a counseling transaction, it is too inclusive to be useful.

A number of investigations, of which Walter B. Miller's studies of street gangs [7] are illustrative, indicate subcultures and subgroupings

[6] Marshall P. Sanborn and Robert M. Wasson, "Guidance of Students with Special Characteristics," in *Review of Educational Research*, 36, No. 2 (April, 1966), p. 316.

[7] Walter B. Miller, "Lower Class Culture as a Generating Milieu of Gang Delinquency," in *Sociology of Crime and Delinquency*, eds. Marvin E. Wolfgang, Savits and Johnston (New York: John Wiley & Sons, Inc., 1962), pp. 267-276.

within so-called disadvantaged populations. Further, as emphasized by Marcus de Leon [8] in discussing the problems of the Mexican-American in southern California, the degree of acculturation of the population to be studied may have significant bearing on research findings. Joseph D. Lohman [9] refers to another kind of subculture created "... as a result of the technological revolution and automation, of people who are permanently indigent, ... in perpetual and abiding poverty, deep-seated within the culture of the lower classes, and with a culture which keeps many living within their own race ... many young people [of which race] are conditioned to exclusion and denial ... proposing an adolescent subculture. ... There evolves a single subculture representing the hostile, the unregenerate, and those who pose themselves as problems."

2. Selection of a representative sample specific to a proposed study also poses a hurdle for sound research about disadvantaged. Until recent years, data about the size and characteristics of the disadvantaged population and its various subgroups were not systematically compiled. In fact, school systems frequently avoided data about the ethnic composition of their pupil population in the interest, they explained, of avoiding discrimination. Data collected for a research about a particular population may not be comparable to other studies' findings, nor may there be a representative sample of the population in question. Indeed, because of the multiple factors involved, sampling procedures may need to account for such characteristics as ethnic group, socioeconomic class, estimate of degree of acculturation, and amount of education of parents, for example. A selected sample may, otherwise, turn out to be more heterogeneous than had been assumed. Hidden or extraneous factors could distort research findings. Present studies should be examined to see if they truly represent the populations to which they purport to refer.

3. Evaluation of the effectiveness of counseling is frequently couched in terms of gains in achievement or ability. Measurement of degree of deprivation is likewise frequently expressed in some kind of measurement. Evidence of change or lack of it may be sought by means of the very tools that a deprived child uses least well. In fact, if a study of the counselor-counselee interaction is made, and data are expressed in terms of conventional kinds of achievement information, there are at least three ways in which the research tools limit the findings. First, achievement

[8] Marcus de Leon, "Transculturation and Tacos—What Does It Mean?" in *Conference on Education of Spanish-speaking Children and Youth* (California: El Rancho High School, May 15-16, 1964. Los Angeles County Superintendent of Schools Office. Mimeographed).

[9] Joseph D. Lohman, *Cultural Patterns of Differentiated Youth: A Manual for Teachers in Marginal Schools* (Berkeley, California: Joint Project of Univ. of Calif. School of Education and School of Criminology. Multilith).

and ability are defined and demonstrated in terms of communication styles least familiar to the subject; second, there is a strong possibility of a poor reporting of whatever ability and achievement may exist because of the problems of communication from subject to researcher; and, third, the perceptual background of the researcher and the frame of reference from which his study may be designed emphasize verbal kinds of achievement and ability least characteristic of the subject.

4. The complex relations of cultural disadvantage to measurement of abilities and achievement has the further problem posed by the question, Which is cause; which is effect? The interaction of factors of poverty, deprivation, low aspiration level, and, if applicable, ethnic group membership confuses the focus of research that hopes to find out how counseling might be of influence. The factors cited are likely to be identifiable on either or both sides of the input-output equation; they are also likely to contribute to the downward cycle of mobility and achievement frequently discussed in connection with problems of disadvantage.

5. Conventional assessment designs as well as conventional patterns of counselor-counselee behavior may be ill-adapted to obtain research information. Research in related disciplines from which Fred L. Strodtbeck draws his discussion of the "Hidden Curriculum in the Middle-Class Home" [10] indicates that there may be dynamics of lower class child-rearing patterns—a generalized fear of formalistic social relations as well as problems of public and formal language for communication—that should be accounted for in considerations of research on counseling disadvantaged children. Such dynamics may inhibit or at least neutralize outcomes of the counseling transaction. Expectations of family loyalty,[11] styles of relating to adult authority, or problems of nonverbal communication [12] may all influence the counseling of disadvantaged children and would appear to be worthy of consideration in research on counseling.

Much of the use of counseling with culturally disadvantaged relates to actions involving assumptions about communication, power relations, perceived organizational roles, patterns of training about choice making, initiative, and other aspects of child-adult interaction. Implications from Strodtbeck's discussion in which he draws on his own and others' research suggest the existence of important differences between middle class and

[10] Fred L. Strodtbeck, "Hidden Curriculum in the Middle-Class Home," in *Learning and the Educative Process*, ed. J. D. Krumboltz (Chicago: Rand McNally & Company, 1965).

[11] Ruth M. Landes, *Culture in Education*, in Appendix, *The Mexican Family Structure*.

[12] Charles M. Galloway, "An Exploratory Study of Observational Procedures for Determining Teachers' Nonverbal Communication" (Doctoral dissertation, University of Florida, 1962).

lower class socialization processes, all of which have a direct bearing on behavior and achievement in school, and probably on the counseling activity as well.

Cary's discussion of class socialization patterns and their relation to learning further indicates the problems of counseling disadvantaged children. "In the middle-class child there is an early development of symbol-expressive behavior, whereas the lower-class child's behavior is more action-expressive." [13]

6. The planning for research about counseling disadvantaged pupils needs to anticipate possible levels of emotionality and defensiveness not so customary when counseling other kinds of pupils. Cary points out the lower class adults "who have felt the frustration encountered in their own difficulty with middle-class standards in school . . . convey some of these negative attitudes to their children." These attitudes may be specifically directed toward education because of its association with resented middle class standards and their representatives. [14] Kardiner and Ovesey also describe emotional content potentially present when there are ethnic differences in a counseling transaction. "The discrimination Negroes must live with results in psychological damage to them . . . [they] must adapt to the same culture and accept the same social goals as the white [person], but without the same opportunity to achieve them. The self-esteem of the Negro suffers because he is constantly receiving an unpleasant image of himself from the behaviors of others toward him. This is the subjective impact of social discrimination. A person who is discriminated against tends to react aggressively. But to survive in a world of the white, the Negro finds he must replace aggressive activity with more acceptable behavior, such as ingratiation and passivity." [15]

Even when counselor and counselee are of the same ethnic group, there may still be emotional factors present, according to the discussion of Kardiner and Ovesey. There is a tendency for the Negro to take the white as his "ideal." Accepting the white as ideal is a recipe for perpetual self-hatred, frustration, and for tying one's life to unattainable goals. Self-hatred generally requires some form of projection outward in an attempt to stay its damaging effects. The simplest form it takes in the Negro is hatred of other Negroes. [16]

Dr. Daniel Feder describes the problem of emotionality further: "The counselee who is defensive for any reason whatsoever, will be watching avidly for clues as to the counselor's acceptance or rejection of him. The

[13] Gene L. Cary, M.D., "Class Socialization Patterns and Their Relation to Learning," *School and Society* (October 29, 1966), p. 350.

[14] *Ibid.*, p. 352.

[15] Abram Kardiner and Lionel Ovesey, *The Mark of Oppression* (Cleveland, Ohio: World Publishing Company, 1951).

[16] *Ibid.*

developing body of highly intriguing information concerning the potency of non-verbal communciation is the best argument that need be advanced for the conscious structuring of openness in the counseling relationship. ... The importance of neutralizing the grounds for potential defensiveness is such as to warrant the extra time and the departure from conventional procedures. Just how this neutralization may be accomplished best remains yet a matter to be explored experimentally and experientially." [17]

7. Dr. Martin Deutsch [18] suggests an important limitation on the kind of research study that would involve comparing Negro and white children. "Even when it is possible to control the formal attributes of social class membership, the uniqueness of the Negro child's experience would make comparability impossible when limited to class factors." In another section of his paper, Dr. Deutsch continues, "School is an experience which for children in the experimental group (primarily Negro, lower-class children) is discontinuous with the values, preparation, and experience they receive from their homes and particular community; it represents society's demands that they bridge social class orientations for a few hours a day, five days a week. No catalyst is provided for this transition, and few plans have been made to facilitate the child's daily journey across the chasm."

8. Differences in value orientation on the parts of the counselor, the school system of which he is a part, and the disadvantaged counselee—especially if he is from an ethnic subgroup—may be a barrier to research findings about counseling. Lohman asks that the core culture agent, in this case the counselor, look at himself. "We are often tempted to refer to our troubled students as maladjusted, to focus on something which is individually distinct. The truth of the matter is that our developing knowledge of the behavioral sciences reveals that deviance or departure from the generally accepted norms of the wider community represents a kind of adjustment, rather than a failure to adjust. Thus it is the perspective in which we see deviant young people that makes them different. It is our perspective that attributes to them different aims and views and prevents us from understanding what is really going on within them. ... [It is important that we] come to grips with our own view of this problem: with the terms and conditions of our experiencing of the

[17] Daniel Feder, "Counseling Some of My Best Friends ...," manuscript-lecture reproduced in multilith form in the volume, compiled and edited by Robert C. Fredericks, *Proceedings of Delta Workshop on Counseling Minority Youth.* Sponsored by Delta Sigma Theta and the Cortland Continuation Center, General Extension Division, Oregon State System of Higher Education (Portland, Oregon: August 13-17, 1962), pp. 11-12.
[18] Martin Deutsch, "The Disadvantaged Child and the Learning Process, Some Social Psychological and Developmental Considerations," a paper prepared for the Ford Foundation, *Work Conference on Curriculum and Teaching in Deprived Urban Areas* (New York: Columbia University, July 10, 1962. Mimeographed).

problem, the terms and conditions of the structures and organizations through which we address the problem." [19]

9. A further problem in dealing with research about counseling the disadvantaged lies in the very rapid change that has been taking place among some of the groups of disadvantaged as federally funded programs are becoming active. Customary kinds of status studies and comparisons may not give an accurate picture of change. Lohman cited the possible effects of recent improvements during a discussion with teachers working in a project for marginal schools.[20] Feder expressed a similar thought as early as 1962 in his lecture before the Delta Workshop in Counseling Minority Youth. "The events of the past few years suggest that social movement with reference to the Negro integration problem is moving with the speed of revolution rather than that of evolution. This being the case, we cannot afford to trust completely data which were derived from studies performed before the beginning of this revolution. By the same token, we may safely assume that the revolution in itself has created totally new problems at the same time that it was providing solutions for others. Obviously, there is no time for historical perspective. Nor is there time to perform the kind of on-going study now which might permit the evolution of trends and the evaluation of changes. The changes which are taking place are too important to the fabric of our society to be impeded." [21]

In summary, the difficulties in conducting research about counseling revolve around issues of behavioral definition of the counseling process and the unavailability or inappropriateness of instruments to use. The variability of the input and output factors in the counseling situation also impedes comparability of findings from one study to another.

When the question of "disadvantaged counselees" is added to the sizeable problems of research cited above, more limitations are recognized. The definition of the population or subgroup to be studied, and the question of locating a representative sample are basic hurdles to sound research outcomes. In addition, the currently predominant manner of expressing effectiveness of counseling is couched in terms of some demonstration of achievement. There are strong indications that such a criterion may be misleading in the case of a "disadvantaged" population. Further, the whole question of cause and effect may color interpretation of findings, especially where counselees involved are at the upper elementary years or beyond.

The dynamics of family-rearing or class socialization patterns as well

[19] Lohman, *Cultural Patterns of Differentiated Youth*, pp. i-iv.
[20] *Ibid.*, p. 328.
[21] Feder, "Counseling Some of My Best Friends."

as problems of nonverbal and verbal communication between pupil and counselor may be influential in unsuspected ways for children from non-core culture or non-middle class groups. As indicated above, the counseling transaction appears to make certain assumptions regarding such important questions as communication, power relations, patterns of training about choice making and adult-child relationships. In any of these aspects of socialization evidences of considerable difference may be found among disadvantaged group members and the group represented by the counselor.

Several writers comment on the possibility that emotional content in a counseling situation may grow out of such factors as feelings about self, experiences of discrimination, and fear of tension in minority-majority contacts. There is, indeed, considerable weight in discussion that points out the lack of equality between minority and majority group experiences even when such group comparisons are equated for a number of objective factors. Even with factors of age, ability, and social class held constant, the experiential content of the lives of Negro and Caucasian children may differ considerably because of discrimination.

COUNSELING DISADVANTAGED, A MATTER
OF CONTENT AS WELL AS PROCESS

A dimension of the counseling transaction that deserves attention when considering problems of research is described by Trueblood.[22] "The school counselor . . . has a two part role to play—process and content. There is among professional counselors and guidance workers an intellectual and traditional argument as to whether the counselor is not indeed the same figure to all clients. The argument posits that the techniques and skills applied in the counseling or guidance situation are everywhere the same, that the individuality of the counselor should not affect these techniques, and that the psychosociological background of the client, though admittedly probably different, should not affect the techniques which the counselor will use or the role which the counselor will play."

The idea of "process" as well as "content" having specific meanings for minority group and/or disadvantaged counselees needs considerable exploration. Research appears to have little to contribute as far as clarifying the differences or likenesses of the counseling function between "regular" and "disadvantaged" students, whether for the "content" or the "process." In this context, it is appropriate to recall Feder's comment, quoted above, about counselors who are defensive.

[22] Dennis L. Trueblood, "The Role of the Counselor in the Guidance of Negro Students," *Harvard Educational Review*, 30, No. 3 (Summer, 1960), 252-269.

Some adaptation in the process or technique of counseling, as well as its content is suggested by Trueblood's discussion of the particular role of the counselor with the Negro student:

... while they may remain basically the same as those used for other groups, [the process or technique of counseling] will be affected by the special needs of a particular population group [content]. It seems defensible, therefore, to state that the role of the counselor in the guidance of Negro students must be affected by his special knowledge of the needs of Negroes. . . . With such knowledge and the knowledge about experiences of other educators in the guidance of the Negro student, the counselor, in terms of both process and content, will be better able to function successfully with the Negro student.[23]

The need to change the nature of the counseling process with disadvantaged youth is also emphasized by Feder. He states that one cannot escape the conclusions

... that our central concern is . . . counseling an individual. In this relationship, matters of race, color, creed, socio-economic status, and all the myriad elements which make us a nation of countless minorities pale into insignificance as we are confronted with one human being who seeks our help. Nevertheless, the cogent elements of adjustment and reaction to a special kind of social environment which exists for an individual who is in some significant way "different" from the majority of his peers, must be reckoned with in our efforts to perform the helping function.

Most strikingly meaningful in the meager evidence at hand is the urgency that the counselor who seeks to work effectively with minority youth must enter the relation with a full awareness of his own prejudices and must be willing to depart from the rigid restrictions of ultra-permissiveness and adopt a conscious program of seeking to establish rapport with the counselee on the basis of frank facing of their own mutual differences as a first step in the establishing of a relationship. Within this framework of technique, then, the challenge to the counselor is to serve every counselee in such a way as to assist him toward maximum self-understanding and self-realization.[24]

There are but scattered research evidences to support appropriate direction for change in either process, content, or both, for disadvantaged counselees. When students in an urban-centered school reported how they viewed their counselors' behavior, they cited behaviors interpreted by some of the members of the integrated student body as prejudicial—enough in some cases to interfere with the counselor's effectiveness. Counselors in the same school population were questioned about their confidence in the success of students with marginal grade averages. Some said that they were more confident with success for Caucasian students with marginal averages than they were for Negro students with similar

[23] Trueblood, *Harvard Educational Review,* Vol. 30, p. 254.
[24] Feder, "Counseling Some of My Best Friends," pp. 15-16.

marks. Barney and Hall reported that the counselors' own reports reflected less confidence in Negro students' chances for success and college.[25]

Phillips[26] conducted a study of problems in counseling minority youth. A group of twelve 17 year old Negro boys who had been repeatedly referred for asocial and uncooperative acts were divided among Negro and white counselors for interviews. Later in the semester, all of the counselors were compared for success in reaching the twelve boys. Reports of lack of success in identifying with Negro students' behaviors came more frequently from white counselors. The small number of counselors and counselees leads to questions about the conclusions; the attempt to study a significant question in the counseling process with minority groups is, however, recognized.

There is considerable agreement that the "content" of the counseling transaction needs alteration for the disadvantaged; but there is little agreement about the nature of that content, or what it should be. One can assume, however, that it should rest on the most respectable, the best documented, the most recent research available. For instance, if the content in question is to pertain to entrance requirements for higher education or the diversity and specializations of such institutions, then assuredly the most reputable information, both for local and for nation-wide opportunities, should be continually and readily available for the counselor and the counselee. Demographic data on which counselors may rely for trends and patterns of opportunity for minority youth must reflect the reputable and recent, both for a specific locality and for sections of the country. One example of this kind of information is provided by the Los Angeles County Commission on Human Relations in their publication, *The Urban Reality—A Comparative Study of the Socio-Economic Situation of Mexican-Americans, Negroes, and Anglo-Caucasians in Los Angeles County.*[27] The study is representative of the kind of current data needed.

Alternation of both "process" and "content" is needed according to Trueblood. He urges recognition of the fact that the function of the counselor in the guidance of Negro students is greatly complicated by the complexities of cultural and social class differences. He favors a broad approach and lists thirteen activities related to the direct act of counseling, such as "advise about occupational and educational choice on the basis of national trends," "use test data with caution," "use a variety of data in attempting to identify the capabilities of the Negro student, i.e.,

25 O. Pat Barney and Lurel D. Hall, "A Study in Discrimination," *Personnel and Guidance Journal,* **43** (March, 1965), 708-709.

26 Waldo B. Phillips, "Counseling Negro Pupils: An Educational Dilemma," *California Journal of Educational Research,* X, No. 4 (September, 1959).

27 *The Urban Reality, A Comparative Study* (California: County of Los Angeles, Commission on Human Relations, June, 1965), p. 54. Multilith.

performance, aptitude, family occupational and educational background," "learn about financial aid available for continuing education beyond high school," and "study talent search programs and components, steps, minimum essentials," as well as "utilize community resources to help in the guidance of Negro students." [28]

Vital to a counselor's background is another kind of basic research summary, of which *Race and Intelligence, A Scientific Evaluation,*[29] is an example. Here a panel of four scientists react to questions pertaining to racial differences in mental capacity as well as issues about testing and predicting school achievement. The fundamental concepts about race and intelligence detailed and documented by the panel are basic to any counselor-counselee interaction involving disadvantaged or minority group children. Their point of view is summarized by Dr. Stanley Diamond in the following excerpt. "All of the historical and psychological evidence scrutinized by anthropologists leads to one conclusion: there is no differential capacity for the creation and maintenance of culture on the part of any population large enough to be sensibly called a race, in the traditional sense of that term. Mongoloids, Negroids and Caucasoids have been physically and culturally interfertile through the history of modern mankind. Moreover, none of these groups is exclusively associated with any given cultural phenomenon. Nor has any genetically based differential capacity in intelligence among these major populations ever been established. On the contrary, the doctrine of racial equality is fully supported by scientific and historical inquiry." [30]

Valid and reliable information about ability and achievement of disadvantaged children is a vital part of the counselor's tool kit and becomes operative "content" in the counseling transaction. A number of writers support the concept that ordinary use of school measurement and test interpretation procedures is inadequate for counseling minority or disadvantaged youth. If used, they may lead to inappropriate expectations for such groups or individuals, and hence to inappropriate or inadequate programs for them.[31] Cultural differences create semantic differences that may cause invalidation of tests of interest or personality adjustment if these are used wtih disadvantaged children.[32] Because ability and achievement data are frequently used to evaluate the success of counseling, such research on the effectiveness of counseling the disadvantaged

[28] Trueblood, "The Role of the Counselor in the Guidance of Negro Students," p. 268.

[29] Melvin M. Tumin, ed., *Race and Intelligence, A Scientific Evaluation* (New York: Anti-Defamation League of B'nai B'rith, 1963).

[30] Tumin, ed., *Race and Intelligence,* p. 10.

[31] Martin Hamburger, in *Review of Educational Research,* 1960, p. 319.

[32] Anne Anastasi, "Cultural Differences," in *Encyclopedia of Educational Research* (3rd ed.) (New York: The Macmillan Company, 1960), pp. 350-358.

could hardly be expected to have merit if basic information used in that counseling were in question.

In a paper presented at the 1964 Educational Testing Service Invitational Conference on Testing Problems, Martin Hamburger called attention to three types of measurement issues that should concern counselors working with disadvantaged children. He questioned the scientific-technological assumptions about the use of a "normal curve" frame of reference when applied to test performance of minority groups. Some basic concepts about the nature of human ability were also to be questioned, as well as the matter of creating a concept of human ability in terms of the instruments used to measure it.[33]

There are three principal difficulties in using the current standardized tests with groups of disadvantaged or minority group children. Too often these instruments have been developed for the intellectual and social ways of the middle class children. Test answers considered deviant from the viewpoint of a majority culture may be typical of a minority group. Children from a culture of poverty may not possess certain of the characteristics that affect test performance—verbal fluency, competitiveness, self-confidence, motivation for academic achievement, to cite a few. As a result, they tend to do poorly in tests; assumptions are made that exclude them from opportunities for training; such exclusion tends to continue and heighten the deprivation already in existence.[34] Individualized followup studies revealed that students had responded randomly or without comprehension rather than admitting to the counselor that they did not understand the meaning intended.[35] Lennon [36] states that the attitude with which the use of tests is approached is most important: the deprived children's feelings of alienation from the school should be lessened, and motivation should be increased.

SELECTED READINGS

1. Barney, O. Pat, and Lurel D. Hall, "A Study in Discrimination," *Personnel and Guidance Journal*, **43** (March, 1965), 708-709.

2. Cottle, William, *Review of Educational Research, Guidance, Counseling and Personnel Services*, **27**, No. 2 (April, 1957).

[33] Hamburger, *Review of Educational Research*, p. 318.

[34] Joshua Fishman *et al.*, *Guidelines for Testing Minority Group Children*, Society for the Psychological Study of Social Issues, American Psychological Association, June, 1963: and in *Journal of Social Issues*, XX, No. 2 (Ann Arbor: University of Michigan, 1964), pp. 127-145.

[35] Feder, "Counseling Some of My Best Friends," p. 14.

[36] Roger T. Lennon, "Testing and the Culturally Disadvantaged Child," in *Problems in Education of Culturally Disadvantaged* (New York and Burlingame: Harcourt, Brace and World, Inc., 1964).

3. Fishman, Joshua, *et al.*, "Guidelines for Testing Minority Group Children," *Journal of Social Issues,* XX (1964), 127-145.

4. Krumboltz, J. D., ed., *Learning and the Educative Process.* Chicago: Rand McNally & Co., 1965.

5. Miller, S. M., *The American Lower Class: A Typological Approach.* Syracuse University Youth Development Center, 1963.

6. Patterson, Cecil H., "Methodological Problems in Evaluation," *Personnel and Guidance Journal,* 39 (December, 1960), 270-274.

7. Rothney, John W., and Gail Farwell, *Review of Educational Research, Guidance, Counseling and Personnel Services,* 30, No. 2 (April, 1960).

8. Schreiber, Daniel, *Guidance and the School Dropout.* Washington, D.C.: National Education Association, 1964.

9. Stefflre, Buford, ed., *Theories of Counseling.* New York: McGraw-Hill Book Company, 1965.

10. Trueblood, Dennis L., "The Role of the Counselor in the Guidance of Negro Students," *Harvard Educational Review,* 30, No. 3 (1960), 252-269.

11. Tumin, Melvin M., ed., *Race and Intelligence, A Scientific Evaluation.* New York: Anti-Defamation League of B'nai B'rith, 1963.

12. Tunnel, J. W., *What Research Says About the School Dropout.* Lubbock, Texas: West Texas School Study Council, 1963.

13. U.S. Department of Labor, Bureau of Labor Statistics, *Factbook on the School Dropout in the World of Work.* Washington, D.C.: Government Printing Office, 1963.

15

COUNSELING:
AN OVERVIEW

PAUL MUNGER AND RICHARD MELLOH

In recent years the American public has come to view school counselors as significant contributors to over-all personal and educational development of youth in school. The public believes that counselors make things happen, and that the counseling experience affects many of the everyday activities of school age youth. The counselor is viewed as a person to whom a youngster may turn for support, for direction, for help in adjusting to the present and in planning for the future. The continued demand for the employment of counselors in schools is one indication of the success of counseling in the eyes of the public. In most secondary schools counselors are considered an integral part of the educational program; the third side of a triangle, with administrators and teachers representing the other two sides. School counselors have worked extensively with adolescents in schools, but have had little opportunity to work with adolescents who are out of school. In the emphasis on schools and those who go to schools, counselors have inadvertently tended to ignore the concerns of the adolescents who simply were not around. School dropouts, the economically disabled, the culturally deprived have rarely been the clients of school counselors.

Society has now become concerned with those who frequently are not in school, who are not in the middle class, and who are called the disadvantaged. Through congressional action, a new look at the disadvantaged or culturally deprived has brought about a new emphasis in counseling. Counseling has assumed increased importance in legislation such as the Economic Opportunity Act, the Manpower Development and Training Act, the Vocational Education Act, the Mental Retardation Facilities Act, and the extension of the National Defense Act. Counselors are key personnel in Youth Opportunity Centers and in Job Corps Centers; they have been given greater responsibilities in Employment Services offices. In all of these new activities, counselors have been called upon to duplicate the efforts that seem so successful in schools. In this endeavor, they are attempting to help the disadvantaged to find their potential and to develop better lives. In short, society has asked counselors to enable such clients to acquire new values and reach higher levels of being.

COUNSELING AS A RELATIONSHIP

All members of the helping professions are enablers in the sense that when they are successful their clients achieve more satisfying lives. The counselor helps the client to look at himself and his concerns, to explore his experience, both past and present, for new meaning. He enables the client to perceive himself in more realistic and more productive ways. All counseling is based on a professional understanding of the client, a skill developed by working with many clients. Ideally, the counselor and the counselee, working together, attempt to discover the counselee's potentialities and to make plans for developing these potentialities. The counseling relationship is one in which the counselor creates an atmosphere of permissiveness, one in which he attempts to understand the client, and to give positive regard to the client, enabling the client to better understand himself, his motives, his goals, his behavior, and his environment. Such understanding enables the client to assess himself and to make changes in his pattern of perception and in his pattern of living.

To counsel is to foster self-understanding, self-acceptance, and self-direction on the part of a counselee by means of a carefully structured relationship. Though similar relationships occasionally occur elsewhere in our culture, only in counseling is there a systematc, organized effort to establish them. It is such interaction that distinguishes counseling from other educational activities.

To offer this unique relationship to others, a counselor must possess a number of firmly established attitudes toward human beings generally, and toward his clients particularly. He must view each counselee as a person of dignity and worth who is in no way required to demonstrate his claim to that dignity and worth. By virtue of his humanity alone, each counselee is deserving of the counselor's acceptance and unconditionally positive regard. A second deeply seated attitude required of the counselor is acceptance of the client's right to self-direction. This attitude must be based on the realization that, possibly superior intellect, extensive preparation, knowledge of "best" values, and more intensive or extensive experience notwithstanding, no human being ever knows enough to walk in another's shoes. A third and equally important attitude required of a counselor is an acceptance of himself. The counselor's helpfulness to others is limited by his own personal security; he must have no reason to use his counselees in ways that enhance his own worth or satisfy his own needs.

The attitudes of the counselor toward himself, toward others, and toward his purposes determine the kind of relationship that he will offer his clients. The techniques that a counselor uses to communicate these attitudes seem to be of secondary importance. Appropriate attitudes are not superficial techniques that can be switched on by the counselor when he begins a counseling relationship; they are a continuing way of life. Combs and Soper [1] have studied the relation between counseling effectiveness and the ways in which counselors themselves perceive interpersonal relations, their goals, and other persons outside of a counseling setting. Ratings of the following 12 variables were found to be related significantly to ratings of counseling effectiveness:

A. With respect to their general perceptual orientations, good counselors will be more likely to perceive:

1. *From an internal rather than from an external frame of reference.* The protocol writer's general frame of reference can be described as internal rather than external; that is to say, he seems sensitive to and concerned with how things look to others with whom he interacts and uses this as a basis for his own behavior. He is concerned with perceptions of others as well as their overt behavior.

2. *In terms of people rather than things.* Central to the thinking of the subject is a concern with people and their reactions rather than with things and events.

B. With respect to their perceptions of other people, good counselors will perceive others as:

1. *Able, rather than unable.* The subject perceives others as having the capacities to deal with their problems. He has faith that they can find adequate solutions as opposed to doubting the capacity of people to handle themselves and their lives.

2. *Dependable rather than undependable.* The subject regards others as being essentially dependable rather than undependable. He shows confidence in the stability and reliability of others and does not need to be suspicious of them.

[1] Arthur W. Combs and Daniel W. Soper, "The Perceptual Organization of Effective Counselors," *Journal of Counseling Psychology,* **10,** No. 3 (Fall 1963), 222-226.

3. *Friendly rather than unfriendly.* The subject sees others as being friendly and enhancing. He does not regard them as threatening to himself, but rather sees them as essentially well intentioned rather than evil intentioned.

4. *Worthy rather than unworthy.* The subject tends to see other people as being worthy rather than unworthy. He sees them as possessing a dignity and integrity which must be respected and maintained rather than seeing people as unimportant, whose integrity may be violated or treated as of little account.

C. With respect to their perceptions of self, good counselors will perceive themselves as:

1. *Identified with people rather than apart from people.* The subject tends to see himself as a part of all mankind; he sees himself as identified with people rather than as withdrawn, removed apart or alienated from others.

2. *Enough rather than wanting.* The subject generally sees himself as enough; as having what is needed to deal with his problems. He does not see himself as lacking or unable to cope with problems.

3. *Self-revealing rather than self-concealing.* The subject is self-revealing rather than self-concealing; that is, he appears to be willing to disclose himself. He can treat his feelings and shortcomings as important and significant rather than hiding them or covering them up. He seems willing to be himself.

D. With respect to purposes, good counselors will perceive their purposes as:

1. *Freeing rather than controlling.* The subject's purpose is essentially freeing and facilitating rather than controlling, dominating, coercing or manipulating.

2. *Altruistic rather than narcissistic.* The subject appears to be motivated by feelings of altruism rather than narcissism. He is concerned about others and not merely about self.

3. *Concerned with larger rather than smaller meaning.* The subject tends to view events in a broad rather than narrow perspective. He is concerned with larger connotations of events, with larger, more extensive implications than the immediate and specific. He is not exclusively concerned with details but can perceive beyond the immediate to future and larger meaning.

It seems to the authors that the core and essence of all counseling is the relationship. This is especially true in counseling with the culturally deprived. It is relatively easy for the counselor to offer acceptance and understanding to other middle class persons who hold the same values the counselor holds. It is more difficult to counsel with persons whose values are quite different, who speak a different language. Yet the counselor of the culturally deprived frequently will need to accept and to give unconditional positive regard to persons who are usually rejected by the middle class.

A requisite of any counseling relation is an empathic understanding of the client by the counselor. The counselor must seek to share the unique perceptions of the client from moment to moment as the client is willing to share his experiences. The concept of empathic understanding in a counseling relation includes both the understanding of each client's unique perception, and also the communication of this understanding in a language and a manner or emotional tone that permits the client to recognize the accuracy of the counselor's understanding. Katz [2] describes the effect of empathy upon our social relations.

What do we ordinarily derive from empathy? It serves us in two ways. First, it helps us to understand the other person from within. We communicate on a deeper level and apprehend the other person more completely. With this kind of communication we often find ourselves accepting that person and entering into a relationship of appreciation and source of personal reassurance. We are reassured when we feel that someone has succeeded in feeling himself into our own state of mind. We enjoy the satisfaction of being understood and accepted as persons. It is important for us to sense that the other person not only understands our words but appreciates the person behind the message as well. We then know that we are recognized and accepted for the particular kind of person we are. When friends fail to empathize, we feel disappointed and rejected. . . . When empathy is lacking, our self-awareness and self-respect are diminished. We then experience ourselves more as objects and less as persons.

The experienced counselor has developed his skill in offering empathic understanding to a high degree. Through the phenomenon of empathy, he is able to understand the client and, in the communication of his understanding to the client, the counselor conveys his acceptance.

INTRAPERSONAL CONCERNS

Every human being is beset by certain feelings of concern that arise within awareness. These feelings result from conflict among values held, needs experienced, and pressures felt. These values, needs, and pressures come from within the individual and from the environment. Some are fleeting; others, enduring. Such feelings of uneasiness are often a result of immediate problems to be solved or decisions to be made. At other times, these feelings are of ill-defined dissatisfaction, unrest, or uneasiness.

Confronted by such vague (or well-defined) feelings, a person may try to do something about his uneasiness in one of several ways. He may meditate, or introspect in isolation. He may seek the advice of friends or associates whose views he respects, whose interest and understanding can be anticipated, and from whom confidence can be expected. Frequently such recourse provides him with a passable solution, or time seems to lessen his concern. In some instances neither of these approaches proves adequate, nor does time alleviate the concern. Within himself he finds only further question. When he turns to others, he may receive advice reflecting the bias of a differing value system. His closest friends may

[2] Robert L. Katz, *Empathy: Its Nature and Uses* (New York: The Free Press of Glencoe, Inc., 1963), pp. 7-8.

be unable or unwilling to understand as he had expected: self-disclosure may actually push them away from him.

If such a troubled individual is fortunate, he is able to establish with a counselor the very kind of relationship he seeks. It is the counselor who offers him understanding, acceptance, and confidentiality.

As he strives to communicate to the counselor the uneasiness he is experiencing, and as the counselor assists in the clarification of ideas, the counselee often becomes aware of the circular reasoning that had previously prevented his thinking the problem through to a solution of his own. The counselor deliberately avoids introducing into the relation any of his own values or biases, except those relating to his genuine concern, high regard, and unconditional acceptance of the individual as a human being.

COUNSELOR'S VIEW OF MAN

There is probably no single factor that will influence the behavior of a counselor more than the counselor's view of the nature of man. If human behavior is seen exclusively as the product of forces exerted by the environment upon the individual, then there seems to be no alternative but for the counselor to become still another force in the lives of his counselees. The nature and direction of the force introduced by the counselor will depend wholly on environmental forces the counselor has experienced, and over which he presumably has had no control. Such a view of human nature eliminates all possibility of any personal responsibility for behavior on the part of either the counselor or the counselee. There is no possibility of personal choice.

In contrast, if human behavior is seen exclusively as the product of personal choice, of internal forces operating in isolation from the environment, then there seems to be no possibility for a counselor—who is really only another aspect of the counselee's environment—to influence the behavior of another. To hold such a view of human behavior necessitates a denial of the results of most of the research into human behavior to date, and the hypothesis upon which such research has been based: that human behavior is lawful.

The most logically tenable view of directive forces influencing human behavior is that such forces arise from a number of sources, both within and without the individual. From outside the individual comes the press of the physical environment and the cultural milieu; from within the individual arises the press of physiological and psychological needs, wants, and drives. Most important among the forces that arise within the individual and affect his behavior is the capacity to choose. The existence of such volitional power is assumed in our Judaeo-Christian system of morals and our democratic ethic. Courts of law determine guilt and innocence and even degrees of responsibility on the basis of the amount of freedom to exercise this volitional power that an individual possessed at a given point in time. The difficulty in assessing the effect of the myriad external and internal forces that delimit the individual's freedom to choose, to act, or not to act, immensely complicates our judicial process and a behavioral approach to psychology as well.

The amount or degree of free choice that an individual may exercise is affected by all of the many other forces influencing behavior. It appears reasonable to assume that certain direct relations exist between volitional power and the other behaviorally significant forces. With greater amounts of intellect, physical health, psychological health, economic opportunity, and cultural advantage are found greater degrees of freedom of choice. In keeping with most observations of human behavior, there is a tendency toward such direct relations, but such direct relations are not universally true.

If a counselor accepts the capacity to choose as an inherent power in each of those whom he counsels, his behavior in the counseling relation will be determined by his view of the direction toward which the counselee's freedom of choice will lead. If the counselor views man as essentially evil, then the counselor may see his task as manipulating the counselee in such ways that the counselee will not do the very things that he, the counselor, would freely choose to do. This raises the disquieting question of who manipulates the counselor.

In contrast to an orientation holding that man is essentially evil is a more positive and hopeful view of the direction of human behavior, a view that is accepted by the present authors. This view suggests that man has the capacity of free choice and that, when he is free from the inhibiting effects of threat, man will select the choices most enhancing to himself and to his fellow man. Such choices, however, can be made only from among the alternatives available to an individual within the limits of his perceptions at a given point in time. It is the function of a counselor to offer to his client a relationship that will provide a threat-free opportunity to explore the meaning of experience, to alter perceptions of experience, and to elect new ways of responding to experience.

It is the function of a democratic society, primarily through its educational system, to enrich the experience of every individual to the fullest extent. American society is now attempting to enrich the experiences of the underprivileged who in many ways have been bypassed by the educational system. New choices of behavior become available to the underprivileged when they are furnished with new opportunities for learning.

Enduring and meaningful changes of behavior are possible only when the individual has the opportunity to explore experience in terms of his own personal perception of that experience and its relation to his perception of himself. An adolescent who has come to identify himself with a segment of society that supports itself only with outside subsidies, belittles initiative, and rejects most of the middle class values, can be persuaded, because of societal values, to participate in a subsidized training program. Such a program may enrich in various ways his knowledge of a skill and an awareness of his own potential. However, whether or not he rejoins his former cultural group or moves toward the mainstream of society will depend on how he perceives himself. He may take as personally meaningful some of the new experiences to which he has been exposed. In a counseling relation, such an adolescent may look at what he has experienced, the kinds of experiences that have been satisfying, and those that seem to lead toward the kinds of things he would like to experience in the future.

If this adolescent is able to sense genuine concern for his well-being on the part of the counselor, if he senses an acceptance of himself as he really is, if he can sense that this acceptance is not dependent on his making certain choices to please the counselor, the adolescent can personally experience the responsibility for decision. He is then able to make a choice, to move in a direction toward which he has a genuine commitment and a real sense of involvement.

Not all of the choices made by such an individual in counseling are in keeping with our middle class values. However, if the counselor has been successful in offering the right conditions in the counseling relation, the choice made by the counselee is the best choice available within the limits of the counselee's current perception. The counselor may well offer information within the counseling relation as he is aware of the counselee's willingness to accept such information. It is not, however, the function of the counselor to persuade or to coerce the counselee in any particular direction.

Counselor's View of Self

The counselor's acceptance of himself is not to be confused with self-satisfaction, complacency, or resignation. Self-acceptance is rather a forthright acknowledgment of one's strengths and weaknesses, one's successes and failures, and an open awareness of one's limitations and potential. True self-acceptance must include a realization of the dynamic aspects of human nature and the capacity for change.

Often one observes in himself a tendency to present to others only certain aspects of his personality, while he carefully hides from view the details he is ashamed of. He may be fearful that, if others knew him as he really is, they would think less of him and even reject him completely. At such times he is unable to accept himself and, in turn, he cannot accept others. His attention may be so strongly focused upon fostering and maintaining this illusory self that he may perceive those about him only as objects to be manipulated. He may not be interested in sharing the perceptions of others, or in expressing warmth and understanding. He may be greatly preoccupied with self and, if this preoccupation is carried to an extreme, he may sink into depression. With each added effort to maintain the illusory self, he may find that his productive efficiency is impaired.

Acceptance of self is a critical requisite for every counselor. He cannot afford to expend his efforts on pretense. He must be so secure in his own person that he is able to focus full attention to understanding the unique perception of his counselee, and to offering his counselee the same kind of acceptance that he offers to himself. In a secure relationship, one in which there is freedom from judgment, the counselee learns that he can be more and more his true self. The counselor accepts him as he is. There is no need to portray a role. By being himself and finding that this previously hidden self is acceptable to the counselor, the counselee can become more acceptant of himself and progressively devote less of his energy to maintaining an illusion.

COUNSELOR RESPONSIBILITIES

In most agency settings, the counselor is one member of a team—often the most important member, since he is the one who relates most closely with the client. Since he is the one who knows the client best, as a result of having entered into a counseling relation with him, he is frequently given the task as well as the responsibility of arranging for the implementation of client decisions. With counselors in short supply, agencies should examine for efficacy policies of utilizing counselors for client facilitating activities that less trained persons can do. The professional counselor frequently cannot do all the client-aiding tasks for which he has been assigned responsibility. Rather, he should leave the task of helping the client to progress in the direction the client has selected to others whose training qualifies them for such work.

Identification of Clients

Typical responsibilities of the counselor include the identification of those who should be counseled, and acquainting people who need counseling to the availability of such a service. In many agencies that offer a counseling service, the counselor has little to do with the selection of those he sees in counseling interviews. Agencies may have others whose purpose it is to refer and, in fact, to make appointments for counselors.

However, counselors should be able to control the kinds of clients they see. Certain kinds of clients should be referred to the counselor, and others should be referred for noncounseling services.

Therefore, it is the counselor's responsibility to see that people who make referrals to counselors know the purposes of counseling and are aware of what counselors can do. At the same time, the counselor in an agency needs to tell these persons how to identify those who can benefit from counseling. In other words, the counselor is responsible for enabling clients to see him and for referring to appropriate services those who do not need counseling. This responsibility can be facilitated by providing information to persons who make referrals to counselors, and by employing a receptionist who is generally knowledgeable about whether different individuals can benefit from counseling, or whether they should be referred to another service.

While the identification of persons who should receive counseling is the counselor's responsibility, he must depend either on others within his office or on those he contacts from other areas served by his office. However, there are times when he must take this action himself.

Appraisal of Clients

Another responsibility of the counselor in many agencies is the gathering of information about the individual client. Interpreting these data is called appraisal. It should be pointed out that such appraisal of a client should actually be with him rather than of him. While the gathering of information about the client remains the responsibility of the counselor, he may see to it that others conduct the intake interview establishing the life history, and administer tests, if these techniques are used by the counselor. The merit of collecting a life history from every client must be weighed against the feelings of threat and resentment the process generates in some clients. The counselor cannot relinquish the interpretation of appraisal data to others. Appraisal can be a part of counseling. Tyler [3] has pointed out that the appraisal of possibilities as the client sees them within counseling is really counseling.

Routine testing for all is a common practice in many agencies. Some agencies have tests as legal requirements for enabling the client to progress in his chosen direction, e.g., training. However, all clients do not need testing. To test all clients indiscriminately does not fit the concept of the individual nature of counseling.

In many agencies, interest, ability, and achievement tests are frequently used for purposes of gathering information about the client; they seem to have some credence as "reality testing" devices for persons who

---

[3] Leona E. Tyler, *The Work of the Counselor* (New York: Appleton-Century-Crofts, Inc., 1964), p. 85.

hold middle class values. Recently, some counselors who have worked with disadvantaged youth have expressed doubt about the validity of such tests in actual practice. It has been found that so-called culture-free tests are not culture-free, and counselors have had to discard such tests and depend on the counseling relation alone.

Wrenn has stated that even though tests are carefully developed and standardized, test results are assumed to provide only a fraction of the picture of a person. He said that:

Occupational appraisal is far more than aptitudes. Motivation cannot be determined with assurance from what a person says about himself. For a counselor to attempt to do his job with a few aptitude tests and some informational booklets would be analogous to a surgeon's operating with only a scalpel.[4]

In discussing the same topic Arbuckle stated that the most obvious reason for a counselor to use tests would be to acquire information about the client that he could not get more accurately and quickly in some other way. He stated that when

Counselors of various orientations discuss clients . . . they normally have the results of test data, and the psychologist is often considered to be the fellow who provides the counselor with this information. The counselor who feels that he needs this information must need it either to pass on to the client or to help him in his work with the client. In any case, this is counselor directed procedure, in which there is no doubt that the counselor has decided that he needs to know more about the client; he determines what clients will be tested, when they will be tested, and how they will be tested.[5]

Arbuckle goes on to say that frequently counselors who have made such diagnoses have little use for some other counselor's diagnosis. The authors believe that most counselors who currently use tests use them as extensions of themselves in trying to understand their clients, rather than as probing devices for relatively exact measurements of the traits and characteristics of the client. The question of whether or not tests should be used may be answered by asking whether the tests are able to help the client make decisions about himself, and whether the direction taken is that of the client.

Arbuckle suggested situations that may arise in which the counselor would eventually supply the client with test information.

In more cases than not, however, the original request for testing need not actually develop into testing unless the counselor is so unskilled as to miss the feelings being expressed, and blunders ahead with a voluminous discussion of tests and testing without ever giving the client a chance to get closer to what

[4] C. Gilbert Wrenn, *The Counselor in a Changing World* (Washington, D.C.: American Personnel and Guidance Association, 1962), p. 53.

[5] Dugald S. Arbuckle, *Counseling: Philosophy, Theory and Practice* (Boston: Allyn & Bacon, Inc., 1965), p. 259.

he was trying to say when he tentatively asked the question about testing. Even when the client comes in for the sole purpose of testing, as often occurs in a vocational guidance center, more often than not the client is in need of counseling—possibly vocationally oriented, but still counseling, rather than vocational testing. The client who, after a number of counseling sessions, rather consistently raises the question of testing, may feel secure enough so that he can go to the point of taking a look at some test data; or, of course, he could, becoming more threatened, be looking for an easier way out. The good counselor, however, should be able to help the client to see just why he wants test information. When the client can see this, he may have no further need for testing; or, on the other hand, he may be even more certain, but for possibly different reasons, that it would be good for him to take a battery of tests.[6]

One of the best discussions of appraisal has been done by Tyler. She discusses drawing on all possibilities in the life of the client and using these in a tentative sense. In fact she describes the skill of tentativeness as a particular skill in counseling.

To be able to introduce a new idea very tentatively, withdrawing it if one senses actual hostility to it, presenting another thought but not insisting on it, is a kind of trial-and-error behavior that is learned only through experience.[7]

This is the art of appraisal that helps the client to gain new perceptions—to see his possibilities in a new light.

Working with information about the client is counseling. The counselor cannot give information to the client unless the client is ready to accept it. Readiness is as necessary for the counselor as it is for the client. To say the counselor knows the client is not enough. The counselor can impart personal information, such as the results of tests, only when he perceives as the client perceives.

The counselor, by means of his skill in sharing the perception of the counselee, is able to introduce information that has meaning for the latter at a given moment. By information is here meant factual data rather than opinion or value judgment. Along with the tentativeness that Tyler has suggested in offering such information, it is important that the counselor refrain from identifying himself with such informaton. To the degree that the counselor invests part of himself in the information he conveys, he denies the freedom of the counselee to reject it. Having offered information for consideration, it is important for the counselor to share the counselee's perception of that information and, if necessary, to correct inaccuracies conveyed in communicating the information.

[6] Dugald S. Arbuckle, *Counseling: Philosophy, Theory and Practice,* p. 263.
[7] Leona E. Tyler, *The Methods and Processes of Appraisal and Counseling, in the Professional Preparation of Counseling Psychologists,* Report of the 1964 Greystone Conference (New York: Teachers College, Columbia University, 1964), pp. 85-86.

Occupational and Related Information

In many respects the informational aspect of counseling and guidance is historically the oldest service offered to clients. Occupational information has been one of the principal contributions of the Employment Service. Information may be broken down into the three general areas: occupational, educational, and social. Norris, Zeran and Hatch describe them as follows:

> Occupational information is valid and usable data about positions, jobs, and occupations, including duties, requirements for entrance, conditions of work, rewards offered, advancement patterns, existing and predicted supply of and demand for workers, and sources for further information. . . .
> Educational information is valid and usable data about all types of present and probably future educational or training opportunities and requirements, including curricular and co-curricular offerings, requirements for entrance, and conditions and problems of student life. . . .
> Social information is valid and usable data about the opportunities of the human and physical environment which bear on personal and interpersonal relations. It is that information about human beings which will help a student to understand himself better and to improve his relations with others. Included, but not constituting the whole, are such broad areas of information as "understanding self" and "getting along with others," as well as such specific areas as boy-girl relations, manners and etiquette, leisure-time activities, personal appearance, social skills, home and family relationships, financial planning, and healthful living.[8]

The counselor is responsible for providing occupational and related information for the client. As with appraisal information, the counselor must be able to perceive what the client perceives. The counselor himself may not actually relate the information to the client. He may refer the client to reference materials, or he may refer him to specialists in the appropriate area. The use of specialists in the area of occupational information is frequently necessary since the counselor cannot hope to gather all pertinent information, or be informed of all the changes taking place in the community. He may make use of clerks who gather and file information under his supervision.

Some clients may find information about occupations quite to their liking; others may feel threatened and defeated by it. Feelings about such information need to be discussed. Factors related to an occupation, such as salary, working conditions, education, and place of residence, are important to the client's self-concept, and to his need to have the opportunity to be the kind of person he wants to be.

[8] Willa Norris, Franklin R. Zeran, and Raymond N. Hatch, *The Information Service in Guidance* (Chicago: Rand McNally & Company, 1960), pp. 22-23.

Referral

In the same way, a client may realize, for example, that his present environment is detrimental to his future and that he needs to remove himself from it. For instance, the counselor can help him to understand his feelings with regard to moving, and what moving to a different area within a city may mean. If the client feels unable to manage such an action because of lack of knowledge, the counselor may help the client to express his concerns, but will eventually refer him to a specialist who can assist with the indicated arrangements. Clients may be referred to specialists such as placement and training officers, remedial specialists, and community service workers.

The counselor's responsibility in an agency does not end with referral to others. He is also responsible for periodic follow-up of the client. He must frequently find out whether the client is progressing in the plan of his decision. While this is not usually done by the counselor, he can discover by inquiring of others, such as the placement specialist or the school administrator, how the client is progressing. He should be available for further counseling with the client, and he should enable the client to find new sources of assistance in carrying out his goal.

COUNSELOR AS RESEARCHER

The counselor needs to be continuously aware of research developments in counseling and their implications for counseling theory and practice. He should be aware of the research being done with and about the persons he counsels. If he works with the culturally deprived, he must keep abreast of new developments concerning the culturally deprived not only generally, but—since he must be aware of the local environment of his clients—in the geographical areas they come from.

He must also be able to review what he has done as a counselor. While introspection may be of some minor help in his practice, he needs to have more objective evidence in order to evaluate his own proficiency. Certainly, having an experienced supervisor who serves as his counselor for this purpose is ideal. Too often, assigned supervisors are not of this kind, nor are they qualified to serve in this role. Often consulting another counselor is the most practical way to make this kind of evaluation. Tape playing and discussion of alternatives with another counselor serve the purpose of self-appraisal as a counselor, and can result in changes in the counselor's own counseling behavior.

Ideally, the counselor should be a researcher. He should be able to do research about the counseling process in the area or agency in which he works. If several counselors work in an office with a large enough number of clients, well-designed research projects can be conducted. Practically, counselors do not often do research because they are not usually trained for research unless they have doctoral degrees; furthermore, they are usually so busy with the service of counseling that they have little time for research activity. Research on counseling should be done in each of the many agencies in order to discover the effects of counseling with different cultural groups, and the effects of different amounts and types of counseling with different groups.

WHERE COUNSELORS HAVE WORKED

Counselors have worked in hospitals, in private agencies, and in community agencies. They have been employed by state and local rehabilitation agencies, by the Veterans Administration, by the Employment Services of 50 states, by secondary schools and some elementary schools, and by colleges and universities. In all these settings, counselors have worked with the culturally deprived with varying success. In some settings the counselor has been an enabler by helping clients to understand themselves as worthwhile human beings, able to make progress toward satisfying long-range goals and satisfying lives. In other settings counselors have worked with clients who have had more immediate concerns, such as suitable training or employment. In still other settings the counselor has worked for the client to the point of providing services beyond those of counseling.

Every counselor who has worked with the culturally deprived has felt that certain of these individuals would be immediately better off if they were given help, including money. Some counselors have wanted to use their own perceptions of clients and their environments, rather than clients' perceptions, as a basis for manipulating the clients and their environments.

It is the contention of the authors of this chapter that the counselor's enabling function is best utilized in providing an opportunity for the client to explore his experiences and determine the direction in which he will go. Unless the client recognizes that the counselor accepts him as a person, regardless of his class or race, the counseling relation will not be established. The authors recognize that ease in counseling occurs as a result of experience in a particular setting, and familiarity with clients from a particular type of environment; but the counselor who establishes the counseling relation will be able to work with clients from any cultural group. The counselor who has never worked with culturally different clients will find that, once he has acquired an ease in communication, counseling as a relationship is the same for any group of clients.

The counselor, then, is an enabler in that he enables the client to understand and be himself. He is not a manipulator of his client's life.

LIMITATIONS OF COUNSELING

The federal government has undertaken a massive program of aid to underprivileged and culturally deprived citizens. The intended recipients of these services are viewed by legislators and by the majority of the general public as inadequate individuals who are incapable of achieving a self-sustaining role in society without the intervention of public funds and agencies in their behalf.

The underprivileged of our nation are seen for the most part as having had little, if any, opportunity to exercise choice in the mode of their existence. Environmental factors have literally condemned succeeding generations of such persons to watch helplessly, and often with frustration and hostility, as the rest of the nation moves onward to ever higher standards of living.

In the several legislative actions supporting America's war on poverty, considerable emphasis has been placed on counseling services. If counseling is accepted as a useful and an essential means of enabling individuals to understand themselves and their environments, to accept themselves and to assume self-direction, then it is fitting that counseling services become a significant part of any antipoverty program. However, there appears to be a very real danger that persons providing the counseling services included in a program having as its goal the forceful manipulation of masses of people might become little more than another aspect of the gigantic manipulative effort.

The very helplessness of the underprivileged that provoked the federal program of assistance becomes a source of pressure for the counselor to do for people, rather than to assist them to do for themselves. The cultural barriers to communication, the seemingly insurmountable ignorance of and resistance to middle class values, and the naturally exhaustible patience of the counselor, along with the sometimes overwhelming desire to help, constantly goad the counselor to intervene. Under such circumstances, it appears highly possible that counselors in programs for the culturally deprived may be described in terms very similar to those used by Patterson to depict the behavior of a rehabilitation counselor:

He *determines* the eligibility of clients as clients and the feasibility of their rehabilitation; he *appraises* the client's vocational potential and the probability of his success; he *evaluates* the suitability of various jobs; he *interviews* the client *toward realistic* (as defined by himself) goals; he *develops* a vocational rehabilitation plan with all its parts; *he carries out* the plan, implementing and administering its various aspects; *he makes referrals* to related services. One might ask: "What is the client doing all the time?" Too often he is literally doing nothing except what he is told to do by the counselor.[9]

In counseling children of elementary school age, the job seeker, the handicapped, and the underprivileged, similar pressures that are experienced by the counselor move him toward assuming responsibility for the direction of a client's behavior. It is necessary and highly desirable that persons in our society assume such responsibility for those who, because of age or disability, or for any reason beyond their control, are unable to be responsible for themselves. However, when a counselor regards another individual as inadequate for the task of self-direction, and presumes to supply direction on the basis of his personal system of values or on the basis of societal values, he is not functioning as a counselor, but as a parent, a guardian, a teacher, an administrator, a therapist, a physician, a social worker, or as a policeman.

SELECTED READINGS

1. Arbuckle, Dugald S., *Counseling: Philosophy, Theory and Practice.* Boston: Allyn and Bacon, Inc., 1965.

2. Beck, Carlton, *Philosophical Foundations of Guidance.* Englewood Cliffs, N.J.: Prentice-Hall, Inc., 1960.

3. Bergin, Allen E., "Some Implications of Psychotherapy Research for Therapeutic Practice," *Journal of Abnormal Psychology,* 71, No. 4 (1966), 235-246.

4. Blum, Milton L., and Benjamin Balinsky, *Counseling and Psychology,* Englewood Cliffs, N.J.: Prentice-Hall, Inc., 1951.

5. Bordin, Edward S., *Psychological Counseling.* New York: Appleton-Century-Crofts, 1955.

6. Carkhuff, Robert R., "Counseling Research, Theory and Practice—1965," *Journal of Counseling Psychology,* 13, No. 4 (1966) 467-480.

7. Combs, Arthur, and Donald Snygg, *Individual Behavior.* New York: Harper and Row Publishers, 1959.

8. Combs, Arthur, and Daniel W. Soper, "The Perceptual Organization of Effective Counselors," *Journal of Counseling Psychology,* 10, No. 3 (Fall, 1963), 222-226.

9. Cottle, William C. and N. M. Downie, *Procedures and Preparation for Counseling.* Englewood Cliffs, N.J.: Prentice-Hall, Inc., 1960.

10. Ehrle, Raymond A., *Counseling in the Employment Service.* Washington, D.C.: Leviathan Publishers, 1966.

[9] C. H. Patterson, *Counseling and Psychotherapy: Theory and Practice* (New York: Harper & Row, Publishers, 1959), p. 11.

11. Evraiff, William, *Helping Counselors Grow Professionally.* Englewood Cliffs, N.J.: Prentice-Hall, Inc., 1963.

12. Katz, Robert L., *Empathy: Its Nature and Uses.* New York: The Free Press of Glencoe, Inc., 1963.

13. McGowan, John F., *Counselor Development in American Society.* Conference Recommendations from Invitational Conference on Government-University Relations in the Professional Preparation and Employment of Counselors, University of Missouri, 1965.

14. ———, and Thomas L. Porter, *An Introduction to Employment Service Counseling.* University of Missouri, 1964.

15. ———, and Lyle D. Schmidt, *Counseling: Readings in Theory and Practice.* New York: Holt, Rinehart & Winston, Inc., 1962.

16. Norris, Willa, *et al., The Information Service in Guidance* (rev. ed.). Chicago: Rand McNally & Co., 1966.

17. Patterson, C. H., *Theories of Counseling and Psychotherapy.* New York: Harper and Row, Publishers, 1966.

18. ———, "The Counselor's Responsibility in Rehabilitation," *Journal of Rehabilitation,* **24** (January-February, 1958), 7-11.

19. Rogers, Carl R., *Client-Centered Therapy.* Boston: Houghton Mifflin Company, 1951.

20. ———, *On Becoming A Person.* Boston: Houghton Mifflin Company, 1961.

21. Stefflre, Buford, *Theories of Counseling.* New York: McGraw-Hill Book Company, Inc., 1965.

22. Tyler, Leona E., *The Work of the Counselor* (2nd ed.). New York: Appleton-Century-Crofts, 1961.

23. Williamson, E. G., *Vocational Counseling: Some Historical, Philosophical and Theoretical Perspectives.* New York: McGraw-Hill Book Co., Inc., 1965.

24. Wrenn, Gilbert C., *The Counselor in a Changing World.* Washington D.C.: American Personnel and Guidance Association, 1962.

16

WHERE DO WE GO

FROM HERE?

JEAN D. GRAMBS AND WILLIAM E. AMOS

Predicting the future has always been hazardous. Today one can state with certainty only that many old problems will remain unsolved and new ones will appear. This truism applies with particular felicity in the field of counseling youth—whether from suburbia or inner city. The older generation has always had trouble with its offspring; the generational gap grows wider with each decade. At the same time, however, we are fortunately more aware of, and more sensitive to the facts and appearances of the problem. We may be puzzled by youth, baffled, frustrated, and indignant, but we are in a far better position than ever before to gain access to the world of youth, thereby gaining some wisdom about how we can best guide them toward satisfying adulthood.

The chapters in this volume are strong evidence that we have much information at hand about the particular and unique problems of the children of poverty, so that we can put into practice what we preach as well as what we know. Thus, given the data and experience available, excuses for lack of implementation must be sought elsewhere. In attempting to summarize what has been stated in the body of this volume, it seems fruitful to take a look, first, at the institutional and societal barriers to change—to putting into practice what we know—and then delineate some unsolved or unresolved problems that practitioners still face.

1. *Institutional Inertia*

Wherever the counselor operates, he is not a private entrepreneur who seeks out clients to buy his services, and adapts to the market he finds. Rather, he is part of a system, whether it be a school system, a government employment office, a nonprofit guidance center, or a specially constructed "War on Poverty" program. The older the institution, the harder it will be to effect change in the counselor's role, except in relatively minor aspects. The school system is probably the prime example of a tradition-bound institution in which counselors may find role expectations so rigid and so clearly defined that shifts to accommodate the special needs of a particular group may be all but unachievable. For instance, as has been pointed out over and over again in this volume, many disadvantaged youth are school push-outs (or dropouts), potential or actual. There are numerous ingenious ideas for counselor intervention to assist these young people to find a place in the world of work or their own families, and still keep in touch with the school and further their education. Yet it is just as clearly documented that few schools permit or encourage broad attempts to provide flexibility of scheduling, of curriculum, or other adaptations that would achieve the above goals.

The school counselor, besides being burdened with an impossible case load, is expected to be particularly responsible for the college-bound group, to be the expert on testing as well as (in many instances) the administrator of test programs, to be the schedule maker and troubleshooter. Small wonder that he has little time left over for the time-consuming work involved in establishing and supporting more work-study programs, specially tailored educational work, and the other adaptations effective with culturally disadvantaged and educationally discouraged students.

Similar restrictions may bind the counselor operating in other agencies. Job descriptions may be so tightly constructed that the innovating counselor is unable to work outside the narrow range of defined activities. In private agencies, as in the schools, lay boards may be unsympathetic to many of the approaches to counseling suggested in this book.

Like many of his colleagues, the counselor talks mainly with other counselors, and what he writes is read by other counselors. To overcome institutional inertia or ignorance, it is essential that counselors take upon themselves a more aggressive and educational role. It is clearly self-defeating for professional people to beat their breasts about all that they cannot do which they know they should do, and place the blame elsewhere as they continue business as usual. It is incumbent upon the counselor and his colleagues to become active proponents of new programs, to seek ways of influencing the changes in their institutional settings that will permit such programs to operate, and to provide data of local relevance, demonstrating that newer approaches are indeed procedures whereby both money and human lives are saved.

In the newer agencies, such as those that have sprung up like mushrooms in the War on Poverty programs, there appears to be little excuse for counselors who accept traditional solutions to new problems, when the evidence is clearly at hand that traditional procedures just do not work. Here the barrier to change is the individual himself.

2. Counselor Inertia

One might venture a guess that the failure to practice what we preach is roughly half the fault of institutional barriers; but at least the other half is the product of individual unwillingness or inability to change. Those who have read the preceding chapters have undoubtedly found themselves saying, "It's all very well, but . . ." and thinking of all the many reasons why one could not organize such programs in one's own area.

Experience itself may be a hazard. As is so often the case, an older worker views an innovation as a threat: established procedures might be junked, new forms developed, new contacts established; furniture may have to be moved, partitions put up or taken down—a whole host of "new" things must be done. If, as seems to be agreed by the experts writing in this volume, individual counseling with the disadvantaged has distinct limitations, then facilities must be provided for working with several youths at a time, or for extended group counseling. The private cubbyhole in which the counselee pours forth his woes is not the prototype of an effective milieu for counseling with many of these disadvantaged young people. Indeed, as one writer (Gordon) suggests, the counselor must take himself to the job site where the new worker is having his first adequate work experience, and give him supportive assistance the minute he walks off at the end of the day. Will many counselors transport themselves to the site of the new construction work in order to "catch" a counselee, perhaps to drive him home and reinforce, en route, the value of the work experience, and respond to the counselee's fears about the new situation? "Why, I can't leave my office!" is a common cry; how many counselors are so office-bound that the outside world is really foreign country? Yet it is in this world that the true work with disadvantaged youth must take place.

For the counselor trained in case work methods or individual counseling approaches, dependent on objective or other kinds of tests to furnish basic data about a given counselee before he even sees him, the approaches suggested here will probably be resisted. Test-dependence is a critical dimension of counselor behavior which, in the light of the comments by Cody (Chapter 3), needs serious re-examination. Group procedures in counseling are qualitatively different from individual counseling procedures. Thus the counselor untrained in group process would need retraining; and there comes a time in the lives of all of us when learning new tricks hardly seems feasible or possible. We can rationalize all we wish, but the fact remains that such retraining is essential.

The immunity of counselors from the real world of the disadvantaged has been described at much length in this volume, from a number of points of view. What is indeed difficult is to gain effective entry into the world of disadvantaged. Very few individuals will choose to live in a slum in order to learn the slum code or the slum language. Yet these men and women are needed for adequate counseling of persons raised in such a subculture. The anthropologist, who spends years submerged in a different and alien culture in order to learn its ways, considers this period necessary to his professional training. It might be useful to consider ways of becoming "counselor-anthropologists" in learning about the culture of the poor. This culture, of course, will differ depending on whether one is working with youth from Harlem, San Antonio, a Sioux reservation in South Dakota, or the isolated subsistence farms of Vermont. How does one pick up the cues to what will work with these diverse kinds of children of poverty? And how willing is the counselor to get from behind his desk to do some anthropological snooping to find out?

While more counselors are needed at every level, from early childhood to old age, recruiting more personnel of the same stripe is not going to solve the problem. It is obvious that well-trained teams of counselors intent on achieving change would seem ludicrous if they did in a rural village in India the kinds of things they would do in Scarsdale; yet the analogy does not always seem as clear to the counselor who moves from Scarsdale to the Cardozo area of Washington, D.C. The mere fact that the "natives" speak more or less the same language, when pressed, does not mean they move to the same tune.

3. Community Apathy

Community apathy is apparent in all of the "communities" in which the counselor must work. The power community—the one that sends representatives to sit on boards of education or welfare agency boards— is often more keenly aware of and interested in programs that support its own kind (e.g., the school's college-bound groups), or keep the poor out of sight and out of mind. It is clearly demonstrable that it costs more to keep a person in prison or an asylum than it does keep him in school or even college; yet the amount of money spent for preventive action (before incarceration) is minimal. It may be no accident of planning that prisons and asylums are typically far, far removed from population centers, and particularly from places where the middle class and affluent may see them.

Since the power community sits on school boards, its representatives are often, as Cottle (Chapter 9) points out, reluctant to publish figures on their dropouts, and may be extremely uncooperative in research efforts to determine the causes for such dropouts. A strong attitude still prevails that the dropout is innately lazy, shiftless, no-good, that he deserves a miserable life. The fallacy here, regardless of the assumption about what can be innate in human nature, is that, ultimately, the public does pay for these miserable and "shiftless" persons—via welfare, by maintaining them in public institutions, and by similar drains on the public purse. Again, the apathy or unwillingness of the power community to face the disagreeable facts of the public cost of poverty must, by default, rest upon the counselors who are nearest to the problem.

The middle class community, like the power community, is often equally uninformed and equally uninterested, if not downright opposed, to dealing forthrightly, imaginatively (and expensively) with the problems of the poor. Many middle class persons are themselves only a generation or so removed from the bottom of the social ladder. In reaction to an article about the need to re-think some school programs for the disadvantaged Negro slum child, one Polish-American wrote a bitter letter to the effect that no one had bled for him, and he had risen from severe poverty to respectable status as a teacher, so why should he go about bleeding for the Negro? Let him help himself as the respondent had! There are innumerable such individuals in the middle class community. They resent and often actively oppose programs that will aid the current crop of victims of poverty.

Finally, the community of poverty, by its very nature, is defeated by feelings of powerlessness, helplessness, and lack of faith in anything that will make life better. Today's victims of poverty, as documented in this volume and many others, live in a different world from that of yesterday's immigrant poor, and have had different educations in the possibilities of the good life. They are nonbelievers. They are distrustful. They are victimized—and they know it—by individuals and institutions who profit from their helplessness. The energy and artifice needed to overcome these kinds of defeats are in scarce supply among the poor. But by reading such poignant reports as Hertha Riese's *Heal the Hurt Child* [1] one can begin to glimpse what generations of disabling poverty can do to individuals.

[1] Hertha Riese, *Heal the Hurt Child* (Chicago: University of Chicago Press, 1962).

Indeed, poverty and its rituals become a way of life.[2] The skills learned by the individual are those that serve him well in his closed world. To suggest, much less insist, on a way out, is to push the individual into a world where the skills he has acquired to cope with his own culture will not serve him at all. Where he is strong on the street, he will be vulnerable, weak, and exposed as inadequate in the routine world of everyday work. The trauma that prevents some children from ever being able to leave home, figuratively or literally, afflicts the youth of poverty, their parents, and the other adults with whom they associate. "It's just no use, man," they say, speaking from accurate knowledge of their own eroded personalities, and from observing those around them.

Thus the many communities that make up our social world stand as barriers to effective counseling programs such as those described in this volume. Each community, in its apathy, inertia, or active resistance, poses a different problem for the engineer of social change. Since counselors do not, typically, conceive of themselves as engineers of social change, it is hardly surprising that little change in the effectiveness of counselors has come about.

4. *Insufficient Data*

Although we have asserted that we have at hand ample documentation to show that new programs will work, there is still a disgraceful lack of hard research in the field of counselor effectiveness with the disadvantaged. The guides that must be relied upon are the testimonials of those who report their own programs. Many good working programs are reported in this volume. Yet each is attested to as being successful by those who were responsible. What about the programs that failed? Why is there such a void when it comes to follow-up data? As the Smallenbergs (Chapter 14) point out, research in the field of counseling the disadvantaged is practically nonexistent. The same may be said for many areas of human behavior. We know a great deal more about the diseases of pigs than we know about the health of human beings. We know more about how to raise a pullet to market size than we know about how to educate a child to enter the world of adults.

Again, the allocation of that scarce resource—research personnel—is determined as a matter of the interest of those with the power to make decisions, not those about whom the decisions are being made (in this case counselors, and the children of the disadvantaged). Education as a whole has been short-changed in research efforts. Where research has been extensive, it is typically in the tight, statistically pure, doctoral dissertation type of study, with results published in limited circulation journals for consumption by similar-minded colleagues and superiors. The

[2] Jules Henry, "White People's Time, Colored People's Time," *Trans-Action*, 2 (March-April, 1965), 31-34.

broad and complex research and data gathering that would serve counselors working in the area of the disadvantaged are notably undersupported. One can only observe that there appears to be considerable wishful thinking operating here: if we don't really pay much attention to the problem, perhaps it will just go away!

The lack of data, however, provides a ready excuse for those who do not see or do not want to see the need for different programs. Thus the inertia of institutions, of individuals, and of the community rests on a fairly solid ground of past experience with very little in the way of new information to disqualify outmoded procedures. Therefore, the counselor who understands the value of trying new approaches must become, also, his own researcher. It is folly (though a pervasive one) for government programs to have funds for performing various functions, but little or no funds for *adequate,* objective, sound evaluation of results. In working with youth in the counseling area this kind of research effort must include a major component of follow-up studies; what worked today may, in a few years, be less effective than some other procedure. Only time can tell us; yet longitudinal and follow-up studies are among the most costly, the most needed, and the most lacking, in the literature.

Issues and Prospects

The enumeration of barriers to change has undoubtedly had a familiar sound. These barriers are not insurmountable, and numerous individuals are already well at work in getting around or over them, as the previous chapters attest. Certain unresolved issues, however, require further study and further examination. A few of the most impressive and pertinent, in the view of this author, are listed below.

1. *What is the counselor's role in prevention?*

Typically, the counselor who works with disadvantaged youth appears in the life of the young person when the individual is far along the road to nowhere. In many cases, a counselor knows only too well that he has too little to offer, and that it comes too late. Many counselors feel very successful if, as far as they know, half of their clientele succeed. And the other half? They marry, breed, and the vicious cycle continues.

Data from studies of behavior and growth, notably those of Bloom,[3] Kagan and Moss,[4] and Hess and Shipman [5] point repeatedly to the impact

---

[3] Benjamin S. Bloom, *Stability and Change in Human Characteristics* (New York: John Wiley & Sons, Inc., 1964).

[4] Jerome Kagan and Howard A. Moss, *Birth to Maturity* (New York: John Wiley & Sons, Inc., 1962).

[5] Robert D. Hess and Virginia Shipman, "Early Blocks to Children's Learning," *Children,* 12, No. 5 (September-October, 1965), 197-198; Fred L. Strodtbeck, "The Hidden Curriculum of the Middle-Class Home," in *Urban Education and Cultural Deprivation,* ed. C. W. Hunnicutt (Syracuse, N.Y.: Syracuse University Press, 1964).

of early experiences in determining future development. Thus, if we were to put into practice what these research studies show, our major efforts would be directed toward the very young child and the elementary school student. After sixth or seventh grade, we are told, or even after third grade, patterns of learning, of coping with the world, or relating to other people, are so firmly set that intervention is bound to be futile. Counselors, then, instead of working with disadvantaged youth, should be located where their services and help will really make a difference: in nursery schools, well-baby clinics, elementary schools, homes for abandoned infants; they should also be accessible to children with foster parents. If proper assistance as well as proper diagnosis occurs at early stages in the child's development, the later efforts of counselors will be more effective—and less needed.

Going even further back—or forward, as the case may be—the counselor's most effective role may occur even before a new child enters the world. Perhaps counselors should staff (or assist in establishing) centers in all poverty areas, so that they can work with *future* mothers to educate them in their critical role of educator of the young. It is astounding, when one considers it, that the most significant person in the life of a child—his mother—is very seldom given formal help by educational institutions. The simple facts of child psychology, of child growth and development, of infant nutrition, are only too rarely provided those persons least able to find out what to do for themselves—pregnant women who are poor. As Hess and others have documented, the mother in the lower socio-economic level literally does not talk to her child much, does not provide him with a model of attention, obedience, understanding; thus she cripples him at birth in terms of later intellectual and psychological growth.

Should the counselor working with the disadvantaged identify a more critical point, a point at which his specialized training and service would be of more lasting impact? Since counselors are a scarce commodity, should we not re-examine their allocation in terms of maximizing their influence?

2. *Is the training of counselors relevant?*

Formal academic training of counselors rests on a body of tradition that may itself impede new modes of counselor behavior. If the training is within an academic institution, the counselor has undoubtedly had one or two courses in statistics. Did this provide him with tools to do follow-up studies of his clients? Since we know there is a gross lack of such studies, evidently the kind of research training provided counselors either does not equip them to do such studies, or does not make them feel that performing such studies is an integral part of their day-to-day work.

Because of the traditional reliance on individual counseling (which makes sense, it would seem, to the typical middle class individual), is the counselor equipped with skills to work with two or three or groups of youth at a time—an apparently appropriate technique for working with the disadvantaged? Is there, indeed, as much training time given to group processes of counseling as there is to individual counseling? And is the counselor provided clinical experiences with persons of *varied* socio-economic backgrounds, not just college sophomores? Does the training program itself exemplify the kinds of operations that the counselor should later carry out on his own—that is, follow-up research, continued operational research, and maintenance of a broad community base outside the ivory tower? The kind of clinical practice described by Sarason and associates [6] would appear to be a model for clinical training for counselors in general who must operate, willy-nilly, in a *community*.

Do counselors, in their training, have assistance in understanding the power structure of institutions and of communities? The frustrations of the counselor who seeks to develop new programs can be documented on every side. Is one reason the fact that the counselor does not know how to go about working to change the institutional setting or community climate in which he finds himself? Institutions can change, and individuals can help to make them change, but only if they have insight into the social processes of change, and the structure of organizations. There is a notable lack of both sociological and anthropological orientations in the basic education of most social service personnel. Though they may know the skills of their trade, and have a conscience about what constitutes a good job, they are immobilized because, once they quit the protection of the academic community, they are unable to operate in the "real world." The line of least resistance, then, is to leave the profession (as only too many do), or to grow cynical about the whole thing and become a pencil-pusher, a test-giver, and a defensive apologist for an ineffective operation.

Finally, are counselors in their training permitted to gain windows onto their own souls? The typical resistance of educators to psychology [7] is not overcome by lectures *about* motivation, achievement, values, cultural differences, etc. A few procedures, such as the T-Group method utilized by the National Training Laboratories,[8] are helpful; and it is open to question how many counseling programs include these ways of helping individuals see themselves and gain sensitivity to others. Where

[6] Seymour S. Sarason *et al.*, *Psychology in Community Settings* (New York: John Wiley & Sons, Inc., 1967).

[7] Roger G. Barker, "Difficulties of Communication Between Educators and Psychologists: Some Speculations," *Journal of Educational Psychology*, 33 (September, 1942), 416-426.

[8] Leland T. Bradford *et al.*, *T-Group Theory and Laboratory Method* (New York: John Wiley & Sons, Inc., 1964).

counselors must work with youth of a different socioeconomic class, of a different ethnic, racial and sex group, such sensitivity is a prerequisite for effective work. Yet how many white counselors really feel at home with a Negro client? How many Negroes do not retain hidden hostilities when working with white youth? How much covert anti-Christian bias distorts the perception of Jewish workers? These kinds of feelings are baggage the counselor can least afford to carry into the counseling situation, yet few training programs provide (with academic credit!) a means of unloading them. Similarly, insights into cultural differences is provided, if at all, in what is probably the least effective way devised to understand the culture of another group: the lecture.

3. *What piece of the person belongs to the counselor?*

The phrasing of the above question probably has the effect of a red flag on most readers. "We deal with the whole person," they say heatedly. Of course. Everyone does. Then why the constant referrals? Why do so many disadvantaged youth, and their parents, feel as though they were volley balls tossed from agency to agency, from referral center to referral center?

Rafferty [9] has made the point about the indefensible concept of territoriality when it comes to the helping professions, particularly those having to do with the adjustment, mental health, and guidance of individuals. A person needs help *now*, when he is at the door; he will not come back if he must find his way to another agency across town that has been designated as *the* one for his particular kind of problem. Both the training of the counselor and the counselor's own perception of his role probably are at fault in delineating sharply defined territories in which counselors alone can work, and also defining carefully the territories of others—psychiatrists, social workers, teachers—where one may not trespass. There is also, as every community worker can testify, the problem of whose client belongs to whom. "Send us all the Catholics," may be the hidden message of one agency. "We will help Negroes find jobs; send the others to *their* agency," may be the message of another group. "You take this case; we can't handle it," is the way some hard-core problem cases are shunted from one agency to another. As Sarason so tellingly describes it, this kind of interagency noncooperation results in less help, more tragedy, more cost, than even our blunderings as individuals. [10] Competition among agencies, lack of coordinated effort, plus ignorance of other programs means that some persons get too much attention, some get none, and others are torn by contradictory policies. Counselors, and all other professional personnel who work with disadvantaged youth,

[9] Frank T. Rafferty, Director, Child Psychiatry Service, University of Maryland School of Medicine, in a lecture, 1963.
[10] Sarason, *op. cit.*

need procedures for maximizing interchangeability of programs, plus clear and *instant* ways of coordinating efforts.

4. Can any counselor counsel anybody?

The research indicates that responses differ according to the race and sex of the interviewer. Such research has been repeated enough times in enough different settings to suggest that, indeed, there is something *personal* about being a counselor—an interviewer—that makes a difference in the perception of the one interviewed or counseled. Do Negro students respond with equal validity to white counselors? Are boys as candid with women counselors as they may be with men counselors?

These questions have, it would seem, been answered by some of the research at hand. Yet counselors and counseling training seem to eradicate the differences, or at the least to ignore them. If one is a trained counselor, goes the code, then one is equipped to work with anyone. We have mentioned the need for sensitivity training as an element in the education of counselors. But there is a point beyond which even sensitivity training cannot go. The very real differences in the perceptual and affective world of men and women, for instance, will not soon be breached by any amount of T-Group experience. And few counselors have even this kind of training to help them. Counselors, being people, are not interchangeable parts. Some are good, that is, more effective, with certain kinds of people than with others. Not all counselors are comfortable with a nondirective approach; not all should be. Many counselees are not comfortable with the nondirective interview; and this is especially true of the culturally disadvantaged. Thus screening for counseling roles might well take into account the individual differences that a given counselor brings to a given situation.

Of particular concern in this area, as in many others in education, is the unwarranted assumption that because certain programs work with boys or young men, they will obviously work with girls or young women. Nothing could be further from the empirical truth. As Konopka describes so vividly, the world of the girl in trouble is a very different world from that of the delinquent boy.[11] Yet, using generalizations based primarily on research on delinquent boys (there are more of them, and most researchers are men) the policies and procedures for dealing with both sexes have been similar. There is evidence that treating girls like boys simply does not work.

The counseling assignment in many kinds of situations is heavily loaded with boys and young men. Much of the literature is devoted to their problems; many of the programs described in this volume are those effective primarily with boys. The girls, like other minority groups, are ignored

[11] Gisela Konopka, *The Adolescent Girl in Conflict* (Englewood Cliffs, N.J.: Prentice-Hall, Inc., 1966).

or underestimated as persons with problems and unique needs. Staffing of agency programs, whether school, government, or private, must reflect consideration of the kinds of differences that counselors bring in terms of the cultural expectations of their clients.

WHERE DO WE GO FROM HERE?

It would seem that the massive efforts of government at all levels, and agencies operating on the private sector as well, will in very short order eliminate the need for counseling assistance for the culturally disadvantaged. If all of the well-publicized programs were as effective as claimed, the potential customers for counseling in this category would soon be gone.

Yet, knowing society as we do, our predictions cannot be as optimistic. The poor will be among us for a few more decades; and when they have disappeared in their current guise, a new group of those who are deprived or disadvantaged will need our ministry.

A number of important considerations can provide guidelines for preparation for the future: most of these are implicit in previous chapters in this volume. Let me spell out a few that seem especially critical.

1. *Utilizing the request for innovation in new programs*

Educators and their colleagues in the helping professions have long cried out that if only they had enough money, they could work miracles. Now, and, barring major world wide cataclysms, in the decades ahead, the federal government will invest a great deal of money in the areas of interest to counselors. How will these funds be used?

The chance to be innovating is one that most professional persons have requested; when the opportunity is at hand, persons with fresh ideas and courage to try new things must be ready. Above all, however, such persons must have the support of old institutions, tradition-laden and ivy covered, and bound by United Givers codes! It is in this arena—the struggle between the innovative, and the familiar and the conservative—that the future direction of counseling services will be determined.

It is worthy of note, however, that new ideas are not really born overnight. The innovator who stands any chance of surviving moves forward on the basis of some surety—he knows his business, he knows the research, he has explored what others have done, and he can put old pieces together in a new shape. The tragedy today is to observe millions of new funds supporting old and feeble programs because of lack of new ideas, and lack of support for new ideas where they are forthcoming.

Now, as never before, persons with new ideas must come forward.

2. *The role of counselor is of crucial importance*

Previous generations got rid of their problem people by exploiting them, abandoning them, or incorporating them into the folklore of family eccentrics. Formerly, too, people turned to other family members for help when in trouble: if Junior couldn't stand his Pa, he could go work for Uncle Seth down the road a-piece; if Susy was too wild, she could be sent to the city to live with other Young Ladies in a tightly chaperoned (and exploited) boarding house, and tend the textile looms. Today the family is adrift, with relatives either distant, not interested, or disowning. If anyone is in trouble he turns, not to his own kind, but to some impersonal public agency. School personnel report time and again how many parents grasp the occasion of parent-teacher conferences on report cards as a rare opportunity to pour forth family problems and make wistful appeals for help.

The counselor in the future can expect, therefore, to find that his skills for helping will be called upon by many different people in many different ways. As the world grows more complex, it grows more bewildering to the undereducated and the underexposed. The counselor may appear to be the one person with a beacon to light the way out of darkness. Teachers are judges; police are threatening; even the neighborhood bartender is a stranger. But the person bearing the public label of helper—counselor—will be more than ever called upon. The disadvantaged, whether they be youth or their parents, will seek such help. Thus the counselor may well become the doorkeeper of the future for many, many millions.

3. *The problems of the culturally disadvantaged will become more rather than less severe*

The obvious gap between those who have and those who have not, which can be seen every hour of the day on TV, will become increasingly a part of the behavior and motivations of those who have not. The more they know what they lack, the less able they will be to bear their burdens meekly. One can expect more assertion of rights, more aggressive resistance to lame excuses, and also more dependence on finding a "formula" answer. As we all know, these are contradictory and conflicting forces. There is no formula that will solve all the ills of mankind, let alone one man. Aggression breeds resistance; assertion of rights leads to negation of rights. The counselor may well become the man in the middle, sympathetic with the strivings and needs of the dispossessed, but the symbol and the trained emissary of those in possession.

It is possible, however, to envision a procedure whereby those who need help are helped to help themselves with the professional aid of the trained counselor. The helpless dependence of the poor is decried by those who have made it up the ladder; it just may be that the counselor may find that his best ally is organization. Though the name of Saul Alinsky may be unknown to many, and may cause considerable anguish in others and real anger in some more, what this man personifies is the concept that power leads to amelioration of problems.[12] When the poor feel that they can help *themselves,* they are no longer helpless and, in a real sense, on the way to being poor no more. The specter of organized poor is one that affronts many who have through their own organizations managed to protect their own interests and gain considerable personal benefit and public power in the process! Where will the counselor see his role in this process? Some counselors, knowing the dreadful degradation of powerlessness, will try to assist the poor to gain power; those who feel that "experts" are better judges than the poor of what is good for them will not support the efforts of the poor to organize, but will encourage their continued dependence. Perhaps many of the poor would use power badly, having little knowledge of the meaning of power; thus, some feel, they should not be encouraged to exercise that which they do not understand. Many may prefer dependence. In any event, the counselor may make some critical decisions in this area in the near future. There is little doubt that a confrontation between the haves and the have-nots will occur, particularly in the racial context, and the counselor will need to have some insight, lest he be cast to the sidelines.

4. *Counselors will be selected in a more careful fashion*

As jobs disappear in other areas of life, the helping professions will become the arena of greater and greater job competition. As has been noted by big industry, as it buys into education, here is the growth industry of the future. Included in these growth indices are the numerous personnel, counselors among them, who make up the skilled echelons. There will be, for some time to come, a need for more trained counselors than current programs can fill. But in the not too distant future, supply may well exceed demand. At this point, more stringent screening procedures will be needed. It is at this point, too, that many may be screened out of the profession.

Today, reports indicate, almost anyone with some kind of professional training, whether relevant or not, may find himself behind a desk with the title of "counselor" on the door. Such a state of affairs cannot be tolerated for long; nor will it last long, because of the push of genuinely trained personnel into the field. As opportunities close down elsewhere (and in any event, many college graduates would prefer to be counselors

[12] "The Professional Radical: Conversations with Saul Alinsky," *Harper's Magazine,* June, 1965, pp. 37-47.

than managers of shoe stores), it is probable that counseling will become more attractive. The implications for this shift, in terms of dealing with the culturally disadvantaged, is unpredictable. To the degrees that the new recruit to counseling is himself upward mobile, and his training is as traditional as that typical of today's programs, he will be resistant to the expectations of the lowest segment of society. If training, however, catches up with need, and with what is known about training problems in his field, then increased competition for counseling positions will result in more personnel who are also more able to deal with the real problems of poverty.

5. *Counselors of youth will become counselors of adults who deal with youth*

A new role for the counselor is developing as specialization increases, and as demands for services increase. It is highly probable that the counselor of the future may find that most of his time is devoted to working with other adults who work with culturally disadvantaged youth, rather than to working directly with these young people. He may be a consultant to a group of classroom teachers who want assistance in the educational problems posed by these students; he may counsel with the parents of these youth; he may serve as liaison among a number of agencies dealing with young people in his jurisdiction. Therefore although a counselor's primary concern may be with young people, he may soon find himself increasingly relegated to individual clinical sessions, or mass testing programs, and out of touch with the concerns of the majority of his clientele. As noted previously, counselors working with disadvantaged persons will also find that group process skills will be needed as much if not more than skills of individual interviewing and counseling.

6. *The counselor as bridge to the future*

Finally, the future seems to indicate that the counselor of the deprived—or the advantaged—is likely to find himself as the person most likely to be asked to interpret the future. He does, as a matter of fact, today indicate to young people how their current decisions affect what they will be doing ten years from now; thus he is already functioning as a predictor of the future. This role, however, has not been as carefully assessed as has others. With the coming of more complex technology and the consequent disruption of more and more segments of standard ways of living, the counselor will find his ability to peer into the future called increasingly into account. He will, therefore, have to be a student of the future. He will have to be the first to know of new economic policies, new international policies, and local shifts in technology, that will have implications for those who turn to him for a map of the future.

CONCLUSION

Inevitably, a key person emerges from all proposals for solving the problems of disadvantaged young people: he is the counselor. How can the young person find a way out of his multiple dilemmas if no one is around to give him some guidance, some help, some advice? Yet the very persons who need this help most are those hardest to talk with, hardest to convince of sincerity and genuineness, and least likely to show quick response to attention and assistance.

Thus working with the disadvantaged young person is not as rewarding for either giver or recipient as is working with more amiable and amenable youth. When the going gets tough, the natural inclination is to seek an easier route. For this reason our disadvantaged are doubly disadvantaged, since those who should serve them find them so difficult and, sometimes, seemingly impossible to serve.

In this volume we have, with the help of outstanding practitioners in the field, attempted to give some needed information for the counselor so that the job may be more adequately done. There are no easy formulas, however, and no simple solutions; and there is a tremendous amount that we do not know about our clientele and what works with them. In the long run, only the convergent, persistent efforts of all persons of good will and courage in seeking ways of making the good life more readily available to all will accomplish the work that needs to be done.

APPENDIX I

SOURCES
OF OCCUPATIONAL
INFORMATION*

Educational and vocational information can be gleaned in the formal curriculum. Teachers of all grades and subject areas should comprehend the need for career information on their subjects and its practical work relation. The classroom teachers may give information about work and education not only as it happens to come up for discussion, but as an integral part of the subject they teach.

Occupations classes are held in some secondary schools. Their value is enhanced if similar activities have taken place earlier at the elementary school level. Some literature on the introduction of educational and vocational information in the earlier grades seems well worth further exploration. Activities along these lines can be a source of motivation to students as they study. The relation of a subject to the world of work gives it a new and purposeful meaning. Subjects taken in school are related directly to many occupational families. The creative teacher can do much to show the direct importance of a subject studied in school to various jobs and careers.

A study can be made of what jobs have been attained by youngsters who have graduated, and what courses were most helpful. There are many ways of showing the direct and indirect relations between subject and occupations. Practical applications of a subject and how it relates to

* Compiled by S. Norman Feingold.

369

the world of work can and does give meaning. A subject should not stand in isolation, unrelated to other subjects or to the world of work. It is particularly inappropriate for education and learning on the part of culturally deprived youth.

Young people approaching their teens want to know where they will fit in the world of education and the world of work. Familiarity with concepts about the world of work such as education, division of labor, mobility between occupational groups, job satisfaction, etc., help students to gain essential experience. They can then project themselves into new, expanding educational and vocational roles that are available. Teachers of occupations curricula, or teachers of occupations classes, must be particularly creative. They are in a position to maintain a stance toward youth or adults that will release their potentialities and stimulate them toward creative self-development. The activities that take place in an occupations curriculum are based on planning by the teacher and needs of the student.

Presentation of educational and vocational information appears to be an important aspect of the counseling process. The counselor working with the disadvantaged should have a minimum of basic factual information that youth need as they choose jobs and careers in a changing technological society.

Here briefly are a few places where the counselor can acquire local employment information: the state Employment Agency, the U.S. Department of Labor, the U.S. Department of Commerce, the U.S. Chamber of Commerce, the U.S. Bureau of the Census, and various units within the state governments, local boards of education, local industries, unions and headquarters for Red Feather agencies. These are a bare minimum.

Planning local surveys allows the counselor to know what basic local resources are available that may be helpful to youth and adults. Most of these groups have some printed information or a periodical that may be obtained at little or no cost. Local information can be functional. It is one of the basic tools of the counselor who has a working knowledge of his own community. The counselor should have a sophisticated working knowledge of the local telephone directory (particularly the yellow pages). This is a veritable gold mine of career information in every community.

The counselor must also have a working knowledge of local and national sources of occupational information. There are various publications that can be of considerable help. Lists of these publications may be obtained at no cost from the U.S. Departments of Agriculture, Commerce, Health, Education and Welfare, Interior, Labor, State, Treasury, and Defense (including Departments of the Army, Air Force, Navy, and Marine Corps); the U.S. Employment Service, the Women's Bureau, the Civil Service Commission, the National Science Foundation, the Peace

Corps, the President's Committee on Employment of the Handicapped, the President's Committee on Equal Employment Opportunities, the Veterans Administration, and the Small Business Administration. Many private publishers, too, publish books and pamphlets on careers, and they all distribute a free catalog of their publications. Educational and occupational information may be procured at little or no cost from the following national organizations. A brief, selected list for counselors is as follows:

Alumnae Advisory Center, Street and Smith Publications, 541 Madison Avenue, New York, N.Y. 10022.

American Chemical Society, 1155–16th Street, N.W., Washington, D.C. 20036.

American Council on Education, 1785 Massachusetts Avenue, N.W., Washington, D.C. 20036.

American Dental Association, Council on Education, 222 East Superior Street, Chicago, Ill. 60611.

American Dental Hygienists' Association, 100 East Ohio Street, Chicago, Ill. 60611.

American Dietetic Association, 620 North Michigan Avenue, Chicago, Ill. 60611.

American Federation of Labor & Congress of Industrial Organizations, 815–16th Street, N.W., Washington, D.C. 20006.

American Institute of Biological Sciences, 2000 P Street, N.W., Washington, D.C. 20036.

American Library Association, 50 East Huron Street, Chicago, Ill. 60611.

American Meteorological Society, 45 Beacon Street, Boston, Mass. 02108.

American Occupational Therapy Association, 250 West 57th Street, New York, N.Y. 10019.

American Pharmaceutical Association, 2215 Constitution Avenue, N.W., Washington, D.C. 20037.

American Society for Engineering Education, University of Illinois, Urbana, Ill. 61803.

American Society of Pharmacology, 9650 Wisconsin Avenue, Washington, D.C. 20014.

American Society of X-Ray Technicians, 16–14th Street, Fond du Lac, Wis. 54935.

American Statistical Association, 810–18th Street, N.W., Washington, D.C. 20006.

American Textile Manufacturers Institute, Inc., 1501 Johnson Building, Charlotte, N.C. 28202.

American Trucking Association, 1616 P Street, N.W., Washington, D.C.

American Veterinary Medical Association, 600 South Michigan Avenue, Chicago, Ill. 60605.

Association of Casualty and Surety Companies, 60 John Street, New York, N.Y. 10038.

Bellman Publishing Co., Post Office Box 172, Cambridge, Mass. 02138.

B'nai B'rith Vocational Service, 1640 Rhode Island Avenue, N.W., Washington, D.C. 20036.

Bureau of Labor Statistics, U.S. Department of Labor, Washington, D.C., 20210. (For free publications only. For priced publications released by the Bureau, send check or money order to the Superintendent of Documents at the address shown below.)

Careers, Largo, Florida. 33540.

Charles Pfizer & Co., Inc., 11 Bartlett Street, Brooklyn, N.Y. 11206.

Chronicle Guidance Publications, Inc., Moravia, N.Y. 13118.

Columbia University Press, 2960 Broadway, New York, N.Y. 10027.

Council on Social Work Education, 345 East 46th Street, New York, N.Y. 10017.

Dartnell Press, 4660 Ravenswood Avenue and Leland, Chicago, Ill. 60640.

David McKay Co., Inc., 750 Third Avenue, New York, N.Y. 10017.

Dental Hygienists' Alumni Association, Columbia University, New York, N.Y. 10027.

Department of Employment, State of California, Sacramento, Calif. 95814.

General Motors Corp., Department of Public Relations, 3044 West Grand Boulevard, Detroit, Mich. 48202.

Guidance Center, Ontario College of Education, 371 Bloor Street, West Toronto 5, Ont., Canada.

Indiana University Bulletin, Indiana University, 10th and Morton Streets, Bloomington, Ind. 47405.

Institute of Life Insurance, 488 Madison Avenue, New York, N.Y. 10022.

Julian Messner, 8 West 40th Street, New York, N.Y. 10018.

Los Angeles Junior College of Business, 1601 South Olive Street, Los Angeles, Calif. 90015.

Los Angeles Trade-Technical Junior College, 400 West Washington Boulevard, Los Angeles, Calif. 90015.

Manhattan College, 4513 Manhattan College Parkway, Riverdale, N.Y. 10471.

Manufacturing Chemists Association, 1825 Connecticut Avenue, N.W., Washington, D.C. 20009.

Michigan College of Mining and Technology, Houghton, Michigan. 49931.

Michigan Employment Security Commission, 7310 Woodward Avenue, Detroit, Mich. 48202.

National Association of Manufacturers, 277 Park Avenue, New York, N.Y. 10017.

National Association for Practical Nurse Education, 475 Riverside Drive, New York, N.Y. 10027.

National Education Association, 1201–16th Street, N.W., Washington, D.C. 20036.

National League for Nursing, Committee on Careers, 10 Columbus Circle, New York, N.Y. 10019.

National Science Teachers Association, National Education Association, 1201–16th Street, N.W., Washington, D.C. 20036.

National Science Teachers Association, Project on Information Processing, Box 201, Montclair State College, Upper Montclair, N.J. 07043.

New York Life Insurance Co., 51 Madison Avenue, New York, N.Y. 10010.

Park Publishing House, 4141 West Vliet Street, Milwaukee, Wis. 53208.

Personnel Services, Inc., Post Office Box 306, Jaffrey, N.H. 03452.

Public Health Service, U.S. Department of Health, Education and Welfare, Washington, D.C. 20201. (For free publications only. For priced publications released by this agency, send check or money order to the Superintendent of Documents at the address shown below.)

Registry of Medical Technologists, American Society of Clinical Pathologists, Post Office Box 44, Muncie, Ind. 47305.

Richard Rosen Press, Inc., 29 East 21st Street, New York, N.Y. 10010.

Science Research Associates, Inc., 259 East Erie Street, Chicago, Ill. 60611.

Society for Industrial and Applied Mathematics, Post Office Box 7541, Philadelphia, Pa. 19101.

State Guidance Service, 503 Library Building, Salem, Ore. 97301.

Superintendent of Documents, U.S. Government Printing Office, Washington, D.C. 20402.

United Air Lines, Stapleton Airfield, Denver, Colo. 80207.

University of Missouri, School of Mines and Metallurgy, Rolla, Mo. 65401.

Upjohn Co., Employment Office, 301 Henrietta Street, Kalamazoo, Mich. 49006.

Educational information may be obtained from professional and trade societies and associations. A sample list may be found at the end of this appendix. Local research will provide many more books and pamphlets on counseling the disadvantaged.

RELATING EDUCATIONAL AND OCCUPATIONAL
INFORMATION TO THE CURRICULUM

The emerging, new role of vocational education in the guidance of young people and adults at times needs clarification. The function of vocational education is not to create job opportunities; it is to provide training opportunities appropriate for jobs and careers that exist. This activity has taken place in the United States for more than half a century. Guidance, education, and training of youth must be undertaken with a knowledge of a changing, automated, technological society. Skilled TV repairmen, like typewriter and auto mechanics, are hard to find. We will have even fewer such skilled personnel unless youth and adults receive education and training that is adequate for the times—not training in obsolete skills.

Every worthwhile education program contains a vocational element as well as a cultural one. The United States has been characterized by a very mobile population. Every indication is that career mobility experiences will increase and become even more noticeable in the decades ahead.

During the period of March 1960 to March 1961, over 35 million persons above the age of 1, or 1 out of 5 persons in the population, had moved. More than 11 million people had moved from one county to another or from one state to another. The average family moves eight times. Half of American children are now living in a community different from that in which they were born. A high proportion of these moves involve shifts in employment and schools, and significant personal changes based on each individual family's relocation. Statistics also show that nonwhites are more mobile than whites. Many of the large number of people who now live on subsistence-level farms belong to minority groups; they are primarily Negroes, but also Mexican-Americans and American Indians.

Members of minority groups are handicapped in at least three ways. Some of their behavioral attributes impede their acceptance by the dominant population, which factor makes their search for employment more difficult. Secondly, many of these groups are migrants. The migrant always faces special difficulties in adjustment as he attempts to shed earlier patterns of adjustment and acquire others to meet a new environment. Thirdly, members of minority groups tend to come from environments that do not facilitate access to the wide range of educational and vocational opportunities available in the communities in which they settle. This places them at a further disadvantage both in school and on the labor market.

In society's present state of technological advance, employers prefer workers—whether of middle class or disadvantaged parentage—who can not only perform their immediate tasks, but can learn quickly to operate new equipment or adapt to new functions. Employees need varying skills that also must change in order to meet changing conditions. A girl who can shift easily from check sorter to key punch operator, to tape punch operator, to code-and-edit clerk, is likely to be continually employed by one firm, or in demand by others. The same is true for a young man who can read a bill of lading, follow instructions for truck loading, use judgment on the size of all loads, and exercise caution in handling fragile articles. Such an individual will probably be a good candidate for operator of a fork lift, or any other mechanized equipment when it is introduced by his employer.

The day of the laborer who can offer only a strong body and brute strength has passed. Without flexibility, adaptability, and mobility, he will soon join ranks of the unemployed. Mechanized equipment gradually takes over in an automated society. For many of the disadvantaged, it means starting a second career shortly after the first has begun. The role of counseling is obviously in the center of the arena of helping meet changing times with creative adjustment.

We must realize, too, that many once-flourishing occupations are in a state of decline. The 1960 Census of Population, for example, lists more than 80 occupations, many of them at the skilled level, in which employment has declined since 1950. Examples of these are: loom fixers, cabinet makers, paperhangers, locomotive engineers, shoe repairmen, plasterers, boilermakers, tailors, furriers, stonecutters, and some highly skilled trades personnel.

The ubiquitous Post Office Department may be an appropriate model for presenting educational and occupational information. The mailman is probably the one civil servant with whom almost every adult and child comes into contact. Children's books at pre-primer level have been written about the post office. The local post office is always most cooperative in arranging tours. There is one caveat. To obtain the most value out of a field visit to the post office at any age level, pre-school to high school, meet first with the postmaster or his designated representative. If you tell him the age group of your children and what you hope to accomplish from the trip, he will be able to provide some information to develop with your children before the trip. A visit to the post office is no exception to the rule that all field trips should be prepared for in advance.

The post office has several other advantages besides accessibility. It employs, at most job levels, large numbers of persons of minority groups, thus supplying living models—members of minority groups who are moving upward. The post office offers a wide range of jobs and requires many practical skills of its employees, not the least of which is reading the Postal Directory Code. The counselor and teacher will be surprised at the Code's difficulty. The writer suspects that the range of jobs in the Post Office is wider than most counselors realize. Further, since post offices are being automated, the Superintendent can tell about the changes in employee requirements; and he can probably demonstrate them in his own post office. Another advantage to using the Post Office Department as a source of educational and occupational information is continuity. Meaningful programs may be developed for every age group. For high school age students, the post office is a rich source of part-time and temporary jobs at Christmastime and during summer. Obtaining such part-time jobs can become a goal toward which the students work. What personal traits must they have? What forms must be filled out? How should they dress when they apply for a job? An excellent byproduct of such inquiries might be an attempt to find out what job specialities are employed.

Obviously, the Post Office Department cannot meet the employment needs of all students in a given area; nor will all students want a postal career or job.

ASSESSMENT OF EDUCATIONAL AND OCCUPATIONAL MATERIAL

The counselor needs some help in evaluating the mass of occupational and educational information published annually. G. S. Speer and L. Jasker reported that suitability of occupational choice is improved by work experience, or by guided reading discussed with a counselor.[1] The best choice involves a combination of both methods. Studies at B'nai B'rith Vocational offices point up that a combination of many methods of presenting educational and occupational information offers the most promising results.

Brayfield and Reed analyzed the interest value and difficulty level of 78 samples of occupational literature from the list of those publishers. Almost two thirds ranked at the very difficult, or scientific, level; 32 per cent fell into the difficult classification; approximately the same proportion fell into the dull and mildly interesting categories. Less than 5 per cent were at the reading level of popular national magazines.[2]

Brayfield and Mickelson summarized approximately 6000 references listed in two different indices of occupational materials. The purpose was to ascertain how adequately titles covered the diverse levels of the world

[1] G. S. Speer and L. Jasker, "The Influence of Occupational Information on Occupational Goals," *Occupations,* **28** (1949), 15-17.
[2] A. H. Brayfield and P. A. Reed, "How Readable Are Occupational Information Booklets?" *Journal of Applied Psychology,* **34** (1950), 325-328.

of work in the United States. They discovered that the occupational literature is far too greatly concentrated in white collar and professional fields of endeavor; thus the types of endeavor in which the majority of workers find their life's work receive short shrift.[3]

Watson, Rundquist, and Cottle utilized two readability formulas to evaluate *Occupational Outlook Quarterly*, and three other samples of occupational information selected at random from twelve publishers. Their findings disclosed that most of the material was at the eleventh or twelfth grade level. This is, of course, too difficult for many high school students, and for nearly all of the culturally deprived.[4] At present, efforts are being made to lower the readability levels of all educational and occupational material. This factor is also being considered when new matter is prepared for the elementary and high school levels.

With a wide variety of educational and occupational literature available, a counselor must have standards for judging its relevancy and adequacy. The counselor often recommends what career materials are to be purchased. He can do this intelligently only if he understands how to select helpful material that meets basic professional standards. Special committees of the National Vocational Guidance Association prepared a report, *Standards for Use in Preparing and Evaluating Occupational Literature*. This is an essential guideline for the counselor.[5]

Several publications present annotated reviews and evaluations of current occupational and educational material. They are the *Counselor's Information Service*, published by B'nai B'rith Vocational Service; the *Bibliography of Guidance Materials*, published by the National Vocational Guidance Association, and the *Scholarships, Fellowships and Loans News Service*, published by the Bellman Publishing Company.

SOURCES OF CAREER INFORMATION FOR COUNSELORS

Accounting

American Institute of Certified Public
Accountants'
666 Fifth Avenue
New York, N.Y. 10019

Comptrollers Institute of America
3 Park Avenue
New York, N.Y. 10016

National Association of Accountants
505 Park Avenue
New York, N.Y. 10022

The Institute of Internal Auditors
120 Wall Street
New York, N.Y. 10005

United Business Schools Association
1518 K Street, N.W.
Washington, D.C. 20005

---

[3] A. H. Brayfield and G. T. Mickelson, "Disparities in Occupational Information Coverage," *Occupations*, 29 (1951), 506-508.

[4] D. E. Watson, R. M. Rundquist, and W. C. Cottle, "What's Wrong With Occupational Materials?" *Journal of Counseling Psychology*, 6 (1959), 288-291.

[5] *Guidelines for Preparing and Evaluating Occupational Materials* (Washington, D.C.: National Vocational Guidance Association, 1964).

SOURCES OF CAREER INFORMATION FOR COUNSELORS (*continued*)

Actuary

Career Information Service
New York Life Insurance Co.
Box 51, Madison Square Station
New York, N.Y. 10010

Casualty Actuarial Society
200 East 42 Street
New York, N.Y. 10017

Society of Actuaries
208 South LaSalle Street
Chicago, Ill. 60644

Advertising

Advertising Federation of America
655 Madison Avenue
New York, N.Y. 10022

American Association of Advertising
Agencies
420 Lexington Avenue
New York, N.Y. 10017

Association of National Advertisers
155 East 44th Street
New York, N.Y. 10017

Career Information Service
New York Life Insurance Co.
Box 51, Madison Square Station
New York, N.Y. 10010

Aeronautical Technology

Academy of Aeronautics
La Guardia Airport Station
Flushing, N.Y. 11371

National Council of Technical Schools
1507 M Street, N.W.
Washington, D.C. 20005

Aerospace Technology

National Aeronautics and Space
Administration
Washington, D.C. 20546

Agriculture

U.S. Department of Agriculture
Office of Personnel
Washington, D.C. 20250

Agricultural Engineering

American Society of Agricultural
Engineering
420 Main Street
St. Joseph, Mich. 49085

Agronomy

The American Society of Agronomy
677 South Segoe Road
Madison, Wis. 53711

Air Transportation

United Air Lines, Inc.
School & College Service
P.O. Box 8800
Chicago, Ill. 60666

Airlines

Air Transport Association of America
1000 Connecticut Avenue, N.W.
Washington, D.C. 20036

Airline Stewardess

American Airlines, Inc.
Mgr., Flight Recruitment
Dallas Love Field
Dallas, Tex. 75235

United Air Lines, Inc.
Stewardess Recruitment Section
P.O. Box 8775
Chicago, Ill. 60666

American Red Cross

American National Red Cross
Personnel
Washington, D.C. 20006

Anthropologist

American Anthropological Association
1530 P Street, N.W.
Washington, D.C. 20005

American Sociological Association
New York University
Washington Square
New York, N.Y. 10012

Apparel Design

Fashion Institute of Technology
227 West 27 Street
New York, N.Y. 10001

Apparel Communications
Fashion Institute of Technology
227 West 27 Street
New York, N.Y. 10001

Apparel Management
Fashion Institute of Technology
227 West 27 Street
New York, N.Y. 10001

Apparel Merchandising
Fashion Institute of Technology
227 West 27 Street
New York, N.Y. 10001

Apprenticeship
Bureau of Apprenticeship and
    Training
U.S. Department of Labor
Washington, D.C. 20210

Archaeologist
American Anthropological Association
1530 P Street, N.W.
Washington, D.C. 20005

American Historical Association
400 A Street, S.E.
Washington, D.C. 20003

Architect
The American Institute of Architects
1735 New York Avenue, N.W.
Washington, D.C. 20006

Architecture and Building Construction Technology
National Council of Technical Schools
1507 M Street, N.W.
Washington, D.C. 20005

Astronomy
American Astronomical Society
211 FitzRandolph Road
Princeton, N.J. 08540

Atomic Scientist
Career Information Service
New York Life Insurance Company
Box 51, Madison Square Station
New York, N.Y. 10010

Automotive, Business, Retail
Educational Relations Section
Public Relations Staff
General Motors Corporation
Detroit, Mich. 48202

Automotive, Diesel
U.S. Trade Schools
500 East Eleventh Street
Kansas City, Mo. 64106

Automotive Mechanic
U.S. Trade Schools
500 East Eleventh Street
Kansas City, Mo. 64106

Aviation Hostesses
Trans World Air Lines
10 Richard Road
Kansas City, Mo. 64105

Eastern Air Lines
Miami International Airport
Miami, Fla. 33148

Bacteriologist
American Institute of Biological
    Sciences
2000 P Street, N.W.
Washington, D.C. 20005

Federation of American Societies for
    Experimental Biology
9650 Wisconsin Avenue, N.W.
Washington, D.C. 20007

Bacteriology and Microbiology
American Society of Microbiology
115 Huronview Boulevard
Ann Arbor, Mich. 48103

Baking Industry
American Bakers Association
200 North Wacker Drive
Chicago, Ill. 60606

Banking
The American Bankers Association
90 Park Avenue
New York, N.Y. 10016

Sources of Career Information for Counselors (*continued*)

Barber
National Association of Barber
  Schools, Inc.
750 Third Avenue
Huntington, W. Va. 25701

Beauty Culture
National Association of Cosmetology
  Schools
3839 White Plains Road
New York, N.Y. 10067

Biologist
American Institute of Biological
  Sciences
2000 P Street, N.W.
Washington, D.C. 20005

Career Information Service
New York Life Insurance Company
Box 51, Madison Square Station
New York, N.Y. 10010

Federation of American Societies for
  Experimental Biology
9650 Wisconsin Avenue, N.W.
Washington, D.C. 20007

Office of Personnel
U.S. Department of Agriculture
Washington, D.C. 20250

Employment Officer
U.S. Department of Health, Education
  and Welfare
National Institutes of Health
Bethesda, Md. 20014

Biophysicist
American Institute of Biological
  Sciences
2000 P Street, N.W.
Washington, D.C. 20005

Federation of American Societies for
  Experimental Biology
9650 Wisconsin Avenue, N.W.
Washington, D.C. 20007

Department of Biophysics
Pennsylvania State University
University Park, Pa. 16802

Body and Fender Repair
U.S. Trade Schools
500 East Eleventh Street
Kansas City, Mo. 64106

Botanist
American Institute of Biological
  Sciences
2000 P Street, N.W.
Washington, D.C. 20005

Boys' Clubs
Boys' Clubs of America
771 First Avenue
New York, N.Y. 10017

Boy Scouting
Boy Scouts of America
Personnel Division
National Council
New Brunswick, N.J. 08903

Business Schools
United Business Schools Association
1518 K Street, N.W.
Washington, D.C. 20005

Business for Yourself
Career Information Service
New York Life Insurance Co.
Box 51, Madison Square Station
New York, N.Y. 10010

Camp Fire Girls
Camp Fire Girls, Inc.
65 Worth Street
New York, N.Y. 10013

Chamber of Commerce Management
American Chamber of Commerce
  Executives
1627 K Street, N.W., Suite 315
Washington, D.C. 20006

*Chamber of Commerce and Trade
  Association*
Head, Management Department
College of Business
Oklahoma State University
Stillwater, Okla. 74074

Chemical Engineer
American Institute of Chemical
Engineers
345 East 47th Street
New York, N.Y. 10017

Chemist
American Chemical Society
1155–16th Street, N.W.
Washington, D.C. 20036

Manufacturing Chemists Association,
Inc.
1825 Connecticut Avenue, N.W.
Washington, D.C. 20009

Chiropodist
American Podiatry Association
3301–16th Street, N.W.
Washington, D.C. 20010

Chiropractor
American Chiropractic Association
Department of Information Services
P.O. Box 1535
Des Moines, Iowa 50306

International Chiropractors
Association
741 Brady Street
Davenport, Iowa 52803

National Chiropractic Association
National Building
Webster, Iowa 52335

City and Regional Planner
Career Information Service
New York Life Insurance Company
Box 51, Madison Square Station
New York, N.Y. 10010

Civil Engineering Technology
National Council of Technical Schools
1507 M Street, N.W.
Washington, D.C. 20005

Civil Engineer
American Society of Civil Engineers
United Engineering Center
345 East 47th Street
New York, N.Y. 10017

Civilian Specialist
Department of the Army
Office of Civilian Personnel, EMD-SS
Interchange & Recruitment Coordina-
tion Branch
Old Post Office Building
12th and Pennsylvania Avenue, N.W.
Washington, D.C. 20315

Civil Service Careers
U.S. Civil Service Commission
Bureau of Recruiting and Examining
Washington, D.C. 20415

Clergyman
National Council of the Churches of
Christ in the U.S.A.
Department of the Ministry
475 Riverside Drive
New York, N.Y. 10027

Serra International
Catholic Religious Vocations
22 West Monroe Street, Room 500
Chicago, Ill. 60603

Synagogue Council of America
235 Fifth Avenue
New York, N.Y. 10016

Clerical
United Business Schools Association
1518 K Street, N.W.
Washington, D.C. 20005

Coal Industry
National Coal Association
Coal Building
1130–17th Street, N.W.
Washington, D.C. 20036

Community Organization
United Community Funds & Councils
of America
345 East 46th Street
New York, N.Y. 10017

Commercial Artist
National Association of Schools of Art
50 Astor Place
New York, N.Y. 10003

Commercial Artist (cont.)
National Society of Art Directors
115 East 40 Street
New York, N.Y. 10016

Construction Business
Career Information Service
New York Life Insurance Company
Box 51, Madison Square Station
New York, N.Y. 10010

Cosmetology
National Association of Cosmetology
Schools
3839 White Plains Road
New York, N.Y. 10067

National Hairdressers and Cosmetologists Association, Inc.
175 Fifth Avenue
New York, N.Y. 10010

Counseling
Career Information Service
New York Life Insurance Company
Box 51, Madison Square Station
New York, N.Y. 10010

Craftsman
General Motors Corporation
Educational Relations Section
Public Relations Staff
Detroit, Mich. 48202

Crop Science
The American Society of Agronomy
677 South Segoe Road
Madison, Wis. 53711

Dairy Industry
Purdue University
Department of Animal Sciences
Lafayette, Ind. 47907

Dental Assistant
American Dental Assistants
Association
410 First National Bank Building
LaPorte, Ind. 46350

Dental Hygienist
American Dental Hygienists
Association
100 East Ohio Street
Chicago, Ill. 60611

Dental Laboratory Technician
American Dental Association, Council
on Dental Education
222 East Superior Street
Chicago, Ill. 60611

National Association of Dental
Laboratories
1330 Massachusetts Avenue, N.W.
Washington, D.C. 20005

Dentist
American Dental Association
211 East Chicago Avenue
Chicago, Ill. 60611

Designer
APPAREL
Amalgamated Clothing Workers of
America
15 Union Square
New York, N.Y. 10011

Clothing Manufacturers Association
of U.S.A.
230 Fifth Avenue
New York, N.Y. 10010

International Ladies' Garment
Workers' Union
1710 Broadway
New York, N.Y. 10036

United Garment Workers of America
31 Union Square
New York, N.Y. 10011

INDUSTRIAL
American Society of Industrial
Designers
15 East 48 Street
New York, N.Y. 10017

Industrial Designers' Institute
441 Madison Avenue
New York, N.Y. 10017

INTERIOR

American Institute of Interior
  Designers
673 Fifth Avenue
New York, N.Y. 10022

National Society of Interior Designers,
  Inc.
157 West 57 Street, Suite 700
New York, N.Y. 10019

Dietitian

American Dietetic Association
620 N. Michigan Avenue
Chicago, Ill. 60611

Diesel Technology

National Council of Technical Schools
1507 M Street, N.W.
Washington, D.C. 20005

Doctor

Council on Medical Education and
  Hospitals
American Medical Association
535 Dearborn Street
Chicago, Ill. 60610

Association of American Medical
  Colleges
2530 Ridge Avenue
Evanston, Ill. 60201

Drafting

National Council of Technical Schools
1507 M Street, N.W.
Washington, D.C. 20005

Draftsman

American Federation of Technical
  Engineers
900 F Street, N.W.
Washington, D.C. 20004

General Motors Corporation
Educational Relations Section
Public Relations Staff
Detroit, Mich. 48202

Economist

American Economic Association
Northwestern University
Evanston, Ill. 60201

National Council of Technical Schools
1507 M Street, N.W.
Washington, D.C. 20005

Electrical Power Technology

National Council of Technical Schools
1507 M Street, N.W.
Washington, D.C. 20005

Electronics

Electronic Industries Association
2001 Eye Street, N.W.
Washington, D.C. 20006

DeVry Technical Institute
4141 Belmont Avenue
Chicago, Ill. 60641

National Council of Technical Schools
1507 M Street, N.W.
Washington, D.C. 20005

Electronic Computer Programming

Career Information Service
New York Life Insurance Company
Box 51, Madison Square Station
New York, N.Y. 10010

Electronic Data Processing

Project on Information Processing
Box 201, Montclair College
Upper Montclair, N.J. 07043

Engineer

American Society of Civil Engineers
345 East 47th Street
New York, N.Y. 10017

American Society for Engineering
  Education
Technical Institute Division
University of Illinois
Urbana, Ill. 61801

American Society of Mechanical
  Engineers
345 East 47 Street
New York, N.Y. 10017

American Ceramic Society
4055 North High Street
Columbus, Ohio, 43214

SOURCES OF CAREER INFORMATION FOR COUNSELORS (*continued*)

Engineer (*cont.*)
American Institute of Chemical
Engineers
345 East 47 Street
New York, N.Y. 10017

American Institute of Electrical
Engineers
345 East 47 Street
New York, N.Y. 10017

American Institute of Industrial
Engineers
145 North High Street
Columbus, Ohio 43215

American Institute of Mining, Metal-
lurgical and Petroleum Engineers
345 East 47 Street
New York, N.Y. 10017

General Motors Corporation
Educational Relations Section
Public Relations Staff
Detroit, Mich. 48202

Engineers Council for Professional
Development
345 East 47 Street
New York, N.Y. 10017

Engineers Joint Council
345 East 47 Street
New York, N.Y. 10017

National Society of Professional
Engineers
2029 K Street, N.W.
Washington, D.C. 20006

Institute of the Aerospace Sciences,
Inc.
2 East 64 Street
New York, N.Y. 10021

Scientific Manpower Commission
2101 Constitution Avenue, N.W.
Washington, D.C. 20418

Engineering Technician
American Association of Junior
Colleges
1785 Massachusetts Avenue, N.W.
Washington, D.C. 20036

American Society for Engineering
Education
Technical Institute Division
University of Illinois
Urbana, Ill. 61801

Engineers Council for Professional
Development
345 East 47 Street
New York, N.Y. 10017

National Council of Technical Schools
1507 M Street, N.W.
Washington, D.C. 20005

Farming
B. F. Goodrich Company
500 S. Main Street
Akron, Ohio 44318

U.S. Department of Agriculture
Division of Information
Washington, D.C. 20250

F.B.I.
Federal Bureau of Investigation
Department of Justice
Washington, D.C. 20535

Federal Government Service
U.S. Civil Service Commission
Washington, D.C. 20415

Fine and Graphic Arts
The Cooper Union for the Advance-
ment of Science and Art
Cooper Square
New York, N.Y. 10003

Food Industry
National Association of Food Chains
Educational Council
1725 Eye Street, N.W.
Washington, D.C. 20006

Food Manager
HOTEL
American Hotel and Motel Association
221 West 57 Street
New York, N.Y. 10019

Council on Hotel, Restaurant, and
Institutional Education
Statler Hall, Cornell University
Ithaca, N.Y. 14815

RESTAURANT

Council on Hotel, Restaurant, and
Institutional Education
Statler Hall, Cornell University
Ithaca, N.Y. 14815

Educational Director, National
Restaurant Association
1530 North Lake Shore Drive
Chicago, Ill. 60610

Food Technology

Institute of Food Technologists
Scholarship Center
176 West Adams Street
Chicago, Ill. 60603

Foreign Languages

Occupational Outlook Service
U.S. Department of Labor
Washington, D.C. 20212

Foreign Service

Director, College Relations Staff
Department of State
2201 C Street, N.W.
Washington, D.C. 20520

Forester

American Forest Products Industries,
Inc.
1816 N Street, N.W.
Washington, D.C. 20036

Forest Service
Department of Agriculture
Washington, D.C. 20250

National Lumber Manufacturers
Association
1319–18th Street, N.W.
Washington, D.C. 20036

Society of American Foresters
425 Mills Building
17th Street and Pennsylvania Avenue,
N.W.
Washington, D.C. 20006

Funeral Service

National Association of Colleges of
Mortuary Science, Inc.
Broadway at 71st Street
New York, N.Y. 10023

Geography

Denoyer-Geppert Company
5235 Ravenswood Avenue
Chicago, Ill. 60640

Geological Sciences

American Geological Institute
1444 N Street, N.W.
Washington, D.C. 20005

Geologist

American Geological Institute
1444 N Street, N.W.
Washington, D.C. 20005

Geophysicist

American Geophysical Union
1145–19th Street, N.W.
Washington, D.C. 20036

Society of Exploration Geophysicists
Box 1536
Tulsa, Oklahoma 74101

Girl Scouting

Girl Scouts of U.S.A.
830 Third Avenue
New York, N.Y. 10022

Health Education

American Association of H.P.E.&R.
1201–16th Street, N.W.
Washington, D.C. 20036

Metropolitan Life Insurance Company
Health and Welfare Division
1 Madison Avenue
New York, N.Y. 10010

Health Physics

Atomic Energy Commission
Oak Ridge Institute for Nuclear
Studies
Oak Ridge, Tenn. 37831

SOURCES OF CAREER INFORMATION FOR COUNSELORS (*continued*)

Heavy Equipment Operator
National School of Heavy Equipment
Operation
P.O. Box 8529
Charlotte, N.C. 28208

Historian
American Historical Association
400 A Street, S.E.
Washington, D.C. 20003

Home Economist
American Home Economics
Association
1800–20th Street, N.W.
Washington, D.C. 20009

Hospital Administration
American College of Hospital
Administrators
840 North Lake Shore Drive
Chicago, Ill. 60611

Hotel Administration
Council on Hotel, Restaurant, and
Institutional Education
Statler Hall, Cornell University
Ithaca, N.Y. 14815
The Educational Institute of the
American Hotel & Motel Association
221 West 57th Street
New York, N.Y. 10019

Industrial Engineering Technology
National Council of Technical Schools
1507 M Street, N.W.
Washington, D.C. 20005

Industrial Hygiene
Atomic Energy Commission
Oak Ridge Institute for Nuclear
Studies
Oak Ridge, Tenn. 37831

Insurance
Institute of Life Insurance
488 Madison Avenue
New York, N.Y. 10022

Insurance Information Institute
110 William Street
New York, N.Y. 10005

Internal Auditing
The Institute of Internal Auditors
60 Wall Street
New York, N.Y. 10005

Journalism
School of Journalism
University of Missouri
Columbia, Mo. 65201

Laboratory Assistant
Board of Certified Laboratory
Assistants
9500 South California Avenue
Evergreen Park, Ill. 60642

Law Enforcement
Career Information Service
New York Life Insurance Company
Box 51, Madison Square Station
New York, N.Y. 10010
Director, Personnel Division
Internal Revenue Service
U.S. Treasury Department
12th and Constitution Avenue, N.W.
Washington, D.C. 20224

Lawyer
American Bar Association
1155 East 60th Street
Chicago, Ill. 60637

Legal Secretary
United Business Schools Association
1518 K Street, N.W.
Washington, D.C. 20005

Librarian
American Library Association
50 East Huron Street
Chicago, Ill. 60611

Linotyping
New York Mergenthaler Linotype
School
244 West 23rd Street
New York, N.Y. 10011

Management
United Business Schools Association
1518 K Street, N.W.
Washington, D.C. 20005

Manufacturing Engineer
Career Information Service
New York Life Insurance Company
Box 51, Madison Square Station
New York, N.Y. 10010

Marketing
Sales and Marketing
Executives-International
Youth Education Department
630 Third Avenue
New York, N.Y. 10017

Material Handling
The Material Handling Institute, Inc.
Gateway Towers, Gateway Center
Pittsburgh, Pa. 15222

Mathematician
American Mathematical Society
190 Hope Street
Providence, R.I. 02906

Mathematical Association of America
University of Buffalo
Buffalo, N.Y. 14214

National Council of Teachers of
    Mathematics
1201–16th Street, N.W.
Washington, D.C. 20036

Mechanical Technology
National Council of Technical Schools
1507 M Street, N.W.
Washington, D.C. 20005

Medical Record Librarian
American Association of Medical
    Record Librarians
840 North Lake Shore Drive
Chicago, Ill. 60611

Medical Technologist
Registry of Medical Technologists
American Society of Clinical
    Pathologists
P.O. Box 2544
Muncie, Ind. 47302

American Society of Medical
    Technologists
Hermann Professional Building,
    Suite 25
Houston, Tex. 77025

Medicine
American Medical Association
535 North Dearborn Street
Chicago, Ill. 60610

Medical X-Ray Technician
American Registry of X-Ray
    Technicians
2600 Wayzata Boulevard
Minneapolis, Minn. 55405

Mental Health Careers
National Association for Mental
    Health
10 Columbus Circle
New York, N.Y. 10019

Meteorologist
American Meteorological Society
45 Beacon Street
Boston, Mass. 02108

Mining Engineer
National Coal Association
Coal Building
1130–17th Street, N.W.
Washington, D.C. 20036

Mineral Industry
Chief, Division of Personnel
Bureau of Mines
U.S. Department of the Interior
Washington, D.C. 20240

Motel Administration
American Hotel and Motel Association
221 West 57th Street
New York, N.Y. 10019

Music
Music Educators National Conference
1201–16th Street, N.W.
Washington, D.C. 20036

SOURCES OF CAREER INFORMATION FOR COUNSELORS (*continued*)

National Park Service
Department of the Interior
Career Employment
National Park Service
"C"—18-19th Street, N.W.
Washington, D.C. 20240

Newspaperman
American Newspaper Publishers
 Foundation
750 Third Avenue
New York, N.Y. 10017

The Newspaper Fund, Inc.
44 Broad Street
New York, N.Y. 10005

Nuclear Science and Engineering
Atomic Energy Commission
Oak Ridge Institute for Nuclear
 Studies
Oak Ridge, Tenn. 37831

Nurse
National League for Nursing
10 Columbus Circle
New York, N.Y. 10019

Nurse Anesthetist
American Association of Nurse
 Anesthetists
Prudential Plaza, Suite 3010
Chicago, Ill. 60601

Occupational Therapist
American Occupational Therapy
 Association
250 West 57th Street
New York, N.Y. 10019

Oceanographer
American Society of Limnology and
 Oceanography
Sapelo Island Research Foundation
Sapelo Island, Georgia 51327

Interagency Committee on
 Oceanography
17th Street & Constitution Avenue,
 N.W., Room 1714, Building T-3
Washington, D.C. 20009

Office Worker
General Motors Corporation
Educational Relations Section
Public Relations Staff
Detroit, Mich. 48202

Oil Industry
American Petroleum Institute
1271 Avenue of the Americas
New York, N.Y. 10020

Optometrist
American Optometric Association
700 Chippewa Street
St. Louis, Mo. 63119

Orthoptic
The American Orthoptic Council
4200 North Woodward Avenue
Royal Oak, Mich. 48072

Osteopathy
American Osteopathic Association
212 East Ohio Street
Chicago, Ill. 60611

Paper Industry
American Paper Institute
122 East 42nd Street
New York, N.Y. 10017

Paper Industry Management
 Association
10 North Clark Street
Chicago, Ill. 60602

Pathologist
Career Information Service
New York Life Insurance Company
Box 51, Madison Square Station
New York, N.Y. 10010

Personnel
Career Information Service
New York Life Insurance Company
Box 51, Madison Square Station
New York, N.Y. 10010

Pharmacist
American Pharmaceutical Association
2215 Constitution Avenue, N.W.
Washington, D.C. 20037

Pharmacology
American Society for Pharmacology
and Experimental Therapeutics
9650 Wisconsin Avenue
Bethesda, Md. 20014

Photographer
Professional Photographers of America,
Inc.
152 West Wisconsin Avenue
Milwaukee, Wis. 53203

Physical Education and Coaching
American Association of H.P.E.&R.
1201–16th Street, N.W.
Washington, D.C. 20036

Physical Education for Girls
American Association of H.P.E.&R.
1201–16th Street, N.W.
Washington, D.C. 20036

Physical Therapy
American Physical Therapy
Association
1790 Broadway
New York, N.Y. 10019

Physicist
American Institute of Physics
335 East 45th Street
New York, N.Y. 10017

Physiology
The American Physiological Society
9650 Wisconsin Avenue, N.W.
Washington, D.C. 20014

Pilot, Flight Engineer
Correspondence Inquiry Branch
MS-126, Federal Aviation Agency
Washington, D.C. 20553

Podiatry (Chiropody)
American Podiatry Association
3301–16th Street, N.W.
Washington, D.C. 20010

Political Scientist
American Political Science Association
1726 Massachusetts Avenue, N.W.
Washington, D.C. 20036

Printing Industry
Education Council
Graphic Arts, Inc.
1025–15th Street, N.W.
Washington, D.C. 20005

Production
General Motors Corporation
Educational Relations Section
Public Relations Staff
Detroit, Mich. 48202

Professional Chef and Cook
The Culinary Institute of America,
Inc.
Angell Square, 393 Prospect Street
New Haven, Conn. 06511

Psychiatry
American Psychiatric Association
1700–18th Street, N.W.
Washington, D.C. 20009

Psychiatric Aide
National League for Nursing
10 Columbus Circle
New York, N.Y. 10019

Psychologist
American Psychological Association
1200–17th Street, N.W.
Washington, D.C. 20036

Public Health
Office of Personnel
Public Health Service
Department of Health, Education and
Welfare
Washington, D.C. 20201

Public Relations
Public Relations Society of America,
Inc.
375 Park Avenue
New York, N.Y. 10022

SOURCES OF CAREER INFORMATION FOR COUNSELORS *(continued)*

Public Relations (cont.)
Career Information Service
Public Relations Society of America
845 Third Avenue
New York, N.Y. 10022

Public Servant
Career Information Service
New York Life Insurance Company
Box 51, Madison Square Station
New York, N.Y. 10010

Public Welfare
American Public Welfare Association
1313 East 60th Street
Chicago, Ill. 60637

Purchasing Agent
Career Information Service
New York Life Insurance Company
Box 51, Madison Square Station
New York, N.Y. 10010

Radio
National Association of Broadcasters
1771 N Street, N.W.
Washington, D.C. 20006

Recreation
American Association of H.P.E.&R.
1201–16th Street, N.W.
Washington, D.C. 20036
National Recreation Association
8 West 8th Street
New York, N.Y. 10011

Recreation Therapist
National Recreation Association
Consulting Service on Recreation for
the Ill & Handicapped
8 West 8th Street
New York, N.Y. 10011

Refrigeration, Heating and Air Conditioning Technology
National Council of Technical Schools
1507 M Street, N.W.
Washington, D.C. 20005

Rehabilitation Services
Career Information Service
New York Life Insurance Company
Box 51, Madison Square Station
New York, N.Y. 10010

Retailing
Career Information Service
New York Life Insurance Company
Box 51, Madison Square Station
New York, N.Y. 10010

Safety Education
American Association of H.P.E.&R.
1201–16th Street, N.W.
Washington, D.C. 20036

Sales and Marketing
Sales and Marketing
Executives-International
Youth Education Department
630 Third Avenue
New York, N.Y. 10017

Salesman
Career Information Service
New York Life Insurance Company
Box 51, Madison Square Station
New York, N.Y. 10010

Sanitary Engineering
Department of Health, Education and
Welfare
Public Health Service
Washington, D.C. 20201

Science
Denoyer-Geppert Company
5235 Ravenswood Avenue
Chicago, Ill. 60640
General Electric Company
Dept. MWH, Educational Relations
Schenectady, N.Y. 12305
Occupational Outlook Service
U.S. Department of Labor
Washington, D.C. 20212
Scientific Manpower Commission
2101 Constitution Avenue, N.W.
Washington, D.C. 20418

Science Teaching
National Science Teachers Association
1201–16th Street, N.W.
Washington, D.C. 20036

Scientist
General Motors Corporation
Educational Relations Section
Public Relations Staff
Detroit, Mich. 48202

Secretary
United Business Schools Association
1518 K Street, N.W.
Washington, D.C. 20005

Social Science
Occupational Outlook Service
U.S. Department of Labor
Washington, D.C. 20212

Social Security Administration
Chief, Employment Branch
Room 1-P-23A, Operations Wing
Social Security Bldg.
6401 Security Boulevard
Baltimore, Md. 21235

Social Worker
Career Information Service
New York Life Insurance Company
Box 51, Madison Square Station
New York, N.Y. 10010

Council on Social Work Education
345 East 46th Street
New York, N.Y. 10017

National Association of Social Workers
95 Madison Avenue
New York, N.Y. 10016

National Commission for Social Work
Careers
345 East 46th Street
New York, N.Y. 10017

Sociologist
American Sociological Association
New York University
Washington Square
New York, N.Y. 10012

Soil Science
The American Society of Agronomy
677 South Segoe Road
Madison, Wis. 53711

Space Scientist
Career Information Service
New York Life Insurance Company
Box 51, Madison Square Station
New York, N.Y. 10010

Special Librarian
Special Libraries Association
31 East 10th Street
New York, N.Y. 10003

Speech and Hearing Disorders
American Speech & Hearing
Association
1001 Connecticut Avenue, N.W.
Washington, D.C. 20036

Statistician
American Statistical Association
810–18th Street, N.W., Suite 700-704
Washington, D.C. 20006

Surveyor
American Congress on Surveying and
Mapping
Woodward Building
Washington, D.C. 20005

American Society of Photogrammetry
44 Leesburg Pike
Falls Church, Va. 22044

Teaching
American Association of University
Professors
1785 Massachusetts Avenue, N.W.
Washington, D.C. 20036

American Council on Education
1785 Massachusetts Avenue, N.W.
Washington, D.C. 20036

Board of Education of your town or
city.

National Association for Retarded
Children, Inc.
420 Lexington Avenue
New York, N.Y. 10017

SOURCES OF CAREER INFORMATION FOR COUNSELORS (*continued*)

Teaching (*cont.*)
National Commission on Teacher Education and Professional Standards
National Education Association
1201–16th Street, N.W.
Washington, D.C. 20036

National Education Association
1201–16th Street, N.W.
Washington, D.C. 20036

State Education Department in the capital of your state.

U.S. Department of Health, Education and Welfare
Washington, D.C. 20201

Technician
General Motors Corporation
Educational Relations Section
Public Relations Staff
Detroit, Mich. 48202

Television
National Association of Broadcasters
1771 N Street, N.W.
Washington, D.C. 20006

Tool and Die
National Tool, Die & Precision
Machining Association
1411 K Street, N.W.
Washington, D.C. 20005

Traffic Management
Academy of Advanced Traffic, Inc.
50 Broadway
New York, N.Y. 10004

Trucking Industry
American Trucking Association, Inc.
1616 P Street, N.W.
Washington, D.C. 20036

United States Air Force Officer
Director of Admissions
United States Air Force Academy
Colorado Springs, Colo. 80912

United States Air Force Reserve Officer
Commandant, Air Force ROTC
Maxwell Air Force Base, Ala. 36112

United States Army Nurse
Army Careers
CONARC
Fort Monroe, Va. 23357

United States Army Officer
Admissions Division
United States Military Academy
West Point, N.Y. 10996

United States Army Reserve Officer
Department of the Army
ROTC Division
Office of Reserve Components
Washington, D.C. 20310

United States Coast Guard Officer
Director of Admissions
United States Coast Guard Academy
New London, Conn. 06320

United States Merchant Marine Officer
Admissions Officer
U.S.M.M. Academy
Kings Point, N.Y. 11024

United States Navy Officer
Chief of Naval Personnel
Navy Department
Washington, D.C. 20370

U.S. Navy-Marine Regular Officer
Chief of Naval Personnel
Department of the Navy
Washington, D.C. 20370

Veterans Administration
Veterans Administration
Department of Medicine and Surgery
Washington, D.C. 20420

Veterinarian

American Veterinary Medical
Association
600 South Michigan Avenue
Chicago, Ill. 60605

Vocational Rehabilitation Administration

Office of Vocational Rehabilitation
Department of Health, Education and
Welfare
Washington, D.C. 20201

Watch Repairing

American Watchmakers Institute
P.O. Box 70, Station A.
Champaign, Ill. 61824

Welding

American Welding Society
345 East 47th Street
New York, N.Y. 10017

Hobart Welding School
Troy, Ohio 45373

X-Ray Technology

American Society of Radiologic
Technologists
537 South Main Street
Fond du Lac, Wis. 54935

Y.M.C.A.

Personnel Services
National Council of Y.M.C.A.'s
291 Broadway
New York, N.Y. 10007

Y.W.C.A.

Personnel Services
National Board of the Y.W.C.A.
600 Lexington Avenue
New York, N.Y. 10022

Youth Services

Career Information Service
New York Life Insurance Company
Box 51, Madison Square Station
New York, N.Y. 10010

CASES

FOR DISCUSSION*

The following cases are included for the purpose of stimulating discussion on the techniques used in counseling disadvantaged youth. Some of the techniques used in these cases illustrate problems or procedures to be avoided, rather than optimal counseling practice. It is hoped that, after thorough and careful discussion, trainees will be able to identify both the "good" and "bad" aspects of the counseling procedures followed in these cases.

Suggested discussion questions are listed after the cases. These questions were designed to encourage discussion of the salient points in the case. The following are general areas suggested for discussion with all cases:

1. Nature and depth of vocational problem or problems involved.

2. Techniques apparently used by the counselor. Discussion should attempt to determine whether different or additional techniques might have been used by the counselor. The reasons for using such techniques, and purposes for using them should be discussed.

3. Appropriateness of tools used, including Interest Check List, GATB or other tests, and references such as *Occupational Outlook Handbook*, should be considered. Other possible suitable tools should be explored and their appropriateness to the particular case considered.

* Reprinted with the permission of the United States Employment Service, U.S. Department of Labor.

4. The effectiveness of the counseling as a whole should be considered in the light of the following:

   a. Depth of exploration by the counselor.

   b. Insight apparently gained by the counselee into his own problems and how to go about solving them.

   c. Suitability of suggested alternate fields of work or courses of action.

   d. Clarity and feasibility of the vocational plan.

   e. Action taken to put the plan into effect.

   f. Validity of the relation between the problem, the information secured about the counselee, and the plan worked out with him.

CASE NARRATIVE NO. 1

Gloria was barely 17 years old when she came to the local office. She completed the sophomore year in high school and was well into the junior year when she decided to quit school. She claimed she had been too ill to take the semester tests; and as a result, she had not received credit for the first semester. She seemed quite discouraged.

The counselor noted Gloria's listless behavior, her unkempt appearance, and her "everybody hates me" attitude. Gloria told the counselor she dropped out of school because her family could not afford to carry her. She wanted a job so she could help out at home. A discussion of her interest indicated mild enthusiasm for typing, but nothing else. Gloria had never had any part-time jobs. As the counseling session proceeded, Gloria became more and more aware that she had nothing to offer an employer.

After Gloria left the office, the counselor contacted the school and Gloria's mother to verify the information. The principal indicated that Gloria's attendance was poor, and that she did poor work, but that she was quiet and unobtrusive. The mother denied the need for financial assistance, and indicated she preferred Gloria to either stay in high school or transfer to a business school.

On her next visit to the counselor, Gloria took the typing test and scored below average in speed and accuracy. This really discouraged her. The counselor then explored the possibility of Gloria's return to school to gain additional skills. Gloria was reluctant but felt obligated to try because of her mother's insistence. The high school refused re-entry. Gloria's mother then enrolled her in a business school, but she withdrew after only three days. Back at the local office, she requested to see the counselor.

A job order search yielded a substandard order for a one-girl office. The job required a person to answer the telephone, and do minimal filing and typing. The counselor asked Gloria if she would be interested. She was. Then the counselor became quite directive regarding Gloria's appearance. Did she think an employer would be interested in someone whose hair needed combing and whose clothes needed cleaning and pressing? Gloria agreed to go home and return to the office the following morning, fresh and ready to go job hunting.

The following morning Gloria arrived early. Her appearance had improved but still left much to be desired. However, for the moment Gloria's attitude was changed. She was not as listless or as negative as she had been. The counselor decided to take a chance and arrange for an appointment with the employer.

Gloria got the job, partly because she was referred by the local office, and partly because the employer was aware that he had limited his choice of applicants by the low pay offered. Gloria has been on the job now for two months. She feels a sense of accomplishment; and the employer, for the time being, seems satisfied.

Suggested Discussion Questions

1. What do you think Gloria's problems are? Do you think the counselor saw her problems as you see them? Consider counselor attitudes as they apply in this case.
2. Should Gloria be considered "culturally deprived?" Why?
3. What is Gloria's self-image? Why does she feel that everyone dislikes her?
4. What kind of help did Gloria need? What kind of help did she get?
5. What sort of attempt could have been made to build up Gloria's self-image? To create positive conditions rather than the negative ones described here?
6. Was it proper to contact mother and principal? How should this be done? How would you use the information secured in this way?
7. Could the GATB have been used to advantage? Was it wise to give a typing test?
8. How could a consultation (case conference) have been helpful in this case? Who would you include in such a conference?
9. How should the counselor handle the conflicting information received from Gloria and her mother on the economic situation?
10. What is your reaction to the counselor's summing up in the last paragraph?

Case Narrative No. 2

Phillip W. was first known to the agency when he registered for employment. He was given a code for Elemental Work and his application kept pending until he was referred to the counseling section. He was 20 years old and had left school after the ninth grade.

Phillip was referred to counseling because of his withdrawal from school, and because it was felt that his employment potential could be increased by further study and/or training.

Phillip had worked for two weeks at a carnival where he had earned $1 per hour operating a ride for children, taking tickets, etc. He had also worked at two different Steak 'n Shake establishments for periods of less than one week.

Phillip stated he left the above jobs because of low pay. In discussing his reasons for leaving school, Phillip cited financial reasons: specifically, his family had not been eligible for ADC allowance in his behalf since his eighteenth birthday. It was pointed out that his withdrawal from school had not, in fact, increased the family's income. However, there are no incidental school expenses for him.

Phillip has a slight build, blond hair, blue eyes. He has an appealing manner and is very anxious to please. A worker suggested MDTA registration to him. He was very enthusiastic about such a course stating he planned to marry within a year and a half; he showed the worker a picture of his girl, who is an elementary school student.

Phillip had decided he wanted to take up welding, his only reason being the comparatively high wage received by welders. In discussion with counselor and worker, he said he would be satisfied with other work if it paid him "good wages," and offered steady employment.

GATB was administered with the following scores: G-77; V-88; N-90; S-101; P-113; Q-95; K-62; F-64; M-80.

Counselor discussed the counseling session with worker. Counselor felt that the applicant was not particularly suited for his preferred occupation of welding, suggesting, however, that a generalized shop course would benefit the applicant, both in developing manual skills and providing time for him to fully decide the kind of life work he prefers. Counselor felt that applicant had been too selective in the type of job he was willing to accept, or keep after being hired. (Counselor had emphasized that the pay accompanying the type of work Phillip is able to get is not unusual for such jobs.)

On this date applicant was given an explanation of MDTA Training Course by the MDTA Coordinator. Phillip indicated his desire to participate, and plans were made for him to discuss it with his mother before final decision was made.

The counselor visited the family's residence. The family is composed of Phillip, the applicant, his mother and stepfather, Mr. and Mrs. F., and nine other children who range in age from 3 months to 17 years. Phillip and Daryl, 17, are Mrs. F's children by her first marriage which ended in divorce. Daryl is attending high school and, during the past year, had a part-time job secured under the auspices of the Ford Foundation. A half-sister, 15, is at the same high school.

The worker met only Mrs. F. and the children. Phillip's stepfather did not appear during the visit.

Phillip gets along well at home and takes responsibility for the younger children for his mother. He demonstrates a great deal of pride, and said the family would need a new linoleum carpet for the living room if the counselor called there. On the day of the visit, Phillip said he hoped the kids had not messed up the house in expectation.

The family are native to the city. Their present home is a large two-story, red brick building in the northern part of the city. It has reached a bad state of deterioration. The family has been making payments on the purchase of this house for the past eight years. The counselor saw only the living room area, but it was obvious that the whole house, which shows results of poverty and neglect, is in a very poor state of repair. Large holes were noticed in the plastered walls and ceilings. The walls were covered with drawings and scribbling made by the children. The home appeared sparsely furnished with dirty, upholstered, overstuffed pieces, of colors indeterminable because of filth and dirt.

Mrs. F. stated that the family's income consists of ADC grants totaling $224 per month that she receives in behalf of eligible children. In addition, Mr. F., who is partially blind, receives a grant of $70 from the State for permanent and total disability.

Mrs. F. says that it is difficult for her to manage on this amount because the family has a great deal of medical expense. Since her last child's birth, Mrs. F. has been bedridden most of the time; she had had a Caesarean section, and had miscarried one birth prior to the youngest baby's birth.

Mrs. F.'s attitude appears to be one of resignation and apathy. She has a pleasant disposition and is very cooperative, discussing the family's situation quite freely with the worker. Phillip's situation was discussed with her and she felt that, while her son was in need of additional training, she could not provide funds for it. However, when the MDTA training course that was being contemplated for Phillip was explained, Mrs. F. felt that he would benefit from such a course, and that the allowance he would receive would relieve the family's financial condition to some degree.

Phillip will enter MDTA Training Course for general shop work in September. After completion of this session, applicant states he plans further training if eligible. He will receive $17 a week, which will defray the cost of incidental expenses incurred in connection with this course.

Counselor plans to contact Phillip at end of the three-month period, and on completion of all training received, to determine employment status. In the meantime, applicant will seek part-time employment. Application will be kept active for this purpose.

Suggested Discussion Questions

1. What do you consider to be Phillip's learning capacity?
2. Would you consider GATB results a valid measure of Phillip's attitude? Why?
3. How do you feel about Phillip's "training readiness?" Do you consider welding a good choice? What other fields would you explore?
4. What essential information about Phillip do you find missing from this narrative?
5. Do you feel that Phillip is well motivated? Give the reasons for your answer.
6. What alternatives could be offered Phillip if he fails in the MDTA course?
7. What do you see as the objectives in counseling Phillip? Were those objectives attained?
8. How could you broaden Phillip's vocational horizons?

Case Narrative No. 3

Linda Sue is 18 years old. Her mother, Effie, died ten years ago. Her father, Robert J., a service station attendant, soon remarried. A good relationship exists between Linda and her stepmother and the five older step- and half-siblings. Linda is now living temporarily with her married stepsister who has four small children.

Mr. J. earns under $4000 a year; his wife is unemployed, and chronically ill. Both the elder J.'s were born in rural Arkansas, and neither completed high school. They are apathetic, soft-spoken people with a dejected air about them. In fact, the J.'s did harvest crops for a living some years ago in Arizona, Texas, and other southwestern areas.

Linda is a high school dropout, who completed less than two years of secondary schooling. She attended high school in Arizona, withdrew in the middle of the year. Linda stated that, with the exception of a half-year of sewing, she felt that high school was "a bore and a waste," and she "just never did like school anyway."

Linda later revealed that one reason for the family's migration to Arizona was Linda's health. During her stay in Arizona she was treated for a spot on her lung (tuberculosis), which she refers to as a "black lung." She is now an arrested tubercular, but is under no regular medical care.

Linda was taken into custody for the first time at age 15, for shoplifting. She had taken a pair of shoes from the self-service counter of a store in Chicago. She was placed on probation with the juvenile authorities for an indefinite period; but before the probation had ended, Linda committed another offense. At age 16, she ran away from home and hitchhiked, with two other girls, through Illinois, Kentucky, and Indiana. She was returned home by juvenile officers, and once again placed on probation.

A year later, Linda, now no longer a juvenile but still a minor, was arrested for consuming intoxicating beverages at a noisy party in a private home, to which police had been called by neighbors. Linda was again on probation. She managed to complete this probation period successfully.

In August, Linda was arrested on a similar charge in a tavern along with two older female companions. She feels that she was a bad influence on these older women, rather than the other way around, as was implied by the judge in the court proceedings. Linda is still under this two-year parole to a city probation officer.

Linda is a stocky, brown-eyed, fair-skinned girl—about 5′ 5½″, weighing over 140 pounds. She wears her straight brown hair in an unimaginative, stubby ponytail. She is friendly and out-going, speaks rapidly and readily, but with frequent lapses in grammar. The girl is clean, but not smartly groomed. She rarely wears hose or pays strict attention to coordinating colors in her attire. She wears no makeup, but has good clear skin. She wears very flat-heeled shoes and sleeveless blouses that tend to make her limbs look even heavier. Much more could be made of Linda's personal appearance, if she could be tactfully motivated.

Linda was referred to the Employment Service by the Metropolitan Service Association for Women, an organization concerned with the rehabilitation of women in prison or on parole.

Linda's work experience is scanty: she has actually held only two regular jobs, and both of these were of short duration. While still in high school, Linda had a temporary summer job as a waitress in a restaurant in Arizona. The salary was less than $1 an hour and, according to Linda, the hours were quite long. She had also doubled as dishwasher and short-order cook, when necessary.

For two weeks in August, Linda had worked on the assembly line at a baby carriage company, dipping carriage panels in paint. She had quit after a dispute with the personnel manager over an item on her application form about "other relatives employed by company." It seems that Linda did not consider her stepsister a "relative" and the personnel manager did. It was about this time that Linda became involved with the law, and it is not clear which incident precipitated Linda's sudden discontinuance of employment.

Linda has a seven-month old son, born to her out of wedlock. His name is Robert Gregory, and his father is a married man residing in Chicago with his wife and family. The father has never seen his child, although he was aware of Linda's pregnancy. According to Linda, she and the married man had carried on a brief and casual affair early last year; neither had been sorry to end the relationship, no thought ever having been given to marriage by either party, before or after Linda's pregnancy.

The baby is now with Linda's aunt. However, this arrangement is a temporary one, since the aunt is quite poor and has nine children of her own to support. Linda says she visits her son frequently, but does not now have definite plans for the child's care and custody.

At the time of Robert's birth, Linda's father was already having financial woes. He was obliged, due to his overwhelming indebtedness, to skip town, deserting Linda and her stepmother, the latter being ill at the time with ulcers and an infected abdominal tumor. Linda's baby was in the home then, and two months old. With only $2 between the family and total destitution, Linda decided then to send baby to her aunt and to move into the home of her married stepsister, where she resides now. Fortunately, Mr. J.'s defection lasted only a short while; within a few weeks he returned to his wife and took employment as a service station attendant, where he presently works. Linda returned again to her father's home, but only briefly.

Linda was seen by a counselor, who also scheduled her for the GATB and Kuder in September. Linda failed to report for testing on the prearranged date. The counselor called the J.'s home and learned that Linda and her father had had a violent quarrel, and that Linda had moved again from the house, taking her baby with her. (It appears that Linda had retrieved her son from the relatives and brought him back to Chicago with her.)

This is what precipitated the argument between Linda and her father —the fact that Linda has no means of support for either herself or her son, and Mr. J.'s feeling that it is unfair to expect him to support them both.

Linda was finally reached at her sister's home, and a new testing appointment was set up for two days later.

Counseling notes read as follows: "Youth interested in factory job. Very limited experience and knowledge of the types of jobs available in this field. Also, mentions a great deal of interest in artistic endeavors which she might or might not be interested in exploring vocationally."

Linda's GATB scores are: G-103, V-94, N-91, S-120, P-117, Q-95, K-89,

F-108, M-98. According to the counselor, the Kuder scores indicate that Linda would possibly be adaptable to artistic, mechanical, sales, or social service work particularly. On the whole, the entire test battery bears this out.

In October, Linda was given two referrals by the ES specialist; she had been counseled in advance about clothes, coiffure, and makeup. She appeared in the office, quite changed in appearance, and obviously enjoying the compliments she received from the staff. She wore a bright green wool skirt, neatly pleated and pressed, a black long-sleeved sweater, black walking shoes and *dark hose*. She had had her hair cut and arranged attractively in a bouffant style. Cosmetics were tastefully applied, although the mascara was perhaps a little overdone. Linda explained that she was desperately in need of work at this time, due to the pressing expenses of keeping the baby in the home. She is willing to accept either full- or part-time work.

Linda was sent out on a cashier opening, part-time with chance of becoming permanent. She was also sent to a retail store on a stock girl order. Duties here consisted of labeling and packing small leather products.

It was learned from the order-holding interviewer with whom the above named job orders originated that Linda was not hired at the retail store because of "too much makeup." The personnel man there felt she was a "hard type." The other employer took her application "under advisement." No reason given.

Linda was then referred to a cafeteria for a $40 per week job as steam table girl. Information received indicated that the employer did not hire Linda because he felt that she was "not a wholesome type of girl like those [they] generally employed, and therefore, would not fit in." The main objection appeared to be her injudicious use of mascara.

Linda called the ES specialist, quite distressed and despondent because of her failure to hear from any of her recent referrals. She was told that she was not hired, and the reasons given by the employers. After a short lecture on cosmetics and proper usage thereof (to enhance, not camouflage), Linda stated that hereafter she would "try to look like sweet sixteen."

Two referral cards were mailed to Linda for nurse's aide jobs at hospitals. The counselor telephoned Linda to get results of these referrals, and was informed by the sister, Tylese, that Linda had secured a job on her own at a beading company that manufactures buttons and bows for shoes. Tylese would have Linda return the call at her earliest convenience.

Linda called the ES specialist to report that she had been laid off at the beading company due to a slowdown in work, and that she now desperately needed work. She added that the presence of her infant son in the home is again causing family difficulties, and that the approaching (expensive) Christmas season emphasizes her lack of funds to support herself and child. Linda plans to move away as soon as she becomes re-employed. Before any action was taken by the Employment Service, Linda was rehired at the beading company.

Two months later Linda came in again, looking well, but wearing rumpled black trousers and dark print overblouse. She wore no hose in spite of rather blustery weather. She had a swollen jaw due to an abscessed tooth.

Linda reported that she had been laid off again; that it may be permanent, due to the company's apparent slowdown in working schedules. Linda's sister is now unemployed, too, due to pregnancy.

Linda was referred through a placement officer on a factory trainee job at a paper company, where she thought she would be able to work the required third shift whenever slated, anticipating no transportation problem. If hired, she might move closer to the factory.

Linda called: hired at the paper company, hopefully on a permanent basis. Her baby is back with the aunt again.

Suggested Discussion Questions

1. What is Linda's motivation? How could you either use this motivation positively, or change Linda's motivation into more productive channels?
2. How would you go about achieving rapport with Linda?
3. Is Linda ready to work? Give your reasons for your answer.
4. What are the various aspects of Linda's problem? Are her problems all within the province of the ES counselor?
5. Were Linda's problems solved at the end of the counseling? Give your reasons for your opinion.
6. Were Linda's referrals timely and suitable? Why?
7. Discuss the various actions taken with Linda Sue. Were they suitable? Timely? Successful? Why?
8. Should prospective employers be told about Linda's police record? Why do you think as you do?
9. What is Linda's vocational plan?

Case Narrative No. 4

John S. is a Negro boy, 21 years of age. He is slight of build (5' 5", 121 pounds) and has made a neat, presentable appearance on all contacts with this office. He wears slacks and a sweater, and has a beard and moustache. He is in good health and appears capable of handling the maximum workload for an average person of his size. He is quiet, pleasant in manner, and cooperative during interviews. Though somewhat slow to respond at first, apparently due to timidity in the interview situation, he warmed up and related well to the counselor.

John came to St. Louis four and a half years ago, and since then has lived with his aunt. John's parents reside in Texas and are, presumably, tenant farmers. (Whenever questioned about his parents or family background, John becomes vague and very evasive. On different visits John has stated his father's occupation as a farmer, laborer and that "he worked for a farmer," so it is merely assumed that he works as a sharecropper or tenant farmer. John usually said his mother was a housewife; however, on his last visit he disclosed that his mother was a "laborer and helps my father.") John has several brothers and sisters, most of whom have been "farmed out" with relatives throughout the country. John isn't sure of their number, nor does he know their ages or location. Apparently John has had no contact with either parent, nor with any members of his immediate family since he was sent here five years ago.

John is unsure of his aunt's source of income, although she does supply his clothes and a small amount of spending money. John is extremely vague as to whether or not his uncle resides with his aunt, or whether his aunt has any children of her own that reside with her.

Presumably, John's aunt is completely responsible for him and his actions; however, she seems to be quite elderly and usually unsure of John's daily whereabouts and activities. In trying to reach John by phone on several occasions, conversations were exchanged with the aunt, who never knew where John could be reached or when he would return, except that "He usually comes back before very late at night." She seemed unaware that John was seeking work, and either neglected to take the messages left for John or failed to give them to him upon his return. The conversations were somewhat strained, as it was difficult for John's aunt to understand the purpose of reaching him. Failing memory, or inability to read or write may have accounted for her failure to relay the messages.

John seems to be a quiet boy, usually keeping much to himself except when with a few close friends. He enjoys dancing and drawing, but apparently takes little part in group activities. John seems to be having some difficulty in making an adjustment to the community, as well as in accepting himself as a person who, in turn, is acceptable to the community.

When he came to St. Louis, John entered a technical high school as a freshman. He made a C average and said that English and mathematics were his best subjects. He also took two years of commercial art, which was his favorite subject.

He dropped out of school at the end of his junior year to get a job, but has only had casual jobs—carrying out packages in a supermarket and work as a relief janitor. He didn't particularly like or dislike this work.

John asked for clerical work. He thinks he would like to work with figures.

John's problems are twofold. As indicated, he has not fully accepted himself as a competent person, or as an acceptable member of the community. Secondly, he does not know how to seek work. John has many good qualities, but he chooses to dwell only on his faults and shortcomings, and has developed quite an inferiority complex. Also, he feels that as a Negro he will not be accepted in the labor market, particularly in the clerical field; and he feels that there is little point in even trying to seek work. Consequently, he has built up such a fear of employers and personnel workers that, in his words, "Sometimes I'd look at ads and go to the places, but before the interview, I'd get scared and leave."

John first contacted the local office in March. He was registered and classified for clerical work. His need for counseling was not recognized, although he made five local office visits between March of one year and August of a year later. He came into the office in August after having been out of school a year and a half to ask about MDTA programs. At that time he was referred to a counselor.

John was given the GATB with the following results:

G	V	N	S	P	Q	K	F	M
80	82	88	81	83	90	93	102	101

The test results showed that John made the pattern for Orderly and Waiter. The scores also indicated that John would probably be successful as a flat-work folder, photostat operator, or in related occupations.

The test scores and aptitude patterns, along with his own doubts about his opportunities in the clerical field, convinced John that he is best suited for work in the fields mentioned, and would probably be happiest in these newly considered fields of work.

John returned for subsequent discussions about filling out application forms, interviews with prospective employers, etc. He seemed to gain some confidence in himself and his opportunities in the newly revealed areas, but was not sure enough to agree to go out on an actual interview. However, after a period of role playing in a simulated job interview, John agreed that he was ready to see an employer.

An opening for an orderly in a local hospital, preferably experienced, was found in the office files. Through a telephone contact with the personnel interviewer in the hospital, an interview was arranged for John. His difficulties in an interview situation were also discussed, and the hospital interviewer said that the matter would be taken into consideration.

There seemed to be a good possibility that John would be considered for a job as a trainee orderly.

Several unsuccessful attempts were made to reach John by telephone, his aunt apparently failing each time to deliver the message. Finally he was reached at home, and he agreed to come to the office for referral to the hospital. He accepted the referral card.

Late the next afternoon the counselor called John's home. He stated that he had not gone on the interview because he had received his draft notice that day and had spent the day at the Army recruiting office. He thought he would "probably leave in a week or two."

John was drafted into the U.S. Army and will begin basic training on August 30.

Suggested Discussion Questions

1. Why did it take so long for John's counseling need to be recognized? What should have alerted the receptionist or the employment interviewer to refer him to a counselor?

2. What were the possible effects of John's long unemployment on him? How do you think he felt about his contacts at the Employment Service? Why did he come back?

3. Do you see any significance in John's wearing a beard? In his evasiveness in discussing his parents' occupation?

4. Do you believe that there was good rapport between the counselor and John? Support your point of view?

5. Would you suggest directive or nondirective counseling with John? Why?

6. What areas of information would you explore further? Can you suggest new areas for exploration?

7. Do you believe GATB results accurately measure John's aptitudes? Why?

8. What was the basis for the vocational plan? Is this sound?

9. Would you have discussed with John the same fields of work chosen by the counselor? Why?

10. Do you believe that John had any part in the planning of his "career"?

11. Do you believe that John will come in to see the counselor when he returns from the army? Why do you think so?

12. If John had not entered the armed forces, how long do you think it might have been necessary for a counselor to work with him in order to achieve some success?

CASE NARRATIVE NO. 5

Willie James P. is a Negro boy 19 years of age. He and his father, Willie Sr., live alone; his mother, Luella, died of cancer ten years ago. Willie has an older half-sister, Doris Jones, who is married and lives elsewhere.

Mr. P., Sr. was born in Atlanta, Georgia, but spent most of his life here in this city. He worked for many years as a chauffeur for private families, retiring in 1961. His monthly OASI benefits of about $60 now constitute the only regular income in the home.

The home is in a two-family upstairs flat, located in a blighted residential area where the houses range from fairly well-kept old brick structures with small, spotty lawns, to older frame dwellings with peeling paint and splintering porches. In the small commercial area nearby are numerous billiard parlors, chop suey restaurants, laundromats, and package liquor stores.

Willie and his father make their home in three rooms: two rooms contain sleeping accommodations, and the kitchen is a total disaster. Willie and his father cook and clean for themselves, and the home is in a state of complete deterioration. Furnishings are old and in need of repair or replacement. Lighting and ventilation are practically nonexistent.

Willie has attended three high schools. He was expelled from two high schools for smoking and/or gambling in the buildings. After enrolling in a third high school, he was selected for the football team. This lasted for less than a single semester because, Willie states, his "grades were low in everything except English" and he "played around too much" during football practice. After four or five temporary suspensions for minor infractions, Willie was finally excluded permanently for refusing to take his transistor radio from a classroom and for insulting a woman instructor.

Willie exhibits no remorse concerning his unhappy school career, and has the fatalistic attitude that "Whatever happens will happen anyway." He carried this same attitude over into our discussion of his penal record.

Willie is currently marking the second year of a two-year probation for a burglary, stealing, and concealed weapon charge. He was involved with two other boys in the burglarizing of a service station; the attendant had seen them escaping; knives had been flourished. Although Willie has never been incarcerated, he also has a juvenile record for trespassing, stealing, and destruction of property.

Willie is a tall, slender, dark boy, with long untidy hair and a slight acne condition on his face. He is also sprouting a sparse unsightly growth of hair on his chin which he refers to as a "goatee." He is not talkative, often says "I don't know," or "I don't remember," emphasizing the words with a shrug. His rare smile reveals many gold fillings in his teeth, which he says were affixed in early childhood, although he doesn't remember ever having had dental trouble.

In the office visit, Willie wore dusty woolen trousers and a fairly clean blue shirt, sleeves rolled to the elbow. He wore chamois sneakers and had to be reminded to remove a black felt hat from his head.

Called to task by the ES specialist about his generally unkempt appearance, Willie agreed that he certainly could and would make a change in some of his personal habits before he returned to our office. He was amazed to learn that a man is supposed to remove his hat on certain occasions.

During our discussion of "respect for women and girls," Willie displayed an unusual contempt for the niceties of everyday living and the social graces. He insists that most girls of his own age group were "not deserving of respect from men," and claims he'll "never marry." He spoke of his late mother with grudging affection, but had little praise for his older half-sister, whom he actualy doesn't seem to know very well. Willie simply slumped lower into his chair and toyed with his hat while being lectured on these matters.

Willie's only significant employment was a part-time job as a busboy-porter, which he held while going to high school. He doesn't remember the name or address of his place of employment, except that it was a "restaurant in Gaslight Square." He earned $28 a week, but was laid off after two months. He has not worked since that time, but he did tell the counselor that he would like to become a waiter eventually.

Willie was referred to the local office by his parole officer. After his first contact with the office, he was not heard from again until, a year later, he inquired about MDTA. An appointment for initial counseling and testing was set, but Willie failed to appear on that date. He said he lost his green appointment slip and then "forgot" the appointment. He was given a second appointment. After his initial counseling interview he was scheduled for GATB two days later, but he arrived half an hour late and could not be tested. He was scheduled for another testing session later that day and was given the GATB. His scores were:

G	V	N	S	P	Q	K	F	M
80	82	80	88	74	78	87	86	91

The counselor said that no further counseling was needed at this time. Willie was listed to be included in MDTA beginning in September.

Willie was called at his home for referral to an automotive company as a part-time stock clerk. He promised to see the employer early in the morning. He was instructed to clean himself up, paying particular attention to his hair and shirt collar. He agreed to do his very best, and he seemed enthusiastic about the job.

Later Willie called with a long tale of woe regarding the referral. He said he had arrived too early at the auto company and found the premises locked. After waiting more than an hour, he had seen the owner, who had told him to come back later in the afternoon to see another man. When Willie returned, the owner had insisted that he had never seen Willie before in his life. The other owner had appeared and had told Willie to go home, that he was "not the boy they were expecting." Willie was quite puzzled.

We will continue to try to locate part-time work for Willie, who will start evening classes in September.

Suggested Discussion Questions

1. What is the probable significance of Willie's behavior at school?
2. What does Willie need?
3. How would you approach Willie as a new counselee?
4. Do you think the counselor aided or deterred rapport by asking Willie to remove his hat? By being "called to task" for his personal traits? By being lectured?
5. Why do you think Willie arrived late for GATB?
6. How could the counselor have prevented Willie's unfortunate experience at the auto company?
7. Evaluate Willie's "training readiness."
8. Do you feel that GATB results adequately reflect Willie's potential? Give your reasons.
9. In what ways might group counseling be useful with Willie?

SELECTED BIBLIOGRAPHY

BOOKS AND PAMPHLETS

1. American Oil Company, *American Traveler's Guide to Negro History* (3rd ed.), Chicago: The Company, 1963.
2. Ames, William C., Halsey, Van R., and Brown, Richard H., *The Negro Struggle for Equality in the Twentieth Century*. Boston: D. C. Heath & Company, 1965.
3. Amos, William E., and Wellford, Charles F., eds., *Delinquency Prevention, Theory and Practice*. Englewood Cliffs, N.J.: Prentice-Hall, Inc., 1967.
4. ——— Manella, Raymond, and Southwell, Marilyn A., *Action Programs for Delinquency Prevention*. Springfield, Ill.: Charles C Thomas, Publisher, 1965.
5. Berenson, Bernard G., and Carkhuff, Robert, *Sources of Gain in Counseling and Psychotherapy: Readings and Commentary*. New York: Holt, Rinehart and Winston, 1967.
6. Blocker, Donald H., *Developmental Counseling*. New York: The Ronald Press Company, 1966.
7. Bloom, Benjamin S., Davis, Allison, and Hess, Robert, *Compensatory Education for Cultural Deprivation*. New York: Holt, Rinehart and Winston, 1965.
8. Briggs, William A., and Hummel, Dean L., *Counseling Minority Group Youth: Developing the Experience of Equality Through Education*. Columbus: The Ohio Civil Rights Commission, 1962.

9. Burchill, G. W., *Work-Study Programs for Alienated Youth*. Chicago: Science Research Associates, Inc., 1962.
10. Burgess, Elaine, and Price, Daniel, *An American Dependency Challenge*. Chicago: The American Public Welfare Association, 1963.
11. Caplovitz, David. *The Poor Pay More: Consumer Practices of Low-Income Families*. New York: The Free Press of Glencoe, Inc., 1963.
12. Carter, R. L., Kenyon, D., Marcuse, P., and Miller, L., *Equality*. New York: Pantheon Books, Inc., 1965.
13. Caudill, Harry M., *Night Comes to the Cumberlands: A Biography of a Depressed Area*. Boston: Little, Brown and Company, 1963.
14. Chester, Mark, and Fox, Robert, *Role Playing Methods in the Classroom*. Chicago: Scientific Research Associates, Inc., 1966.
15. Clark, Kenneth B., *Prejudice and Your Child*. Boston: Beacon Press, 1955.
16. ———, and Plotkin, Lawrence, *The Negro Student and Integrated Colleges*. New York: National Scholarship Service and Fund for Negro Students, 1963.
17. Clemons, Lulamae, Hollitz, Erwin, and Gardner, Gordon, *The American Negro*. St. Louis: Western Division, McGraw-Hill Book Company, Inc., 1965.
18. Conant, James B., *Slums and Suburbs*. New York: McGraw-Hill Book Company, Inc., 1961.
19. ———, *The American High School Today*. New York: McGraw-Hill Book Company, Inc., 1959.
20. Conference on Economic Progress, *Poverty and Deprivation in the United States, the Plight of Two-Fifths of a Nation*. Washington, D.C.: The Conference, 1962.
21. Conference on Unemployed Out-of-School Youth in Urban Areas, *Social Dynamite*. Washington, D.C.: National Committee for Children and Youth, 1961.
22. Crow, Lester D., Murray, Walter I. and Smythe, Hugh H., *Education of the Culturally Disadvantaged Child*. New York: David McKay Co., Inc., 1966.
23. Davis, Allison, *Social Class Influences Upon Learning*. Cambridge: Harvard University Press, 1948.
24. Delli Quadri, Fred, ed., *Helping the Family in Urban Society*. New York: Columbia University Press, 1963.
25. Denver and Jefferson County Public Schools, *Joint Board Report, Metropolitan Youth Education Center*. Denver: The Schools, May 1964.
26. Denver Public Schools, *Emily Griffith Opportunity School*. Denver: The Schools, 1962.
27. Duhl, Leonard J., ed., *The Urban Condition*. New York: Basic Books, Inc., Publishers, 1963.
28. Educational Policies Commission of the National Education Association, *Education and the Disadvantaged American*. Washington, D.C.: The Association, 1962.

29. Federation Employment and Guidance Service, Richard J. Bernard Memorial Library, *A Guide To Resources for Anti-Poverty Programs: A Selected Bibliography.* New York: The Service, April 1965.
30. Ferman, Louis A., Kornbluh, Joyce L., and Haber, Allan, eds., *Poverty in America.* Ann Arbor: The University of Michigan Press, 1965.
31. Fichter, Joseph H., *Negro Women Bachelors.* Chicago: National Opinion Research Center, University of Chicago, 1965.
32. Flesch, Rudolf F., *Why Johnny Can't Read—and What You Can Do About It.* New York: Harper & Brothers, 1955.
33. Frazier, E. Franklin, *The Negro Family in the United States.* New York: The Dryden Press, 1951.
34. Friedman, Rose D., *Poverty—Definition and Perspective.* Washington, D.C.: American Enterprise Institute for Public Policy Research, 1965.
35. Frost, Joe L., and Hawkes, Glenn R., *The Disadvantaged Child: Issues for Innovations.* Boston: Houghton Mifflin Company, 1966.
36. Galbraith, John K., *The Affluent Society.* Boston: Houghton Mifflin Company, 1960.
37. Giles, H. Harry, *The Integrated Classroom.* New York: Basic Books, Inc., Publishers, 1959.
38. Ginzberg, Eli, *The Negro Potential.* New York: Columbia University Press, 1956.
39. Gordon, Margaret S., ed., *Poverty in America.* San Francisco: Chandler Publishing Co., 1965.
40. Goslin, Willard, *Learning to Plow a City Street.* Washington, D.C.: National Education Association.
41. Gowan, John Curtis, and Demos, George D., *The Disadvantaged and Potential Dropout.* Springfield, Ill.: Charles C Thomas, Publisher, 1966.
42. Graham, Jory, *Handbook for Project Head Start.* New York: Anti-Defamation League of B'nai B'rith, 1965.
43. Grambs, Jean D., *Schools, Scholars, and Society.* Englewood Cliffs, N.J.: Prentice-Hall, Inc., 1965.
44. Guilford, J. P., *The Nature of Human Intelligence.* New York: McGraw-Hill Book Company, Inc., 1967.
45. Handlin, Oscar, *The Newcomers.* Cambridge: Harvard University Press, 1959.
46. Harrington, Michael, *The Other America: Poverty in the United States.* 191 p. New York: The Macmillan Company, 1962.
47. Health and Welfare Council of the National Capital Area, *Child Rearing Practices Among Low Income Families in the District of Columbia.* Washington, D.C.: The Council, May 16, 1961.
48. Hentoff, Nat, *The New Equality.* New York: The Viking Press, Inc., 1965.
49. Hollingshead, August B., *Elmtown's Youth.* New York: John Wiley & Sons, Inc., 1949.

50. Information Retrieval Center on the Disadvantaged, Graduate School of Education, Yeshiva University, *The Education of Socially Disadvantaged Children and Youth: A Brief Introduction and Bibliography.* New York: The Center, 1965.
51. Job Corps, *Education in Job Corps Youth Conservation Center.* Washington, D.C.: Office of Economic Opportunity, 1965.
52. Kahn, A. J., *Planning Community Services for Children in Trouble.* New York: Columbia University Press, 1963.
53. Kardiner, Abram, and Ovesey, Lionel, *The Mark of Oppression: A Psychological Study of the American Negro.* New York: W. W. Norton & Company, Inc., 1951.
54. Kolko, Gabriel, *Wealth and Power in America: An Analysis of Social Class and Income Distribution.* New York: Frederick A. Praeger, Inc., 1962.
55. Kvaraceus, William C., Gibson, John S., Patterson, Franklin K., Seasholes, B., and Grambs, Jean D., *Negro Self-Concept: Implications for School and Citizenship.* New York: McGraw-Hill Book Company, Inc., 1965.
56. Lewis, Oscar, *The Children of Sanchez.* New York: Random House, Inc., 1961.
57. ———, *Five Families.* New York: Random House, Inc., 1959.
58. Loretan, Joseph O., and Umans, Shelley, *Teaching the Disadvantaged.* New York: Teachers College Press, Teachers College, Columbia University, 1966.
59. Lyman, Howard B., *Test Scores and What They Mean.* Englewood Cliffs, N.J.: Prentice-Hall, Inc., 1963.
60. May, Edgar, *The Wasted Americans.* New York: Harper & Row, Publishers, 1963.
61. McClelland, David C., *et al., Talent and Society.* New York: D. Van Nostrand Co. Inc., 1958.
62. McGrath, Earl J., *The Predominantly Negro Colleges and Universities in Transition.* New York: Teachers College Press, Teachers College, Columbia University, 1965.
63. McQueen, Mildred, research ed., *Research Report, Parts 1-5.* Chicago: Science Research Associates, Inc., 1965.
64. Michigan State University Cooperative Extension Service and U.S. Department of Agriculture cooperating, *Job Guide for Future Workers.* East Lansing: The Service.
65. Miller, Herman P., *Income of the American People.* New York: John Wiley & Sons, Inc., 1955.
66. Miller, S. M., *The American Lower Class: A Typological Approach.* Syracuse: Syracuse University, Youth Development Center, January 1963.
67. Morgan, James N. *et al., Income and Welfare in the United States.* New York: McGraw-Hill Book Company, Inc., 1962.
68. Myrdal, Gunnar, *Challenge of Affluence.* New York: Pantheon Books, Inc., 1963.

69. National Association for the Advancement of Colored People, *Negro Heroes of Emancipation*. New York: The Association, 1964.
70. National Catholic Welfare Conference, *A Religious View of Poverty*. Washington, D.C.: The Conference, 1964.
71. National Medical Fellowships, Inc., *New Opportunities for Negroes in Medicine*. Chicago: The Fellowships, April 1965.
72. National Merit Scholarship Corp., *The Merit Scholar*. Evanston, Ill.: The Corporation, October 1964.
73. National Society for the Study of Education, *Vocational Education, Part I*. Chicago: University of Chicago Press, 1965.
74. National Vocational Guidance Association, *Guidelines for Preparing· and Evaluating Occupational Materials*. Washington, D.C.: The Association, 1964.
75. Northrup, R. Herbert, and Rowan, Richard L., eds., *The Negro and Employment Opportunity*. Ann Arbor: Bureau of Industrial Relations, University of Michigan, 1965.
76. Office of Economic Opportunity, *Head Start Child Development Programs*. Washington, D.C.: The Office, 1965.
77. ————,Project Head Start, *Head Start Resource Series I–IX*. Washington, D.C.: Head Start, 1965.
78. ———— and U.S. Office of Education, *Education: An Answer to Poverty*. Washington, D.C.: The Offices, 1965.
79. Orshansky, Mollie, and Karter, Thomas, *Economic and Social Status of the Negro in the United States*. New York: National Urban League, 1961.
81. Parker, Seymour, and Kleiner, Robert J., *Mental Illness in the Urban Negro Community*. New York: The Free Press of Glencoe, Inc., 1966.
82. Passow, A. Henry, ed., *Education in Depressed Areas*. New York: Bureau of Publications, Teachers College, Columbia University Press, 1963.
83. President's Task Force on Manpower Conservation, The, *One-Third of a Nation*. Washington, D.C.: Government Printing Office, 1964.
84. Public Affairs Committee, *Children Who Never Had a Chance*, Public Affairs Pamphlet No. 183. New York: The Committee, 1952.
85. Rainwater, Lee, *And the Poor Get Children*. Chicago: Quadrangle Books, Inc., 1960.
86. Riese, H. P., *Heal the Hurt Child*. Chicago: University of Chicago Press, 1962.
87. Riessman, Frank, *The Culturally Deprived Child*. New York: Harper & Row, Publishers, 1962.
88. Schlesinger, Benjamin, *Multi-Problem Family*. Canada: University of Toronto Press, 1963.
89. Schorr, Alvin L., *Slums and Social Insecurity*. Washington, D.C.: Government Printing Office, 1963.
90. Schreiber, Daniel, ed., *The School Dropout*. Washington, D.C.: National Education Association, 1964.

91. ――――, *Guidance and the School Dropout*. Washington, D.C.: National Education Association, 1964.
92. Science Research Associates, Inc. Rodman Job Corps Training Center (New Bedford, Mass.), *Fact Sheet*. Chicago: The Associates, March 1965.
93. Sexton, Patricia C., *Education and Income*. New York: The Viking Press, 1961.
94. Shostak, Arthur B., and Gomberg, William, eds., *New Perspectives on Poverty*. Englewood Cliffs, N.J.: Prentice-Hall, Inc., 1965.
95. Shriver, Sargent, *Poverty*. Reprint from the Encyclopedia Americana. New York: Americana Corp., 1965.
96. Sicault, George, ed., *The Needs of Children*. New York: The Free Press of Glencoe, Inc., 1963.
97. Silberman, Charles E., *Crisis in Black and White*. New York: Random House, Inc., 1964.
98. Sinclair, Donald A., *The Negro and New Jersey*. New Brunswick, N.J.: Rutgers University Library, 1965.
99. Standler, C. B., *Children of Brasstown*. Urbana: University of Illinois Press, 1949.
100. Strom, Robert D., *Teaching in the Slum School*. Columbus, Ohio: Charles E. Merrill Books, Inc., 1965.
101. Subcommittee on Employment and Manpower of the Committee on Labor and Public Welfare, U.S. Senate, *Toward Full Employment and Manpower Policy for the U.S., A Report*. Washington, D.C.: Government Printing Office, April 1964.
102. Sutton, Elizabeth, *Knowing and Teaching the Migrant Child*. Washington, D.C.: National Education Association, 1962.
103. Syracuse University Youth Development Center, *The American Lower Class: A Typological Approach*. Syracuse: The Center, 1963.
104. Theobald, Robert, *The Challenge of Abundance*. New York: Mentor Books, 1962.
105. Therkildsen, Paul T., *Public Assistance and American Values*. Albuquerque: University of New Mexico Press, 1964.
106. Thomas, R. Murray, *Social Differences in the Classroom*. New York: David McKay Co., Inc., 1965.
107. Tucker, Shirley, *Mississippi from Within*. New York: Arco Publishing Co., Inc., 1965.
108. Turner, B. A., *Occupational Choices of High School Seniors in the Space Age*. Houston: Texas Southern University, 1964.
109. U.S. Children's Bureau, *Children of Working Mothers*, Publication No. 382. Washington, D.C.: Government Printing Office, 1960.
110. U.S. Congress. *Manpower Development and Training Act of 1962, As Amended (42 U.S.C. 2571-2620)*. Washington, D.C.: Government Printing Office, 1965.
111. U.S. Department of Agriculture, Economic Research Division, *Employment, Unemployment, and Low Incomes in Appalachia*, Agri-

cultural Economic Report No. 73. Washington, D.C.: Government Printing Office, 1965.

112. U.S. Department of Commerce Area Redevelopment Administration, *Information Sources for Locating Industrial Prospects.* Washington, D.C.: Government Printing Office, 1964.

113. U.S. Department of Health, Education and Welfare, *Education and Training, the Bridge Between Man and His Work.* Washington, D.C.: Government Printing Office, 1965.

114. ———, Office of Education, *The Vocational Education Act of 1963,* OE-80034. Washington, D.C.: Government Printing Office, 1965.

115. ———, and U.S. Housing and Home Finance Agency, *Services for Families Living in Public Housing.* Washington, D.C.: Government Printing Office, 1963.

116. U.S. Department of Labor, Bureau of Labor Standards, *The Youth You Supervise.* Washington, D.C.: Government Printing Office, 1965.

117. ———, Office of Manpower, Automation and Training, *Occupational Training: Pathway to Employment.* Washington, D.C.: The Office, 1964.

118. ———, Office of Policy Planning and Research, *The Case for National Action: The Negro Family.* Washington, D.C.: Government Printing Office, March 1965.

119. ———, Women's Bureau, *Negro Women Workers in 1960.* Bulletin 287. Washington, D.C.: Government Printing Office, 1964.

120. ———, ———, *Trends in Educational Attainment of Women.* Washington, D.C.: The Bureau, January 1965.

121. U.S. Welfare Administration, Department of Family Services, *Children and Neglect ... Hazardous Home Conditions.* Washington, D.C.: U.S. Department of Health, Education and Welfare, 1963.

122. ———, *Children in Migrant Families,* Report to U.S. Senate Committee on Appropriations. Washington, D.C.: U.S. Department of Health, Education and Welfare, December 1960.

123. Union Theological Seminary, The Auburn Library, Urban Education Collection, *The Negro in American History and Culture: A List of Resources for Teaching.* New York: The Library, March, 1965.

124. University of Chicago Committee on Human Development, *Growing Up in River City.* New York: John Wiley & Sons, Inc., 1962.

125. University of Delaware, Pre-Vocational Institute. *Teacher's Vocational Series* prepared in connection with Teacher Training Institute for Non-Achieving Junior High School Students. Dover: State Department of Public Instruction, Vocational Division, 1965.

126. Warner, W. L., *et al., Who Shall Be Educated?* Harper & Brothers, 1944.

127. Warren City Schools, *Educational Program for Project Head Start.* Warren, Ohio: Office of Assistant Superintendent, June 1965.

128. Washington, Bennetta B., *Youth in Conflict*. Chicago: Science Research Associates, Inc., 1963.
129. Watson, G., *No Room at the Bottom*. Washington, D.C.: National Education Association, 1963.
130. Watts, Lewis G., Freeman, Howard E., Hughes, Helen M., Morris, Robert, and Pettigrew, Thomas F., *The Middle-Income Family Faces Urban Renewal*. Boston: Division of Urban Renewal, Department of Commerce and Development, The Commonwealth of Massachusetts, 1965.
131. Weller, Jack E., *Yesterday's People*. Lexington: University of Kentucky Press, 1965.
132. Welsch, Erwin K., *The Negro in the United States: A Research Guide*. Bloomington: Indiana University Press, 1965.
133. Wilner, D. M., *et al.*, *The Housing Environment and Family Life*. Baltimore: The Johns Hopkins Press, 1962.
134. Wrenn, C. Gilbert, *The Counselor in a Changing World*. Washington, D.C.: American Personnel and Guidance Association, 1962.

ARTICLES

1. American Educational Research Association, "Education for Socially Disadvantaged Children," *Review of Educational Research*, Washington, D.C.: The Association, XXXV, No. 5 (December 1965).
2. Amos, William E., "A Study of the Occupational Awareness of a Selected Group of Ninth Grade Negro Students," *Journal of Negro Education*, XXIX, No. 4 (Fall 1960), 500-503.
3. ———, "A Study of Self-Concept: Delinquent Boys' Accuracy in Selected Self-Evaluations," *Genetic Psychology Monographs*, Vol. 67 (1963), 45-87.
4. ———, and Perry, Jane, "Negro Youth and Employment Opportunities," *Journal of Negro Education*, XXXII, No. 4 (Fall 1963) 358-366.
5. ———, "Job Adjustment Problems of Delinquent Minority Group Youth," *Vocational Guidance Quarterly*, Winter (1964-65).
6. ———, and Southwell, Marilyn A., "Dropouts: What Can Be Done?" *Federal Probation*, XXVIII, No. 1 (March 1964), 30-35.
7. Appel, J. J., "American Negro and Immigrant Experience: Similarities and Differences," *American Quarterly*, Vol. 18, No. 1 (1966), 95-103.
8. "A Proposed Program for National Action to Combat Mental Retardation," *President's Panel on Mental Retardation*. Children's Bureau, Department of Health, Education and Welfare (Reprint October 1962), Washington, D.C.: Government Printing Office.
9. Asbell, Bernard, "A Surprising Report on Our Worst Schools: Not Like Other Children," *Redbook*, Vol. 121, No. 6, October, 1963.
10. Ausubel, David P., "Ego Development Among Segregated Negro Children," *Mental Hygiene*, XLII, No. 3 (July 1958), 362-369.

11. Axelrod, Joseph and Grambs, Jean B., "Time Out for Training," *Adult Leadership*, Vol. 2, June, 1953.
12. Bagdikian, Ben H., "Poverty: A Special Report—The Invisible Americans," *Saturday Evening Post*, December, 1963, 28-33.
13. Barber, Gertrude A., "Guiding the Low Ability Student," *NEA Journal*, March, 1961, 38-39.
14. Barron, Milton, ed., "What Hate Does to the Victims," in *American Minorities*. New York: Alfred A. Knopf, Inc., 1957.
15. Berkman, Sigmund S., "Appalachia—Rebirth of a Region." *Training Facts No. 14* (Reprint No. 6). Washington, D.C.: U.S. Department of Labor, Manpower Administration, Office of Manpower, Automation and Training, 1964.
16. Boehm, Leonore, and Nass, Martin L., "Social Class Differences in Conscience Development," *Child Development*, Vol. 33, No. 3 (September 1962), 565-574.
17. ———, "The Development of Conscience: A Comparison of American Children of Different Mental and Socio-Economic Level," *Ibid.*, 575-590.
18. Boocock, S. S., "Toward a Sociology of Learning: A Selective Review of Existing Research," *Sociology of Education*, Vol. 39, No. 1 (1966), 1-45.
19. Brittain, C. V., "Preschool Programs for Culturally Deprived," *Children*, Vol. 13, No. 4 (1966), 130-134.
20. Bronfenbrenner, Urie, "Socialization and Social Class Through Time and Space," in *Readings in Social Psychology*, eds. E. Maccoby, T. Newcomb, and R. Hartley. New York: Holt, Rinehart and Winston, 1958.
21. Burchinal, Lee, Gardner, Bruce, and Hawkes, Glenn R., "Children's Personality Adjustment and the Socio-Economic Status of their Families," *Journal of Genetic Psychology*, Vol. 92 (1958), 149-158.
22. Cervantes, L. F., "Parental Authority and the Dropout," *Sociological Analysis*, Vol. 27, No. 1 (1966), 27-37.
23. Charters, W. W., and Gage, N. L., eds., *Readings in the Social Psychology of Education*, Section 1, "Social Class and Family Influences." Boston: Allyn & Bacon, Inc., 1963.
24. Clark, Kenneth, and Clark, Mamie, "Racial Identification and Preference in Negro Children," in *Readings in Social Psychology*, eds. E. Maccoby, T. Newcomb, and R. Hartley. New York: Holt, Rinehart and Winston, 1958.
25. Clarke, A. D. and Clarke, A. M., "Some Recent Advances in the Study of Early Deprivation," *Child Psychology and Psychiatry*, Vol. 1 (1959), 26-36.
26. Cohen, Albert K., and Hodges, Harold M., "Characteristics of the Lower-Blue-Collar-Class," *Social Problems*, Vol. 10, No. 4 (Spring 1963), 303-333.
27. Cohen, Jerome, "Social Work and the Culture of Poverty," *Social Work*, Vol. 9 (January, 1964), 3-11.

28. Cohen, Wilbur J., and Sullivan, Eugenia, "Poverty in the United States," *Indicators.* Washington, D.C.: U.S. Department of Health, Education and Welfare (February, 1964), vi-xxii.
29. Della-Dora, D., "The Culturally Disadvantaged: Educational Implications of Certain Social-Cultural Phenomena," *Exceptional Child,* Vol. 28 (1962), 467-472.
30. Deutsch, M., Fishman, J. A., *et al.*, "Guidelines for Testing Minority Group Children," *Journal of Social Issues,* XX, No. 2 (April, 1964), 129-145.
31. Deutscher, Max, and Chein, Isidor, "The Psychological Effects of Enforced Segregation: A Survey of Social Science Opinion." *Journal of Psychology,* Vol. 26, No. 2 (October, 1948), 259-287.
32. "Disadvantaged: A Symposium." Bibliography. *NEA Journal.* Washington, D.C.: National Education Association, April, 1963.
33. "Disadvantaged Children and the World of Work," *The American Child,* Vol. 40, No. 4 (November, 1958). New York: National Committee on Employment of Youth.
34. Douvan, E., "Social Status and Success Strivings," *Journal of Abnormal and Social Psychology,* Vol. 83 (1963), 137-157.
35. Doverman, M., "Today's Legal Revolution: The Reformation of Social Welfare Practice," *Social Service Review,* Vol. 40, No. 2 (1966), 152-68.
36. "Educating the Culturally Deprived in the Great Cities," Special Feature, *Phi Delta Kappan,* November, 1963.
37. Epstein, Leonore A., "Some Effects of Low Income on Children and Their Families," *Social Security Bulletin,* Vol. 24, No. 2 (February, 1961), 12-17.
38. Faltermayer, E. K., "Who Are the American Poor?" *Fortune,* March, 1964, 118-119.
39. Farnsworth, K. E., "Application of Scaling Techniques to the Evaluation of Counseling Outcomes," *Psychological Bulletin,* Vol. 66, No. 2 (1966), 81-93.
40. Frazier, E. Franklin, "Problems and Needs of Negro Children and Youth: The Negro Child and Youth in the American Social Order," *The Journal of Negro Education,* Vol. 19, No. 3 (Summer, 1950), 269-277.
41. Gleuck, Sheldon, and Gleuck, Eleanor, "Working Mothers and Delinquency," *Mental Hygiene,* Vol. 41 (1957), 327-353.
42. Goldsmith, H. F., and Lee, S. Y., "Socioeconomic Status Within the Older and Larger 1960 Metropolitan Areas," *Rural Sociology,* Vol. 31, No. 2 (1966) 207-215.
43. Gottlieb, David, *The First Thirty,* Job Corps, Corpsman Report No.1. Washington, D.C.: Office of Economic Opportunity, Job Corps, January, 1965.
44. Grambs, Jean D., "The Community and the Self-Governing Adolescent Group," *Journal of Educational Sociology,* Vol. 30, October, 1956.

45. Grambs, Jean D., "Rural Youth Are Citizens Too," *Extension Service Review.* Washington, D.C.: U.S. Department of Agriculture, August, 1963.

46. ———, "The Culturally Deprived Child Achieving Adequacy Through Education," *National Elementary Principal*, Vol. XLIV, November, 1964.

47. "Guidelines for Testing Minority Group Children," *The Journal of Social Issues*, XX, No. 2 (April, 1964).

48. Havighurst, Robert J. and Davis, Allison, "A Comparison of the Chicago and Harvard Studies of Social Class Differences in Child-Rearing," *American Sociological Review*, Vol. 20, No. 4 (1955).

49. Herzog, Elizabeth, "Some Assumptions About the Poor," *Social Service Review*, Vol. 37, No. 4 (December, 1963).

50. Hollingshead, August B., "Class Differences in Family Stability," in *Social Perspectives on Behavior*, eds. Cloward and Klein. New York: The Free Press of Glencoe, Inc., 1963.

51. Howard, Jack, "Neighborhood Youth Corps," *Occupational Outlook Quarterly.* Washington, D.C.: U.S. Department of Labor. Vol. 12, No. 4 (December, 1964).

52. Jencks, Christopher, "Johnson vs. Poverty," *The New Republic*, March 28, 1964, pp. 15-18.

53. Kelly, J. G., "The Mental Health Agent in the Urban Community," in *Urban America and the Planning of Mental Health Services, Symposium.* No. 10 of the Group for the *Advancement of Psychiatry*, 1964, pp. 474-494.

54. Kemp, Barbara H., "The Youth We Haven't Served." U.S. Department of Health, Education and Welfare, Washington, D.C.: Government Printing Office, 1966.

55. Kephart, William M., "Occupational Level and Social Disruption," *American Sociological Review*, Vol. 20, No. 4 (1955), 456-465.

56. Keyserling, Leon, *Poverty and Deprivation in the United States.* Washington, D.C.: The Conference on Economic Progress, 1962.

57. Kohn, Melvin, "Social Class and the Exercise of Parental Authority," *American Sociological Review*, XXIV (June, 1959), 352-366.

58. ———, "Social Class and Parent-Child Relationships," *American Journal of Sociology*, Vol. 68, No. 4 (1963), 471-480.

59. Kvaraceus, William C., "Poverty and Undereducation: What School and Community Can Do," *Occupational Outlook Quarterly*, Vol. 8, No. 3. Washington, D.C.: U.S. Department of Labor, September, 1964.

60. Levinson, P., and Schiller, J., "Role Analysis of the Indigenous Nonprofessional," *Social Work*, Vol. 11, No. 3 (1966), 95-101.

61. MacDonald, Dwight, "Our Invisible Poor," *The New Yorker*, January 19, 1963, p. 108 ff.

62. MacDonald, M. E., "Reunion at Vocational High: An Analysis of Girls at Vocational High; An Experiment in Social Work Intervention," *Social Service Review*, Vol. 40, No. 2 (1966), 175-189.

63. Miller, S. M., "Poverty and Inequality in America: Implications for the Social Services—An Essay Review of *The Other America.*" *Child Welfare*, Vol. 42 (November, 1963), 442-445.

64. ———, and Riessman, Frank, "The Working Class Sub-Culture: A New View," *Social Problems*, Vol. 9, No. 1 (Summer, 1961), 86-97.

65. Miller, Walter B., "Implications of Lower Class Culture for Social Work," *Social Problems*, Vol. 33 (September, 1959), 219-236.

66. Muir, Donald E., and Weinstein, Eugene A., "The Social Debt: An Investigation of Lower-Class and Middle-Class Norms of Social Obligation," *American Sociological Review*, Vol. 27 (August, 1962), 538.

67. Murray, Evelyn M., "Work: A Neglected Resource for Students," *The American Personnel and Guidance Journal*, XLI, No. 3 (November, 1962), 229-233.

68. NAACP Department of Public Relations. "The Negro Heritage Library," *The Crisis*, May, 1965.

69. National Committee on Employment of Youth, "Women in Poverty," *American Child*, May, 1965. New York: The Committee.

70. National Council of Teachers of English, "More Sources of Free and Inexpensive Material," *The English Journal.* Champaign, Ill.: The Council. September, 1964.

71. National Employment Counseling Association, "Appraisal Measures Needed for the Educationally and Culturally Deprived," *Journal of Employment Counseling*, Vol. 2, No. 2 (1965). Washington, D.C.: The Association.

72. Orshansky, Mollie, "Children of the Poor," *Social Security Bulletin*, Vol. 26, No. 7 (July, 1963), 3-13.

73. ———, "Counting the Poor: Another Look at the Poverty Profile," *Social Security Bulletin*, January, 1965. Washington, D.C.: U.S. Department of Health, Education and Welfare.

74. Phillips, W. B., "Counseling Negro Pupils: An Educational Dilemma," *Journal of Negro Education*, XXIX, No. 4 (Fall, 1960).

75. "Poverty: Skeleton in the National Closet," *Senior Scholastic Magazine*, March 13, 1964. pp. 6-8. New York: Scholastic, Inc.

76. Rae-Grant, O. A. F., Gladwin, T., and Bower, E. M., "Mental Health, Social Competence and the War on Poverty," *American Journal of Orthopsychiatry*, Vol. 36, No. 4 (1966), 652-664.

77. Rein, M., "Poverty and Income," *The American Child*, Vol. 48, No. 3 (1966) 1-10.

78. Richmond, Charlotte, "The Job Corps—What It Is and How It Works," *Occupational Outlook Quarterly*, Vol. 9, No. 1 (February 1965). Washington, D.C.: U.S. Department of Labor.

79. Riessman, F., and Miller, S. M., "Social Change vs. the Psychiatric World," Reprint from *American Journal of Orthopsychiatry*, January, 1964.

80. Schnore, L. F., "The Rural-Urban Variable: Urbanite's Perspective," *Rural Sociology*, Vol. 31, No. 2 (1966), 131-143.

81. Sherman, S. N., "Family Treatment: An Approach to Children's Problems," *Social Casework*, Vol. 47, No. 6 (1966), 368-372.
82. Silberman, Charles E., "Give Slum Children a Chance: A Radical Proposal," *Harper's Magazine*, May, 1964, pp. 37-42.
83. Snyderman, George S., "Serving the Hard-to-Place Youth," *Employment Security Review*, Vol. 26, No. 3 (March, 1959), 27-28.
84. "Social-Class Influences on American Education," A Bibliography. *Sixtieth Yearbook, National Society for the Study of Education, Part 2*, 120-43. Chicago: University of Chicago Press, 1961.
85. "Stirrings in the Big Cities," *NEA Journal*, January-May, 1962. Washington, D.C.: National Education Association.
86. Toby, Jackson, "Orientation to Education as a Factor in the School Maladjustment of Lower-Class Children," *Social Forces*, Vol. 35, No. 3, 259-265.
87. Trueblood, Dennis, "The Role of the Counselor in the Guidance of Negro Students," *Harvard Educational Review*, XXX, No. 3 (Summer 1960).
88. U.S. Department of Health, Education, and Welfare. Office of Education. "... The First Work of These Times ..." A Description and Analysis of the Elementary and Secondary Education Act of 1965. *American Education*, April, 1965.
89. Elementary and Secondary Education Act of 1965, *American Education*, April 1965. Washington, D.C.: The Office.
90. U.S. Department of Health, Education, and Welfare, Social Security Administration. "Who's Who Among the Poor: A Demographic View of Poverty." *Social Security Bulletin*, Vol. 28, No. 7 (July 1965). Washington, D.C.: Government Printing Office.
91. U.S. Department of Health, Education, and Welfare. "Converging Social Trends—Emerging Social Problems," *Welfare Administration Publication No. 6*, 1964. Washington, D.C.: Government Printing Office.
92. "Vocation Counseling and the Hard-to-Reach," *The American Child*, Vol. 41, No. 1 (January, 1959). New York: National Committee on Employment of Youth.
93. Washington, Bennetta B., "Growth and Cultural Conflict," *The Vocational Guidance Quarterly*, Vol. 12, No. 3 (Spring, 1964), 153-158.
94. Weiner, R. B., "Adolescent Problems: Symptoms of Family Dysfunction," *Social Casework*, Vol. 47, No. 6 (1966), 373-377.

SUPPORT PERSONNEL FOR THE COUNSELOR: THEIR TECHNICAL AND NONTECHNICAL ROLES AND PREPARATION

A STATEMENT OF POLICY ADOPTED BY THE AMERICAN PERSONNEL AND GUIDANCE ASSOCIATION, NOVEMBER, 1966 *

RATIONALE FOR SUPPORT PERSONNEL FOR COUNSELORS

The extensive forces for change in American society are having critical impact upon our educational, manpower, welfare, and other institutions. A growing series of federal laws assigns a fundamental and greatly broadened role to the counseling and guidance movement in meeting the needs of additional groups of people in a variety of life situations. The problems of helping people progress in education, and relate themselves to productive work, requires professionals and para-professionals to do different tasks, with various skills.

Recent federal legislation creating greatly increased demand for personnel to provide relevant services includes the Manpower Development and Training Act, the Economic Opportunity Act, the Vocational Education Act, amendments to the National Defense Education Act, amendments to the Vocational Rehabilitation Act, the Elementary and

* Reprinted with the permission of the American Personnel and Guidance Association.

Secondary Education Act, and the so-called "Cold War G.I. Bill." These necessitate new approaches to the provision of services so as to make more efficient and effective use of personnel now providing these services.

This has resulted in the development of a new group of personnel positions variously referred to as auxiliary, technical, nonprofessional, para-professional, or support personnel. The concept of such positions is not new. It has been accepted by many professional groups. However, the systematic programming of support personnel roles is new in connection with the work of the counselor.

Before we can determine the duties of support personnel, it is necessary to consider previously published policy statements that outline the role and functions of professional counselors. A general policy statement has been prepared by the Professional Preparation and Standards Committee of APGA, and several of the divisions have published policy statements concerned with the work of the counselor in specific settings.

These reports and a series of related articles on counselor role and function have been published in a manual entitled *Counseling, A Growing Profession.* *

It is the position of the Association that appropriately prepared support personnel, under the supervision of the counselor, can contribute to meeting counselees' needs by enhancing the work of the counselor. The appropriate use of such personnel will facilitate the work of the counselor and make the total endeavor more effective.

GUIDING PRINCIPLES

It is the purpose of this document to identify the principles and concepts that undergird the roles and preparation of support personnel. It provides guidelines for the development of specific functions within specific settings. There is no intention of providing detailed job descriptions for such personnel. This document, however, should provide guidelines for the development of such job descriptions.

The concept of support personnel does not refer to reciprocal lateral relations between the counselor and representatives of collaborating occupations, such as social workers, psychologists, physicians, or placement directors.

This statement deals only with a discussion of relations between the counselor and various support personnel. This approach is not based upon a lack of interest and/or understanding of the importance of "reciprocal lateral relations between the counselor and collaborating occupations." It is based upon a recognition of the importance and scope of such rela-

---

* J. W. Loughary (ed.), American Personnel and Guidance Association, 1605 New Hampshire Ave., N.W., Washington, D.C., 1965.

tions, which means that each of these occupations may establish policies relative to support personnel, and finally, that the concept of reciprocal relations is by itself quite worthy of separate research and study.

Career patterns must also be considered in delineating the difference between the counselor and support personnel. Support personnel jobs may or may not be terminal. In the event that support personnel wish to be upgraded to full professional status, it is to be understood that they must meet the necessary academic and personal characteristics of professional counselors.

Even though agency policy and hiring practices may ultimately determine the actual role of support personnel, the counselor must have a voice in determining what specific duties can be performed by such personnel. There are certain services, such as the establishment of a formal counseling relationship, for which the counselor must maintain responsibility and which only a counselor can provide. There are certain other services—such as orientation, outreach and recruitment activities, follow-up, development of job readiness, and improvement of personal appearance—that may be more appropriately provided by specially oriented and adequately prepared support personnel. It is essential that a coordinated pattern of professional and support services be provided.

The activities of support personnel differ from the work of the counselor in several basic respects:

1. The counselor performs the counseling function described in the professional policy statements cited above, while support personnel may perform important and necessary activities that contribute to the overall service.

2. The work of the counselor involves synthesis and integration of interrelated parts of the total range of services with, and in behalf of, the counselee. The work of support personnel tends toward the particular and becomes an integral part of the larger whole only as this is developed under the leadership of the counselor.

3. The counselor bases his performance on the use of relevant theory, authoritative knowledge of effective procedures, and evaluation of the total endeavor. Functions of support personnel are characterized by more limited theoretical background, and specialization in one or more support functions.

TYPICAL ACTIVITIES OF SUPPORT PERSONNEL

The role of the counselor is subtly but constantly changing, a fact that is characteristic of any dynamic profession. Since the definition of roles for support personnel is dependent on their relationship to the counselor's role, it is inevitable that support personnel roles will also change. Today, however, it is advisable to consider an analysis of the total complex of roles and responsibilities involved, in order to identify supporting activities or duties that may be performed satisfactorily by support personnel rather than by the counselor. Such activities or duties are related to specific clusters, which may be called functions, in the total complex of the professional role.

Nothing in this paper should be construed as meaning that support personnel should take the place, or responsibility, of the counselor. However, the performance of identified activities by support personnel will contribute to the work of the counselor. Sometimes the tasks supportive of counselor functions are assigned to persons who are not working in support personnel positions. On other occasions, enough supporting activities can be logically related to constitute a full-time support personnel position. The counselor is, nevertheless, responsible for incorporating all such tasks into a meaningful pattern of services to the counselee.

Direct Helping Relationships

A number of support personnel activities involve direct person-to-person helping relationships, but they are not identical or equivalent to counseling as conducted by the counselor. Prominent among these functions and activities would be the following:

1. Individual Interviewing Function:
   a. Secure information from an interviewee by means of a semistructured or structured interview schedule. The information elicited would tend to be factual and limited in nature.
   b. Give information prepared in advance and approved by the counselor for its appropriateness for the interviewee. Such information would usually be factual rather than interpretative.
   c. Explain to the counselee in practical lay terms the purposes and procedures involved in the services.
   d. Engage the counselee in informal, casual discussion as a means of putting him at ease and establishing an openness to counseling. Such dyadic activity may be especially important when performed by an interviewer who is making initial contact with potential counselees who are hostile toward, or apprehensive of, counseling.
   e. Provide informal follow-up support to a former counselee.

2. Small Group Interviewing or Discussion Function:
   a. In structured groups with a largely preplanned program, guide discussions as a discussion leader.
   b. Describe staff and material available to the group, as an information resource person, or tell the group how and where to acquire needed resources.

   c. Act as recorder in a variety of small group discussion or counseling situations, under the supervision of the counselor.

   d. Observe verbal and nonverbal interaction in groups, following pre-determined cues and procedures for making observations.

   e. Participate in informal, superficial social conversation in a small group of counselees to help put them at ease and to establish the beginning of helping relations that may be provided by forth-coming counseling.

   f. Informally provide information and support to former counselees.

   g. Perform outreach activities.

Indirect Helping Relationships

Most of the activities of support personnel appear to provide help indirectly rather than directly to counselees, even though some of these activities do involve face-to-face relations with counselees. Among the functions and activities may be these:

1. Information Gathering and Processing Function:

   a. Administer, score, and profile routine standardized tests and other appraisal instruments (nonclinical-type).

   b. Obtain and maintain routine information on the scope and character of the world of work with current reference to employment trends, in accordance with instructions established by the counselor.

   c. Contact various sources for needed records and related information relevant to counseling.

   d. Search for new sources of information about counselees and/or the environment, under direction of the counselor.

   e. Prepare educational, occupational, and personal-social information for visual-auditory verbal and graphic presentation, or transmittal to others, for use in accordance with instructions established by the counselor.

   f. Under the counselor's supervision, search for new sources to which the counselee may be referred.

   g. Secure specific special information about former counselees upon request and under the supervision of the counselor.

   h. Operate technical communications media involving printed and electronic processes of a visual-auditory nature for the counselee's benefit.

2. Referral Function:

   a. Initiate general contacts with specific referral agencies.

   b. Initiate contacts for specific individuals with given referral agencies.

   c. Aid individuals in making proper contact with referral agencies.

3. Placement and Routine Follow-up Function:
   a. Through appropriate channels, establish and maintain working relations with organized placement agencies in the community.
   b. Develop specific placement opportunities (under the supervision of the counselor) for the individual cases not handled through cooperation with other placement agencies.
   c. Maintain continuous surveys of placement conditions and trends as requested by the counselor.
   d. Search for new placement resources that may be useful to counselees.
   e. Secure follow-up information of a routine nature according to a general follow-up plan.

4. Program Planning and Management Function:
   a. Perform routine collecting and analytical statistical operations as a research assistant.
   b. Procedure and prepare supplies of materials of various sorts for the counselor.
   c. Prepare standardized reports of contacts with counselees, potential counselees, referral, placement, and follow-up agencies and persons.
   d. Maintain appropriate personnel and information records for the counselor.
   e. Supervise and coordinate the activities of clerical or other skilled personnel under the general supervision of the counselor.

THE PREPARATION OF SUPPORT PERSONNEL

The preparation of support personnel will vary according to a number of factors. Among those that must be considered are the following:

1. People who wish to become support personnel must be selected for their potential ability to perform specific duties, and for their suitability for working with counselors and counselees in particular settings. Selection must not be restricted to those who may be capable of earning academic degrees since, in actual practice, many of these positions may be terminal in nature. Such people will come from a wide variety of educational and experiential backgrounds. It may be possible to find people who already possess the necessary competencies, depending upon the local setting, and the accumulation and organization of specific duties and/or tasks into payroll jobs. Preplanning by supervising counselors and agency, or institutional administrative personnel, relative to the development of support personnel payroll jobs, will be imperative.

2. The duration of preservice preparation for support personnel will be fairly brief—that is, a matter of weeks or months, compared to years for the counselor. In-service preparation of support personnel on the

job is essential to the ultimate success of the program. Such preparation should be initiated on a carefully planned basis.

3. The activities to be learned may be rather concrete and specific. In most cases this will imply an inductive approach to the development of background, theoretical, and philosophical understandings. There may be a necessary emphasis upon frequent practice or drill. The preparation must utilize field settings and/or laboratory simulations.

4. At least the final portions of a preparation program must involve opportunities to work under the field supervision of counselors. There should be supervised preparation as members of a team of support personnel.

5. The staff for support personnel preparation programs should include experienced, highly successful support personnel, counselors, and counselor educators.

6. It would be advantageous to support personnel preparation programs and to counselor education programs, if they could be coordinated in terms of content, time, and physical proximity.

INDEX